PRAISE FOR

Genius of Place

"Engaging . . . Mr. Martin is good at shedding light on the less familiar aspects of Olmsted's life." —*Wall Street Journal*

"Martin has succeeded brilliantly in bringing to detailed life the man he calls the greatest American that most Americans have never heard of." —*Minneapolis Star Tribune*

"A comprehensive journal of Frederick Law Olmsted's life written with great precision and exhaustive historical specifications; but these elements do not get in the way of a well-told tale. . . . Highly recommended." —*New York Journal of Books*

"A wide-ranging, surprisingly revealing biography." —*Boston Globe*

"A fast-moving and fascinating narrative of the life of one of America's great visionary figures." —*Buffalo News*

"Martin does an excellent job of tracing the development of this multitalented genius." —*Christian Science Monitor*

"The story of Olmsted's life offers today's readers an opportunity to see what effect one energetic and imaginative person had on the formation of today's nation . . . invites the reader to complete the book in one sitting—and then ask for more." —*Roanoke Times*

"A fine job in presenting the life of a fascinating American."
—*Providence Journal*

"Reading *Genius of Place* feels like listening to Olmsted's best friend dishing about the private life of a real person."
—*Charleston Post and Courier*

"Exhaustively researched and clearly written, this volume should become the standard for students of both history and design."
—*Landscape Architecture*

"*Genius of Place* offers more than the legacy of a man who accomplished 'more than most people could in three lifetimes.' Martin provides an intimate portrayal of the man himself, whose life was both blessed with genius and plagued by tragedy."
—*E: The Environmental Magazine*

"[An] ardent biography . . . Martin presents Olmsted's era in all its glory, with the intimate affairs and staggering accomplishments of the great man unfolding against the vivid backdrop of nineteenth-century America."
—*Publisher's Weekly*

"Justin Martin's lively biography creates a rich portrait of complex, multitalented Frederick Law Olmsted." —*Seattle Times*

GENIUS *of* PLACE

ALSO BY JUSTIN MARTIN

Greenspan: The Man Behind Money

Nader: Crusader, Spoiler, Icon

GENIUS *of* PLACE

THE LIFE OF
Frederick Law Olmsted

Justin Martin

A Merloyd Lawrence Book
DA CAPO PRESS
A Member of the Perseus Books Group

Designed by Brent Wilcox
Set in 11.75 point Adobe Garamond Pro by the Perseus Books Group

Library of Congress Cataloging-in-Publication Data
Martin, Justin.
    Genius of place : the life of Frederick Law Olmsted / Justin Martin.—1st Da Capo Press ed.
        p.   cm.
    "A Merloyd Lawrence book."
    Includes bibliographical references and index.
    ISBN 978-0-306-81881-3 (hardcover)—ISBN 978-0-306-81984-1 (e-book)
    1. Olmsted, Frederick Law, 1822–1903.   2. Landscape architects—United States—Biography.   3. Social reformers—United States—Biography.   4. City planning—United States—History—19th century.   I. Title.
SB470.O5M37 2011
712.092—dc22
ISBN 978-0-306-82148-6 (paperback)

                                                                           2011002246

First Da Capo Press edition 2011
First Da Capo Press paperback edition 2012
Published as a Merloyd Lawrence Book by Da Capo Press
A Member of the Perseus Books Group
www.dacapopress.com

Da Capo Press books are available at special discounts for bulk purchases in the U.S. by corporations, institutions, and other organizations. For more information, please contact the Special Markets Department at the Perseus Books Group, 2300 Chestnut Street, Suite 200, Philadelphia, PA 19103, or call (800) 810-4145,ext. 5000, or e-mail special.markets@perseusbooks.com.

"There's a great work wants doing," said FLO.
This book is dedicated to my twin sons, Dash and Theo,
and those are words to live by.

CONTENTS

Photo Credits   ix
Acknowledgments   xi

Introduction: Why Olmsted Matters   1

I
"An Enthusiast By Nature"
GROWING UP, 1822–1851

1 So Very Young   6
2 At Sea   21
3 Uncommon Friends   35
4 A Farmer and Finite   48
5 Two Pilgrimages   61

II
"The Cause of Future Freedom"
SOUTHERN TRAVELS AND JOURNALISM, 1852–1857

6 "The South"   74
7 *Tief Im Herzen Von Texas*   89
8 A Red-Hot Abolitionist   103
9 The Literary Republic   108

III
"A People's Pleasure-Ground"
CONCEIVING CENTRAL PARK, 1857–1861

10 "Is New York Really Not Rich Enough?"   124
11 Right Man, Right Place   135
12 A Park Is Born   148
13 Growling Green   161
14 Swans   172

IV
"Heroes Along with the Rest"
CIVIL WAR SERVICE, 1861–1863

15 In Search of a Mission   178
16 In the Republic of Suffering   196
17 Antietam to Gettysburg   211
18 "The Country Cannot Spare You"   223

V
"There Seems to Be No Limit"
CALIFORNIA, 1863–1865

19 Gold Dust   232
20 Yosemite   244
21 *Un*settled in the West   254

VI
"Where Talents and the Needs of the World Cross"
SHAPING THE NATION, 1865–1877

22 New Prospects   270
23 City Planning: Buffalo and Chicago   287
24 Battling Boss Tweed, Splitting with Vaux   303
25 Blindness and Vision   313

VII
"I Have All My Life Been Considering Distant Effects"
SUMMITS AND SORROWS, 1877–1903

26 A Troubled Wander Year   328
27 Stringing Emeralds   335
28 Saving Niagara, Designing Stanford   347
29 Big House in the Big Woods   359
30 A White City Dreamscape   369
31 "Before I Am the Least Prepared for It"   387
32 Fade   399
    Epilogue: Olmsted's Wild Garden   401

    Notes   407
    Index   437
    Appendix: The Olmsted Views   453
    About the Author   461
    Photo insert follows page 210

PHOTO CREDITS

FLO's three children (The Frances Loeb Library, Harvard Graduate School of Design)

FLO with signature (National Park Service, Frederick Law Olmsted National Historic Site)

World's Fair 1893 (Courtesy of Peter Marsh)

FLO and Marion (National Park Service, Frederick Law Olmsted National Historic Site)

FLO's Sargent portrait (Courtesy of The Biltmore Company, Asheville, North Carolina)

The Biltmore (The Biltmore Company, Asheville, North Carolina)

McLean (Courtesy of McLean Hospital)

The frontispiece on page vi is a woodcut image that appeared in Frederick Law Olmsted's *A Journey Through Texas*. It was based on a sketch by Olmsted, featuring himself and his brother John camping on the prairie.

ACKNOWLEDGMENTS

It starts with my subject—thanks to Frederick Law Olmsted. Fresh from college, on my very first day in New York City, I followed a hectic round of job interviews by seeking refuge in Central Park. At the time, my thoughts went something like this: "Who created this amazing place?" This launched an interest in Frederick Law Olmsted that, with time, has only grown. I was married in Central Park, his masterpiece. After my twin sons were born, I moved to Forest Hills Gardens, New York, a 147-acre planned community that is Frederick Law Olmsted Jr.'s masterpiece.

Writing this book was a huge project, and I can honestly say that my two years steeped in Olmsted's story were a pleasure. Thanks again, FLO, for leading such a large, varied, interesting life. It made my job fun.

A great big thanks is also due my friend Catherine Fredman. After Catherine landed a gig as a guide for the Central Park Conservancy, I accompanied her on a number of her excellent tours. My Olmsted fascination grew, and I began to think about writing a biography. Once the project got under way, Catherine continued to help: reading drafts, chasing down hard-to-find facts, cheering me on.

At my publisher, Da Capo, it was a great pleasure to work once again with Merloyd Lawrence. She's an old-school editor in the very best sense. The rap on publishing these days is that harried editors have no time to shape books. Happily, that was not my experience. From the germ of an idea to finished book, this was truly a collaboration. Every single page of this text features changes, additions, and literary flourishes wisely suggested by my editor. Thanks, Merloyd!

At Da Capo, I also wish to thank Lissa Warren, publicist nonpareil. Well into the Internet age, Lissa remains a pro at getting attention for books. Kudos to Jonathan Sainsbury for the gorgeous cover design and to Brent Wilcox for such an elegant design of the book's interior. I also want to thank Annette Wenda for a thoughtful and meticulous job of copyediting, which served to further refine and clarify the text. Annie Lenth: Thanks for keeping things rolling in production.

To write a book on Olmsted, you really need to visit his creations. I wish to thank a number of people for conducting me through various Olmsted sites. What follows can't help but read like a list. But that's an injustice. All of these people gave generously of their time and shared their knowledge while showing me around the assorted majestic works of FLO.

Julia Bachrach of the Chicago Park District brought the 1893 World's Fair vividly to life during our visit to modern-day Jackson Park; Lonnie Sacchi provided a superb walking tour of Riverside, Illinois, a model suburb designed by Olmsted; my appreciation to Tim O'Connell, a peerless historian, for a thoroughly memorable and memorably thorough survey of the Rochester park system; Alan Banks of the National Park Service provided valuable domestic details on my subject at Fairsted, Olmsted's home in Brookline, Massachusetts; Jeanie Knox of the Emerald Necklace Conservancy guided me through the Back Bay Fens and other gems of the Boston system; Lanae Handy introduced me to Boston's Franklin Park, and Chris McArdle led me around the Arnold Arboretum; I spent a wonderful morning with Dennis Evanosky and Barbara Smith at Oakland's Mountain View Cemetery, a graveyard with a scenic setting that's simply unrivaled; thanks to David Lenox for the tour of Stanford, one of the world's most striking campuses; historian Bill Alexander provided invaluable perspective on the incomparable Biltmore Estate, and Susanne Woodell showed me around its grounds; Steve Livengood of the U.S. Capitol Historical Society gave me fresh perspective on a place I'd visited countless times—the Capitol grounds—revealing all kinds of hidden and inspired Olmsted touches; Christian Zimmerman and Amy Peck of the Prospect Park Alliance gave me a great tour of this timeless Brooklyn green space; and thanks to Terry Bragg for guiding me through the historic landscape of McLean Hospital, whose grounds evoke both sadness and hope.

I also want to give a special thanks to Francis Kowsky, who provided a wonderful tour of the Buffalo park system. Throughout the project, Dr. Kowsky, author of the excellent *Country, Park, and City: The Architecture and Life of Calvert Vaux*, went above and beyond, fielding my assorted questions.

An invaluable resource, while working on this biography, was the Olmsted papers, a multivolume collection of park plans, letters from private collections, unpublished manuscripts, and assorted Olmsted-alia. My appreciation to project editor Charles Beveridge and his team for this decades-long enterprise, still under way. I am also grateful to Laura Wood Roper, a pioneering Olmsted biographer who generously donated many letters she unearthed to the Library of Congress.

My uncle David Mel Paul, a researcher guidance volunteer at the LOC, helped me get rolling at this incredible institution. I appreciated the opportunity to stay with him and my aunt Margareta while visiting Washington, D.C. In the course of doing my research, I also visited a number of other archives and libraries and found the librarians and other staffers unfailingly helpful. I especially want to thank Mary Daniels of the Frances Loeb Library at Harvard University's Graduate School of Design. With my deadline fast approaching, she generously arranged for me to work in the special collections outside normal hours. Mary also described John Olmsted, FLO's adopted son, as "dutiful to the point of masochism," a line so irresistible that I simply cribbed it for my book.

I'm indebted to Larry Hott of Florentine Films, who is working on an Olmsted documentary that will air on PBS. I'm serving as a consultant to the project, a role that has greatly helped me to clarify my thoughts on Olmsted. I also want to thank Marjorie Perlman for her support, which included inviting me to speak before the Friends of the University of Rochester Libraries.

Rex and Donna Martin, my parents, are architecture aficionados who have made recent trips to such far-flung places as Riga, Latvia (stellar examples of art nouveau), and Bartlesville, Oklahoma (Frank Lloyd Wright's only skyscraper). They happily joined me for my Buffalo and Chicago research junkets. My dad is an emeritus philosophy professor and my mom a book editor who has lately allowed herself the luxury of slowing down (ever so slightly). My parents provided all kinds of help with choosing words and checking facts. Most of all, they have believed in me and loved me for . . . oh, only my entire life. I also want to thank my in-laws, Sylvia Charlesworth and Gerald Kressman, for their constant encouragement. On my worst days of writing, I'd remind myself there were people who truly wanted me to finish this book—Sylvia and Mr. K. That always helped; thank you both. I also want to thank my cousin Brett Perkins, a superb writer. His book, *Frantic Francis: How One Coach's Madness Changed Football*, and our insanely free-ranging conversations helped shape this book.

My friend Scott Marcus points out that authors invariably close their acknowledgments by thanking their spouses for "putting up with them through the grueling process of writing this book." Very astute, Scott. I want to thank my wife, Liza Charlesworth, for putting up with me during the grueling process of writing this book. Of course, Liza did so much more. She is my partner, my collaborator, my toughest critic, my biggest fan, my best friend, the love of my life. It ends with Liza, as always.

INTRODUCTION

Why Olmsted Matters

ON MARCH 25, 1893, a gala dinner was held in honor of Daniel Burnham, driving force behind the Columbian Exposition, a World's Fair about to open in Chicago. Various artists and architects who had worked on the project gathered for this lavish event.

But when Burnham took the stage to be feted, he chose to deflect credit away from himself and onto someone else instead. "Each of you knows the name and genius of him who stands first in the heart and confidence of American artists, the creator of your own parks and many other city parks," said Burnham. "He it is who has been our best adviser and our constant mentor. In the highest sense he is the planner of the Exposition—Frederick Law Olmsted." Burnham paused to let that sink in. Then he added: "An artist, he paints with lakes and wooded slopes; with lawns and banks and forest-covered hills; with mountain sides and ocean views. He should stand where I do tonight, not for the deeds of later years alone, but for what his brain has wrought and his pen has taught for half a century." A collective roar went up among those assembled.

Burnham's tribute provides a sense of Olmsted's stature and importance. But effusive as it is, it still fails to do him full justice. His life and career were just too sprawling and spectacular. Ask people today about Olmsted, and they're likely to come back with a few stray details—best case. But his achievements are immense. Olmsted may well be the most important American historical figure that the average person knows least about.

Olmsted is best remembered as the pioneer of landscape architecture in the United States. He created New York City's Central Park and a

1

number of other green spaces, often in collaboration with his sometime partner Calvert Vaux. Olmsted designed the grounds of scores of private estates, Stanford and assorted college campuses, several mental institutions, and a pair of cemeteries. For these achievements alone, Olmsted would have a measure of lasting fame. At a time when open space is at a premium, he's left a legacy of green in city after city across America and in Canada, too.

But he was also an environmentalist. This is a separate role from landscape architect. "I was born for a traveler," Olmsted once said, and he managed to roam most of the country in the course of his lifetime. Along the way, he became aware that some of the most striking natural landscapes were under siege. Olmsted played a crucial role in the early efforts to preserve Yosemite and Niagara Falls, for example. Over time, he began to bring environmental considerations to his park work as well. He designed Boston's Back Bay Fens not only as a park but also as America's very first effort at wetlands restoration.

Preserving wild places is different from crafting urban spaces, and it's a vital Olmsted role that is often overlooked. I devoted a great deal of research time and did abundant spadework in an effort to reconstruct this aspect of his story. This biography is designed, among other things, to give Olmsted his due as a pioneering environmentalist.

But he was so much more. Olmsted was a sailor, a scientific farmer, and a late bloomer nonpareil. During the Civil War, he did a stint as the head of a battlefield relief outfit. (In the postwar years, the outfit—after many twists and convolutions—became the basis for the American Red Cross.) He also took a fascinating detour, moving out to California and managing a legendary but ill-starred gold-mining enterprise.

Olmsted was no dilettante, though. He simply did a lot of different things and did them well. It was the nineteenth century, and a younger America was in the grip of a frontier mind-set. All things seemed possible; all hands on deck. During this era, people didn't have to carve out narrow areas of specialization. It was an ideal time for someone of Olmsted's gifts. Seeking varied experience was his essence, as surely as Mark Twain's essence was to turn a phrase.

At the same time, there's a common theme that runs through many of Olmsted's diverse endeavors. First, last, always, he was a reformer. No disrespect to Americans who came of age in the 1940s, often called the "Greatest Generation," but Olmsted's cohort (those who came of age in the 1840s) was pretty great in its own right. It was an especially socially conscious period in the country's history, and it produced people who fought for the rights of the physically disabled and the mentally ill and—in the North—for the freedom of slaves.

Olmsted was very much a part of his generation. Thus, he didn't become a scientific farmer merely as a way to make a living. He did so because, at a time when America was a predominantly agricultural nation, the vocation represented a chance to benefit society by demonstrating the latest cutting-edge practices. He became a park maker because, at a time when cities were especially dense and teeming, it was a way to provide recreation and relief to the masses.

When it comes to reform, however, there's no question that some of Olmsted's most notable contributions came from yet another erstwhile vocation—journalist. That's what Burnham alluded to when he said "his pen has taught" in the tribute to Olmsted.

During the 1850s, Olmsted traveled throughout the American South as a reporter for a brand-new paper, the *New-York Daily Times*. (The paper later dropped *Daily* from it name.) His mandate was to approach the region almost like a foreign correspondent. In the course of his travels, Olmsted interviewed both white plantation owners and black slaves and produced a series of extraordinary dispatches—balanced, penetrating, humane. As a consequence, Olmsted managed to lay bare the evils of slavery in a way that other more polemical works of the era often did not. For Northerners anxious to understand the South in the years right before the Civil War, Olmsted's dispatches were one of the best windows.

When war finally erupted, Olmsted's writings from the 1850s continued to furnish a vital perspective, this time to British readers. Britain was on the fence at the beginning of the conflict, uncertain whether to side with the Union or the Confederacy. In 1861, Olmsted's *The Cotton Kingdom*—an updated compendium of his collected Southern writings—was published in England. *The Cotton Kingdom* helped sway British public opinion toward the Union cause.

Olmsted did eventually settle down as a landscape architect, exclusively. Demand for his designs was such that he really didn't have a choice. But when finally forced to pick a career, he brought the sum of all the wildly varied experiences that had come before. That's why Olmsted's work is so gorgeous, so inspired, so dazzlingly set apart. It draws on the numerous disciplines to which he'd been exposed. When Olmsted created the landscape for the Biltmore Estate near Asheville, North Carolina, in the 1890s, for example, he looked to memories of his long-ago travels throughout the antebellum South. When he designed the grounds for the 1893 World's Fair, he drew on his experiences in China, as a sailor, a half century earlier.

For this book, I also wanted to bring Olmsted's personal life into clearer focus. Previous accounts have tilted into hagiography, casting Olmsted as a kind of radiant figure—a deeply devoted husband and sweet, gentle father. Such portrayals conflate his pastoral park creations with his personal demeanor, which is a mistake. Yes, he created beauty, but he was capable of being a very hard man.

I consulted pertinent letters from five separate archives and spent hours poring over them, deciphering the distinctive handwriting of Olmsted and various intimates, often with the aid of a magnifying glass. That furnished the grist for a more accurate and more human portrait of Olmsted. He was a great artist and a hard-driving reformer, to be sure. He also happens to have had a strained marriage and serious tension within his family. In many ways, the two things were related.

Olmsted had a big life, but also a tough one. He faced more—much more—than his share of tragedy, even by nineteenth-century standards. He contended with the untimely deaths of children, close relations, and dear friends. He suffered various physical ailments, such as the ravages of a near-fatal carriage accident. And he endured assorted forms of psychological torment: insomnia, anxiety, hysterical blindness, and depression. "When Olmsted is blue, the logic of his despondency is crushing and terrible," a friend once said. Olmsted spent his final days in an asylum; in a great irony, it was one for which he had earlier designed the grounds.

But first he accomplished more than most people could in three lifetimes. As a park maker, environmentalist, and abolitionist, Olmsted helped shape modern America. This is his extraordinary story.

I
"An Enthusiast by Nature"
GROWING UP, 1822–1851

CHAPTER 1

So Very Young

ON APRIL 26, 1822, John and Charlotte Olmsted welcomed a baby known variously as "Fred" and "Fred-Law." He was born in the boom-town of Hartford, Connecticut, at a time when America itself was still in its infancy.

There were twenty-four states then, Missouri being the westernmost, and the United States was still working out its border with the Canadian territories to the North. The country was so sparely populated that on av-erage there were only about twelve people per square mile.

Fred's father had been born in 1791, during George Washington's first term as president. Fred's mother was born in 1800, the dawn of a new century that would bring such innovations as the train, the telegraph, the revolver, and baseball. Fred was the first child for John, age thirty, and Charlotte, age twenty-one. He was named after Frederick Olmsted, John's older brother who had died a few years earlier, and Jonathan Law, Charlotte's adoptive father.

Even the notion of giving a child a middle name, as in Frederick *Law* Olmsted, was new in this era. Records show that virtually no one born during colonial times had received one. John Quincy Adams, America's sixth president, was the first to have a middle name. Over time, Ameri-can parents began latching onto this long-standing practice of the Euro-pean gentry, whiff of pretension and all. The year 1822 produced a bumper crop of middle-named babies; Fred-Law's exact contemporaries include Rutherford Birchard Hayes (the nineteenth president), noted ex-plorer Edward Fitzgerald Beale, and Henry Benjamin Whipple, who would grow up to be the first Episcopal deacon of the future state of Minnesota.

Fred was born into a comfortable household on College Street in Hartford. Circa 1822, the state's capital was a good-size city with a population of nearly 7,000. The place was thriving, thanks to its fortunate location along the banks of the Connecticut River, which flows into Long Island Sound and onward to the Atlantic. This made Hartford perfect as an inland port for shipping traffic between the United States, Europe, and even the Far East. The American insurance industry first took root in Hartford to serve merchants looking for financial protection in the event their wares were lost in shipwrecks. During this period, Hartford also included its share of blacksmiths, saddlers, tailors, masons, and wagon makers. There were thirteen doctors and twenty-two lawyers. There were twelve churches and fourteen taverns.

Fred's father was part owner of Olmsted and King, which occupied a prime location, corner of Main and Pearl streets, right near the statehouse. The store specialized in fabrics that arrived by ship, such as silk from France and wool from Germany. These fabrics were used for everything from curtains to neckties to carpeting. John Olmsted had started the store during the War of 1812. By the time of Fred's birth, it was prospering.

The senior Olmsted was a big man with broad shoulders and a kind of Abe Lincoln–like awkwardness in both dress and manner. He had a keen mind for business, despite receiving little formal education. He was extremely meticulous, too, and kept a diary of sorts, filled with crabbed-script notations on the finances of both his store and his household. Occasionally, he'd add the briefest mention of something of a more personal flavor, such as an illness or his surprise at an uncharacteristically early spring thaw.

At times, John Olmsted could appear very gruff. In social situations especially, he would often retreat to the periphery, where he'd sit quietly and uncomfortably. But the reticence masked perhaps *the* defining trait of Fred's father. At heart, he was a soft man, capable of real sweetness toward those he loved. His feelings for his young family were fervent.

John Olmsted also felt an intense patriotism for his native Hartford. This he expressed through generous charitable contributions to such Hartford institutions as the nation's first public art museum and third insane asylum. Such was his duty, as a seventh-generation descendant of one of the city's founders, James Olmsted.

In 1632, this original Olmsted set out from Essex, England, aboard the ship *Lyon*, bound for America. He had buried his wife and lost four of his seven children. Anxious for a fresh start in the New World, he settled first in the colony of Massachusetts. But in 1636, he joined an expedition led by the Reverend Thomas Hooker that headed south on foot to found a new community. The group wound up in the Connecticut Valley and settled in a place they named Hertford, after a town in England. (It was later Americanized to "Hartford.") As part of a land distribution, James Olmsted was given 70 acres along a road that became Front Street.

When Fred was a baby, James Olmsted's colonial-era house was still standing. Generation upon generation of Olmsteds were inextricably tied up with the history of Hartford. Joseph Olmsted was the city's first deacon. Captain Aaron Olmsted was the first in the community to own a piano. Voting records show that even into the 1800s, Olmsted remained the second most common name in Hartford after Hill. Olmsteds were everywhere: Ashbel Olmsted served a term as town clerk; George Olmsted was secretary of the local Temperance Society.

The Olmsted line on his father's side may have dominated the civic life of Hartford, but Fred's very first memory involved his mother. He was about three years old. His mother was sitting under a tree sewing while he played at her feet. It's a hazy little reminiscence, but poignant when one considers what happened soon after.

On February 28, 1826, Charlotte Olmsted died of an overdose of laudanum. Laudanum is a tincture consisting of opiates dissolved in alcohol. It was a common patent medicine, a mainstay in many nineteenth-century American households, used to aid sleep, suppress coughs, relieve menstrual cramps, and myriad other things. Laudanum was also highly addictive and frequently lethal. Charlotte's death happened just six months after the birth of a new baby, John Hull Olmsted. This was her second child—Fred's baby brother.

Supposedly, Charlotte overdosed accidentally, while battling the flu. One wonders whether she took her own life. Maybe she was suffering from postpartum depression, a syndrome entirely unrecognized in that time. Or perhaps she was reeling from the religious revival, which she had attended only a few weeks before her death. Such revivals were part of a fevered effort to stiffen religious conviction that swept across America during the first half of the 1800s. They were highly public events, in which participants were called upon to demonstrate the purity of their faith to the satisfaction of the community. Participating in a revival was known to pitch people into terrible bouts of self-doubt and recrimination.

Olmsted's second memory is clearly from his mother's deathbed. "I chanced to stray into a room at the crisis of a tragedy then occurring and turned and fled from it screaming in a manner adding to the horror of the household," he later recalled. "It was long before I could be soothed and those nearby said to one another that I would never forget what I had seen."

Even as a small boy, Fred began working to blot out the memory. For the rest of his life, his mother's death was something he refused to discuss in any detail. Charlotte Olmsted took an accidental overdose of laudanum. That was that.

Following his wife's death, John Olmsted briefly stopped writing in his diary, a silence that spoke volumes. Then he picked back up with: "No a/c kept of expenses from Feb 24 to March 12." And he added the following brief notation: "Tues Feb 28 at ½ past 5 p.m. my dr wife died & was buried Sunday following."

A grieving John Olmsted left the care of his two young sons to a live-in nurse. After a few months, four-year-old Fred was enrolled in a "dame school." Dame schools offered instruction—often, very casual instruction—at the homes of women in a community. They served as a kind of nineteenth-century version of nursery school. In some cases, the schooling extended through what today would be the first few primary grades. Fred attended Mrs. Jeffry's dame school. There, his days consisted mostly of playing in a nearby brook, chasing frogs, and building dams to trap small fish.

John Olmsted would be a widower for a little more than a year before wedding Mary Ann Bull. His new wife—Fred's stepmother—was twenty-six and came from a prominent Hartford family. Her father was a druggist. A contemporary account calls her a "celebrated beauty of the day" and goes on to describe her as "the leading singer in the Centre Church choir," with a "rich soprano voice." For John, this second marriage appears to have been more of a practical arrangement, hardly a love match. He was raising two small boys. He needed help.

Mary Ann Olmsted was organized, focused, intense. She was extremely devout, to the point of being puritanical. In fact, she and Charlotte had been friends, and together they had attended the religious revival. Apparently, John hoped that his new wife would provide a hard line, realizing all too well that he was inclined to be soft toward his two sons. Furthermore, while John Olmsted was a regular churchgoer, he had failed to experience a genuine conversion—that mysterious but undeniable signal held by Connecticut Congregationalists as proof of true faith. He seems to have hoped that Mary Ann would set an example for his boys, where he was lacking.

Two weeks after the wedding, both Fred and his brother, John, were baptized. Not long after that, Fred was moved to a school run by Naomi Rockwell, considered a more disciplined dame school. He was six now and small compared to his schoolmates. There was a shut-off quality about him that was heartrending, making others want to reach out to him. An older girl named Anne Charlotte Lynch used to pick Fred up at his house and walk him to Miss Rockwell's. She later remembered him as having blue eyes, thick blond curls, and chubby dimpled arms, invariably dressed in a short-sleeved frock.

At Miss Rockwell's, Fred was introduced to a curriculum that drew largely on pedagogical works by residents of Hartford. This was remarkable and rooted in Connecticut's Puritan origins. The first Puritan settlers had been fervent about education on the theory that if they taught their children to read and reason, their principles might be passed along to subsequent generations. As the capital and as an economic and cultural center, Hartford had a long, distinguished history of producing schoolbooks. The homegrown works that Fred studied also happened to be the standard texts adopted by teachers throughout the young nation.

To learn grammar, Fred used *The American Spelling Book* by Noah Webster, the trailblazing lexicographer and Hartford native. Webster's "blue-back speller" was *the* text for generations of American school kids. It is arranged according to syllables, starting out with entire passages written in single-syllable words and working its way to five-syllable doozies. Webster was a very pious man, and the "blue-back speller" includes ample religious instruction, even in monosyllabic form:

The way of man is ill.
My son, do as you are bid.
But if you are bid, do no ill.
See not my sin, and let me not go to the pit.

To learn what was where, Fred used *A Geography and Atlas*, a brand-new book by Hartford resident Jesse Olney. By introducing children first to observable details such as lakes and hills and then moving to the more abstract, such as countries and continents, Olney revolutionized the way that geography was taught. His book quickly became a mainstay in virtually every school in the United States—dame, public, private, or otherwise.

According to notations in John Olmsted's diary, Fred also read various books featuring "Jack Halyard, the Sailor Boy" at Miss Rockwell's school. These fictional tales packed with moral instruction were the work of Hartford's own Samuel Goodrich, who wrote under the name Peter Parley. He was the J. K. Rowling of nineteenth-century America. Parley was mobbed by children during his frequent reading tours, and he sold millions of Jack Halyard tales.

While Miss Rockwell's specialized in one kind of instruction, Fred was receiving equally valuable lessons from his parents. If there's one area where John and Mary Ann Olmsted connected emotionally, it was in their shared appreciation for nature. The couple frequently took their

two young boys on horseback rambles through the Connecticut countryside. Even though the Olmsteds were city dwellers, natural splendor
was very close at hand. Hartford—bustling civic center that it was—
consisted of a mere thirty streets. It was possible, within a matter of minutes, to leave the town utterly behind and travel across broad meadows
and over rolling hills, soaking in the beauty of the hinterlands.

Fred rode with his father, sitting on a pillow placed on the saddle.
There was little conversation. John and Mary Ann preferred to take in the
scenery with a kind of hushed reverence. These quiet family expeditions,
devoted to appreciating the landscape and its beauty, made quite an impression on young Fred. Often, the family would stop near a stream so
that Fred and his brother could bathe. Or they might have a picnic. The
boys would gather wild berries while their stepmother arranged a spread
beneath the shade of a tree.

One time, Fred and his father were walking across a meadow as
evening was falling, after a long day's ramble. Fred was tired, so his father
scooped him up. Fred made a few comments about their surroundings,
but his father didn't respond, carrying him in silence. Suddenly, Fred
pointed to a star up in the sky. His father hugged him close and mum-
bled something about the "infinite love" he felt for his son.

That moment stuck with Fred, too. He'd remember it—cling to it
even—for the rest of his days. It was a solid marker in a life that would
be filled with so much change.

John Olmsted's diary entry for February 8, 1829, was ostensibly a brief
note on the weather: "Sunday rain." Then, almost as an afterthought, he
scrawled: "Miss Naomi Rockwell buried. Died Friday Eve from burns by
clothes taking fire."

Fred's dame-school days were over, just like that. His parents packed
him off to North Guilford, Connecticut, to study with the Reverend
Zolva Whitmore. For nearly the next decade, from the age of seven to the
age of sixteen, Fred would have a series of boarding arrangements, living
with ministers who ran schools, with relatives while attending schools,
serving a vocational apprenticeship. There was nothing unusual about
this. It was a common practice in this era for parents of comfortable

means to send their children away for schooling. What's more, as of 1829, John and Mary Ann had just had a new baby. In the years ahead, they would have five more. The household would grow increasingly crowded and hectic, filled with young children. It made sense to send Fred away.

Where to send him was more of an issue. Apparently, John and Mary Ann disagreed about how young Fred should be educated. She was troubled that her husband's paltry formal schooling had been deficient on matters of faith. She didn't wish to repeat the same mistake with Fred. Much of his schooling in the years ahead would emphasize religious training.

As for the sheer number of different schools that Fred tried out—now, that was unusual. He would prove a tough placement. As he grew, he developed a restless intelligence—hard for his teachers to channel—and became increasingly difficult to discipline. Consequently, Fred would recall: "I was strangely uneducated—miseducated. . . . I was left at the most important age to 'run wild.'"

Off in North Guilford, Fred quickly discovered that although Whitmore was a religious man, he was far from strict. He was just a poor country parson running a one-room school for twelve boys in an effort to make a few extra dollars. Frequently, the reverend delegated the task of teaching to one of the older boys, while he attended to his parson duties. Fred soon discovered there was a lot of latitude. In fact, the boys were allowed to go barefoot at all times except for Sunday services.

Fred headed out on a series of solitary rambles throughout the countryside. He chased after rabbits and crafted figure-four traps out of sticks and string, hoping to catch quail. He paused before an open meadow to watch as a decrepit old militia regiment from the War of 1812 drilled in their faded uniforms. He peered through a window as some people who had traded pelts for rum drank themselves into a stupor.

One evening, he slipped out of the parsonage and walked to the grave of a little girl who had recently died. The death had consumed the parsonage throughout the previous days. Fred had been present when a man arrived, announcing that his little daughter was dead. The man banged three times on an iron triangle that hung by a strip of cowhide from the belfry beams of the meetinghouse, thereby alerting the community of the sad event. Next day, lessons were canceled, and Fred tagged along with his schoolfellows to watch as the coffin was made. It was tiny, crafted from pine boards, and stained red—the smell of the varnish was overpowering. Whitmore enlisted his pupils to help with funeral preparations. He delivered the eulogy, and the boys walked in the procession.

It was during the wake that Fred had slipped out to visit the little girl's grave. He knelt before it and prayed to God to bring her back to life. He planned to lead her to the parsonage and reunite her with her devastated parents. The night grew still, and Fred could hear whippoorwill cries. He chased fireflies for a while. Then he returned to the parsonage and went to bed—no one even asking any questions.

Free to come and go as he pleased, Fred often went to the country store, where he would sit quietly and listen as his elders talked. Sometimes, he'd pay an impromptu visit to one of the many Olmsteds who lived in the countryside surrounding Hartford. "I was under no more constraint than a man," Fred would recall. "Every house, every room, every barn and stable, every shop, every road and byway, every field, orchard and garden was not only open to me but I was every where welcome. With all their hard working habits no one seemed to begrudge a little time to make life happy to such a bothering little chappie as I must have been."

After a year, Fred was yanked out of Whitmore's overlax parsonage and parked in the home of Benjamin and Content Olmsted, his paternal grandparents. The plan was for him to live with them and attend Hartford Grammar School. Benjamin Olmsted, age seventy-nine, was one of Fred's favorite relatives. For church, the man's Sunday best consisted of a ruffled shirt, knee breeches and stockings, and shoes with silver buckles. He'd tie back his gray hair in a pigtail. He had fought in the Revolutionary War and was like the living embodiment of history itself. About the only thing missing from the ensemble was a three-corner hat. Even that Fred discovered in the attic, gathering dust.

Fred enjoyed the society of older people, much more than a typical child. Benjamin was happy to oblige his grandson, spinning out reminiscences about marching through the Maine woods under Benedict

Arnold to lay siege to Quebec, one of the earliest and bloodiest battles of the Revolution. Fred asked whether he had ever been forced to cook and eat his own boots. His grandfather laughed and laughed.

On a warm spring day, Benjamin led Fred outside and pointed to an elm. He had helped his own father plant the tree, he explained, and it had once been a mere sapling. But just look at it: It was a tall tree. The old man stood there, leaning on his silver-topped Malacca cane, shaking his head in wonderment.

Fred was nine years old now. His blond hair had turned brown; the curls had loosed into waves. His baby fat was all gone; his chubby, dimpled arms had grown lean and sinewy. But he remained a small boy, with dark eyes and a tight-coiled nervousness about him. A report from Hartford Grammar School assessed Fred as very bright but unwilling or unable to focus on his studies.

He found other, more informal, ways to supplement his schoolwork. Fred explored his grandmother's book collection and at a tender age waded into such dense fare as *The Vicar of Wakefield* by Oliver Goldsmith and Laurence Sterne's *Sentimental Journey Through France and Italy*. During this time, he also made frequent visits to the Hartford Young Men's Institute library, which his father helped fund with charitable contributions. Here, he discovered works such as William Gilpin's *Remarks on Forest Scenery* and Sir Uvedale Price's *Essay on the Picturesque, as Compared with the Sublime and the Beautiful*. These were rarefied texts on landscape aesthetics—highly precocious subject matter—but young Fred found himself drawn to them nonetheless.

He also felt the pull of *Solitude* by Johann Georg Zimmermann, a favorite book he'd return to throughout his life, but one that he read for the first time while living with his grandparents. Zimmermann, a Swiss physician, argued that it was necessary to periodically retreat from humanity into nature for the sake of spiritual replenishment.

Then, all too soon, it was good-bye Grandfather Benjamin, good-bye Grandmother Content. Fred was off to Ellington, a brand-new school that promised "strong discipline" in its ad in the *Hartford Courant*. Perhaps Fred simply needed a firm hand to rein him in. "I was very active, imaginative, inventive, impulsive, enterprising, trustful and heedless,"

Fred would recall. "This made what is generally called a troublesome and mischievous boy."

At Ellington, what he got instead was a cruel hand. Shortly into his first term, a minister grabbed Fred by both ears and pulled until they bled. The event was sufficiently brutal to prompt one of the older students to write a letter describing the event to Fred's father. Time to move yet again, this time to a school run by the Reverend Joab Brace in Newington, Connecticut.

Brace was a tall, severe man with coal-black eyes and an intimidating demeanor. He held a degree in divinity from Williams and spoke Latin, Greek, and Hebrew. He had a reputation for preparing his charges for both Christian conversion and college education. Despite his erudition, he was yet another poor preacher who ran a school and worked a farm, both as ways to supplement his small income. The reverend wasn't averse to mixing his two sidelines by requiring his pupils to help out on the farm.

Fred lived with three other boys in a rickety little building that sat beside Brace's parsonage. The building's cellar was piled high with cabbages and roots. On the ground floor, there was a workshop for the farm, full of harnesses and other equipment. The boys' desks for study and beds were crowded into the upper story. Winds whipped through the warped clapboards and swirled about their meager quarters.

Fred's days were mostly given over to chores. During cold weather, for example, he would be up before dawn chopping logs. He'd haul wood into the parsonage and the school building and have to maintain fires in the heating stoves throughout the day. Fred did this every fourth day, rotating with the other three pupils. On the other days, there were other chores; there was always endless work to be done.

Nighttime was set aside for actual course work, often on the heels of a full day of farm labor. Brace's students were required to pore over books such as *Adam's Latin Grammar* and the *Young Men's Book*, which offered moral instruction. Fred found that he simply couldn't abide this regimen, especially after enjoying such freedom at Rev. Zolva Whitmore's school and his grandparents' home. Sometimes at night, he would entertain his fellow pupils with made-up adventure stories. He'd spin these tales in the barest whisper because Brace was in the habit of sneaking into the little building where his pupils lived. The reverend would slip off his shoes, creep up the stairs, and stand at the threshold, silently listening. If he detected discussion of anything save for lessons, he'd burst through the door and whack the boys about the shoulders with a broom handle. Invariably, he'd shout, "Oh, the depravity of human nature!"

Hot water was provided on Saturday nights only. The boys were expected to wash their ears, necks, and feet. Twice a day, for prayers, the boys knelt on the cold, bare floor of the parsonage kitchen.

Fred was soon joined at Brace's country school by John, his younger brother. John was growing into an attractive boy—also small for his age—with tousled hair and a winningly casual demeanor. He was very smart, but he didn't scuff against the world like Fred. Nor did he share Fred's lack of focus. At Brace's school, John would continue on an academic course that would take him to Yale, where he'd study medicine. In the years ahead, the bond between the two brothers was destined to grow tighter. The two of them were set apart, after all, as the only children born to Charlotte Olmsted before she died.

As for Fred's half-siblings back home in Hartford, he knew them only fleetingly. They were more like cousins. Three of the six children born to John and Mary Ann Olmsted would die before reaching maturity. These departed half-siblings would be little more than dimly recalled shadows for Fred, whose young life was already a study in inconstancy.

Another big blow soon followed. At age fourteen, Fred developed a severe rash from coming in contact with the plant poison sumac. The infection spread to his eyes, and soon his vision was seriously impaired. He feared that he was going blind. Naturally, he had no choice but to withdraw from Brace's school.

Fred was urged to pursue a course of "hydrotherapy"—then all the rage. In Fred's case, a regimen of ocean bathing—exposing his eyes to saltwater—seemed the best approach. Off went Fred to the seaside town of Saybrook, Connecticut, where he boarded with the Reverend George

Clinton Van Vechten Eastman, who was to oversee his cure and also act as his tutor.

The better Fred's eyesight became, the more he was required to study with Eastman. Not surprisingly, his improvement was slow. So Fred's father took him to New York City to consult with a doctor. The doctor suggested that Fred continue with the hydrotherapy. Apparently, the man also recommended that, given Fred's delicate eyesight, he should scrap any plans of going to college. During the 1800s, kids frequently went off to college in their midteens—at fourteen or fifteen. By now, Fred had fallen desperately behind in his studies anyhow.

Gradually, Fred regained his eyesight, thanks to the wonder of his hydrotherapy sessions in Saybrook. Or perhaps the healing was achieved by the simple passage of time, accompanied by very little stress, on a beach. Either way, Fred was done with formal schooling. He had a doctor's orders to prove it. But if he wasn't going to college, he needed to learn a trade. Fred selected surveying. Of course, surveying requires eagle-sharp eyesight in order to spot topographical details and render precise maps. There wasn't much logic in any of this. But his father was willing to entertain anything, anything at all, to get Fred moving again.

Fred entered into an apprenticeship with F. A. Barton, a surveyor who also happened to be studying to become a minister. This seemed an ideal combination. Fred could learn a profession under the tutelage of someone who could also look out for his spiritual development. Neither of Barton's qualifications seems to have made an impact on Fred. John Olmsted wrote Fred a letter, gently suggesting that his son had reached an age where "we begin to feel that the time is come for us to throw off boyish notions and habits." His father added hopefully, "Even surveying begins to have some interest in your mind."

Fred learned the basics from Barton. But he was more interested in laying out imaginary cities. Even this activity lost out to one of the biggest draws of surveying—it was outdoor work. Under the guise of learning a useful trade, Fred engaged in the things he truly loved—hiking and swimming and hunting and fishing.

Then Fred simply returned home to live. It was an unfathomable move, the kind of thing that able-bodied young men simply did not do in the 1840s. He was a boomerang child when the concept simply did not exist. His father was exhausted and confounded but welcomed him back. What other option was there? His stepmother was tolerant, but barely.

Fred had become a source of puzzlement to those who knew him. He was a person of such obvious intelligence, yet he was entirely adrift. He was a wastrel, yet he wasn't a difficult person or mean-spirited. More than anything, he just seemed to lack any real sense of urgency. It was as if he was following his own private calendar, and he behaved as though he had all the time in the world. "I hear Fred'k coming (whistling)," wrote John Olmsted in a letter. "He works in the garden (with great moderation) in the morning and this P.M. has been breaking the laws of our town, shooting poor blackbirds."

To some degree, at least, Fred's maddening indolence appears to have been a front. During this time, his brother John was off studying in Paris, an opportunity furnished by a family friend. This seems to have secretly eaten at Fred. Here, after all, was his younger brother, leaving him behind, quite literally. "Dear brother," begins a letter from Fred to John in Paris. "I have nothing particular to write to you about." In another letter, Fred first offered a piece of national news. (There had been a big flood in Natchez, Mississippi.) He followed this with a piece of Connecticut news (the legislature was about to adjourn) and closed with local news from Hartford (gutter work in progress). And that was all. Signed, Fred.

In his own strange way, Fred seemed to be communicating embarrassment in this letter by not bothering to include a solitary detail about himself or his current life. Or maybe it was an act of emotional withholding: *You think you're better, away in Paris—well, I'm not even going to bother to tell you about myself, living at home, in Hartford.* Certainly, there's something off-kilter about writing such an impersonal letter to one's brother.

Ultimately, John's Paris trip may have goaded Fred back into the world. While his brother was away, Fred got a job at Benkard and Hutton, an importer of high-quality French silk located at 53 Beaver Street in Manhattan. Benkard and Hutton was a supplier to his father's store. Fred's father, in turn, used his connections to land the job for his son.

At age eighteen, Fred moved to Brooklyn, New York, where he took a room in Mrs. Howard's boardinghouse on Henry Street. It was his first time living on his own. Rent, breakfast, and laundry service cost $3.50 per week. Fred was desperately lonely. After work, he'd sit by himself, slowly picking his way through dinners taken at Pine's Coffee Rooms. Back in Brooklyn, he spent his time on the roof of his boardinghouse, looking after a pair of doves that he adopted.

He hated the job at Benkard and Hutton. He hated the twelve-hour workdays. He hated the six-day workweeks. He hated sitting at a desk. He hated the rules and regimentation. But Fred's job required him to go onboard ships anchored in New York's harbor to inventory their cargoes of silk, and it was while visiting these ships that he began to form an idea of something else he might do with his life.

CHAPTER 2

At Sea

FRED RESOLVED TO become a sailor. If he had to choose a trade, this made far more sense than the other professions in which he'd briefly dabbled. It was outdoor work, unlike clerking, and it promised a great deal more adventure than surveying. Besides, going to sea was in his blood. Trace his father's line back over those many generations, and it was sailors, sailors everywhere.

Among the most notable was Aaron Olmsted, Fred's great-uncle. As captain of the *Huntress* and one of the first Americans involved in the China trade, he established a shipping route to Canton, amassing a fortune along the way. Captain Gideon Olmsted was another great-uncle. As a boy, Fred sat on the captain's knee and listened to his yarns about various ocean adventures, one of which was particularly dramatic and noteworthy. In 1777, Olmsted was one of several prisoners who staged a revolt on a British warship, where they were being held captive. Olmsted seized control, diverted the ship to the New Jersey coast, and turned it and its British crew over to American authorities. The brave feat made him a Revolutionary War hero. Years back, he'd even published a book about the episode, *The Journal of Gideon Olmsted: Adventures of a Sea Captain During the American Revolution*. More recently, Fred's nautically inclined cousin Francis had written *Incidents of a Whaling Voyage*.

Fred had read both of these books. Despite his piecemeal schooling, Fred was—and would remain—a voracious reader. He had also recently read *Two Years Before the Mast*, Richard Henry Dana Jr.'s classic account of a voyage from Boston to California, by way of Cape Horn. The book had created a sensation upon its publication just two years earlier, in 1840. The striking parallels between his own life and Dana's were not lost on Fred. As a child, Dana had studied under a cruel schoolmaster, who one time nearly pulled off his ear. Later, complications from measles— leading to a condition called ophthalmia, characterized by temporary blindness—prompted Dana to drop out of Harvard. On recovering his vision, he decided to take an ocean journey.

Among Dana's well-heeled peers, it was in vogue to travel to Europe as a passenger on a luxury ship and embark upon a "grand tour." He chose instead to enlist on a merchant ship as an ordinary seaman, the better to have a genuine adventure. Fred wanted to do the same.

Securing a job on a ship proved a challenge. First, there was the matter of Fred's chosen destination. Fred concluded that he wanted to sail to China. Great-uncle Aaron and his grandfather Benjamin had both made this voyage, so it was something of a family tradition. But choosing China meant that Fred had to wait some months for the timing to be right. In those days, in order to avoid the most treacherous monsoon winds, ships bound for China from ports on the East Coast of the United States tended to depart in the spring. So Fred came home to Hartford and passed some more idle months in waiting.

As spring drew nearer, Fred faced the not inconsiderable challenge of finding a ship's captain willing to hire him on. He teamed up with Jim Goodwin, a Hartford friend who had the experience of a single voyage under his belt. With his stories of fierce storms and exotic ports, Good-win seemed like a ship-worn veteran to Fred. The pair took a trip to New York City and visited the offices of various maritime trading companies. They stopped by the Sailor's Home, where members of ships' crews hung out during shore leave. Together, Fred and Jim canvassed the Manhattan waterfront, looking for leads to a job aboard a ship.

They were much encouraged by a talk with a principal at Gordon and Talbot, an outfit involved in the China trade. The man informed them that the *Ronaldson*, a ship operated by his firm, would be leaving within a matter of days. Some additional hands were needed, he suspected, and he urged Fred and his friend to go meet with the captain at once.

On meeting Captain Warren Fox, Jim Goodwin was immediately hired. The captain wasn't so sure about Fred. He expressed concern about taking on a "green boy," someone who had never before been to sea. Now pushing twenty-one, Fred was hardly the typical green boy. In response, Fred pulled out all the stops. He explained that although he lacked experience, he came by his yen to sail honestly, as one of the seafaring Olmsteds of Hartford. And he promised to work hard and to follow orders. Presently, he wore down Captain Fox and was hired as an apprentice sailor. Salary: roughly $5 a month.

During their interview, Captain Fox impressed Fred as immensely capable. He seemed to have thought of everything. The *Ronaldson* was a bark, a medium-size vessel with three masts, and for the voyage to China it would have a crew of about twenty men. Captain Fox explained that he did not like the seasoned sailors to mix with the younger, less experienced hands. They could be a corrupting influence. In fact, one of his primary rules was that no cursing was allowed on his ship. He planned to set aside separate sleeping quarters for the voyage's four youngest sailors. To Fred, Captain Fox gave the appearance of a deeply honorable man.

Fred was elated. After being hired, he remained on the dock on Manhattan's East River where the *Ronaldson* was anchored to get a good, long look at the ship that would be conveying him to China. Standing there, he dashed off a letter to John, who was back from his Europe trip and enrolled at Yale. At last, Fred had some news of himself to share with his brother: "Now's the time, as I have a sailor with me, to describe the ship. Bark, I should say. She is of about 330 plus tons, pretty good form, but nothing clipper. Rakish rigging, long black yards (main royal up)." Fred carried on for several more paragraphs, breathlessly cataloging the features of the *Ronaldson*: "[The ship] has a long boat, quarter boat & whale boat. Carries two bulldogs (6 lb. carronades or so), wheel of the best construction under cover (when wanted) & is about two years old, having been but two voyages to Valparaiso or thereabouts. Mr. Coghlin [the first mate] says she is the best calculated for Canton of any ship he ever saw except the 'Morrison.'"

The *Ronaldson* was scheduled to depart in two weeks for a journey that would last eight months, minimum. Fred made a whirlwind visit back to Hartford to say good-bye to his family and prepare for his voyage. He bought an almanac, a sea chest, cloth pants, and three flannel shirts. From a Hartford doctor, he obtained a homeopathic remedy for seasickness. His spinster aunt Maria voiced concern that Fred might be "drowndered," as she termed it. So he also bought a life preserver. As a final touch, a local artist was hired to sketch Fred in his sailor's uniform.

On April 24, 1843, the *Ronaldson* set sail from New York. Fred's father and brother, who had accompanied him down from Hartford to see him off, stood on the Pike Street wharf, waving.

It was a perfect day for sailing, sunny with a light breeze. As a result, nearly thirty other ships departed at the same time as the *Ronaldson*. It was like a flotilla, heading out of New York Harbor. For a while, the *Ronaldson* sailed alongside a packet called the *Albany*. The crews yelled back and forth, and Fred learned that the other boat was sailing to Havre. When they pulled up beside another ship, the *Pilot*, he learned that this one was bound for Batavia. All these ships, sailing to all these different destinations—it seemed very glamorous. Fred noticed a spout in the distance. It turned out to be a whale.

The *Ronaldson* was packed with fur pelts, machine-spun cloth, and other "Yankee notions," as Fred termed them. These were to be sold in China, though specific buyers had not been lined up. Rather, the *Ronaldson* planned to anchor in China and open up for business to whoever came onboard. That was the standard practice. Fred's ship was like an amphibious Wal-Mart.

Of course, the fuller the ship, the more goods one could hawk. Prior to embarking, Captain Fox had stuffed every available spot, even sleeping quarters, with saleable wares. The *Ronaldson* was almost comically overloaded. Once the ship hit open water, when it was safely away from the prying eyes of the captains and crews of ships such as the *Albany* and *Pilot*, a kind of rejiggering of the cargo took place under the direction of Captain Fox. To shed some weight, he ordered the men to toss overboard barrel after barrel of salt beef and other rations. Food was getting jettisoned in preference for saleable merchandise. Never mind that U.S. maritime law prescribed that a ship must carry a certain allotment of rations to feed the crew.

As for the separate quarters Captain Fox had promised Fred, meant to keep impressionable young sailors away from morally suspect veterans, this proved quite a comedown. Even following the food toss, the *Ronaldson* remained incredibly overloaded. Many of the cabins, while designed for human habitation, were actually filled up with China-bound wares. Fred and three other young hands were crammed into a tiny, foul-smelling space deep belowdecks.

Fred was put to work on a head pump. Hours before dawn, he was out on the ship's undulating deck, squatting low to open a spigot, filling a bucket with bilge water, closing the spigot, walking a few teetering steps to dump the water into a tub, where it was used to clean the decks. Repeat. By 8:00 a.m., he was already exhausted. The ship's carpenter was working nearby, and Fred asked if any kind of break was in sight. The carpenter simply laughed.

Fred kept going. His hands grew raw and blistered from opening the spigot and carrying the bucket. His clothes were soaked through with spray. And then the nausea began to set in. Now, he really was a green boy. His discomfort grew over the next couple days, until it got so bad that he was ordered to leave off work and go below deck.

But he couldn't get to his sea chest. During the cargo shuffle, his chest—containing his seasickness remedy, changes of clothes, everything—had gotten wedged somewhere deep in the bowels of the ship, completely inaccessible.

Fred staggered into his tiny quarters and vomited. Then he lay down and tried to shut out the ship's agonizing pitch and yaw. Fortunately, Fred's Hartford friend Jim Goodwin was there to look after him. When Fred was well enough to eat again, Jim brought a tin pot of food, specially prepared by the ship's cook.

Fred took a bite. "Bah!"

"What's the matter?"

Fred explained that the food tasted really sour. But Jim assured him that the bad taste was in his own mouth from being sick.

"It will taste better in a minute," Jim said. "You must get it down. It will do you a great deal of good."

So Fred tried again. But the food still tasted awful. Had it maybe been prepared with saltwater? No, said Jim, the cook had most certainly used fresh rainwater collected in the ship's scuttlebutt. Fred tried one more time. But it was so repulsive that he couldn't choke down a single bite. So Jim decided to give it a try. The moment the spoon reached his mouth, he made a horrible grimace.

"Why, there is something wrong," he said.

"I knew there was," said Fred, and then he joked: "Try a little more; perhaps it will taste better."

Turns out, the cook had viewed Fred's "special" dinner as an opportunity to unload some old meal that had gone sour. In fact, it was left over from the *Ronaldson*'s previous voyage.

While he recouped, Fred was put on light duty, filing rust off the ship's cutlasses and blunderbusses. Encountering pirates was always a possibility; the ship's crew might have to use these weapons. Meanwhile, Jim separated out the palatable parts of meals—things like beans—and brought them to Fred. When Fred could keep down scouse, a thin stew made with cod and chunks of hard biscuit, the worst was finally behind him.

Fred had gotten his sea legs—or sea stomach, rather. He began to get into the flow of life on a ship. Water was forever collecting in the hull, and this bilge water had to be pumped. The decks were forever getting dirty and had to be swabbed. Fred took his turns on watch and was initiated into one of the great sailor's arts, learning to tie and splice various knots.

Fred soon gleaned that the crew of the *Ronaldson* worked hard, harder than crews aboard other ships. The weather had been calm so far, and Captain Fox was keen to take advantage by quickly covering as much distance as possible. As a result, the men were placed on extralong shifts, putting in eighteen-hour days, six days a week.

As the days bled one into another, Fred found that the thing he craved most, more even than a decent meal, was sleep. The vast unbroken sky, the sea stretching endlessly in all directions, the ceaseless rocking motion—it was like the ultimate soporific. As he worked, Fred constantly caught himself nodding off. But the lure of sleep was balanced by a powerful disincentive. He'd snap to instantly. Two of the younger sailors dozed off while on duty and had been "rope's ended" as in: flogged.

A month into the journey, the *Ronaldson* crossed the equator. By now, Fred was growing comfortable going aloft, shimmying up ropes and edging out along narrow wooden spars, squaring the sails to catch the wind. Sometimes he'd climb more than one hundred feet above the deck. He was learning the lingo—"set the lee foretopmast stud'n sail" and "clew up main-royal" and "haul down flying jib," directions for positioning the ship's twenty or so sails.

Part of the flow of life on a ship is sudden change. As the *Ronaldson* rounded the tip of Africa, it encountered a stretch of dreaded "Cape weather." There was driving rain and wind so fierce that the main topsail was ripped to ribbons. This gave way to a blinding snowstorm. Because weather in the Southern Hemisphere is the reverse of weather in the Northern, the crew spent the day of July 4, 1843, battling a blizzard at sea.

The sleep-deprived men soon grew woozy. A sailor lost his purchase on a spar and pitched to the deck. It wasn't such a long fall, and his trajectory was fortunate. Had the sailor fallen a few feet farther over, he would have plunged directly into the roiling, frigid sea—and certain death.

Then Fred fell. He lost his grip on an icy rope and tumbled to the deck. He actually fell farther than the other sailor; he, too, could easily have been killed, had it not been for a piece of luck. His impact was cushioned when he landed on a coil of manila rope. Fred got right up, sustaining only an injury to his hand. In the biting cold, the hand soon stiffened and was useless.

This was the worst storm that anyone onboard had ever seen. Every man was needed; Fred was placed on watch, duty that could be performed by a one-handed sailor. Because the *Ronaldson* was so grossly overloaded, with each swell, huge volumes of frigid saltwater washed across the deck. Wind pelted the sailors with snow. When even the most hardened crewman began to show anxiety, Fred became alarmed. It looked like the *Ronaldson* might sink.

Captain Fox gave the order to furl the sails. The *Ronaldson* was nearly impossible to control at this point anyway. The sails had become useless, a detriment even, simply catching the wild winds and driving the ship this way and that. For several terrifying days, the crew huddled below deck and waited while the naked-masted *Ronaldson* contended with the elements without any human guidance whatsoever. The ship was like a tiny cork bobbing on an infinite turbulent sea.

Then the storm lifted as suddenly as it had come on. The *Ronaldson* completed its turn around the Cape of Good Hope and started north through the warm waters of the Indian Ocean.

Traveling through the Sunda Strait, between the Indonesian islands of Java and Sumatra, Fred was thrilled to spot land. It was literally the first time he had seen land since leaving New York. The *Ronaldson* anchored at Anjer, but Fred and most of the crew were required to stay on-board. It was to be the briefest of port calls, as Captain Fox was in a hurry to reach China.

The sailors pooled some money from their small wages and chose a couple of their number to go ashore on a supply run. One sailor came back with rum. But Fred was more interested in food. For weeks now, the crew had been subsisting on wormy bread and the odd scrap of meat. Fresh vegetables and fruit had run out long ago. In fact, much of the supply of such items had been tossed overboard at the beginning of the voyage to make room for saleable merchandise. When the sailors returned to the *Ronaldson* bearing rice, fowl, coconuts, plantains, and tamarinds, Fred prepared for a feast. The centerpiece was to be two live green turtles.

But Fox seized the best of these items, claiming captain's-table prerogative. He and his top lieutenants ate the coconuts, leaving the husks for the lowly crewmen to pick over. And they ate one of the turtles. The other, they tossed overboard, claiming it was sickly. Fred watched in famished horror as the supposedly ailing turtle swam away at a very healthy clip.

By now, Fred had spent enough time with Captain Fox to form an opinion of the man. In the close confines of the *Ronaldson*, he'd learned to fear and despise him. Not only was the captain cruel, but he was a hypocrite to boot. During their first meeting in New York, Fox had taken pains to convey to Fred that he was deeply involved in the welfare of his crewmen, even down to their moral health. Clearly, he didn't care a whit.

About the only thing that had remained consistent was Captain Fox's aversion to swearing. Even this practice he tolerated among the seasoned hands. They swore like, well, sailors. Among the younger hands, however, it was wholly unacceptable and drew immediate and severe punishment. Strangely, Captain Fox did not swear himself. He perceived himself as a very pious man, and even aboard a ship in the middle of the sea, he knelt down every Sunday to utter a lengthy prayer. The rest of the week, Fred noted, appeared devoted to lunging at his men, striking them, flogging them, and, in casually sadistic moments, Fox seemed to delight in heaping on the verbal abuse.

Yet through it all, he never uttered a profanity. He was capable of acts of intense brutality while saying nothing saltier than "blast ye," "old granny," "oh, you marine," and "want your petticoats?" His gravest insult was "infernal soger"—*soger* being slang for someone who is shirking duty. "Well, he's a most incomprehensible man, truly," Fred concluded in a letter to his brother. Letters, by the way, were handed off to ships the *Ronaldson* encountered that were sailing west, headed for America. Such correspondence had to survive a treacherous ocean passage, followed by dispatch over land, to reach their intended recipients.

The *Ronaldson* passed through the Sunda Strait and continued on to the South China Sea. The ship had now entered some of the world's most pirate-infested waters, a legendary and terrifying stretch for sailors. Given everything that had happened so far on the voyage, it would have been only fitting if those well-burnished blunderbusses were needed to fend off an attack.

Instead, the crew had to contend with the other thing the South China Sea was known for during the maritime era: some of the world's most treacherous and confounding wind patterns. The *Ronaldson*'s voyage had been timed to avoid the worst of the monsoons, but what the crew encountered was challenge enough. The wind would whip one way. Then it would abruptly change course, blowing from the complete opposite direction. Navigating in such conditions—making any kind of forward progress—required skill and endurance. Fred and the other sailors scampered over the rigging, setting and resetting sails to take advantage of whatever winds prevailed at the moment. Balanced high on a spar, way in the distance, Fred could see waterspouts, deadly seafaring tornadoes. Fortunately, none came too close to the ship.

The *Ronaldson* spent nearly a month crossing the South China Sea. Then it left the ocean and headed up the Pearl River, weighing anchor at a place called Whampoa Reach. Beyond this point, the river was too shallow to accommodate a large seagoing vessel. The *Ronaldson* was now roughly a dozen miles south of the city of Canton (now known as Guangzhou). Captain Fox hired a translator, who in turn helped hire a team of local laborers. The laborers unloaded goods purchased from the ship onto smaller boats, which transported the merchandise up to Canton.

The *Ronaldson* had arrived in China at a time of heightened suspicion toward the West. The first opium war between China and Britain had only just ended in 1842, the year before. The opium wars—another would start in 1856—were clashes with Britain, which was using its colony in India as a base to ship opium into China. This trade continued, despite China's prohibition against the drug. Captain Fox had to hire a comprador to help navigate the maze of bureaucratic and customs issues that confronted a foreign ship in China at this most delicate time.

Fred was itching to go ashore. But he soon discovered that Captain Fox expected a green boy, such as he, to continue working onboard even while the ship was anchored. Fred had been cooped up in the ship for months, had sailed thousands of miles enduring much hardship, and the only possible compensation was the opportunity to visit an exotic land. Now he found himself patching the sails and slushing the masts—that is, coating the wooden poles in goopy pine tar to prevent rot from setting in.

All the while, China was in plain view. Anchored at Whampoa Reach, he could see people working in a rice paddy, tantalizingly close. But all he got of China was mosquitoes, which swarmed onto the ship and ate him alive. "My opportunities of observation & investigation are very similar to those enjoyed by Mr. Pickwick while a resident in his Majesty's Fleet Prison," he wrote his father.

The reference is to the *Pickwick Papers*, Dickens's first novel. For now, Fred had to content himself with trying to learn something about China from the many natives who came aboard the *Ronaldson*. In a letter to his brother John, he wrote: "I've heard much more than I've seen, to be sure."

The *Ronaldson*'s oversized load of merchandise sold quickly. But there were delays in purchasing the tea that the ship would haul back to America to sell on the other end of the voyage. Still, there was plenty to keep Fred busy. He was put to work going over sales invoices and preparing the ship's books. What a nightmare: It was as if Benkard and Hutton, the Manhattan desk job that Fred had so despised, had pursued him to the other side of the world.

An entire month ticked by before Fred was allowed to set foot in China. Even then, he was able to make only three very brief visits. He made the most of them. He soaked up every sight, sound—and taste. He dined on fresh ham and eggs, tried such novel fare as ginger and loaf sugar. He visited various shops, where he purchased souvenirs to bring home such as a mandarin cap, a sword, and a pair of chopsticks. He even wandered into a schoolroom while class was in session and paused for a long while watching the children as they recited from their textbooks in an impenetrable language.

Most of all, Fred appears to have been intrigued by the people he saw as he wandered around. The letters that he wrote for the benefit of his family are full of descriptions of merchants in their silk robes and black-satin skullcaps and little boys, their black hair pulled into tight queues, their fingernails surprisingly long. When three Chinese ladies passed him on the street, he noted their footwear: "But I was glad enough to have an opportunity of seeing 'em hobbling (exactly as if with wooden legs) on their tiny peg tops—what would you call 'em—not feet certainly—about three inches long."

During these visits ashore, Fred proved a keen observer with an insatiable curiosity. He noticed vivid details, which he communicated in exuberant letters that were also characterized by curious syntax and curiouser spellings—the result, no doubt, of his idiosyncratic education. He also showed an unusual sensitivity to the culture of China. At one point, he visited a temple in the company of some of his fellow sailors.

The sailors milled about, talking loudly. Fred stood quietly, even took off his hat. "What are you taking your hat off for in a heathen temple?" sneered one of his shipmates.

Because Fred was behaving so differently from the others, an old man singled him out and, after bowing deeply, walked up to him. The man spoke only a few words of pigeon English, but he beckoned Fred to follow. He led the way into a little room where he opened up various religious texts and invited Fred to look at them. He pointed out the decorative banners on the walls and showed Fred various implements used in the temple's services. Meanwhile, Fred's shipmates wandered about, tugging on lanterns and mindlessly banging on a ceremonial gong.

Fred spent Thanksgiving on the *Ronaldson*, still anchored at Whampoa Reach. He was ill once again, this time suffering from fever, chills, and exhaustion. Whatever the ailment was, Jim Goodwin had it even worse. Fred was able to return a favor, caring for the friend who had looked out for him during his earlier bout with seasickness.

Fred wrote a plaintive letter, describing the Thanksgiving dinner he pictured in progress, 8,000 miles away in Hartford. "It's just about the right time of day, & I am imagining you just about well to work on the turkeys & cranberry," he scrawled. "I suppose Mother has the 'boiled & oyster,' as usual, while Father performs on the roast & criticizes the dressing." Then he added, "Take care, Bertha," a nod to his half-sister. "That's a big drum stick, but I guess you'll manage it with one hand."

Fred had been away for nearly seven months now. He was ready to head home. On Thanksgiving Day, his father wrote the following brief entry in his diary: "Fred's company much wanted."

On December 30, 1843, the *Ronaldson* finally set sail for America, preposterously laden with a huge load of Chinese tea.

Among sailors, convention holds that return voyages are easier: Spirits are buoyed by the promise of familiar shores; discipline grows laxer. Certainly, that's what Fred expected.

It didn't happen. Thanks to market forces—the fresher the tea, the higher the price it would command—Captain Fox was hell-bent on making incredible time. Ordinarily, passage from China to the United States took about 120 days. He was aiming for 100 days. If anything, the crew would suffer greater privations during the trip home.

Food was scarce, as always. That was a given on a Captain Fox-piloted ship. But the lack of fresh water became the bigger issue. The captain grew concerned that he didn't have a sufficient supply onboard to last the entire voyage. At the same time, he didn't want to lose so much as a minute by stopping at a port to take on fresh water. So Captain Fox simply cut the sailors' ration of water severely, leaving them with minuscule amounts for drinking, making coffee, washing their clothes, and other needs.

By midjourney, the *Ronaldson*'s crew was hungry, thirsty, tired, and enraged. An episode occurred that brought them to the brink of mutiny.

Captain Fox ordered one of the young hands punished for that offense of offenses—cursing. The captain held the sailor while the first mate flogged him repeatedly. Fred looked on in horror, and one of his shipmates counted aloud: "Twenty-three, twenty-four . . . "

Another crewman yelled: "We are no men if we stand it longer!"

Suddenly, all around him, sailors took up handspikes and knives. Fred fully expected the crew to kill Captain Fox and the first mate.

Likely they would have, had one of the ship's most experienced hands not begun yelling: "Avast! Avast! . . . what do you want to run your head into a halter for? Can't you wait till we get home and let the law serve them out?"

His argument was simple: Engaging in mutiny was a foolish and self-destructive act that would surely result in the crew members being hung. Better to wait until the ship reached port and exact revenge on Captain Fox in a court of law. With his plea, the man managed to stop the uprising, and order was restored.

On April 20, 1844, the *Ronaldson* arrived in New York. The voyage had taken 104 days.

The crewman who had urged legal recourse over violence immediately set off for the Sailor's Home. There, he requested a voluntary lockdown to prevent himself from going on one of the alcoholic benders that

usually accompanied his shore leaves. He wanted to maintain a clear head
so that he could testify at the trial of Captain Fox.

The trial would happen surprisingly quickly. Fox would be convicted
of using excessive force and ordered to pay $1,000 to the sailor that he
had flogged.

As for Fred, he arrived home just shy of his twenty-second birthday,
looking yellow and skeletal, racked by scurvy. His head was shaved. At
first, his father didn't even recognize him.

"Well, how do you like the sea?" Fred had asked rhetorically in one of
his letters. Now, he had an answer: not very bloody much.

He'd endured seasickness, illness, and a fall from a spar; he'd battled
wind and water and snow; he'd been hungry, thirsty, and weary beyond
imagining. Unlike some other notable Olmsteds, sailor was not a vocation for Fred. The sea didn't call to him, and he'd never again consider a
life aboard a ship.

Yet, hard as it was, the voyage aboard the *Ronaldson* also changed
something essential about Fred. He'd faced a formidable challenge and,
for once, had stuck with something to completion. He may have appeared a gaunt and diminished figure on the wharf that April day. But he
was larger somehow, too, having perhaps bulked up in terms of inner
strength. He still had a long way to go; plenty of dead ends lay ahead, and
settling into adulthood was going to be drastically more difficult for him
than for most people. But Fred had taken the first steps toward filling
out that grand name, Frederick Law Olmsted, and all the ambition that
it implied.

CHAPTER 3

Uncommon Friends

THE VERY FIRST PHOTOS of Olmsted date from 1846, during the period after he returned from his ocean voyage. There's a pair of pictures from the same sitting. Both are group shots featuring the same cast of characters: Olmsted, his brother John, and three other young men.

Photography was brand-new at this point, having been invented in France less than a decade earlier. Getting one's portrait taken was a fad then sweeping across America. In fact, this same year, 1846, marks the first time a photo was ever taken of a young congressman from Illinois—Abraham Lincoln. These earliest photographic images are known as daguerreotypes, and the process for creating them was painstaking. It required bulky camera equipment and tiresomely long sittings by subjects, spent coaxing an exposure to appear on a copper plate spread with a thin film of chemicals.

In Olmsted's case, the daguerreotypes were created in New Haven, where John was repeating his sophomore year at Yale after withdrawing for a time to recover from a mysterious respiratory ailment. Home from the sea, Olmsted had taken to hanging out on the college campus with his younger brother. The three other men in the picture were Yale students and friends of John who became Fred's friends as well. Olmsted and his companions sat nearly an entire day in order to obtain a small array of images, a pair of which—both very similar—have survived.

The daguerreotypes capture the five young men in dark suits, vests, and cravats. There's a table in front of them on which an open book has been placed—a prop of sorts, intended to communicate that these are substantial persons committed to serious scholastic endeavors. The composition is extremely formal, yet these two images manage to capture key attributes of each of the subjects' characters with uncanny accuracy.

Brother John is dark-eyed and handsome. He's the only one smiling, but it's an enigmatic smile, ever so slight, and seems calculated to convey an air of nonchalance. Charles Loring Brace, by contrast, comes across as straightforward in the most literal sense. The photos find him staring directly ahead with a burning and thoughtful intensity. Meanwhile, Olmsted isn't even looking at the camera. Instead, his head is turned to the side, and he's peering off in a different direction from the others. Typical. His hair sweeps off his forehead in a wave, and his features are small and fine, lending him an almost ethereal quality.

In one of these existing takes, while Olmsted gazes off into the mysterious middle distance, he also has an arm thrown around Charley Brace's shoulders. This, too, is fitting. Growing up, Olmsted was passingly acquainted with Brace (no relation to his old teacher Joab Brace). When Brace became his brother's roommate at Yale, Olmsted got to know him even better. And in the years ahead, Brace would become one of Olmsted's own closest friends and would play a big role in his life.

Like the Olmsted brothers, Brace came from a family that traced its Connecticut roots back for many generations. Brace also lost his mother at an early age, a circumstance that certainly helped forge a bond between him and the Olmsted brothers. There, the similarities ended. Where the senior Olmsted was a well-to-do merchant with only a smattering of education, Brace's father was a Williams graduate, known for his erudition. He was a teacher by trade and had gained renown in Connecticut as a pioneering educator of women. Teaching was noble work, but it didn't bring in much money. Brace grew up in a household that was both less financially secure and more formally intellectual than Olmsted's. Where John Olmsted Sr. took his sons on hushed rides through the countryside, John Brace read to young Charles from the classics of literature or works about history. Then he would quiz his son on the passages. By the time he entered Yale, Charley Brace was proficient in five languages.

Olmsted and Brace quickly fell into a rapport that would characterize their friendship forever onward. Something about their particular chemistry drew them into fevered intellectual argument. They were a kind of closed two-man debating society. The pair argued with one another endlessly on topics such as religion and politics, while the other members of the circle—brother John, particularly—looked on in bemusement.

Olmsted and Brace came at subjects from very different angles. Olmsted tended to be idiosyncratic, drawing on the books he'd read in the course of a haphazard education, along with real-life experience such as his brief clerkship in New York. Brace, four years his junior, was far more doctrinaire. Brace could work his way up to a kind of moral mandate that was hard to refute. "Intense earnestness in whatever he undertook was the characteristic and, one might say, the keynote of his life," Frederick Kingsbury, another of the five friends, would recall of Brace.

Kingsbury, for his part, was the pragmatist of the group. In the years after the photo was taken, he would become first a lawyer and then a businessman. John Olmsted and Fred Kingsbury had a special wink-wink friendship, rooted partly in observing the excesses of the other two. John would frequently turn to Kingsbury for perspective when his brother's idiosyncrasy or Brace's idealism simply grew too ridiculous.

Last and least, there was Charley Trask. Every odd-numbered group needs someone to fill Trask's inglorious role: he was the fifth wheel. Even in the old daguerreotypes, he seems aware of his station, standing off to the side. Besides being credited with a genial manner, Trask appears to have made little impression on Olmsted and the others. Maybe he simply acted as a kind of social lightning rod, necessary to disperse the energy created by the other four. "We are a most uncommon set of common friends" is how Brace described this group.

While Olmsted managed to fall in with a vibrant social circle, he did not yet have a profession, or even a fixed address. During visits to New Haven he stayed with his brother John or others in the group, all of whom were several years younger. Olmsted visited so often that they dubbed him an "honorary member of the Class of '47." He also served a couple of brief apprenticeships on nearby Connecticut farms, one run by an uncle, David Brooks, the other by Joseph Welton, a friend of the Kingsbury family. Otherwise, he continued to live at home in Hartford—downright bizarre for a man now in his mid-twenties. Olmsted's lax father accepted the arrangement, reminding himself that at least his son was good-natured and full of enthusiasm. Mary Ann Olmsted gritted her teeth and prayed for her stepson to find his way in the world.

For a brief spell, it looked like that might actually happen. Olmsted decided to enroll in Yale. Certainly, he was spending enough time on campus. Why not take some classes along the way? Despite his spotty academic record, Olmsted was admitted as a "special student." He was allowed to sit in on classes on a kind of audit basis.

Olmsted approached the opportunity in his own quirky fashion. For course work that captured his interest, he proved willing to go to extraordinary lengths. Olmsted was fascinated by a class in chemistry taught by Benjamin Silliman, one of nineteenth century America's most distinguished science professors. The class was lecture only, with no lab work required. On his own initiative, Olmsted spent hours in the lab doing self-directed experiments, even recruited John and his friends into what he dubbed the "Infantile Chemistry Association." Other subjects such as mineralogy and architecture, strangely enough, failed to capture his interest, and he didn't even bother to do the required reading.

The whole Yale experiment lasted just three months. Then Olmsted withdrew, citing as the reason a concern that he might be suffering from apoplexy. *Apoplexy* is an arcane medical term for heightened nervous excitement. No doubt, Olmsted was capable of achieving such a mental state, though as a reason for quitting something—yet again—it seems like a mere excuse.

Olmsted wrote a letter to Kingsbury summing up his piecemeal schooling: "I have a smattering education—a little scum, from most everything useful to such a man as I—learned as I took a *fancy* to it. Of Arithmetic, I cipher slow and without accuracy. Grammar I know nothing of—nor the rules of Rhetoric or writing. Geography, I know where I have been. History, nothing but my own country, except what I have got incidentaly." Referring to *incidentaly*, he added: "I can't even spell such a word as that right."

During this time, Olmsted began to pursue various romantic possibilities, though his approach was similarly scattershot. He accompanied a variety of different young women to a variety of different events, such as lectures, book-club meetings, hymn sing-alongs, and Sunday sociables. In Puritan New England, for someone of Olmsted's background, these were the kind of chaste—and frequently chaperoned—activities that were available. But Olmsted made the most of it. Yale, one of his main stomping grounds, was an all-male university at this time. Between Hartford and New Haven proper, however, there seemed to be an endless stream of prospects to choose among.

Olmsted mooned over Abby Clark, a student at the Hartford Female Seminary. He went to a dance with Sarah Cook. And in New Haven, he went on a group picnic with a young woman that he identified only as Anna. "'Twas a fine day and I believe we all, particularly the girls enjoyed very much," he wrote to his brother. "Capital dinner on the rocks. Siesta (charming with Anna's lap for a pillow). Smoke, reading, pomp, sentiment, and ride home by moonshine."

Of course, Olmsted wasn't what one would call an eligible bachelor. His career prospects weren't exactly sterling. Then again, he wasn't really looking to get married at this point. Rather, he seemed thrilled by the opportunity to spend time with witty and cultivated young women. His various companions, in turn, seemed to appreciate that he already had some real-life experience, and his time at sea made for especially vivid stories. Maria Mounds had also been on an ocean voyage, and the pair had a "few yarns to spin," as Olmsted termed it.

Yet another object of Olmsted's affections was Frances Condit. At one point, he arranged to meet up with her at a social gathering at a house in Hartford. He stayed way beyond the household's calling hours. Mary Ann Olmsted, who had accompanied him, left early and fretted that her stepson had committed a faux pas. To John Sr., she confided that Fred appeared smitten in the wake of his overlong stay: "He has dreamed about her regularly every week since. I know not whether the admiration is mutual."

As he often would in the course of his life, Olmsted had gotten caught up in a kind of frenzy—a frenzy of courtship. He wrote to Brace: "I am desperately in love—now, and no mistake, only for the life of me I can't tell who it's with—the whole of 'em, I believe."

Still, there was one particular woman who stood apart, as a special object of his affections, dispersed as they were. Elizabeth Baldwin was beautiful, refined, and deeply religious, and she came from one of the most distinguished families in Connecticut—in the whole United States, for that matter. Olmsted's circle of friends called her "Miss B." as a token of their awe and respect. Her great-grandfather was Roger Sherman, the only person to sign America's four seminal documents: the Continental Association, the Declaration of Independence, the Articles of Confederation, and the Constitution. "Mr. Sherman, of Connecticut, a man who never said a foolish thing in his life," is how Thomas Jefferson described him. Her father had until recently served as the governor of the state.

Olmsted met Elizabeth Baldwin at a literary evening held at her home in New Haven. From the outset, he recognized that he was utterly overmatched. Still, he was deeply flattered that she took him seriously. She recommended some books to him by Emerson and Lowell. Years later, Olmsted would credit her with helping to "rouse a sort of scatter-brained pride and to make me realize that my secluded life, country breeding and mis-education was not such a bar to an 'intellectual life' as I was in the habit of supposing."

At one point, Olmsted happened to run into Elizabeth Baldwin in Hartford, on the street right outside his father's store. She had traveled from New Haven to visit some friends. Olmsted went on a walk with her, which left him downright giddy. "Governor's daughter. Excellent princess," he wrote to Brace. "She's a dove. Whew! I shall fill up my letter with her."

Later in her visit, they took a long carriage ride together, under a heavy blanket, and engaged in a "thick talk," as he put it. The experience emboldened Olmsted. He wrote a letter to John that begins by requesting that his brother mention to Miss B. that another such "private opportunity" would be possible, when next he visited New Haven. But Olmsted recognized that he needed to be careful. In the very next sentence, thinking as he wrote, he scrawled his concern that Baldwin might take this the wrong way. He then retracted his request in the same letter. Under no circumstances was John to tell Miss B. about a private opportunity. Olmsted was all over the place. He just couldn't help it. He was "right smack & square on dead in love with her," he confessed to his brother, "beached & broken backed."

As for why Olmsted included these various sentiments in letters, well, that has everything to do with the times. Olmsted, his brother, and the other friends had ample opportunity to see one another. It certainly was possible to discuss these matters in person, and they did. But letters provided a formal means of composing one's thoughts and feelings, as well as a way to demonstrate verbal dexterity and wit. Consequently, letters were constantly exchanged among Olmsted and the other members of the "uncommon set."

Meanwhile, Connecticut was swept up in one of the frequent paroxysms of faith that rolled across the nation in the first half of the nineteenth century. By this time, America was at the tail end of the so-called Second Great Awakening. The first awakening began in the 1730s and launched into prominence such firebrand preachers as Jonathan Edwards, famed for his "Sinners in the Hands of an Angry God" sermon. These awakenings were rooted in the notion that America provided an opportunity to cleanse Christianity, thanks to its unique circumstances. In Europe, the religion was weighted down by centuries of tradition and corruption. But America—it was a new nation. Why, even the landscape itself was pristine, Edenic. In New England, the push for a newer, purer faith also helped spur such movements as abolitionism, temperance, and calls for rights for the mentally ill.

Responses to the Second Great Awakening varied from region to region across the United States. In the South, for example, a tradition grew up of camp meetings, woolly, free-form events full of proselytizing and mass baptisms. New Englanders, by contrast, favored a more dour approach. Among Connecticut Congregationalists (an offshoot of the original Puritans), the practice was to listen silently to sermons, all the while scouring one's soul for a sign of being "under conviction." Had a person legitimately and authentically accepted Christ?—that was the question. These could be agonizing events for participants.

As mentioned earlier, Charlotte Olmsted, Fred's mother, had participated in a revival in New Haven in 1826, just three weeks before her death from an overdose of laudanum. That same revival was attended by Harriet Beecher Stowe, whose son later characterized the event as an instance where "self-examination was carried to an extreme that was calculated to drive a nervous and sensitive mind well-nigh distracted." The bar for genuine faith was set punishingly high, he added, because "there might be something wrong in the case of a lamb that had come into the fold without being first chased all over the lot by the shepherd."

As a fresh New Haven revival got under way, during the spring of 1846, Mary Ann Olmsted's fondest hope was that her stepsons would take full advantage. Here, at last, was an opportunity for the young men to achieve the pure faith that their father had never managed. She dashed off a letter to Olmsted's brother: "I think there is nothing he [John Sr.] so much desires for Frederick and yourself as to see you firmly established in religious principles. I do not doubt he regrets exceedingly that he did not take a decided stand when *young*, and knowing from his own experience the difficulties to be encountered at a later period of life, he is the more anxious you should improve the present most favourable opportunity for securing your present and eternal happiness." Mary Ann Olmsted signed the letter: "The prayer of your still anxious, Mother."

In keeping with her wishes, Olmsted attended the revival in New Haven. He sat through marathon sermons. Dutifully, he spent hours praying for the salvation of his soul, as well as for the souls of his brother and friends. They, in turn, spent hours praying for him. Elizabeth Baldwin was present at the New Haven revival. To his great pleasure, she focused her prayers intensely on him, his brother, and the others in their set—well, everyone save for Charley Brace. His faith was already confirmed as true and pure, so he joined forces with the virtuous Miss. B.

Mary Ann Olmsted noted "how highly bless'd has Miss Baldwin been in her efforts for the good of others."

"Thank God for Miss Baldwin," exalted Olmsted. "What an angel she will make! How glad I am!"

For Olmsted, the prim flirtation he shared with Miss B. along with his very soul hanging in the balance must have made for a heady—and bewildering—mix. He prayed all the more fervently. He uttered religious phrases that had never before and would never again pass through his lips. To his brother, he wrote, "I feel, John, that God's fever attended me in New Haven. . . . I *am* much happier than ever before. My faith is much increased; it is surety."

Mostly, he sounds like a man trying to convince himself. At one point during the revival, he felt a terrible throbbing in his temple. Was this, he wondered, that divine signal at last? In the weeks afterward, he concluded that it was simply a headache. Like his father, Olmsted appeared constitutionally unable to fall "under conviction." Maybe he'd experienced too much cruelty at the hands of country parsons, not to mention the hypocrisy of Captain Fox, never uttering a curse word while beating the holy hell out of his sailors.

Even so, Olmsted's New Haven experience didn't cause him to reject religion outright. Rather, he found himself unable to meet a strict standard of faith in a highly organized setting. The revival didn't stick. His romantic life wasn't exactly progressing, either. When Olmsted requested that Miss B. enter into a formal correspondence with him, she demurred, deeming such an intimacy "neither right nor best."

Fresh from this pair of personal setbacks, Olmsted dusted himself off, looked around, and, in what was becoming a clear pattern for him, simply lit out in a new direction. He decided to become a farmer, a choice that made great sense. As of 1846, America was an agricultural nation, and farming was *the* profession, occupying nearly 70 percent of the labor force. Along with surveyor, clerk, and sailor—all jobs he'd tried—this was another line open to someone with Olmsted's "smattering education." What's more, he'd recently served two brief agricultural internships.

Olmsted didn't want to become just any kind of farmer, though. Inspired, in part, by his brief stint at Yale and the Infantile Chemistry Association, he decided to become a scientific farmer. He intended to make use of the latest farming technology and innovations in horticulture and animal husbandry. "Really, for a man that has any inclination for Agriculture the occupation is very interesting," he'd once written Brace. "And if you look closely, you will be surprised to see how much honorable attention and investigation is being connected with it. . . . Scientific men of the highest distinction are there devoting their undivided attention to its advance." He added: "For the matter of happiness, there is no body of men that are half as well satisfied with their business as our farmers."

Olmsted saw an article in a newspaper about a man named George Geddes, who had received a first-place commendation for the best-cultivated farm from the New York State Agricultural Society. He wrote to Geddes and arranged to work for him through the end of the fall harvest.

Geddes ran a farm called Fairmount, located in the Finger Lakes region of New York, near the town of Camillus. He lived in a large stone manor just a few hundred feet from the spot where the house in which he'd been born had once stood. He'd inherited the farm from James Geddes, his father. The elder Geddes had helped survey the route for the Erie Canal and had done some engineering work on the project. During its earliest days, some of the locals referred to the waterway as the "Geddes Canal." The Geddes name loomed large in this stretch of western New York state.

Olmsted arrived at the farm late in the spring of 1846. It was a sprawling enterprise, covering 300 acres. Geddes grew a huge variety of different foodstuffs: corn, oats, wheat, lettuce, beets, cherries, apples, and quinces. He raised cattle, sheep, and pigs. The farm was a model of efficiency. Geddes owned a Pitt's Corn and Cob-Cutter, a newfangled portable tool that could "grind a bushel of long clean ears in four minutes!" as Olmsted breathlessly informed his father. He was the inventor of the Geddes' Harrow and the Geddes' Swinging Gate. He was thirty-seven years old, thirteen years Olmsted's senior. Olmsted intended to learn everything he possibly could from him.

Work began each morning at the crack of dawn. Yet Olmsted stayed up to all hours reading. He pored over issues of the *Cultivator*, a recently launched journal that was part of a wave of new publications aimed at scientific farmers who could read (unlike many traditional farmers) and were anxious to stay abreast of the latest agricultural advances. He was cramming, trying to get up to speed in his chosen field.

Still, there was a limit to how regimented Olmsted was capable of being, at least at this point in his life. During his nighttime reading sessions, he also fell utterly under the spell of a novel called *Sartor Resartus* by Thomas Carlyle. This was an experimental work by the acclaimed Scottish author, blending fact and fiction, with a kind of meta device thrown in as well, designed to make readers aware that fact and fiction were being mixed and to force them to question which was which, and to contemplate whether such distinctions really even exist. Nearly a decade earlier, upon initial publication, *Sartor Resartus* had been met with critical puzzlement, and sales had been slow. Over time, the book had found its audience: Ralph Waldo Emerson became a serious devotee of the book, and *Sartor Resartus* is often credited with helping shape the transcendentalist philosophy.

Sartor Resartus was just the kind of work that Olmsted, with his peculiar self-directed approach to reading, was likely to find his way to. As often happens with favorite books, it seemed to Olmsted to clarify, to an almost eerie degree, some of the issues he was grappling with in his own life. "I do think Carlyle is the greatest genius in the world," he wrote to his father from Fairmount. " . . . I perfectly wonder and stand awe-struck as I would at a Hurricane."

The main character of *Sartor Resartus* is a German philosopher named Diogenes Teufelsdröckh, which translates roughly to "God-born devil-dung." Unable to find a proper course in life, Teufelsdröckh leads a dissolute youth, something that certainly resonated with Olmsted. The character also finds himself unable to achieve blind religious faith—check. He even woos a beautiful woman from a prominent family only to be rebuffed, an episode that reminded Olmsted of his own courtship of Miss B.

Teufelsdröckh's ultimate conclusion: All is chaos, and one's only option is to construct meaning, as best as possible. He chooses to do so through work. And not just any kind of work, but rather work that has helping others as its stated goal. For Olmsted, this peculiar piece of British metafiction was like a grand theory of everything. In two separate letters written from Fairmount that summer, Olmsted referred to himself as having "faith" in being a farmer. The word choice is no accident. He'd failed to confirm his faith during the recent New Haven revival. But to Olmsted, *Sartor Resartus* suggested another route to salvation. He could throw himself into work, meaningful work, as a farmer.

"Up, up! Whatsoever thy hand findeth to do, do it with thy whole might," writes Carlyle. "Work while it is called To-day, for the Night cometh wherein no man can work." Olmsted was so taken with this passage that he copied it into a letter to his brother.

Of course, late nights might be devoted to reading about farming and the spiritual benefits of labor, but by day, there was actual work to be done. Geddes was a demanding boss. He had strong views about the best and most efficient means of doing any given task. Olmsted learned how to prepare soil and plant seed and tend crops. He learned how to use various implements such as tills and hoes and harrows and how to do so the right way.

A special challenge was washing and shearing sheep. Olmsted wrestled for the better part of a morning with Maggie, a large and unruly prize Merino. He grew exhausted, was soon covered in dirt, but he didn't give up. Finally, he emerged victorious with exactly four pounds and seven ounces of fleece.

The long hours of farmwork were followed by a ritual that Olmsted found immensely appealing. Geddes ended each day by scrubbing up and sitting down to a large and sumptuous meal. It was often lamb or veal, fresh milk flowed freely, and there might be a currant pie for dessert. Sometimes there were even pineapples, an exotic delicacy grown in hot-houses on neighboring farms. The table was set with "silver forks every day," Olmsted noted with wonder. Subsistence farming, this was not.

At dinner, Geddes invariably held forth on a variety of topics. He was a man of broad interests who made a point of staying informed about issues of the larger world, far beyond the realm of farming. In 1846, war had just broken out between the United States and Mexico. Geddes believed that both armies (all the world's armies, for that matter) should be disbanded. He was an avid follower of Elihu Burritt, a blacksmith who was one of the founders of the pacifist movement. Just as the food at Fairmount wasn't typical, Olmsted noted, neither was the conversational fare.

Like his father, Geddes was also involved in the community. During Olmsted's stay at Fairmount, Geddes was overseeing the construction of a plank road connecting several nearby small towns with Syracuse, New York, a major center. This was one of the first plank roads in the United States. It was a critical piece of economic development; without this modern road, the region was in danger of becoming isolated. Geddes was taking the lead in making sure his fellow farmers had a modern trade route to transport their goods to market. The plank road was the younger Geddes's Erie Canal.

Olmsted took measure of all to which he was exposed during that summer at Fairmount. Of this he grew increasingly certain: He wanted to be like Geddes. He wanted to be a farmer making a difference.

CHAPTER 4

A Farmer and Finite

WHEN THE HARVEST was over, Olmsted decided he was ready to embark on his career as a scientific farmer. George Geddes was impressed with Olmsted's commitment, and he tried to convince him to settle on some acreage near Fairmount. That way, Geddes could provide guidance as an older and more experienced farmer. But Olmsted was set on returning to Connecticut. Farming was about a passionate attachment to land, after all. Geddes had enjoyed the luxury of spending his entire life on the same 300 acres. But Olmsted had no ties to the Finger Lakes region of New York State. Rather, the land of Connecticut was in his blood.

Olmsted could picture various places throughout the state—the sites of his boyhood wanderings—and had formed a very clear idea of the kind of farm he wanted. As he spelled out in a letter written from Fairmount, the fields should be situated right on the ocean. A seaside farm in Connecticut—it was a picturesque notion and also very specific.

What he lacked was money. But his father agreed to buy him such a farm, even to stake him to the funds necessary to purchase tools, seed, and other necessities. John Senior's dry goods store continued to be highly profitable, and he could afford to help out. Olmsted had tried out so many different lines of work. Buying a farm was a worthwhile expenditure, if only it would help get his son settled, at last.

The farm Olmsted chose was on Sachem's Head, a little spit of land that juts out into Long Island Sound. It was only about fifteen miles from New Haven, where John was finishing up his final year at Yale. Charley Brace had just started Yale Divinity School, and Fred Kingsbury had just entered the law school. His home in Hartford was just a couple hours away on horseback. Olmsted would be in easy range of his "uncommon set" of friends and his family as well.

But the farm itself was a less attractive proposition. It cost $4,000, hardly cheap, and only a fraction of the 60 acres was even usable, with much of it given over to rocky coastline. Where actual farming was possible, Ebenezer Bartlett, the previous owner, had been completely unimaginative, alternating corn and potatoes year after year. By the time Olmsted took over, the soil was much abused and depleted of nutrients.

There was a modest little clapboard farmhouse, unpainted and riddled with cracks and holes. Drainage was terrible, and run-off water from the fields flowed right past the front door on its way to the sea. When it rained hard, the house sat in a swamp. "Real juicy" is how Olmsted described his new living conditions. The barn was on the verge of collapse.

Still, from the highest point on the property, the view across Long Island Sound was breathtaking. Olmsted had grand plans for the little farm. Olmsted hired a man named Henry Davis to serve as his helper, paying him one dollar a day. Davis had a wife and a small baby. Because even a small farm requires ample work, Olmsted also brought in a field hand and a maidservant, who worked in exchange for board. These five people and Olmsted were now all packed into the cramped farmhouse. As part of that modest one-dollar fee, Davis's wife agreed to do the cooking for the household. Olmsted and his help set to fixing up the farm, as much as that was possible.

John came down from New Haven late in the spring of 1847 to visit Fred. While the Sachem's Head spread was anything but a model farm, he was immediately struck by how his older brother seemed to have taken to the agrarian life. Olmsted had grown deeply tanned from working long hours in the sun. And his conversation was full of references to the price of potatoes and the best method of turning a furrow. Olmsted had even gone and bought the perfect farm dog, a big Newfoundland that he'd named "Neptune"—"Nep" for short.

At the same time, John couldn't contain his amusement at Fred's newly adopted sartorial air. When not working the fields, Olmsted went in for a tweedy, country-squire look that included a nice jacket, a cap even. In a letter to their mutual Yale friend Kingsbury, John described the scene as his brother loaded a cart in preparation to travel to the nearby town of Guilford on some farm business. He recounted what Fred was wearing, before offering slyly, "I don't believe there is much danger of his losing his dignity."

In another letter to Kingsbury, John pondered whether Fred should have devoted more effort to college. Perhaps he should have spent more than three months at Yale. Maybe farming was a poor choice, given his brother's admittedly "fine capabilities." Then again, Fred seemed capable only of pursuing interests that engaged his passions. These were so fickle. In still another letter John wrote, "I hope the present object of his affections i.e. the farm will not be as ephemeral as most of them seem to have been."

Here, John was talking about his brother's professional life, but he might as well have been talking about his love life. Olmsted was an intriguing character, no question. His foibles, his quirky behavior, his wild notions—all provided rich fodder for discussions behind his back among the uncommon set of friends. In this flurry of letters to Kingsbury, in the sheer amount of ink John devoted to his brother and the new farm, one also detects the hint of something else—sibling rivalry, the illicit thrill of feeling superior to another person, maybe both.

"It is pretty much all true what you say about Fred," Kingsbury replied. "But living and growing and experience will have to answer for him instead of college discipline. He is an enthusiast by nature though, and all the Greek and Latin in the world wouldn't have driven that out of him."

Olmsted dove into farm life with aplomb. He put all his effort into making a success of the farm at Sachem's Head. To go along with the staple potatoes, he planted new crops such as onions and turnips. He even wrote letters to various publications seeking advice on farming. These letters are the very first published works by Olmsted. There's one to the *Boston Cultivator* from a "young farmer" inquiring about the merits of using seaweed and fish as fertilizer. And there's another to the *Horticulturist*, a new publication run by Andrew Jackson Downing, a celebrated arbiter of rural style and taste. The *Horticulturist* letter asks advice about planting fruit trees in a coastal setting. Signed: "F. L. Olmsted, Sachem's Head, Guilford, CT." Downing responded by suggesting some varieties of apples that might be appropriate.

During this time, Olmsted also wrote a letter to Brace, exhorting him, "There's a great *work* wants doing in this our generation, Charley, let us off jacket and go about it." It's a high-flown sentiment, a call to action. It also has clear echoes of the personal resolve Olmsted had formed while apprenticing with Geddes and reading that strange novel, *Sartor Resartus.* He was laying down a challenge for Charley and a challenge to himself: They must embark on great works for the benefit of others.

Even so, Olmsted had spent precious little time on his own as a farmer at this point. He was hardly in a position to do any noble outreach to the surrounding community. He'd barely made the acquaintance of any of his fellow farmers. Those few he'd met, he found clannish and close-minded.

Fortunately, Sachem's Head House was within walking distance of his farm. Head House, as it was known, was the finest resort along the Connecticut coast, a place frequented by well-to-do lawyers and merchants. Olmsted was familiar with the place, having gone there as a boy on family trips to the shore. Head House held regular afternoon tea and formal evening dances. Olmsted became a frequent attendee. He began spending time in the company of Ellen Day, an eighteen-year-old woman who was visiting the resort with her family. But he wasn't so certain that his infatuation wasn't instead with her big sister, Mary Day.

Then autumn set in. The Head House closed, and the summer visitors scattered, returning to their lives.

Olmsted, stuck on the farm, grew terribly lonely. The hired help was pleasant enough, but he had nothing in common with any of them. Davis's wife was an atrocious cook who prepared the same meal of cold potatoes and cold pork again and again. Evenings, they all sat around in the cramped little farmhouse, made still more cramped by the presence of Nep, the dog, and Minna, Olmsted's cat, and her litter of kittens. The cold sea winds whipped through the cracks between the clapboards. The Davis infant shrieked, and the cats yowled.

Earlier, Olmsted had told Brace that his farming career was off to a rollicking start. He'd bragged that his crops "so far look bountifully," and he was in proud possession of a barn full of hay. Come harvest time, he'd been forced to reevaluate this optimism. Olmsted had invested $1,000 of his father's money in seed and tools and other costs, to see only a $200 return. The farm was really only the thinnest reed, Olmsted was now forced to admit, on which to hang his newfound idealism about agriculture. Sporting a fancy jacket and cap was all well and good. The truth was undeniable: Sachem's Head was no Fairmount.

But here's another passage from Kingsbury's earlier letter to John Olmsted: "Well, the world needs such men [as Fred], and one thing is curious, disappointments never seem to trouble them. . . . Many of his favorite schemes will go to naught but he'll throw it aside and try another and spoil that and forget them while you or I might have been blubbering over the ruins of the first." This comment is especially discerning. Kingsbury perceived that Olmsted was one of those people who simply keep going. If one thing didn't work out, he'd be on to the next. And the next after that.

At Thanksgiving, Olmsted paid a visit home to Hartford to spend time with his family. His father was distressed at the fate of the Sachem's Head farm. He recognized that drastic measures were needed, ones in the opposite direction from where his son was headed.

Earlier in the autumn, Olmsted had actually taken the extraordinary step of contacting Alexander Jackson Davis about designing a new farmhouse at Sachem's Head. Davis was one of the few people in America involved in the rarefied field of architecture. He was known for his country houses; his creations dotted the Hudson River Valley. A decade hence, he would win acclaim as designer of Llewellyn Park in West Orange, New Jersey, one of the first planned communities in the United States.

Nothing had come of the consultation . . . yet. John Olmsted recognized—as a practical businessman—that the time had arrived to cut and run. Fred's farm was a dismal little place with no hope of profits, and an architecturally notable house wasn't going to change that. As a father, however, he was considerably less practical. He had a soft spot for Fred and his schemes. As it happened, the senior Olmsted had learned that a farm was for sale on Staten Island. Maybe his son could become a successful farmer on a better piece of land in a more suitable location. He told Fred to go take a look. Inspect the foundations of any buildings, he urged him. Find out what is included in the price. Would various tools and implements be thrown into the deal? Only look at the property, he concluded. Don't make any kind of commitment. Just to be certain, he sent younger brother John to accompany Fred on the trip.

Predictably, Olmsted returned from the scouting expedition with a glowing report. This was the perfect farm! Had he once insisted that he could live only in Connecticut? Nonsense. Staten Island was the place for him! So his father made a trip himself to pursue the matter further. It turned out that the farm had belonged to Dr. Samuel Akerly, onetime superintendent of the Deaf and Dumb Asylum in New York City. He had died two years earlier after enjoying a working retirement on the farm. Now, his relatives were trying to unload the place. They were asking $12,000, the same price Dr. Akerly had paid back in 1837. The property was somewhat dilapidated, the result of being unoccupied for two years, but otherwise appeared sound—a pretty good deal, all in all.

On January 1, 1848, John Olmsted completed the purchase, though this time he took out a mortgage on the property. And this time, he required his son to sign a note laying out terms for reimbursing him over time. He simply put Fred's Connecticut farm on the market and was eventually able to sell it for $4,000, the price he'd paid earlier.

The new farm was situated on the south shore of Staten Island and, at 125 acres, was more than twice the size of Olmsted's previous spread. The farmhouse was quirky but spacious. The original structure, a little Dutch cottage with thick stone walls, made up the ground floor. Dr. Akerly had built a modern wooden addition on top of this stone house, completely throwing off the proportions of the place. But the addition featured nine bedrooms. Olmsted would have ample space to put up visiting friends and family. He would have ample space if he chose to start a family of his own.

Once again, Olmsted's farm commanded a splendid view. From the farmhouse, the land traveled in a steady, gentle slope down to the bay.

Looking out across the water, the Sandy Hook lighthouse was visible in the distance as well as Atlantic Highlands, New Jersey, where explorer Henry Hudson had once anchored the *Half Moon*.

A farm such as his demanded a proud name like Fairmount. Olmsted considered "Entepfuhl," after the village where Teufelsdröckh, hero of *Sartor Resartus*, passed his idyllic boyhood. He also briefly toyed with "Hartford" and with "Connecticut" as well. "Here I am now, actually obliged to feel myself at home out of Connecticut," wrote Olmsted to Kingsbury. "Do you believe it? No Sir-ey."

Ultimately, Olmsted decided to call the place Tosomock Farm. This was a corruption of Tesschenmakr, as in Petrus Tesschenmakr, the farm's first occupant who had moved there in 1685. According to local legend, during a later incarnation of the farm, George Washington had stayed in the little stone house while examining fortifications for Staten Island. This place had so much history. And it had so much more promise than Sachem's Head. "One thing, Fred will become a real farmer," his brother wrote to Kingsbury with unconcealed amazement.

Olmsted hired several Irish hands to help out on the farm, and his spinster aunt Maria came down from Hartford to serve as a live-in house-keeper. Nep and Minna, the dog and cat, joined him as well. Olmsted immediately set to work transforming the property from a wheat farm into one devoted to fruits and vegetables.

This was a crucial step. The 1840s were a time of cutthroat competition in the agricultural economy. Much of this was driven by transportation innovations such as railroads and canals. This broadened the market for nonperishables such as wheat. It meant that a Pennsylvania wheat farmer might face competition in the Philadelphia market from wheat transported in from Ohio.

Dr. Akerly, Olmsted's predecessor, didn't have to worry if his wheat crop was undercut. He'd been a retiree with a hobby farm. But Olmsted knew he had to make this work—and fruits and vegetables were the key. Farmers who grew these crops didn't face competition from outside their region. Such foodstuffs couldn't be transported long distances because refrigeration methods were very primitive. Rather, the challenge was finding a market for the produce before it spoiled. But Olmsted was right on the doorstep of New York City, a vast and ready market for his crops. Olmsted planted cabbage, lima beans, turnips, corn, grapevines, and peach trees.

Living on Staten Island, Olmsted had very different kinds of neighbors than he'd had on Sachem's Head. The Dutch had first settled this area in the early 1600s, and he was surrounded by their descendants, people with names like Sequin, Guyen, Van Pell, and Vanderbilt. William Vanderbilt, eldest son of the Commodore himself, worked a nearby farm as a kind of über-gentleman farmer. Obviously, this was a mere sideline for someone destined to inherit a fortune that would make him the richest man in the world.

Increasingly, Staten Island was also becoming popular as a site for New York City's wealthy to build summer homes or to retire, as Dr. Akerly had. Its original rural character was fast disappearing. By 1848, Staten Island was a mixed community, composed of both farmers and exurbanites, with a population of 15,000. Among Olmsted's other neighbors were William Cullen Bryant, the romantic poet and editor of the *New York Post*, and book-publishing magnate George Putnam. Putnam was actually a cousin of Olmsted's deceased mother, Charlotte, though Olmsted didn't know him very well at this point.

Olmsted was thrilled to be in the midst of this charged intellectual atmosphere, even as a farmer on the sidelines. The move to Staten Island had instantly changed his center of gravity, making it New York City rather than Hartford or New Haven. Manhattan was just a quick ferry ride away.

In a fortunate twist, at around the same time that Olmsted moved to Staten Island, both his brother and Charley Brace moved to New York City. John enrolled at the College of Physicians and Surgeons to complete his medical training. He was well on the way to becoming a doctor. Brace was studying at Union Theological Seminary, contemplating a life in the clergy. He was doing outreach work on Blackwell's Island, the old name for Roosevelt Island. This was the site of an almshouse, asylum, penitentiary, and other institutions for the city's outcasts. Brace was preaching to prisoners and impoverished prostitutes in the final throes of disease.

Both John and Charley were frequent visitors to Tosomock Farm, together and separately. They loved the change of pace. They appreciated being in dense, hectic New York City one moment, but with the magic of a quick ferry ride, they could find themselves in another world altogether—Fred's world. Olmsted furnished his guests with slippers, put out a basket of fresh fruit, and set up armchairs outside in full glorious view of the bay. Of course, Fred's world was also one of unbridled enthusiasm, wild plans, and, with Charley Brace—given their unique personal chemistry—endless argument.

In a letter to Kingsbury, Brace described a weekend spent with Olmsted at Tosomock Farm: "But the amount of talking done upon that visit! One steady stream from six o'clock Saturday night till twelve, beginning next day, and going on till twelve the next night, interrupted only by meals and some insane walks on the beach." It was, he added, a "torrent of fierce argument, mixed with divers oaths on Fred's part." Brace, who disciplined himself to always see people in the best possible light, concluded on a generous note: "I must say that Fred is getting to argue with the utmost keenness."

Olmsted began making improvements to the layout of Tosomock Farm. He moved a barn to a new spot behind a knoll, thereby improving the view. He changed the carriage driveway so that it better conformed to his land's topography, approaching the farmhouse in a gentle sweep. When he'd first moved to the farm, there had been a murky little pond that was used to wash off wagons. He shored its edges with stones and planted trees such as ginkgo and black walnut, transforming it into an ornamental pond.

It's fair to say that these efforts represent Olmsted's first foray into landscape architecture. At the same time, the very concept of landscape architecture barely existed, especially in America. There was no vocation called "landscape architect," and there was no set of professional practices to draw upon. Olmsted was simply doing what came naturally to him. Growing up in Connecticut, he'd developed an appreciation for beautiful landscapes. Now he was working to transform his farm into a suitably lovely spot. His neighbors certainly noted the improvements.

William Vanderbilt even requested that Olmsted do some landscaping on his farm in the New Dorp section of Staten Island.

As Olmsted settled into his new environs, he also began to meet his usual stream of courtable young women. He met them at dances and teas and Sunday sociables—his antennae were always up. When Olmsted learned that King Louis Philippe had abdicated the French throne, he was so eager to share the news that he dashed to a nearby farm owned by someone he'd never before met. During this impromptu visit, he made the acquaintance of Cyrus Perkins, a retired New York City doctor. He also met eighteen-year-old Mary Perkins.

Mary was petite, with penetrating blue eyes and an ever-ready wit. She had been orphaned as a small child, and her grandparents Dr. Perkins and his wife had raised her as their own. The Perkins were wealthy, and their household was a model of refinement. Growing up, Mary had been exposed to the best in art and literature. An original painting by Salvator Rosa hung in their home, as did a portrait of Daniel Webster by James Frothingham. In fact, Webster was a distant relative of the Perkins family. As a little girl, Mary had bounced on the great statesman's knee.

Olmsted got to know Mary and found her a challenging companion. As he confided to friends, he thought her more intellectually gifted than even the vaunted Miss B. This was high praise. He wrote a poem to Mary, inspired by her sharp wit and the softer side that he perceived concealed behind it:

Here are two close connected—yet contrasted knives
One let there be—for each of your lives
The first to be lookd at; and we can only say
On acquaintance—it surely grows larger each day.
The steel of the larger, as pure as thy mind
Can be—just as cutting—can not be as kind.

In conjunction with reading the poem to Mary, Olmsted planned to present her with a pair of knives, one sharp, the other blunt. But he doesn't appear to have gone through with this strange little gesture. It seems to have struck him as overly passionate, especially in light of an earlier impression he'd formed of Mary. He'd never really seen her in *that* way. Shortly after their first meeting, he'd described her in a letter to Kingsbury as "just the thing for a rainy day—not to fall in love with, but to talk with."

Meantime, he was ping-ponging between various other romantic interests, confused, per usual. He was well into his twenties now, but in matters of the heart, he was more like a teenager. Olmsted's friends and family wondered if he would ever settle down. Maybe he'd become an "old batch"—a probable fate, he'd recently confided to Brace. He was so flighty, so maddeningly inconstant. And he had impossible standards.

In a letter to Kingsbury, John constructed a lengthy and fanciful list of requirements for Fred's ideal bride. It's a penetrating little passage in terms of its ability to capture some kind of essential truth about Frederick Law Olmsted. It reads like a crazy personal ad:

> A marriageable young lady would be an inducement for Fred. She must have a great deal of common sense, self-control, affection, earnestness, housekeeping-on-a-small-income abilities, capability of silence, capability of speech, comprehension of what is incomprehensible to others, sympathy, . . . small visibility, docility, a broad pelvis, faith, quick antagonism, self-respect, infinite capabilities & longings, power of abstraction, some skepticism, power over appetite, power of seeing a certain distance into a millstone, charity, enthusiasm, self-annihilation, truth, Dr. Taylor's vitus of night, no superior, fondness for sausages, clams, pork & old dressing gowns; all things must be under control of reason; beauty & wealth no object & no objection. If you have such a person mention the time of leaving of the early train.

"Fred is finally rather hard up," John concluded. "He won't be content with less than infinity—while he himself is only finite and a farmer." John was still talking about his brother's love life, though this last comment carries hints about other possible sources of dissatisfaction.

John didn't have nearly such a lengthy list of romantic requirements. While visiting Tosomock Farm, he got to know Mary Perkins, and they began to court. They even went so far as to read *Modern Painters* by John

Ruskin. Reading together constituted quite an act of intimacy during this era. And *Modern Painters*, with its fevered discourse on beauty and the passion of artists, was the kind of work that could really cause one's heart to race and palms to sweat.

While Olmsted remained romantically unsettled, he appeared to have finally found his way to a career. Olmsted really took to Tosomock Farm. He fell into the rhythm. Spring marched toward fall; planting gave way to harvest; 1848 flowed into 1849. A farmer's life was full of rigor, but rewarding, too.

He was forever tinkering with the mix of crops in response to changes in the market. When New York City was flooded with peaches, he made a decision to switch to pears. He began cultivating different varieties. Many of these pears, such as Anjou, were of Gallic origin. Olmsted spoke of them incessantly, and John grew irritated by the parade of foreign names. "We hear nothing but Hog-French continually," noted John. "I hope we shall reap the benefit tho' at some future time."

John got to eat pears, all right, and also plums, raspberries, and everything else his brother chose to grow. Olmsted launched a nursery business, too. He ordered thousands of fruit trees and planted the saplings. This made sense: He could sell fruit trees, and his customers could bear the risk of finding a market for the produce. The nursery served to diversify his business, making him less susceptible to the swings in the prices of crops.

Olmsted labored hard. Where he'd been slothful at times during his teen years, he was developing a formidable work ethic—first aboard the *Ronaldson*, now on the farm—and he wasn't averse to putting in long hours when necessary. He wasn't responsible only for himself. Depending on the season, Olmsted supervised as many as eight hired men. He introduced systems and order to Tosomock Farm. Each morning, he presented the foreman of his crew with a list spelling out the exact time that various tasks should be performed. At the close of each day, the men were required to return all the farm implements to their appointed places.

Olmsted had a genuine talent for this work. The neighboring farmers took note. In 1849, a new organization was formed on Staten Island called the Richmond County Agricultural Society. Olmsted was chosen to act as corresponding secretary. As one of his first acts, Olmsted wrote a lengthy document spelling out the benefits of the new organization and urging others to join. The document was titled "Appeal to the Citizens of Staten Island." And here's a sampling: "We ask you, then, Fellow Citizens, one and all, to associate in this Society. We entreat you to support it. We believe it will increase the profit of our labor—enhance the value of our lands—throw a garment of beauty around our homes, and above all, and before all, materially promote Moral and Intellectual Improvement— instructing us in the language of Nature, from whose preaching, while we pursue our grateful labors, we shall learn to receive her Fruits as the bounty, and her Beauty as the manifestation of her Creator."

In his capacity as recording secretary, Olmsted also pushed for a plank road on Staten Island—just like Geddes; he was doing his mentor proud. One thing that's striking about Olmsted is the speed with which he could inhabit a new role. Blink and he was on the threshold of some bold new endeavor. Blink again and he was deep into it. It wasn't so long ago that Olmsted had served the apprenticeship at Fairmount. Now he was a farmer in his own right. And as he'd once told Brace: "For the matter of happiness, there is no body of men that are half as well satisfied with their business as our farmers."

CHAPTER 5

Two Pilgrimages

BUT THE HALCYON stretch on Tosomock Farm—this, too, could not last. When Olmsted learned that his brother and Brace planned a walking tour of England, he could scarcely contain his envy.

John was going partly in an effort to improve his health. Walking in the countryside would do him well, he hoped, and maybe help quell the lingering respiratory ailment that had been bothering him on and off for several years now. Brace was reeling from the recent death of his younger sister, Emma. Walking would be contemplative, a fitting way to mourn her passing. Brace also viewed the trip as an opportunity to learn about the conditions of the poor in another country.

Olmsted dashed off a letter to his father about this walking tour. The letter starts by striking a note of sober assessment. Olmsted wanted to make it clear that he had his priorities straight. Sure, the idea of a walking tour was enticing. It sounded like a real lark. There was also so much work to be done on the farm. But a few paragraphs into the letter, he could restrain himself no longer: "I have a just barely controllable passion for just what John is thinking to undertake." And he added, "I confess the idea, if I give it the rein of contemplation at all, is so exciting that I can not control it with impartial reason, and so, for the present I try to forget it."

Yet try as he might, he could not forget the matter, not even in that very letter. Olmsted proceeded to scrawl page after page to his father, enumerating all the various reasons that the trip made sense. Though he'd sailed to China, he had never been to England. It would be better to visit now, while he was full of youthful vigor. Then, he could really buckle down to life as a farmer, contented that he'd seen England at least. For that matter, he would surely gain some useful information while visiting the British countryside that he could apply on his own farm. The trip would be good for his health, too, especially in light of a "bowel complaint" he'd been suffering from lately. He could look out for his younger brother. He could look after Charley Brace.

In the letter, Olmsted never comes right out and asks permission from his father. John Sr. held the mortgage on Tosomock Farm, after all, and he was in a position to nix the idea. Instead, Olmsted put together a raft of rationalizations. He would be back in time for the fall harvest. The hired hands could look after the farm during his absence. A trip to England would be a kind of pilgrimage—to an important place, conferring all kinds of benefits—and he simply had to go. "I did not mean to argue the matter much," Olmsted concluded his letter, though he'd certainly done exactly that. As a final touch, he added, "I hope you won't consider my opinions as if they were those of a mere child, nor my desire as senseless romantic impulses only."

By now, John Sr. knew better. He simply gave his blessing. He even agreed to provide Fred with an amount of money sufficient to take a walking tour—a *budget* walking tour. (He'd earlier agreed to pay for John's trip as well.)

On April 27, 1850, the Olmsted brothers and Charley Brace were prepared to embark for England aboard the *Henry Clay*. But the ship failed to sail, despite this being the advertised day of departure. Upon examining their cabin, they discovered yet another problem. The room was half filled up with bales of cotton, bound for England to be sold.

This was billed as a passenger ship, not a merchant ship, but it was shades of the overloaded *Ronaldson*. The Olmsteds and Brace were also informed that they would need to share their cabin with another passenger. They were joined by a young Irish surgeon headed home. Such were the conditions of budget travel. The Atlantic passage was costing them $12 apiece. Three days later the *Henry Clay* finally departed, and three weeks later it arrived in Liverpool.

Fred, John, and Charley spent a little time kicking around Liverpool. On the morning they planned to depart, a baker who was preparing their breakfast rolls told them that, before leaving town, they simply had to see Birkenhead Park. It had opened only three years before and was the very first park in Britain built with public funds. The park was the pride of Liverpool. The designer was a man named Joseph Paxton. Olmsted had never heard of Paxton, knew nothing of this park, but he was taken by the place's winding paths and broad meadows. He was especially impressed to note that people of all classes were mingling in a city park. But soon the three travelers were eager to get going. They took a train a little ways out of Liverpool, threw on their knapsacks, and set out walking.

Olmsted's first brush with the English countryside did not disappoint. From a winding lane, he could see over the tops of little thatched-roof houses to a church spire rising in the distance. It was spring, and the hawthorn hedges were all in bloom. Bees were buzzing, and he could hear a cow munching on grass. His overarching impression was one of greenness, incredible greenness. And everything was softened by a watery mist.

Nothing was really unusual about this scene, Olmsted later noted, yet it had a quiet drama that he found enrapturing. He also experienced a feeling of déjà vu. Here he was at last in countryside he'd read about in the esoteric books of William Gilpin and Uvedale Price at the Hartford Library as a little boy. This was also the land of his forebears. As often happens to American travelers in England, he had the strange and distinct sensation of coming home.

Because they were on a tight budget, Olmsted and his companions were forced to stay in the most modest accommodations imaginable. Theirs was a walking tour, not a grand tour. But this had an unintended benefit. The travelers came in contact with the regular people of England.

This certainly served Brace's purposes. He was deeply committed to the idea of leading a life of service to others. But he hadn't yet figured out how best to accomplish his goal. He was as restless as Olmsted, in his own way. Brace visited a prison at one point in the journey and visited a school for poor children at another. His practice was to split off from Fred and John for these sidelines, planning to rejoin them up the road apiece.

Olmsted also split off from the others frequently, but his stated purpose was to visit farms. Largely on account of England's being an older country than America, at the time of Olmsted's walking tour, it was well ahead of the United States in the critical area of agricultural technology. Back in 1701, Jethro Tull had invented a mechanized seed drill, becoming one of the first people to apply the rigor of science to agriculture. The invention launched a flurry of innovation. Olmsted was in the cradle of scientific farming now, and he intended to make the most of the opportunity.

In fact, he'd set off on the tour carrying letters of introduction to the proprietors of various model farms. He examined livestock and watched cheese being made. He noted various implements used on British farms but not yet available in the United States, such as Crosskill's Patent Clod-Crusher Roller. He even had a consultation with a noted British expert to discuss the latest and best techniques for draining farmland.

During this, his first visit to Great Britain, Olmsted had one other noteworthy visit to a park. In Wales, he got the chance to walk over the manicured grounds of Chirk Castle. Olmsted was amazed: It was a real castle, dating to the late thirteenth century, surrounded by a real moat that was filled with water. It had been home to the Myddelton family for hundreds of years; each successive Myddelton held hereditary titles such as baron of Chirk Castle. Just to visit required some string pulling. Olmsted enjoyed touring the castle and walking over the surrounding parklands on a private tour. He fell into a daydream about what it would be like to live in such splendor. But he snapped out of his reverie just as suddenly. Was it really right for this beautiful place to be so cloistered, he began to wonder, set apart for the enjoyment of the privileged few?

Olmsted was an American, through and through. Besides the sense of coming home, he was having another experience common to Americans visiting England. Having Brace at his elbow during the tour of Chirk Castle no doubt also helped trigger this sudden burst of egalitarianism.

Fred, John, and Charley traveled at a good clip. In the course of about a month, they covered a generous swath of English countryside, mostly on foot, but occasionally by train or coach. And they weren't finished; the companions intended to make the most of this rare opportunity for travel. They had stuck to a bare-bones budget, and money remained. They sailed to France and from there visited Belgium and Germany. They did a brief walking tour through the Rhine Valley. Brace decided to stay on in Germany. He was thinking about studying theology there. On his own, he would later make an ill-advised trip to post-revolution Hungary and wind up imprisoned for more than a month.

Fred and John sailed home from Glasgow. Olmsted had witnessed the beauty of the English countryside, firsthand. He'd visited a public park. He'd visited a private park, too, and been put off by the air of aristocracy that surrounded it. But none of it exactly coalesced. Not yet. He was a farmer still, and these were just more thoughts and observations to churn about in his brain.

The Olmsted brothers arrived in New York on October 24, 1850. According to Fred's accounting, they had spent an average of 71¢ per day for food and accommodations. Throw in the price of ship's passage and other transportation along with incidentals, and the whole trip cost the two of them—cost John Sr., rather—roughly $600.

Olmsted was home for the harvest, and, in subsequent months, he threw himself back into work on Tosomock Farm. He ordered 5,000 fruit-tree saplings to plant in his nursery. As a bonus for placing such a large order, he also received a sampling of ornamental trees. He planted a pair of cedars of Lebanon in front of his farmhouse.

In his capacity as secretary of the county agricultural society, he obtained an innovative British mechanism that he and his fellow farmers could use to make tile. The tile, in turn, could line pipes for drainage on farmland. It was one of the first of these devices ever imported into the United States.

On the surface, Olmsted appeared consumed by the affairs of his farm and by those of his Staten Island neighbors. Yet he found himself oddly detached, less engaged by any of this than he would have expected. He'd gone on the walking tour hoping to quench a kind of wanderlust. *See England as a young man, and it will be easier to buckle down to a farmer's life*—that had been one of the many arguments he'd summoned in that long letter to his father. But he'd found that he really loved traveling. Tosomock Farm seemed terribly drab now. Back on Staten Island, the memories of the walking tour seemed to cast a shadow across his life. Olmsted wrote a letter to Brace, who was still in Europe: "The fact is evident now that when we were traveling we were living a great deal more, getting a great deal more out of the world, loving oftener, hating oftener, reaching a great many more milestones."

In another letter to Brace, Olmsted complained about his stature in life. In the big picture—no, really *big*, cosmic terms—what was the point of being a farmer, he pondered. Was he helping people in any truly meaningful way? Olmsted confessed that he craved influence, longed to be involved in the grand affairs of the world. Yet he was so far away from that. Feeling petulant, Olmsted reflected on his fellow Americans' response to his recent walking tour. "The mere fact of having been to Europe is worth nothing," he groused.

Olmsted had been a farmer—first as Geddes's apprentice, then at Sachem's Head, then on Staten Island—for four years. That was a lifetime in his scheme. Now, that familiar restlessness was starting to intrude. Over the next few years, he'd treat Tosomock Farm as a kind of home base. He would continue to live there, on and off, and farming would remain his primary business. (The hired hands could always pick up the slack if he was involved in something new.) But the walking tour stands as a kind of dividing line in Olmsted's life. For the next few years, he'd be leaning, forever leaning—away from farming and toward other occupations, ones that might prove worthy of his growing but ill-defined sense of ambition.

As it happened, the "mere fact of having been to Europe" was worth something. George Putnam, his Staten Island neighbor and distant relative, was in the process of launching a new line of books. Rather than issuing the standard hardcover, Putnam was eager to try out a recent publishing innovation—the paperback. He planned to publish a variety of different kinds of books in this format: biographies, poetry collections, philosophical treatises, and travelogues. He intended to sell the books for 25¢ apiece.

Putnam approached Olmsted about writing an account of his recent walking tour. Putnam thought it best to focus just on the main leg, across the English countryside. Olmsted accepted immediately. Of course, he had never attempted to write a book. As a first step, he contacted various friends and family members to gather up all the letters he'd sent during his walking tour. In fact, he asked Kingsbury, a friend who had not gone on the walking tour, to send along "every scrap" of correspondence he'd received from him, his brother, or Brace. He knew he'd need these various letters to refresh his memory about where he'd gone, what he'd done, and when. Fortunately, while in England, he'd also taken some "pocket-book notes" that formed a kind of diary, though it was a pretty spare document. But at least this provided another source to draw upon. Olmsted got down to work.

Emboldened by Putnam's book offer, Olmsted also decided to make a pilgrimage to Newburgh, New York, to meet with Andrew Jackson Downing. Downing is not to be confused with Alexander Jackson Davis, the architect whom Olmsted contacted about designing a farmhouse at Sachem's Head. As mentioned, Andrew Jackson Downing was editor of the *Horticulturist and Journal of Rural Art and Rural Taste*, the magazine that had earlier published some letters Olmsted had written seeking farming advice. Now Olmsted was hoping to get some additional writing assignments from Downing's publication.

Downing was a formidable figure. The fact that America was predominantly a rural society coupled with the fact that farming was the leading profession had helped make him one of the most powerful and influential tastemakers in the country during the mid-nineteenth century. His dictates were followed by literate gentleman farmers. Downing was also the source consulted by wealthy city dwellers who owned second homes in the country.

Downing wore his hair in a flowing black mane and had intense dark eyes. He cultivated an air of romantic brooding and made it a practice to rarely smile, and as for breaking into laughter—never. His pronouncements, delivered in the pages of the *Horticulturist*, were taken as gospel: *Houses shouldn't be square boxes. Asymmetry is preferable, as it puts your home in harmony with nature. Don't paint your house white! Don't clear-cut the trees on your property. That's the way subsistence-grubbing pioneers behave. If you're going to lead a virtuous rural life, leave some ornamental trees to beautify your property. But keep it simple. Lavish rural houses are soul distorting, reminiscent of the way landed gentry in the old country live.*

It's hard to overestimate Downing's influence on life in nineteenth-century America. In fact, he is often credited as being the person that popularized the front porch in American homes. He argued that a porch provides a modest, but necessary, transition between one's domestic life and the wider world. "A good house will lead to good civilization" is one of his many, many pronouncements. Olmsted had long been a big disciple of Downing and an avid reader of the *Horticulturist*.

As Downing's star had risen, he'd started receiving requests to put his moral and aesthetic notions into practice. People began asking him to build them suitable country homes. But he wasn't an architect. Rather, he was a gardener, writer, and cultural critic. So he hired a young English-trained architect named Calvert Vaux to help him expand into the design of country homes.

Olmsted's visit to Newburgh occurred during the summer of 1851. Years later, both Olmsted and Vaux would recount having their first brush with one another at this point. But nothing even remotely memorable would stand out for either party. Vaux was simply a novice architect working for the celebrated Downing. Olmsted was simply a farmer hoping to land some writing assignments. That panned out. The *Horticulturist* would publish a brief Olmsted-penned piece titled "A Note on the True Soldat Laboureur Pear."

Not long after the visit to Newburgh, Olmsted also completed his book. It's remarkable how quickly he managed to churn it out, and it was a vast work besides, featuring enough text to fill some seven hundred pages. Of course, this was way too long for Putnam's new line of 25¢ paperbacks. The publisher decided to split the book in two and bring out a second volume at a later date.

Walks and Talks of an American Farmer in England reads like a book that has been dashed off in an unholy hurry. It's a meandering, scarcely organized account of the trip he took with his brother John and Charley Brace. There are long technical descriptions of farm implements. These are often followed by passages of social commentary, maybe bemoaning the conditions of the rural poor. But Olmsted is just as likely to write a comic passage on the manners of a country innkeeper. The first sixty pages are devoted to an account of the sailing-ship voyage from New

York to England aboard the *Henry Clay*. It seems an odd choice for a book intended as an account of a *walking* tour. But as Olmsted would state in the preface to a later edition, he had written his book while standing on "one farmer's leg and one sailor's leg."

Indeed, these were both professions he'd pursued—and his first book was going to cover them, and so much more. *Walks and Talks* can best be viewed as a kind of compendium of the scattershot interests and enthusiasms of its author. Olmsted dedicated the work to George Geddes.

On publication, in early 1852, *Walks and Talks* would garner a handful of notices, mostly lukewarm, and would sell slowly. Still, it's notable for a couple of reasons. Describing the everyday people he encountered in England, Olmsted showed himself to be a keen observer with a good ear for mimicking speech ("Sit ye down now, and take a pint," he quotes one local as saying. "These gentlemen be from Ameriky, and I talks with 'um about going there"). This was reminiscent of the vivid letters he'd sent his family from China.

There's also a prescient passage in *Walks and Talks* that celebrates the fine art of park making: "What artist, so noble, has often been my thought, as he, who with far-reaching conception of beauty and designing power, sketches the outline, writes the colors, and directs the shadows of a picture so great that Nature shall be employed upon it for generations, before the work he has arranged for her shall realize his intentions."

Olmsted was busy writing. He was busy farming. When he finally paused to look around, he was pained to see that nearly everyone he knew seemed to have formed a serious romantic attachment. His brother had gotten engaged to Mary Perkins, the Staten Island neighbor and inspiration for the two-knives poem. After being released from prison in Hungary, Brace had set out for the United States, but he'd stopped in Ireland along the way and fallen head over heels for a woman named Letitia Neill. They would marry in a few years. Kingsbury was about to be married. My God, even Charley Trask—fifth wheel that he was—had somehow managed to get engaged.

That pretty well covered it: Everyone else in the "uncommon set" of friends had found a mate. So, too, had a number of women with whom

Olmsted had earlier enjoyed dalliances. He got the news that Sophia Stevens, a woman to whom he'd been bold enough to read Ruskin's *Modern Painters*, was engaged. The unimpeachable Miss B. was already married— had been for a while. Making matters all the worse, every one of these people was younger than Olmsted, by at least a few years. He was nearly thirty now and he despaired of ever finding a wife. In a letter to Brace, he confessed his predicament: "As it is, I am likely to be all along a bachelor or to marry believing that the 'highest element of love' is not of earth, and so secure from disappointment if I shall not find it." In other words: His idealism was to blame for his being alone. And were he to marry, it would only be after first coming to terms with the fact that pure love doesn't exist in this world. In another letter, he struck a different note: "The sun shines, ice is cold, fire is hot, punch is both sweet and sour, Fred Olmsted is alone, is stupid, is crazy and is unalterably a weak sinner and unhappy and happy. This is my truest most solid and sustainable standpoint."

Lofty sentiments notwithstanding—and loopy sentiments notwith- standing—Olmsted wound up simply doing what people have done since time immemorial: He surveyed the available prospects and settled on the most promising one. Emily Perkins (no relation to Mary Perkins) had grown up on Asylum Street in Hartford, near the Olmsted home. She was in her early twenties, pretty—black hair and soft, friendly eyes— and came from a good family. Her father was a prominent lawyer.

Fred and Emily had courted casually for several years, ever since he had joined a literary group that she belonged to. At one point, he'd taken her on a ride over the ice on a horse-drawn cutter. On another occasion, Olmsted had shown up at her family's home in Hartford at nine in the morning, an absurdly early hour to come calling. But he did that with all the girls. Olmsted had once written to Kingsbury: "The conclusion is that Emily is the most lovely and loveable girl. Oh, she is. Well, I really think she has the most incomparably fine face I ever saw. And she is a real tender sensible downright good woman." Not exactly a description of a love for the ages.

With all his friends settling down, however, Olmsted now sought to heat things up. In February 1851, he asked Emily Perkins to enter into a formal correspondence with him, a very serious step. He'd once made the same request of Elizabeth Baldwin, only to be rebuffed. But Emily agreed. By late summer, they were engaged. Still, she made it clear that she didn't want to announce their engagement to the rest of the world. Apropos of this, she wrote Olmsted the strangest letter. In it, she complained about the annoyance of all the little domestic decisions that they were bound to face, such as buying furniture and picking out carpet. But Olmsted kept after her. Finally, she relented and announced their engagement.

The timing could not have been worse. In early August 1851, John suffered a severe lung hemorrhage and began coughing up blood. He'd been living with respiratory problems for some time now, but the Olmsted family had tried to be hopeful, despite the ominous signs. For years now, John Sr. had regularly told his son to stand up straight. He walked with a slouch, considered a telltale indicator of one of the nineteenth century's most dreaded diseases. But the family had long been in a kind of denial. They had hoped it really was just bad posture. "Sit erect when you sit—shoulders *well back* when you walk," his worried father had once advised him.

Now it was confirmed. John had tuberculosis. On receiving the news, he wrote a letter to Kingsbury that contained the alarming assertion that he had just received a "sentence of death." John had been in training to become a doctor, so he recognized the severity of his diagnosis. But he also managed to strike a philosophical note: "Yet we all have it upon us—& how absurd it is to get worried when the particular mode of death is indicated."

Olmsted tried to be more hopeful. Apparently, John's doctor had indicated that the tuberculosis was an "incipient" form. With the right treatment, there was a possibility that the course of the disease could be slowed, maybe even arrested.

And then another blow: Olmsted received a letter from Emily Perkins's mother, announcing that her daughter wished to break off the engagement. According to this letter, Emily had started to have serious second thoughts about the impending marriage. Apparently, she had experienced a "revulsion of feeling," as it was indelicately put to Olmsted. Likely, the mother and daughter didn't even know about John's diagnosis. Somehow this made it all the worse.

Olmsted hoped that maybe Emily would have a change of heart. He rushed to Hartford and met with Mother Perkins, who assured him that the engagement was off. Olmsted wasn't even allowed to meet with Emily to plead his case. It was simply over. Olmsted was heartbroken yet left with very little to contemplate. He never even received an explanation as to why she had ended their relationship. Even that small satisfaction he was denied. Emily Perkins was packed off to Worcester, Massachusetts, to stay with relatives, clear her head, wait until any gossip about her ill-considered engagement died down.

Everything was so mixed up. John wrote, "I am to be examined by Wednesday, married on Thursday (probably), and am to sail for Italy Thursday week." Mary had stayed with him, despite the diagnosis, and it appeared that they were pressing forward with their plans, and quickly.

On October 16, 1851, John and Mary were wed. On October 22, they sailed from New York aboard the *Asia*, bound for Liverpool. From there, the newlyweds set off for Italy, where they hoped the balmy climate would help keep John's tuberculosis under control.

Back on Tosomock Farm, Olmsted felt devastated and alone. Late in the autumn of 1851, he composed a letter to his father in which he mentioned that he'd been watching ships sail past on the bay. Some of them, he surmised, were no doubt bound for China, a place where he had once gone. And John's ship? Why, it had sailed to Liverpool, the same place they'd sailed together on the happier occasion of commencing their walking tour. Just now, Olmsted confessed to his father, his own life "seems to me somebody else's story." It had been a strange, confusing, painful time.

Outside the farmhouse, on Raritan Bay, the tall ships kept sailing past, headed who knows where.

II
"The Cause of Future Freedom"
SOUTHERN TRAVELS AND JOURNALISM, 1852–1857

CHAPTER 6

"The South"

EVERYBODY WAS READING *Uncle Tom's Cabin*. Olmsted—ever the bibliophile—read it, too. Olmsted wanted to be familiar with this provocative work that had people talking; he was curious to see what the fuss was about. He had no inkling of how this book—and the myriad cultural currents swirling around it—was about to impact his own life.

Uncle Tom's Cabin created a literary mania, the likes of which the world had never before seen. During its first year in print, Harriet Beecher Stowe's opus on slavery sold a record 200,000 copies. That dwarfed the *combined* first-year sales of such earlier literary sensations as *Don Quixote*, *Tom Jones*, and Gibbon's *History of the Decline and Fall of the Roman Empire*. Only the Bible had sold more copies, and that was over the course of centuries. In Boston alone, three hundred newborn girls were christened Eva in 1852, most of them apparently named after a beloved character in Stowe's novel.

Even in the South, Stowe's book was read with avid interest. It was viewed as a window into the Northern mind-set and as a clue to abolitionist intentions. Southern writers rebutted with works like *Aunt Phillis's Cabin*, and a whole body of anti-Tom literature—at least twenty titles strong—was born.

Granted, even many devotees of *Uncle Tom's Cabin* conceded that the book was melodramatic and moralistic. It just happened to be *their* melodrama, jibing with *their* morals. According to detractors—plenty existed in the North as well as the South—the book's portrayal of plantation life was propaganda at best, downright falsehood at worst. But one thing no one could deny: Stowe's timing was perfect. Her book came out during a period when slavery—an issue that had divided America from its inception—had once again exploded into the forefront of the national consciousness.

California had recently petitioned for statehood, threatening to tip a delicate balance: fifteen free states, fifteen slave. The result was the Compromise of 1850. It allowed for California to be admitted as a free state. Among other things, the compromise also spelled out that settlers in western territories such as Arizona and Utah be allowed to make up their own minds about slavery. As a concession to Southerners, a new Fugitive Slave Act was drafted, updating a statute originally passed in 1793. The new act pretty much abrogated runaway slaves' rights, such as they were. Now, one need only claim to own an escaped slave, and the claim had to be honored—no trial, no questions asked. Any person who aided a runaway slave would be subject to a $1,000 fine and up to six months in jail.

The Compromise of 1850 was congressional horse trading, nothing more. It bought time. But simmering tensions remained, and it was virtually ensured that violence would eventually erupt. Citizens of slave states worried about being marginalized and isolated. They had just seen their hopes dashed that California might be split in two, creating a slave state and a free state. Fears ran high that popular sovereignty in territories such as Utah would halt the westward expansion of slavery. An earlier bargain, the Missouri Compromise of 1820, had already arrested slavery's northward expansion, limiting it to below the 36°30' latitude line. (Missouri, though above that line, had been admitted as a slave state. It was supposed to be the lone exception.)

Northerners weren't exactly sanguine about the 1850 act, either. A particular sore point was the recast Fugitive Slave Act. It dictated that Northern abolitionists, following their consciences, could no longer help runaway slaves without risking a fine or jail time. Stowe, who had once lived in the free state of Ohio bordering the slave state of Kentucky, wrote her book specifically as a reaction to the Fugitive Slave Act of 1850.

Amid the maelstrom, despite having read *Uncle Tom's Cabin*, Olmsted remained a gradualist. He believed that slavery should be phased out over time. During the eighteenth century, when slavery was still legal in Connecticut, some of Olmsted's own Hartford forebears had been slave-holders. Partly as a consequence, perhaps, he tended to hold a rather measured view on the subject.

Olmsted was quick to concede that slavery was wrong. But he was-n't certain that immediate freedom was the answer. Maybe it would constitute an unwitting cruelty to emancipate people who were de-pendent and for the most part uneducated. As a farmer and New Yorker, he wondered what would happen if freed blacks seeking em-ployment suddenly swarmed into the North. Furthermore, he wasn't so certain that one region of the country had any right to impose its viewpoints on another. Rather, he believed it was the South's preroga-tive to end slavery on its own terms and in its own time. The United States was a democracy, built on compromise, and in his estimation the spirit of compromise—however imperfect—must be honored. Such gradualism was a common stance, one that Olmsted shared with many of his fellow Northerners.

By contrast, his good friend Charley Brace was a true abolitionist. Brace was descended from a line of educators, intellectuals of modest means. There's no evidence that any of his forebears owned slaves. What's more, Brace's father had been Harriet Beecher Stowe's favorite teacher during her schoolgirl days in Hartford.

Olmsted and Brace had always enjoyed ferocious arguments. It was great sport for them, simply what they did. The year 1852 found Brace back in the United States, recently released from prison in Hungary. He and Olmsted fell back into their old pattern, only now the topic of the day was slavery. Brace argued that slavery was a moral blight that must end immediately; Olmsted countered with a passionate call for, well, a go-slow approach. "I am not a red hot abolitionist like Charley," Olmsted told Kingsbury.

To bolster his case, Brace even went so far as to bring others to back him up for his debates with Olmsted at Tosomock Farm. On one occa-sion, he arrived with Theodore Parker, a preacher who railed against slav-ery. Another time, Brace brought William Lloyd Garrison, the noted abolitionist and editor of the *Liberator*. Even these heavyweights left

Olmsted unmoved. In fact, he perceived the passion that surrounded the issue of slavery as suspect. If either abolitionists or slaveholders were more confident in their positions—if either party relied on facts rather than rhetoric—the volume might go down. "I think both sides very wrong" was Olmsted's conclusion.

Brace wasn't about to give up, however. As the author of a new book called *Hungary in 1851: With an Experience of the Austrian Police*, he had entrée into literary New York. As it happened, Brace knew Henry Raymond, cofounder and editor of the *New-York Daily Times*. When Brace learned that the paper was looking to send a correspondent to the South, he suggested Olmsted to Raymond. Brace recognized that his friend was losing his passion for farm life. Brace also figured firsthand experience of the slave states was just what Olmsted needed to be shaken out of his gradualist stance. For his part, Raymond was glancingly familiar with Olmsted's own recent book, *Walks and Talks*. Raymond was willing to consider Olmsted for the Southern assignment. He agreed to meet with Olmsted for an interview.

At this point, the *New-York Daily Times* was a brand-new publication. It was part of a revolution in newspaper journalism. Between 1800 and 1850, literacy had exploded in urban centers such as New York and Philadelphia. This gave rise to a new kind of newspaper. On the decline were so-called blanket sheets, weekly papers that were large enough to sleep under and filled with commercial notices aimed at a genteel audience. The replacement for these was daily papers, smaller and more portable in size and designed for the now literate masses, on the go.

Newsboys hawked papers on every corner, charging a penny a pop. Competition between publications was fierce. It was necessary to win readers anew each and every day with the best headlines, the freshest scoops. Predictably, papers put a premium on the lurid, the leering, the strange. Editor James Gordon Bennett put his *New York Herald* on the map with exhaustive coverage of the murder of the prostitute Helen Jewett, in the process creating America's first tabloid crime scandal. Meanwhile, the *New York Sun* perpetrated one of U.S. history's great news hoaxes, running a series claiming that life—in the form of a race of man-bats—had been discovered on the moon. When the hoax was exposed, the *Sun* shamelessly took credit for "diverting the public mind, for a while, from that bitter apple of discord, the abolition of slavery."

Into this thicket came the *Times*. The paper was launched in 1851 with the aim of distinguishing itself in a field that was surpassingly yellow. In an era when reporters relied on wild conjecture or just made stuff up, Raymond opted for balance and accuracy. Among the crowded ranks of New York dailies, this was one competitive niche that remained open. A prospectus, used to raise $100,000 in startup costs, contains what amounts to a mandate for the paper that would come to be called the Gray Lady: "We do not mean to write as if we were in a passion, unless that shall really be the case; and we shall make it a point to get into a passion as rarely as possible."

Olmsted's interview with the *Times* lasted less than five minutes. Raymond didn't even inquire about Olmsted's views on slavery. Instead, the editor demanded assurances that Olmsted would base his reporting strictly on observation. Satisfied, Raymond hired Olmsted on the spot, assigning him to travel through the South for many months. He was to receive $10 for each published dispatch.

Raymond could afford to take a chance on Olmsted. In fact, he really had no choice. The *Times* had recently hiked its price to two cents a copy and doubled its pages to eight. Circulation had immediately shrunk from 25,000 to 18,000. Raymond had extra news pages to fill and competitive ground to regain. What better way to make a name for an upstart paper than with a series on *the* topic of the day? While Olmsted's qualifications might appear meager, he was actually a promising choice. He was fresh from a walking tour of England and had produced a book based on his observations—a reasonably parallel exercise. Furthermore, he was a farmer. The South was nothing if not an agrarian society; to make sense of the region's manners and mores, he'd have this common experience to draw on.

In October 1852, shortly after being hired, Olmsted wrote a letter to Fred Kingsbury describing his new job at the *Times* as requiring "matter of fact matter to come after the deluge of spoony fancy pictures now at its height." Translation: Olmsted would need to stick to the facts, avoiding the emotionalism of *Uncle Tom's Cabin* and its ilk, what he here referred to as "spoony fancy pictures."

Critics of Harriet Beecher Stowe were fond of pointing out that she had written her novel with firsthand knowledge of but one slave state, Kentucky. She had never even set foot on a plantation. Olmsted was about to travel all over the South. He was about to see for himself. What he would see would change his thinking utterly.

Olmsted set out on his journey in December 1852, timing his departure for after the fall harvest was done. Though he'd landed a newspaper assignment, he was still a farmer by trade. He planned to be gone for the winter, when nothing of great import was likely to occur. Just to be certain, Brace agreed to periodically check in on Tosomock Farm.

Olmsted traveled first by train to Washington, D.C. There, he experienced something akin to culture shock. While selling slaves had been outlawed within the district—another Compromise of 1850 horse trade—owning slaves was still permitted. This was the U.S. capitol, yet Olmsted was stunned by how much it seemed a southern town. From Washington, he made forays into the Maryland countryside, then down into Virginia.

There was something immensely lonely about this first leg of his journey, as he described it in his accounts. Olmsted ate alone in roadhouses, eavesdropping on fellow diners, trying to gather bits of scuttlebutt. From the town of Richmond, he tailed a funeral procession of slaves as they walked out into the countryside. Standing at a distance, Olmsted watched them heap dirt on the coffin, listened as they broke into a call-and-response dirge, soon broken by wails of grief.

Before coming south, Olmsted had been furnished by friends with letters of introduction to various plantation owners. But plantations proved to be maddeningly absentee operations. Whenever Olmsted called, the owners weren't home. Drawing strangers into conversation, meanwhile, proved immensely difficult.

Olmsted made no effort to disguise either his voice or appearance. He simply identified himself as a traveler, a suitably valid explanation. If someone pursued with further questions, he readily conceded that he was from New York. This was almost a point of honor; Olmsted figured people would open up if he was honest—well, to a point. He stopped short of revealing that he was a reporter. No matter, because at the outset he was rarely able to get anyone to say boo. "You can't imagine how hard it is to get hold of a conversable man," he wrote to Brace, "—and when you find one, he will talk of anything else but slavery &c." Of Southerners, he added, "They are jealous of observation of things that would tell against slavery."

Olmsted recorded his impressions nonetheless and sent them off to Raymond. His initial dispatches were generously padded, full of observations about statues and aqueducts and farm equipment such as Hussey's reapers. Describing Richmond, he included such superfluous detail as this: "The mean temperature in July and August is about 80 Fahrenheit, and in January 44 degrees."

In a letter to his father, Olmsted confessed that he felt like he wasn't doing a very good job. The South was proving hard to penetrate. Olmsted was amazed by how like a foreign country it was, much more so than anyplace he'd visited during his recent tour through Europe. Raymond ran the dispatches anyway, even giving them prominent play. He had a newspaper to fill.

Olmsted's column, "The South," was given a regular spot at the top of page 2. It often alternated with a series that Brace was writing for the *Times* called "Walks Among the New-York Poor." Brace was just then in the process of founding the outfit for which he'd be remembered, the Children's Aid Society. It would revolutionize social services for children in America, providing humane alternatives to almshouses and orphan asylums.

For his dispatches, Olmsted used a pseudonymous byline, as was common practice in those days. "Yeoman" served as a veiled reference to farming, at this point the only profession Olmsted had managed to stick with for any amount of time. It was also an assertion that this particular correspondent could be counted on for earthy, no-nonsense commentary. The convention of using a pseudonym was doubly sensible because it kept Olmsted's identity secret. As a Northerner writing about slavery, he would be in grave danger if his cover got blown. Of course, first he'd need to serve up something beyond the temperature statistics available in any almanac.

Olmsted kept at it. If he possessed one winning quality as a reporter it was unflappability—the very trait that Kingsbury had singled out in a letter about Olmsted years earlier. Ashamed of his flat initial dispatches,

Olmsted took to buttonholing strangers. He tried everywhere to engage people—waiting on train platforms, inside general stores, working in open fields. The law of averages dictated that some would talk. These conversations, in turn, landed him fresh invitations to other plantations, ones where cotton was grown as well as corn, rice, sugar—even a turpentine plantation.

Gradually, the South began to open up before Olmsted. He found it a place of uncommon beauty. Passing beneath a live-oak tree, he paused for several minutes to stare up in wonderment. He noted the strange customs. Corn bread was served breakfast, lunch, and dinner, and he grew to hate it, describing it as "French friterzeed Dutch flabbergasted hell-fixins."

Most of all, the South was complicated. This was a world best rendered in shades of gray. On visiting a plantation along the James River in Virginia, what struck Olmsted most was how harried the owner appeared to be. He was beset by worry about money and crops, forced to manage his slave laborers even on the most trifling matters. "This is a hard life," the man told him. "You see how constantly I am called on, often at night as well as day. I did not sleep a wink last night till near morning; my health is failing and my wife is feeble, but I cannot rid myself of it." Why not hire an overseer? "I cannot trust an overseer," the man continued. "I had one, and paid him four hundred dollars a year, and I had almost as much work and anxiety looking after him as in overseeing for myself." This man may have been a slaveholder, but Olmsted found that he couldn't really see him as wicked. He was merely an overworked farmer, someone with whom Olmsted could easily empathize.

Olmsted proved an open-minded correspondent. He managed to recapture the natural inquisitiveness that had shone through in his letters home during his China voyage years back and, more recently, during his walk across England. He also showed an uncanny ability to capture the quirks and nongrammaticalisms of ordinary speech. His standard practice was to engage in leisurely conversation, then slip off by himself to jot down notes. One time at an inn, he requested a candle for his room. But why did he require a candle in his room? was the puzzled reply. Because, he explained, he needed to write by its light.

Periodically, he'd craft his notes into a *Times* dispatch. He made a practice of preserving the anonymity of his subjects. After all, they hadn't even been aware that they were talking to a reporter. Were their names, attached to their words, to show up in a newspaper article, his subjects might also be in danger of reprisal.

Visiting a rice plantation, Olmsted was intrigued by the generous considerations given to the slaves. The slaves here were comfortably dressed and lived in well-appointed cabins, and there was a nursery where infants were tended while their mothers worked the fields. On this particular plantation, he learned, many of the slaves even owned guns.

Apparently, they used the guns to hunt for game in the nearby woods, a perk that allowed them to supplement their usual food rations. Olmsted was dumbfounded. Here was a white family living in tremendous isolation, miles from the next-nearest white family, and surrounded by two hundred armed slaves. The family didn't even bother to lock their doors or windows, noted Olmsted. When questioned, the owner laughed as though Olmsted was the crazy one. He led Olmsted into a cabin where an elderly female slave was busy separating rice tailings from a pile of chaff. After shooting a grin at Olmsted, the man informed the old slave that he was granting her freedom. The woman protested. "I lubs 'ou mas'r, oh, I lubs 'ou," she cried. "I don't want go 'way from 'ou."

Olmsted—clear-eyed reporter that he was—was left to grapple with this exchange. The rice plantation didn't prove to be an isolated case, either. Strange as it was, a genuine regard seemed to exist, sometimes even approaching familial love, between some owners and their slaves. Meanwhile, it was hypocrisy to pretend that the North's economic system was free of ruthlessness. "Oh God! Who are we to condemn our brother," Olmsted demanded in a *Times* dispatch. " . . . No slave freezes to death for want of habitation or fuel, as have men in Boston. No slave reels off into the abyss of God, from want of work that shall bring it food, as do men and women in New-York. Remember that, Mrs. Stowe. Remember that, indignant sympathizers."

Olmsted remained constantly on the move in the South. Even traveling short distances proved unduly complicated, and frequently it was necessary to transfer from one means of conveyance to another.

At one point, he set off from Norfolk, Virginia, bound for Gaston, North Carolina, about ninety miles. He began his trip on a ferryboat that was supposed to connect with a train. Midway across Norfolk Harbor, the ferry simply stopped running and drifted for fifteen minutes. Apparently, the fireman had fallen asleep and stopped feeding coal into the ferry's engine. Olmsted arrived at the train terminal a half hour late. Fortunately, the train arrived a full hour late.

Chugging along inferior track, the train made an achingly slow journey to Weldon, North Carolina. There, Olmsted hired a stagecoach. The driver, not planning to depart for a while, suggested that Olmsted go eat dinner. He urged Olmsted to leave his luggage, which contained his reporting notes, among other things. Upon finishing dinner, Olmsted discovered that the coach had departed without him. Olmsted broke into a run and was able to quickly overtake the coach. The road was so preposterously rutted that it took four hours for the coach to travel fourteen miles, whereupon Olmsted was summarily turned out. Late that night, he finally arrived in Gaston, exhausted. This was also no isolated incident. Olmsted soon concluded that the South was almost comically inefficient.

Nowhere was this more evident than with slave labor. At any given time, Olmsted observed, only a portion of the slaves on a plantation were capable of work. Prior to the age of twelve, for example, children born to slaves could contribute very little, at most being called upon for such light duty as scaring birds away from crops. Old slaves were also capable of only the most minimal work. Same for a slave that was sick or injured. Female slaves who were menstruating weren't considered fit for the demands of field labor, either. "They are forever complaining of 'irregularities,'" a plantation owner told him. "They don't come to the field, and you ask what's the matter, and the old nurse always nods her head and says, 'Oh, she's not well, sir; she's not fit to work, sir,'—and you have to take her word for it."

Add up all the slaves that *couldn't* work, Olmsted found, and at any given time only about a third remained that *could*—an observation that was borne out in visit after visit to plantations. Yet masters had to house and clothe and feed their slaves, every last one. Moreover, the few slaves working didn't exactly go all out. They broke tools and mistreated the mules, neglecting to give them food and water. One time, Olmsted watched with bemusement as an overseer on horseback rode toward a group of slaves who were shirking. They stepped up their pace, but in the meantime, slaves on the other side of the field had let up.

Olmsted encountered several slave owners who also had experience running farms in the North. These men were in a good position to compare the two systems. All conceded that slave labor was drastically less efficient than hired farm labor. Olmsted did a rough average of the men's varied assessments and concluded that a slave accomplished about half the work of one of the hired hands on his Staten Island farm.

The same clear-eyed approach that had made Olmsted open to the South's charms was demanding that he acknowledge the region's deficiencies. It was becoming increasingly clear to him that slavery wasn't working, but not for the usual reasons. Olmsted's perspective went something like this: Slavery, with its myriad inefficiencies, was a defective system when it came to labor and production. Olmsted's criticism of slavery was uniquely his own and based on empirical observation. As such, it differed greatly from the emotional appeals of abolitionists. Olmsted was growing convinced that slavery was flawed from an *economic* standpoint.

Olmsted's ceaseless travel took him to the North Carolina coast and an unusual operation where slave labor was employed in fishing. Slaves aboard boats used sweep seines to catch herring and shad. Frequently, the nets got fouled by huge underwater cypress stumps. To remove particularly pesky stumps, it was necessary to send down a diver with a crude detonating device, an iron tube packed with gunpowder.

This was demanding work. Olmsted met a fishing boat operator who was in the habit of paying slaves to blow up stumps, giving them a quarter or fifty cents a day. Sure enough, slaves clamored to be selected for this dangerous duty and accomplished it with aplomb. "What! Slaves eager to work, and working cheerfully, earnestly and skillfully?" asked Olmsted in a dispatch. He added, "Being for the time managed as freemen, their ambition stimulated by wages, suddenly they, too, reveal sterling manhood, and honor their creator."

On another occasion, Olmsted was particularly pleased when he got the chance to talk with a slave one-on-one, without a master or anyone else present. At the end of a visit to a sugar plantation, a slave was enlisted to drive Olmsted in a buggy to his next destination. For a white Northern stranger, this was quite a rare opportunity. Olmsted wanted to make sure he didn't blow it. His mind was swirling with questions, but he was careful to let the conversation unfold naturally.

What is your name? he asked the slave.

William.

Where were you born?

Far away, in Virginia.

Olmsted continued on for some minutes in this casual vein. When the moment was right, he slipped it in: *What would you do if you were free?*

"If I was free, massa," said William, immediately warming to the subject, "if I was free I would—well, sar, de fus thing I would do, if I was free, I would go to work for a year, and get some money for myself,—den—den—den, massa, dis is what I do—I buy me, fus place, a little house, and little lot land . . . "

Olmsted had a knack for mimicking speech patterns. And the man's modest dreams touched Olmsted as well. There were slaves, queasy truth be told, who wished to remain slaves. He'd seen as much. But there were probably many more like William, living out their lives in silent rebellion.

Thomas Jefferson once warned that if it continued, slavery would be as damaging to whites as blacks. This Olmsted also found to be true. At the time when he visited the South, more than 70 percent of whites didn't own a single slave. Yet slavery permeated every aspect of society.

Olmsted tried to get an umbrella fixed and was stunned by the ineptitude of the white repairman. The very concept of work had been degraded. This went a long way toward explaining the rutted roads and constant delays encountered everywhere while traveling. Nobody wanted to do anything. Whites didn't value work because work was fit only for slaves. Slaves—lacking incentive—didn't do much of it, either.

Only a select few plantation owners, blessed with fertile land or good luck, really benefited from this system. But the very idea of aristocracy, the notion of one type of person naturally superior to another, was so seductive to many plantation owners that they kept at it, inefficiency be damned. Other plantation owners were simply trapped in a system that didn't really serve them. In unguarded moments, several admitted as much to Olmsted.

For most, it was a hardscrabble life. Passing the night at a planter's "mansion," Olmsted couldn't help but notice that the floors were uncarpeted and the windows covered in paper curtains. On the wall hung a clock, manufactured in his home state, Connecticut. (Everything that required manufacturing came from the North.) The clock was stopped dead. Thus, there wasn't even a ticktock to punctuate the long stretches of silence between Olmsted and his taciturn host.

After a modest meal, Olmsted decided to turn in. He asked for a candle. To Olmsted's puzzlement, the host followed him upstairs to the bedroom and stood there holding the candle. Olmsted reached for it, but the host's grip tightened. That's when it struck him. For thrift's sake, the household was skimping on candles. With the host standing there, Olmsted changed into his nightclothes. Then the man blew out this lone candle and left with an abrupt "Good night, sir."

The next morning, Olmsted stayed for a breakfast of bacon, eggs, and the dreaded corn bread. As he ate, he puzzled over whether this was a representative example of "genuine planter's hospitality." Maybe the man expected to be compensated for the night's stay. He decided to err on the side of offering payment. When Olmsted broached the subject, the man didn't hesitate for a moment, saying, "I reckon a dollar and a quarter will be right, sir."

This episode was one of many that led Olmsted to another of his unique observations: Not only was slavery a flawed *economic* system, but it promoted *cultural* deficiency as well. Sure, this beau ideal existed: the Southern gentleman, possessed of perfect manners and impeccable breeding, enjoying the leisure to pursue refinement in all things. It was a myth, concluded Olmsted. Why, his host had talked of guano, when he had talked at all. Plantation owners simply lived too far apart one from another for any cultural commerce. They were consumed by the mere act of subsisting. This was such a contrast to Northern city life, including his own upbringing in Hartford, where density forced people into contact with each other, and with new ideas. As he traveled the South, Olmsted noted that he rarely saw a book of Shakespeare or a pianoforte or even a picture hanging on a wall.

By March 1853, Olmsted was several months into his journey. He'd covered an immense amount of ground, traveling across Maryland and Virginia, wending his way through the Carolinas and Georgia. He was now deep into the Mississippi Delta. As the historian Edmund Wilson once wrote, "He tenaciously and patiently and lucidly made his way through the whole South, undiscouraged by churlish natives, almost impassable roads or the cold inns and uncomfortable cabins in which he spent most of his nights. He talked to everybody and he sized up everything and he wrote it all down."

There's one thing Olmsted hadn't yet seen. But that would change soon enough. An overseer was giving Olmsted a tour of a cotton plantation on the banks of the Red River, about thirty miles southeast of Natchitoches, Louisiana. As they rode on through a gully, the overseer suddenly pulled up his horse.

"What that? Hallo!—who are you there?"

Someone was lying in the brush, trying to hide.

"Who are you there?" the overseer repeated.

The person rose up slightly. Through the brush, Olmsted could just vaguely make out a figure.

"Sam's Sall, Sir."

The person was a slave, an identity that permeated her whole being. Her name was Sall. And she belonged to Sam.

The overseer demanded that Sall provide an explanation for why she wasn't at work in the fields. She said that her father had locked her in her bedroom. When she woke up in the morning, he had already left. She had pushed on a loose plank and finally had been able to crawl out. As to why she was now hiding in a gully, she was vague.

"That won't do—come out here."

Sall emerged from the brush and stood facing Olmsted and the overseer. Olmsted could now see that Sall was a young woman, about eighteen years old.

"That won't do," repeated the overseer. "You must take some—kneel down."

Sall lowered herself to her knees. The overseer got down off his horse, carrying a rawhide whip in his left hand. He struck the girl repeatedly across the shoulders. Sall took the punishment, not crying out but merely wincing, occasionally saying, "Please, Sir!"

After he'd lashed her about thirty times, the overseer demanded again that Sall explain why she was hiding in the gully. Again, Sall repeated the same story.

"You have not got enough yet," said the overseer. "Pull up your clothes—lie down."

Sall drew up her garments to about her waist and lay down on the ground. She turned on her side, facing the overseer. The man began to strike her again with the rawhide whip, this time lashing her across her thighs and back. "Oh, don't; Sir, oh, please stop, master; please, Sir, please, Sir! Oh, that's enough, master; oh, Lord! Oh, master! master!"

Looking on, Olmsted was overcome with visceral horror mixed with a terrible sense of complicity. The only other time he'd witnessed a scene like this was aboard the *Ronaldson*, when Captain Fox ordered that young sailors be "rope's ended."

The South was a region best rendered in shades of gray, but Olmsted couldn't help but perceive the episode in stark black-and-white: This was so very wrong. Olmsted's horse flared its nostrils and bolted up out of the gully.

CHAPTER 7

Tief Im Herzen Von Texas

OLMSTED COULDN'T AFFORD to miss the spring planting season. He returned to Staten Island in April 1853.

By this time, nine of his *Times* dispatches had already appeared. In the months ahead, while on Tosomock Farm, Olmsted crafted two new dispatches each week, drawing on his travel notes. Ultimately, forty-eight Southern letters would be published. The dispatches were highly successful. Because his accounts were provocative yet balanced—per the original mandate—they grabbed readers' attention, and, as a bonus, they also managed to draw the ire of the Southern press. "The *Times*, however, is not content with the present calm," complained the *Savannah Republican*. "It sends a stranger among us 'to spy out the nakedness of the land.' What is its object, if it be not an evil one?"

Raymond of the *Times* was a classic crusty newspaper editor, sparing with praise. But he was pleased with the Southern dispatches, and even went so far as to communicate this to Olmsted. The series helped the *Times*'s circulation rebound. By the end of 1853, it had returned to 25,000. And circulation would keep growing, soon hitting 40,000, second only to the *Herald* among New York dailies. In the early life of the *Times*, Olmsted's series was a key to establishing the paper's journalistic identity. "The *Times* signaled itself by publishing Olmsted's letters from the South," wrote Edwin Godkin, a correspondent for the paper during its early years and later a friend of Olmsted's.

The success of the Southern series also had an unintended consequence for Olmsted. He grew still more disenchanted with the farmer's life. Increasingly, writing seemed more appealing. Because his letters were published under the pseudonym "Yeoman," few knew that the *Times* pieces were Olmsted's handiwork, save for the people that he chose to tell. But he wasn't shy about sharing this with fellow New Yorkers. (The risk had lain in disclosing his identity to Southerners.)

In the spring of 1853, Anne Charlotte Lynch visited Olmsted at Tosomock Farm. Years back, she had been his classmate at Miss Rockwell's school in Hartford. Now, she was a poet and the host of a Greenwich Village salon, attended by such luminaries as the painter Daniel Huntington, abolitionist journalist Lydia Child, and Felix Darley, the noted illustrator. Before his death in 1849, Edgar Allan Poe had been a regular and had recited "The Raven" before an appreciative gathering. Olmsted confessed in a letter to his father that he didn't care much for Lynch's own poetry. But he was thrilled to reconnect with this childhood acquaintance because she "knew all the distinguished people."

Olmsted tried his hand at a literary work, which appeared in a prestigious new publication, *Putnam's Monthly Magazine*. The magazine belonged to George Putnam, his onetime Staten Island neighbor who had recently moved to Manhattan. Through a separate enterprise, a book publishing company, Putnam had also brought out Olmsted's *Walks and Talks*.

"Gold Under Gilt" is a brief fable (occupying a single page in the July 1853 issue of *Putnam's*) about a wealthy Fifth Avenue couple who drop everything to minister to their gravely ill servants. The couple risks contracting a terrible disease because they feel a moral obligation to do the right thing. The servants still succumb. But as Olmsted concluded, "Here was another 'deed for New-York to be proud of.' Gilt sometimes covers gold."

Olmsted's odd little parable provides a window into his mind-set at this time. It's no coincidence that the setting is New York, his stomping grounds, but also a progressive Northern city. The tale's moral—human values transcend the economic differences that separate people—speaks to his growing sense of noblesse oblige. Perhaps it relates to a nagging conscience as well. Whether witting or unwitting, "gilt covers gold" is a pun on "*guilt* covers gold," as in privileged people such as himself feeling an obligation to those who are less fortunate. Olmsted had been to the South, he'd seen slavery firsthand, and, as Brace had predicted, it had changed his thinking, utterly.

In the summer of 1853, Olmsted's brother returned to America. Since being diagnosed with tuberculosis, John had been living in Italy and Switzerland. He'd hoped that a favorable climate would help arrest the progress of his disease. John and Mary now had a newborn infant son. While overseas, he'd been unable to work as a doctor, the profession for which he'd trained. It was just too demanding, given his illness. He'd made a few dollars writing about Italy for the *Philadelphia Bulletin*. Otherwise, John's travels had been bankrolled by his father. The senior Olmsted could always be counted on to provide help—financial or emotional—to John and Fred.

Fred was there to meet John when his ship, the *Humbolt*, sailed into New York Harbor. John and his family simply moved to Tosomock Farm. They were at loose ends and planned to stay there until they figured out what to do next.

Meanwhile, Fred—also adrift—was on the lookout for a writing assignment that would take him *off* the farm. He approached Raymond with the idea of a London travelogue, or perhaps he could write a series of dispatches on agricultural practices around the United States. Neither idea grabbed Raymond.

How about another Southern swing then? For his last journey, Olmsted had visited such established slaveholding bastions as Virginia and South Carolina, winding up in Louisiana. Why not pick up where his previous trip had left off with a journey through Texas? Texas had joined the United States as a slave state less than a decade earlier, in 1845. Olmsted proposed a trip across this vast new land to document the effects of slavery on a place very different from the Old South—a frontier society. Raymond was sold on this idea and signed up "Yeoman" for a fresh series of dispatches.

John asked to join his brother. Fred immediately agreed. The arid climate of Texas, coupled with the invigoration of outdoor life, was seen as a sensible regimen for a tuberculosis sufferer. Here was the plan: The brothers would visit Texas and perhaps continue west all the way to

California. Mary and the newborn would stay behind in Staten Island. Whatever needed tending on Tosomock Farm would fall to a pair of contract laborers Olmsted had hired the previous spring.

Once again, it made sense to leave after the fall harvest. On November 10, 1853, Fred and John set off together on a new Southern adventure.

The brothers took the unscenic route to Texas. Because Olmsted had already wended his way through much of the South, this time the goal was to get to their destination as quickly as possible. They set out on a westerly course, traveling by railroad, coach, and steamship through Maryland, Ohio, and Kentucky.

Along the way, the pair did find time for one side trip. They made a jog down to Nashville to meet with Samuel Allison, an old classmate of John's from Yale. Allison was that rarest of types in Olmsted's experience, a plantation owner and slaveholder who was truly prosperous. Allison had deep family roots in Tennessee. He lived in a bona fide mansion, set on ample acreage and surrounded by every luxury.

Olmsted found Allison far more garrulous than the planters he'd previously met, such as the man who spoke haltingly of guano. But Allison's views were also disturbing. He argued that slavery must be extended, through a sort of manifest destiny, southward to the Amazon rain forest. He was concerned about impending war in Europe, but chiefly in terms of how it might impact the price of slaves and cotton. Allison was obstreperous. He worked overtime to convince the Olmsted brothers that there had been no gentlemen at Yale and that very few existed in the North, period. On only one occasion, Allison recalled, had he encountered genuine breeding among Northerners. This was when he'd met some Schuylers, members of the old Dutch aristocracy. Olmsted was immensely put off by Allison and was glad to take his leave of the man.

In Nashville, the brothers boarded a steamboat that traveled along the Cumberland River on route to the mighty Mississippi. Lying in his darkened cabin, Olmsted could hear his fellow passengers laughing and playing cards deep into the night. As the steamer pitched to and fro, he wrestled with his recent encounter with the Nashville plantation owner. He got up and tried to compose his thoughts in a letter to Brace. What was it about Allison that provoked him so? Maybe, Olmsted confessed, he was just insecure in the face of the planter's easy convictions. One had to admit that his wealth and luxury were enticing. It would be great to feel that comfort was one's natural station, the fruits of aristocracy. Then again, Allison was so very uncurious. The man seemed to see everything through the narrow prism of his mercantile interests. Sure, he had the financial means to keep more than one candle burning at a time, unlike so many so-called Southern gentlemen. But Olmsted couldn't help noticing that Allison was still in the grip of a kind of poverty, a cultural poverty. What was Allison's higher calling—to *be* a gentleman? What kind of calling was that? If heaven exists, Olmsted posited to Brace, Southerners will be delighted. They will thrive on the leisure. But Northerners will be disappointed. They will just want to get to work. He concluded his letter to Brace with this: "Well, the moral of this damnedly drawn out letter is, I believe, go ahead with the Children's Aid and get up parks, gardens, music, dancing schools, reunions which will be so attractive as to force into contact the good & bad, the gentlemanly and rowdy."

This carries an echo of Olmsted's earlier exhortation: "There's a great work wants doing in this our generation, Charley, let us off jacket and go about it." The two friends were older now and in more of a position to put their words into action. Olmsted was urging Brace to continue his good works with the Children's Aid Society. He himself was traveling through a South sorely in need of reform. In this extraordinary passage, he was also making a bold assertion about the cultural primacy of the antebellum North, a place where it was possible to "get up" parks and dancing schools, a place that drew its vitality from differences, the interplay of the "gentlemanly and rowdy." Of course, "parks" was a curious—and oddly prescient—choice of examples.

After traveling less than a month, the Olmsted brothers arrived in New Orleans. The city was the natural jumping-off point for any trip into Texas. In those days, there were two main ways to go. One could board a ship and travel across the Gulf to the Texas coast. Or one could travel by steamer along the Red River into western Louisiana, then cross into Texas by land. The brothers chose the latter.

At the Louisiana-Texas border, they began to make preparations for a frontier journey. Choosing the right horses was especially important. They were about to set off across a vast prairie, and a horse that grew "jaded"—in the parlance of the day—could leave you stranded miles from help. Fred purchased a roan Creole pony named Nack. John chose a chestnut mare named Fanny.

The brothers also bought a Sharps rifle, a pair of Colt revolvers, and some sheathed knives. Texas was dangerous. There was an ever-present threat of encountering hostile Indians, horse thieves, all manner of outlaws. Texas also was sparely settled. It might be necessary to hunt for food. Fred and John repaired to the outskirts of the tiny town where they'd purchased their weaponry and unleashed a fusillade. "After a little practice," Olmsted boasted, "we could very surely chop off a snake's head from the saddle at a reasonable distance."

This made for compelling adventure writing in a *Times* dispatch. Truth be told, the Olmsted brothers of Hartford would never pass for hardened Texas drovers. (*Drovers* was the appellation for men who drove cattle; the term *cowboy* hadn't even been coined yet.) The brothers bought a pack mule named Mr. Brown. As for packing, they found it quite a challenge to winnow down the accoutrements of civilized life. No way could they part with their gingerbread, and as for getting rid of books— simply out of the question. They improvised, festooning the mule with large wicker hampers, generously stuffed with their possessions.

In San Augustine, the brothers hired a former Texas Ranger to serve as a guide. The man suggested that they replace the laughable mule hampers with an aparejo. An aparejo is a streamlined Mexican pack, consisting of a straw-filled leather sack with loops of rope hanging off of it. Travelers simply place the sack on a mule's back, like a saddle, and secure their possessions with the loops of rope. But the Olmsted brothers stubbornly clung to their mule rig. The townsfolk of San Augustine gathered in the street to see off this quirky traveling party. There was much animated discussion about packs. Onlookers speculated that Mr. Brown the mule would simply collapse after a few steps. By the time they were ready to leave, Olmsted had grown unsure himself. "We should have half Texas hooting at our heels," he observed. "But nothing happened. The mule walked off with as much unconcern as if he had been trained to carry hampers from his birth."

Off they went. They attempted to follow an old Spanish trail, still in use and stretching all the way to San Antonio. But this road, as Olmsted noted, could hardly be called a road. About the only clue that they were still on course were occasional parties of pioneers staggering westward. Invariably, their tawdry few possessions were piled in wagons caked in red mud. To lessen the load for tired horses, the able-bodied travelers made their way on foot. Weary slaves lurched along the road. Weary farmers' wives lurched along beside them. Olmsted had never seen such bedraggled women.

Sometimes, too, they passed wagons laden with cotton, headed the other direction, back East. This was evidence of pioneers who had made lives for themselves in Texas. They had settled a plot of land and worked it with their slaves. Now, they were conveying their cotton to market.

The Olmsted party made slow progress. On a good day, they covered twenty miles. At night, they tried to pitch camp near a farmhouse. This was like an insurance policy. First, they tried to shoot deer and rabbits in an effort to have fresh game for supper. But the Olmsteds weren't the best hunters, and their guide didn't prove such a crack shot, either. Despite their best efforts, they invariably wound up walking to the farmhouse and purchasing their dinner. They had better luck with dimes than bullets, as Olmsted put it.

But even the simple act of eating proved challenging. Bands of ravenously hungry wild hogs roamed the prairie. The horses and mule would be tied at the edge of camp, and the hogs, squealing horribly, took to battling them, stealing their fodder. If a person wasn't on guard, a hog was apt to steal his food, too. One time, a hog dashed into the campfire and snatched a chicken that was cooking on a spit.

This hog problem was confounding. But then, passing through Centerville, Texas, the Olmsteds met an innkeeper who demanded: *What!? You don't own a dog?* Apparently, this was a frontier necessity that had been overlooked. Taking pity, the innkeeper gave them a bull terrier named Judy. "She was made up of muscle, compactly put together behind a pair of frightful jaws," noted Olmsted. With Judy as a traveling companion, the wild hog problem abated.

As they continued west, the prairie began to grow more expansive. They encountered fewer and fewer pioneers. The markers of civilization— farmhouses and hand-lettered roadside signs, "corn heare"—appeared at increasingly long intervals.

A sense of giddiness took over. It was Fred and John, together on the vast prairie. The land crested and dipped, crested and dipped, undulating in all directions like a sea of grass.

On rainy days, the brothers remained in their tent all day, reading from their cache of books and sketching. On clear nights, they sat around the campfire talking for hours.

The sky above was boundless. That didn't surprise Olmsted. Rumors of the big Texas sky had preceded his visit; he'd heard all about it. What was puzzling was that stars seemed closer than he remembered them. It was an odd sensation, but pleasant. The stars just seemed nearer somehow.

On January 9, 1854, the guide took his leave. He had conducted the brothers safely across the prairie and into the Texas hill country. They were now in the town of Bastrop, one of a group of communities in close proximity. Austin was a day's ride away, and they were two days from the thriving metropolis of San Antonio.

Olmsted dropped into a shop in Bastrop. He was surprised to see a copy of a newspaper called the *San Antonio Zeitung*. He didn't speak German. But paging through, he was able to glean that it was a vital publication, full of news of local interest. Olmsted inquired about the paper, but the shopkeeper was stumped. The man didn't have any in- formation about what it was, why it was in his shop, or where it had come from.

A few days later, the Olmsted brothers camped in a live-oak grove near San Marcos. They planned to set out for San Antonio the next day. They stopped by a farmhouse to purchase some fodder for Mr. Brown and the horses. The farmer told them that on route to San Antonio, they could expect to encounter German settlers. Germans again. What were Germans doing *tief im herzen von Texas* (deep in the heart of Texas)? The farmer did his best to satisfy Olmsted's curiosity, but he just didn't have much information.

The brothers set out the next morning, and after about an hour in the saddle, they spied a tidy little log cabin with glazed windows. Then another and another. The fields surrounding these cabins were unlike anything they'd seen in their journey so far. To this point, they'd passed fields given almost exclusively to cotton. But now they saw farms growing cotton in rotation with a mix of other crops. The land was neatly tended. Crops had been harvested in such a way that only the barest stubble poked through the earth. As an experienced farmer, Olmsted recognized this as a telltale sign of rigorous agricultural practices.

Presently, they passed within shouting distance of some farmers, both men and women tending the fields together.

"Good morning," cried the Olmsted brothers.

"Guten morgen," boomed the farmers.

Aha. The picture was starting to grow clearer.

The Olmsteds forded the Guadalupe River with difficulty, then rode up into the hills. Soon they came to a town. The broad main street was lined with workshops and little stores; most of the signs were in German. The brothers' practice was to eat a cold pack lunch on horseback without breaking stride. But Olmsted was curious. When he spotted a cottage with a swinging sign that read "Guadalupe Hotel, J. Schmitz," he had to stop.

The brothers went inside and asked for lunch. The hostess stared at them uncomprehendingly. She spoke only German. Fortunately, an English-speaking customer stepped in and explained their wishes. The hostess seated the Olmsteds at a long oak table and spread a white cloth before them. A few minutes later, she returned with beef sausage, soup, wheat bread sliced warm from the loaf, and freshly made sweet butter. "I have never in my life, except, perhaps, in awakening from a dream, met with such a sudden and complete transfer of associations," noted Olmsted.

It was as if he'd been transplanted to the Rhine Valley, a place he'd visited with John during their walking tour through Europe. There wasn't a cue to tell him otherwise. The walls were hung with lithographs featuring scenes from the German countryside. All around, men with thick pendant beards and flannel shirts sat smoking pipes and speaking animatedly in German. Welcome to the town of Neu Braunfels, Texas.

As it turns out, Germans started pouring into the Texas hill country around 1830. Most of them were desperately poor and received aid from companies organized specifically to resettle Germans in America. The companies, in turn, had the backing of various German princes. This was no casual resettlement plan. Rather, it was a political scheme with a twofold purpose: reduce pauperism in Germany by dumping poor people in wide-open Texas and put a check on American expansionist impulses in the bargain.

In 1844, Prince Carl of Solms-Braunfels led an expedition of 150 families to Texas. The group's destination was a parcel of land purchased sight unseen from a speculator. As the settlers slogged across Texas, it began to dawn on them that their destination was leagues to the west of the existing German belt. They'd been bilked. Upon crossing the Guadalupe River, the weary pioneers decided to proceed no farther. They plunked down and formed a settlement in the hills, naming it Neu Braunfels in honor of their prince and sponsor. By the time the Olmsteds visited, a decade had passed and Neu Braunfels and its environs had grown into a thriving community of 3,000 people, all but about 20 of them Germans.

The brothers spent a whole afternoon at the inn. They fell into conversation with Germans, many of whom spoke English, and found them open and companionable. Olmsted quickly learned another thing about Germans in Texas. Almost to a one, they were free-soilers. They worked their farms themselves without the use of slave labor.

The Olmsteds were charmed by Neu Braunfels and decided to remain at the inn for the night. When they went out to check on Fanny and Nack, they saw that the stable attendant—a white man in cap and jacket—was giving the horses' legs a good rubdown. The animals' snouts were thrust into racks filled with hay, which they were busily gobbling. The whole time they'd been in Texas, the horses hadn't eaten hay. This was so different from the treatment that slave attendants had given their horses during stopovers on the journey.

The brothers repaired to their room and were again pleasantly surprised. The room was clean, had potted plants and a brass study lamp, and best of all—there were two separate beds! The few times the brothers had stopped at inns during this trip, they'd been forced to share a bed.

On one memorable night, they found themselves squeezed together in a narrow bed in a one-room cabin that passed for an inn. A sheet hung between their bed and the next, where the proprietor and his wife slept.

Next morning, as the Olmsteds rode out of Neu Braunfels, they saw more tidy cottages set on well-cultivated land. Now, this tableau was charged with significance.

Encountering the Germans was a real piece of serendipity for Olmsted. The original purpose of his trip had been to document for the *Times* the difference between Old South slavery and slavery as it existed on the Texas frontier. But this topic proved less rich than he'd anticipated. Slavery was slavery. A Texas cotton field wasn't much different from a Louisiana cotton field, and as a consequence, he'd provided scant few details in letters to the *Times*. Thus far, his dispatches had formed more of a travelogue, albeit an interesting one, full of observations about the Texas prairie.

Now, Olmsted had a focus for his reporting. He could compare the free-soil Germans with the slaveholders he'd encountered on his earlier journey. On first glance, the contrast appeared stark. Moreover, the Germans might furnish further evidence that his unique theories about slavery held true. Whereas plantations worked by slaves were economic backwaters, farms worked by Germans appeared to be models of efficiency. Whereas plantation owners fancied themselves refined gentleman but lived in cultural poverty, Olmsted suspected that Germans might be quite different. Going forward, this would be his area of inquiry. This would be his journalistic territory in Texas.

Their next stop was San Antonio, the city where the *Zeitung* was published. That was the paper that Olmsted had noticed in the shop, the one that first piqued his interest in the Germans. San Antonio was neck-and-neck with Galveston for the honor of being the biggest city in Texas. Population circa 1854: about 7,000. It was certainly the most cosmopolitan city, a mélange of nationalities, architectural styles, and religions. "We have no other city, except, perhaps, New Orleans," noted Olmsted, "that can vie in [terms of its] odd and antiquated foreignness."

The brothers visited the Alamo, already a symbol of the independent spirit of Texas. And they dropped by the offices of the *Zeitung*. Of the fifty-seven papers then published in Texas, it turns out that the *Zeitung* had the second-largest circulation. The editor was Adolph Douai. Douai, an immensely cultured man, was fluent in several languages, had once served as principal of a school in Germany, and had also done a stint as a tutor in Russia. During the German revolution of 1848, he had become an outspoken critic of the government and was imprisoned repeatedly for his views. Fed up, he fled to Texas.

Douai was a so-called '48er. The '48ers were different from the types of Texas Germans Olmsted had encountered in his limited experience. Whereas many of the Germans in Neu Braunfels, say, had emigrated in search of economic opportunity, this later wave had come to the United States to escape political persecution. As a rule, the '48ers tended to be highly educated, and many of them had held jobs as teachers, doctors, and lawyers back in Germany. German settlers as a whole were opposed to slavery. But Douai and his fellow '48ers went a step further, as staunch and vocal abolitionists.

Douai took the Olmsted brothers to Sisterdale, Texas, a nearby farming community that was home to many '48ers. Sisterdale was one of five such settlements in the region, the others being Millheim, Latium, Tusculum, and Bettina. Such places were called "Latin settlements" because they were full of impossibly erudite German immigrants, now working as farmers, laborers, and shopkeepers. At Sisterdale, the Olmsteds met Julius Froebel, a mineralogist-turned-farmer, and Ernst Kapp, a geographer-turned-farmer. The brothers arranged to spend the night in the log cabin of Edouard Degener. Degener was the son of a wealthy German banker. He had twice been elected to the parliament in Frankfurt. But he'd lost his home, his land—everything—during the 1848 revolution. He'd come to Texas and was now a farmer.

That night, Degener held an impromptu get-together at his home in honor of the visiting Olmsteds. He had a piano, and one of the guests played passages from Mozart's *Don Giovanni*. As the evening grew looser, there was waltzing. And after the ladies retired, the men got well lubricated, threw their arms around one another's shoulders, and belted out "student songs," as Olmsted termed them. It made him feel very young.

The next morning, Degener was up bright and early, working the fields. He was joined by his two teenage sons. Riding around Sisterdale, Olmsted saw others from the previous night's party, now tending cotton or pushing plows. It was hard work, yet it struck Olmsted that the Germans appeared happy. "But how much of their cheerfulness," asked Olmsted, "may arise from having gained, during this otherwise losing struggle to themselves, the certain consciousness of being courageously loyal to their intellectual determinations—their private convictions of right, justice, and truth."

Using San Antonio as a base, the Olmsteds made several other forays. They traveled to the Gulf coast, going as far as Port Lavaca. They also hired another former Texas Ranger as a guide and took a dip down into Mexico that was by turns dangerous and drab. One night, they stayed at an inn, only to wind up sleeping outside in the courtyard with their Colts and knives placed within easy reach. That was the Ranger's idea. He wanted to stay close to the horses to ward off thieves. They made a few desultory inquiries about joining an immigrant party bound for California, but this came to nothing.

Mostly, they were drawn to the Germans. The brothers decided that maybe they should sell Tosomock Farm and settle in Texas instead. The dry air of the hill country would be a balm for John's tuberculosis. The intellectual climate was certainly to their tastes. They could even take part in a political battle then starting to brew. The original treaty that turned Texas from a separate republic into the twenty-eighth state included the following provision: As the state's population grew, Texas might be split up into as many as five different states. For any new states established, Congress agreed, the all-important slavery question would be determined by popular sovereignty. Of course, the hill country was a stronghold for nonslaveholding Germans. Perhaps the Olmsted brothers could become pioneer residents of the brand-new free state of West Texas. The state, in turn, could act as a bulwark, preventing slavery from spreading through the rest of the southwestern territories. John sent a letter to Staten Island to his wife, Mary, floating the idea. Mary's response has been lost, but it can probably be paraphrased in four words: *Get back here now!*

In April 1854, the Olmsted brothers started home. As they neared the Louisiana border, they sold Fanny and Nack and Mr. Brown. It was hard to say good-bye to the animals that had accompanied them for hundreds of miles of hard travel and high adventure.

The brothers themselves parted way at Bayou Sara, Louisiana. John boarded a steamer and headed north. Fred, a tireless traveler, made his way slowly toward home via the backcountry, the less developed regions of states such as Alabama, Mississippi, and North Carolina. This was about the only part of the South he hadn't covered. He'd walked all over Connecticut as a child; he'd walked all over England a few years back. Now, he was intent on completing his tour of the South; he didn't want to miss anything.

Olmsted could outlast just about anyone, man or beast. John was gone. The horses were gone. The mule was gone. From the Texas party, only Judy, the bull terrier, remained. Olmsted had bought a fresh mount, a stallion named Belshazzar. Judy ran alongside Olmsted and Belshazzar. The dog wore tiny moccasins, fashioned for her worn-out paws.

CHAPTER 8

A Red-Hot Abolitionist

AFTER TAKING HIS TIME traveling the backcountry of the South, Olmsted arrived home to find Tosomock Farm in disarray. Tools were blunted and broken. It had been nearly two years since the pear trees had been pruned, and vines were wrapped tight around their trunks. The peach trees weren't yielding peaches.

One couldn't blame the contract workers. They had been hired as winter caretakers. With the arrival of spring, they had been woefully short-handed—there were only two of them—and they hadn't received adequate direction, besides. Mary had been busy caring for an infant. John had arrived two months before his brother, but he was a doctor by training and in no position to provide guidance.

On his return, Olmsted discovered that he felt a surprising nonchalance about the sorry state of the farm. His passion for the place had utterly dissipated.

More pressing, it seemed, was a message that arrived from the Texas Germans. In September 1854, the Olmsted brothers received a plea for assistance from Adolph Douai, editor of the *San Antonio Zeitung*. Lately, Douai had become more and more outspoken, railing against slavery in the pages of the paper. This had exposed a rift within the Texas German community.

Many of the Germans, while privately against slavery, didn't wish to be so open about their convictions. Life as an immigrant farmer on the frontier was challenge enough, and they wanted to keep a low profile. Douai's incendiary articles might invite the ire of the slave owners that surrounded them everywhere in Texas. The stockholders of the *Zeitung* decided to disassociate themselves from the paper by putting it up for sale.

Douai stepped forward as the buyer. But the financial demands of running a paper—the relentless need for paper stock and printer's ink—quickly sank him into debt. Douai had bold plans for the *Zeitung*, too. He intended to publish an English-language edition. He asked the Olmsteds for a loan.

The Olmsteds were happy to help. Rather than giving Douai a loan, they decided to solicit donations from sympathetic parties in the North and to give the proceeds to Douai as a gift. The Olmsteds circulated a letter, titled: "A Few Dollars Wanted to Help the Cause of Future Freedom in Texas."

The brothers managed to raise more than $200. Brace gave money, as did the proprietor of a New York silk-goods outfit. Olmsted also drummed up subscriptions among his acquaintances to the new English-language edition.

Unfortunately, publishing an English edition ushered in disaster for Douai. Prior to this, the *Zeitung*, despite having the second-largest circulation among Texas papers, had also been an underground publication in a way. After all, most people in the state didn't speak German. Even if Douai had published the most provocative antislavery screed imaginable, it only would have unnerved some of his fellow Germans. The slaveholders could not have read it.

Now they could. The reprisals came fast and furious. Skittish advertisers, afraid to be associated with Douai's vocal abolitionism, fled the paper in droves. Other Texas papers took aim at Douai, including the *Austin State Times*, which published editorials calling for his death, even helpfully suggesting the means of accomplishing this—by drowning. Armed goons showed up at Douai's home and milled around outside, making threats.

Douai simply could not afford the courage of his convictions. He had seven children and an elderly father to support and keep safe from harm. Heartbroken, he sold his printing equipment and fled to the North. In a grim irony, the buyer of the equipment was a Texan, not of German descent, who intended to publish a paper sympathetic to the interests of slaveholders.

The Olmsted brothers helped Douai get settled by providing contacts and letters of introduction. He eventually opened a school in Boston that featured a kindergarten. In the years ahead, Douai would become instrumental in launching the kindergarten movement in the United States. The idea of compulsory public schooling for very young kids was novel in nineteenth-century America and was rooted in German theories about child development and socialization. Douai even wrote a much-read manual on how to run a kindergarten.

This was a time of ratcheting tensions. Even as the Olmsted brothers had made their Southern journey, while they traveled across Texas, a controversial piece of legislation was working its way through Congress, one that would drastically increase the rancor between slaveholders and abolitionists.

On January 4, 1854, Senator Stephen Douglas, later to achieve renown as Lincoln's political and debating rival, introduced the Kansas-Nebraska Act. It provoked several months of ferocious congressional debate and after going through many iterations was finally signed into law by President Franklin Pierce. Back home now, Olmsted would soon become involved in the fallout from this controversial bill.

The act broke the vast Nebraska territory into two territories—Kansas and Nebraska—and specified that in each, the issue of slavery would be determined by popular sovereignty. By opening the possibility of slavery in two territories north of that 36°30' line, the act overturned the earlier Missouri Compromise. Southern slaveholders insisted that the Missouri Compromise had been forced on them, a compromise they'd never abided in the first place. Northern abolitionists were livid, even more exercised than they had been when the new Fugitive Slave Act—the spark for *Uncle Tom's Cabin*—passed in 1850.

Almost immediately, Kansas became disputed territory for people on either side of the slavery divide. So-called border ruffians poured in from the neighboring slave state of Missouri to illegally vote in various territorial elections. Soon, they managed to establish a legislature in the town

of Lecompton. This legislature issued a series of decrees, draconian measures such as the death penalty for anyone speaking out against slavery.
Opponents called them the "bogus laws." These settlers established a
competing legislature in the town of Topeka. The territory of Kansas had
two legislatures now, one free-soil, the other proslavery.

Ruffians from Missouri and even more distant slave states continued
to flow into Kansas, trying to tip the balance. To tip it back, the Reverend Edward Everett Hale helped establish the New England Emigrant
Aid Company. This outfit relocated farmers with free-soil leanings, paying for their passage from states such as Connecticut and Maine to
Kansas. It was a similar model to the German companies that had
dumped paupers in Texas to block U.S. expansion.

The territory of Kansas became a testing ground, a place where the
conflicts that rended the Union played out. And it quickly escalated beyond the novelty of competing legislatures. There was no shortage of violence, and fifty-five people died. In every way, the events of Bleeding
Kansas can be seen as a precursor to the all-out civil war that would erupt
a few years hence.

Olmsted entered into a correspondence with Hale, inquiring about
how he might aid the cause of Kansas. In a truly bizarre twist, Hale was
married to Emily Perkins, the woman who earlier had been Olmsted's fi-
ancée, only to break off their engagement. "I can't well write a word to
you without much emotion even now," closes a letter from Olmsted to
Hale, "but I am anything but a miserable or even a dissatisfied man &
most sincerely. Your friend, Fred. Law Olmsted."

The uneasy relationship proved oddly productive. Through Hale, Olmsted made the acquaintance of James Abbott. Abbott was someone who
had moved to Kansas under the aegis of the New England Emigrant Aid
Company. He was now an officer with a militia, bent on making sure that
if Kansas entered the U.S. as a state, it would be a free state.

Abbott traveled back East seeking funds to purchase weapons for
his militia. After visiting Hartford and Providence, he had raised enough
money to buy one hundred Sharps rifles, a.k.a. "Beecher Bibles." They
were named after Henry Ward Beecher, brother of Harriet Beecher
Stowe, a fiery abolitionist preacher who was in the habit of handing out

these guns to free-soil farmers. Abbott was hoping to raise sufficient funds for an additional hundred Beecher Bibles. In New York, he connected with Olmsted, whom he dubbed as "acting commissioner" of his free-state activities.

Olmsted managed to raise more than $300 from assorted people, including Brace, always willing to support a liberal cause, and Horace Greeley, editor of the *New York Tribune* and coiner of the term *Bleeding Kansas*. Being diligent, Olmsted decided to talk with an expert before purchasing any weapons. He consulted a veteran of European warfare, a man who had fought under Garibaldi during the turmoil that gripped Italy in 1848. In this expert's opinion, Abbott's militia already had enough assault weapons. What they sorely needed was a defensive weapon to stave off an attack.

So Olmsted visited the New York State Arsenal and used the money he'd raised to purchase a mountain howitzer and ammo. Olmsted appears to have gotten caught up in the sub rosa-ness of this activity. To keep Abbott apprised, Olmsted sent him a series of letters employing all too crackable code (such as *h* for howitzer). Olmsted arranged for the weapon to be divided into several pieces—to avoid detection—and shipped west. Abbott referred to Olmsted as a "prompt and energetic friend of Kansas."

Olmsted's howitzer was mounted in front of the Free State Hotel in Lawrence. When the town was sacked, the weapon was seized by a marauding band of South Carolinians. But the free-state militia got it back as part of a prisoner exchange. Quite a picaresque tale for a howitzer, especially one that managed to weather the entire Bleeding Kansas episode without once being fired in battle.

In a few short years, Olmsted had managed quite a transition himself. On the matter of slavery, he'd started out a gradualist, but given all he'd witnessed during his Southern travels, given all the changes to the country at large, he'd come around to Charley Brace's way of thinking. Olmsted was a red-hot abolitionist.

CHAPTER 9

The Literary Republic

HERE'S ANOTHER WAY Olmsted was changing: Weary of the farmer's life, he was eager to commit himself to the writer's life instead.

During 1853 and 1854, Olmsted had received $720 for his *Times* dispatches. That was a goodly chunk of what the farm had cleared over the same period. In fact, Olmsted was forced to rely on a $1,000-per-year subsidy from his generous father just to stay afloat. There had to be a better way. Olmsted began work on a book. It was an account of his first Southern journey, the one that covered the old-line seaboard slave states. He drew on the notes that he'd used to craft the pieces for the *Times*. But it was also necessary to flesh out these anecdotes with economic statistics and details about the history of slavery in the United States. This required him to travel into Manhattan to visit libraries. Olmsted was thrilled by these research jaunts.

For this book, Olmsted intended to use his real name rather than "Yeoman"; he wanted credit for his unique observations and theories about slavery. As the weather turned cold, he devoted still more time to the book, less to farming. Olmsted was "writing as much as he dares," reported his brother.

Dares is an apt word choice. While Olmsted was drawn to writing, he knew it was a risky undertaking. He already had a book under his belt, *Walks and Talks*. It had received some favorable notices but had managed only modest sales. He was thirty-two now and well aware that writing was no sure route to financial independence. But then Olmsted learned about a promising opportunity. *Putnam's Monthly*

Magazine, the highly regarded and innovative publication, had just been sold. This was the magazine where his story "Gold Under Gilt" had earlier appeared. Apparently, the buyer, Dix and Edwards, was looking for another partner.

The principals of Dix and Edwards were very young and very green. They needed capital, and they needed experienced hands, even if the experience consisted merely of being older than they were.

Joshua Dix, just twenty-four, had worked in publishing for George Putnam during most of his brief career. He was also a friend of Charley Brace. Arthur Edwards, age twenty-six, was an upstart dry goods salesman, reputed to be a financial whiz. The pair had bought the magazine from Putnam, Olmsted's onetime Staten Island neighbor, the publisher of his book, and a distant relative to boot. (If it seems that people of this era lived in a tight nexus of interrelationships, that's because it was so. There were simply fewer people, and if one belonged to a particular cohort—cultured northeasterners, say—bumping into others of similar persuasion was ensured.)

Dix and Edwards approached Olmsted about joining their partnership. Becoming part of an outfit that published a magazine, particularly one as esteemed as *Putnam's*, held promise for Olmsted. He could step directly into the writing world but as part owner of a literary property. He'd have a chance to make some real money. During their discussions, Dix and Edwards also made it clear that they intended to expand into other areas, such as book publishing. And yes, the partners agreed: Olmsted's book-in-progress, a serious work about the slave states, would be a perfect fit. This was an added draw. If he joined the partnership, Olmsted might also line up a publisher for his book.

Enticed by this opportunity, Olmsted started making inquiries about selling Tosomock Farm. He was distressed to learn that it would fetch only a paltry $200 per acre. Once again, his father came to the rescue, this time with a plan designed to satisfy everyone involved. He would loan his son $5,000 to buy into the publishing partnership. Because that was a lot of money, even by his generous standards, this loan would need to be *repaid*.

Olmsted, in turn, would sign over the title of the farm to his brother, John. John didn't care a whit about farming. But his tuberculosis was growing worse, and he needed a place to live and a way to make a living. John had a wife to support along with two children now. A daughter, Charlotte, had just been born on March 15, 1855. Hired laborers could do most of the farmwork, and John and his family would be left with a modest income.

On April 2, Olmsted signed the papers, joining an outfit now rechristened as Dix, Edwards & Company. (He was to be a silent partner.) Within days, he moved to Manhattan and rented an apartment at 335 Broadway, two rooms for $200 a year, within easy walking distance of his new job at 10 Park Place. Because finances were tight, he outfitted the apartment with furniture purchased at flea markets and auctions.

John was sorry to see his big brother go. That feeling was mixed with some bitterness. Fred was moving to Manhattan, while he was stuck on Tosomock Farm with tuberculosis. John couldn't help feeling that he'd gotten the worse end of this bargain. "I regret to be left in the lurch," John wrote to his half-sister Bertha.

The two brothers had been close as kids, and they'd built a special bond as adults during their sojourns across Europe and Texas. Staten Island was just a quick ferry ride away, though. Olmsted planned to visit on weekends.

As an owner of *Putnam's*, Olmsted joined another publishing revolution in progress, one equally as profound as the revolution that brought about the *New-York Daily Times*, the paper that sent him on his Southern swing.

An explosion of literacy among the masses had created a demand for inexpensive daily papers such as the *Times*. *Putnam's*, in turn, was part of an upsurge in magazines ushered in by the invention of the cylinder press in 1846. Before this, there had been very few magazines. When Ben Franklin launched his *General Magazine and Historical Chronicle* in 1741, for example, it was only the second magazine in the American colonies, and it was only four pages long. Printing was an arduous process. Creating a long publication for temporary consumption just wasn't very feasible. Lengthy books were printed, of course, as were short newspapers and a handful of short magazines. Still, the whole concept of a magazine—a digest with fiction, reportorial pieces, humor columns, and so forth—couldn't really catch on in such an abbreviated format.

Against this backdrop, Richard Hoe's cylinder press was the biggest printing innovation in the four hundred years since Gutenberg had invented movable type. Now, it was possible to churn out thousands of printed pages an hour. By 1850, there were 650 magazines in the United States, and countless others had started and quickly folded, all part of a "veritable magazine tsunami," in the words of John Tebbel and Mary Ellen Zuckerman, coauthors of a history of publishing.

Harper's New Monthly Magazine began in 1850. *Putnam's* was launched in 1853. The two magazines quickly fell into a fierce rivalry, rooted in their divergent editorial approaches. Because no international copyright law existed yet, *Harper's* simply raided English magazines, obtaining much of the content by theft—*transfer* was the editors' preferred term. Not only was this financially savvy, but it also catered to the literary tastes and cultural insecurities of so many American readers. A steady diet of all things British—that was the road to refinement.

Putnam's took an opposite tack. It chose to distinguish itself as proudly nativist, focused on a new wave of formidably talented American writers. The publication's subtitle further announced that this was a "Magazine of American Literature, Science and Art." By the time Olmsted became an owner, *Putnam's* had already established itself, publishing work by such homegrown talents as Nathaniel Hawthorne, John Greenleaf Whittier, and Henry James Sr. Herman Melville's classic "Bartleby the Scrivener" was originally published in two installments that appeared in the November and December 1853 issues of *Putnam's*. The magazine paid its contributors, too. Melville received an unheard-of $5 per page—$85 for the whole story.

As a first step, Olmsted and Dix made a quick circuit through the Northeast, meeting with some of *Putnam's* regular contributors. They wanted to reassure these writers that the magazine, though under new ownership, would continue to pursue the same high literary standards. They also hoped to get some fresh pieces into the pipeline. Olmsted and

Dix traveled to Boston, where they met with James Russell Lowell and Henry Wadsworth Longfellow. In Concord, they dropped in on Ralph Waldo Emerson. "This is more than half the battle," Olmsted wrote his father. "If we can get the writers, there is little fear but that we shall get the readers."

Olmsted also took the lead on recruiting an editorial staff. Although he had done some writing, he had zero experience editing and recognized that he and his partners were deficient in such skills as shaping someone else's work and figuring out the all-important mix of stories to go in an issue. The worldly and cultivated George Curtis agreed to act as the editor of *Putnam's*. Charles Dana, another experienced hand, signed on as a deputy. In an odd twist, both men insisted on keeping their existing jobs and working incognito for *Putnam's*. That way they could double-dip. Curtis actually wrote the popular "Editor's Easy Chair" column for *Harper's*, the competition. He was one of that magazine's few American contributors, and he was paid handsomely as well. Dana was second in command at the *New York Tribune* and wished to hold on to that job.

Putnam's physical offices reflected this bizarre collaboration between three green owners and two secret editors. Olmsted, Dix, and Edwards had well-marked offices, accessible to all. They were the face of *Putnam's*, as it were. A door in Olmsted's office, meanwhile, led into Curtis's office. That door generally remained closed.

Curtis's office served as a kind of inner sanctum, the site where the real editorial decisions were made. He was often joined there by Dana. The two engaged in learned debates, centering on which pieces to bulk up and which to pare down, what to acquire and what to kill. Curtis and Dana rejected a short story called "The Cited Curate" simply because it was too English in flavor.

With two heavyweights as editors, Olmsted's duties were naturally limited. He acted as a kind of managing editor, crafting manuscript submissions guidelines, corresponding with authors on general subjects such as deadlines, and working with the printer. Another task was dealing with wannabe writers who stormed the *Putnam's* offices demanding answers. "I had just now a call from a queer fellow whose poetry had been rejected," wrote Olmsted to his father, "and who wanted to know why & who struck his breast fearfully and assured me that there must be some mistake for he knew there was no better poetry, and he felt that he had genius."

Curiously enough, Olmsted's most hands-on editorial duty was proofreading. His shoddy schooling had left him an eccentric speller. For this task, fortunately, he could turn to *Webster's: The American Dictionary of the English Language*. In the United States, *Webster's* was quickly gaining favor over British dictionaries. Olmsted's use of it was only fitting since *Putnam's* was a proudly American magazine. What's more, a distant cousin, Denison Olmsted, while teaching at Yale, had been a consultant to the original 1828 edition of *Webster's*, helping craft definitions for technical terms from fields such as astronomy and meteorology.

One of the pieces that Olmsted proofread was the short story "Benito Cereno" by Melville. He made a number of changes such as *mould* to *mold* to reflect American usage as prescribed in *Webster's*. Apparently, though, Curtis was something of a traditionalist on spelling. "It is not yet good use to spell in this hideous Websterian manner," he wrote in a memo. "And, unless you feel that it would too much harm the harmony of the Mag., I will, hereafter, have a U. in my 'mould,' and *my* lustre shall be such and not 'ter.'"

The hideous Websterian spellings stayed, however, and "Benito Cereno" ran in three installments during the autumn of 1855. A Melville story was but one bright flash during a dazzling period for *Putnam's*. The magazine ran a meticulously researched natural history of bees and a lengthy exposition on the Jesuit faith. Poems by Longfellow—"Oliver Basselin," "Victor Galbraith," and "My Lost Youth"—appeared in rapid succession. The magazine even published a Henry David Thoreau work-in-progress that would eventually grow into the book *Cape Cod*. The *Hartford Courant* described *Putnam's* as "higher flight than the *Knickerbocker*, or even *Harper*." At a posh Manhattan literary gathering, William Makepeace Thackeray declared it "much the best Mag. in the world, and better than *Blackwood* is or ever was." Thackeray was a lion of English literature, *Blackwood's Magazine* a much-venerated English publication. For an American magazine, this was high praise indeed.

Yet Olmsted was frustrated. His unusual owner-underling status wasn't the problem. He viewed his role at *Putnam's* as a kind of apprenticeship, little different from the agricultural apprenticeships he'd earlier served. When he wanted to learn about farming, he'd learned from the best, George Geddes. Now, he was learning about publishing from some of the top talent in the field.

The problem was money. Even though *Putnam's* was a hot magazine, generating much talk and interest, circulation was frozen at just under 20,000. Six months into his tenure, the partnership's funds had fallen so low that Olmsted was unable to draw his salary. He had to borrow money from a friend.

In November 1855, Olmsted finished writing his book. When he approached Dix and Edwards about publishing it, per their original discussion, his partners pointed to the depleted coffers. They asked Olmsted to bear the $500 cost of printing his own book. This was too much money to borrow from a friend. Ashamed, Olmsted approached his father again. In a letter, he tried to cast his request in a positive light: "There is a sort of literary republic, which it is not merely pleasant & gratifying to my ambition to be recognized in, but also profitable. It would for example, if I am so recognized & considered, be easy for me, in case of the non-success of this partnership, to get employment in the newspaper offices or other literary enterprises at good wages—to make arrangement for correspondence if I wished to travel, & so on."

The conceit here—the words of a sheepish Olmsted trying yet again to borrow money from his father—is pretty circuitous. But in effect, Olmsted was suggesting that he hoped to crack a "sort of literary republic" that was also potentially "profitable." Pouring more money into cash-strapped Dix, Edwards & Company to publish his book would provide a hedge in case the partnership failed. Then Olmsted would have the book as an entrée and could get a new job in "newspaper offices or other literary enterprises at good wages." John Olmsted Sr. allowed paternal love to trump logic. He put up the money.

An unusual arrangement was struck with Dix, Edwards & Company whereby Olmsted would pay the cost of printing his book and also hand over a small percentage of the sales proceeds to cover expenses such as distribution and marketing. A large percentage of any proceeds would flow back to Olmsted, which was only fair since he—or, rather, his father—was taking all the risk. This was the reverse of the standard agreement, where the publisher bears the upfront costs and the author gets a smaller royalty.

Olmsted put the finishing touches on his book. By now, he'd gone through quite a change in thinking since his initial *Times* dispatches. As a consequence, he stiffened some of his original gradualism, pumping up sentiments such as *slavery is an evil that must end now* and downplaying sentiments such as *allow the South to change over time*. Some of his jabs at Northern hypocrisy, like the passage about how the downtrodden in cities like Boston sometimes starved to death, were simply removed. Still, the book was sprawling. Concerned about the reception awaiting such an overstuffed tome, he wrote a wry note to his father: "This ponderosity becomes a goblin of botheration to me."

A Journey in the Seaboard Slave States was published on January 16, 1856. The 723-page book had an initial run of 2,000 copies.

Olmsted need not have worried. He had made strides as a writer since *Walks and Talks*. He received excellent notices and in a much wider range of publications than his previous title. The *New York Post* wrote: "This remarkable book . . . is certainly the most minute, dispassionate, and evidently accurate description of the persons, places, and social institutions of the southern portion of our confederacy, that we have yet seen." Said the *Boston Daily Advertiser*: "By far the most valuable book we have on slavery and the Southern social system. That book will gradually assume the position of a standard book of reference among all persons, of whatever opinions, whose interest in slavery or in anti-slavery is more than a pretense."

The reviewer's use of the word *gradually* proved somehow prophetic. *Seaboard Slave States* was a big book on a serious topic. The price, $1.25, was five times the cost of *Walks and Talks*. While reviews were uniformly glowing, sales were very slow. Writing wasn't going to pay the bills, apparently; it wasn't going to pay back his father, either.

Meanwhile, things were changing fast in the intrepid new world of magazine publishing. *Harper's* was growing more cautious about stealing English content. Starting with the January 1856 issue, the magazine ran an exclusive serial of the Dickens novel *Little Dorrit*. This generated great excitement and sold tons of magazines, and *Harper's* paid the author for the privilege. Angering Dickens by pirating his work would not have been wise editorial policy, especially because he was immensely popular in the United States. At the same time, *Harper's* was starting to publish a great deal more work by American writers.

When *Harper's* zigged, *Putnam's* zagged. Putnam's editors decided to abandon the patriotic focus, the proud emphasis on American writers and American subjects. It was just too limiting. A new formula was needed, especially in light of the magazine's stagnating circulation and money woes. Time to forge some British literary relationships. *Putnam's* needed a coup to equal its rival's exclusive *Little Dorrit* serial.

On February 13, 1856, Olmsted set sail for England aboard the *Arabia*. The purpose of Olmsted's trip was pretty amorphous, but boiled down to: *obtain some British content*. In addition, he had family responsibilities. Olmsted was joined on the trip by Mary, his twenty-four-year-old half-sister, and he was charged with looking after her. This was an era when it was considered untoward for a young woman to visit a strange city alone. In London, Olmsted met with British magazine publishers, trying to strike deals to reprint their stories in *Putnam's*. He scouted for writers who could become Putnam's contributors. Maybe Dix, Edwards & Company could further diversify into book publishing, printing their works. Or perhaps an English publisher would agree to pay a fee to Dix, Edwards & Company for distributing its titles in America. He explored a number of possibilities. Nothing really took.

When Mary set off for Italy, Olmsted dutifully accompanied her. This was to be a quick travel interlude, and then he planned to return to London and hopefully better luck. In Rome, Mary met up with her younger sister Bertha and Sophia Hitchcock, a family friend. Bertha and Sophia had been living in Italy as students. Olmsted wound up acting as a kind of chaperone, squiring three young women as they took a whirlwind tour through Italy, then on to Vienna and Prague.

Ordinarily, Olmsted thrived on travel. But he didn't really enjoy this trip and was instead dogged by concerns both personal and political. His personal dismay related to the fact that his half-sister Bertha had just rejected a marriage proposal from a man named Edward Bartholomew. Bartholomew was a Connecticut native, living in Rome and working as a sculptor. Olmsted appears to have been put off by what he perceived as a cavalier attitude on Bertha's part. How could she and the other two women jaunt about Europe after something so momentous as a broken engagement? "I should not be much surprised if Bartholomew, supposing he understands Bertha as she meant he should, should be made insane. He is just the man to be ruined by it," wrote Olmsted to a relative.

After parting company with the three women, on his way back to London, he wrote a letter directly to Bertha: "But then it troubles me that the state of mind or conviction on which you acted decisively was but one day old, while as you say your instinct or unreflective 'dream' (state of mind) had all been for weeks previously of an opposite character." Olmsted's prose here is particularly tortured, but he seems to be demanding an explanation. If Bertha felt love for Bartholomew for weeks, how could she decisively break with him based on one day's reflection? Olmsted seems strangely overinvested in the love life of his much younger half-sister. Maybe, behind the judgmental airs, he was still smarting from his own broken engagement to Emily Perkins.

On the political front, a horrifying event occurred in the United States while Olmsted was traveling, and it also colored his experience. On May 22, 1856, Preston Brooks, a South Carolina congressman, walked up to Charles Sumner, a Massachusetts senator, during a recess and proceeded to strike him in the head with a gutta-percha cane. Incredibly, tensions between the North and South had erupted into violence in the very halls of Congress. On about the sixth blow, the cane broke, but Brooks kept whacking Sumner. "Hit him, Brooks, he deserves it," yelled a fellow Southern senator. Meanwhile, a Northern congressman rushed to Sumner's aid. "I'm dead," cried Sumner. "Oh, I'm most dead!" Sumner lived, but he was never the same. It would be more than three years before he was sufficiently recovered to return to his Senate seat.

With the Brooks-Sumner incident as a backdrop, Olmsted found his journey disconcerting. Things felt so much different from his recent walking tour. America was supposed to be a beacon of democracy in hidebound old Europe, but instead his country was an object of scorn. He recorded the following impression: "The position of an American traveling in Europe is just now a most unpleasant one. In railway carriages and other public places when he is not known as an American, he is obliged to hear language applied to his country which it is difficult to allow to pass in silence, and yet which he cannot deny to be just."

Back in London, Olmsted hoped finally to stir up some business for *Putnam's*. He dropped in on John Parker, the editor of *Fraser's*, a supremely serious magazine that featured the work of John Stuart Mill, George Henry Lewes, and the Reverend Charles Kingsley. Olmsted walked away from the meeting with Parker feeling like maybe some kind of deal had been struck. But the details were vague.

A more enticing possibility involved Thomas Gladstone. Gladstone, older brother of the future British prime minister, was a correspondent for the *Times of London*. While Olmsted was in London, Gladstone was in the United States, covering events in Bleeding Kansas. Olmsted read his dispatches with great interest. What if Dix, Edwards & Company were to publish a book based on Gladstone's reportage? Olmsted wondered. This had potential: An Englishman's perspective on Bleeding Kansas was kind of an ideal property for an American publisher seeking to tilt more British.

Olmsted also attended a party that Thackeray threw each year at his home for the editors of *Punch*, a brilliant and merciless British humor magazine. Olmsted showed up at the event overdressed. Absolutely everyone present was in black tie save for Olmsted, who appeared in white tie and tails. "Here comes Olmsted, in a white stock," called out Thackeray. Everyone laughed. Thackeray giveth—with his earlier high praise for *Putnam's*—and Thackeray taketh away. Olmsted was embarrassed. Still, he recovered sufficiently to chat up various *Punch* editors, white tails and all. He sent a letter home suggesting to his partners that maybe it would make sense to publish an American edition of *Punch*. This would come to nothing.

Besides trying to further the interests of Dix, Edwards & Company, Olmsted also used his time in London to promote his own book. He hand-delivered copies of *A Journey in the Seaboard Slave States* to the many editors with whom he met. Like clockwork, reviews began to appear in the months ahead in such publications as the *Athenaeum*, *Fraser's*, and the *Times*. In England, too, Olmsted received glowing notices, but still the book sold slowly. But he was starting to build a small and influential overseas audience for his unique ideas about slavery and the South.

Back on Tosomock Farm, meanwhile, John was using his brother's travel notes and *Times* pieces to stitch together a second book, covering their Texas journey together. The book was to feature Fred's byline, but John would receive two-thirds of any royalties. This easy collaboration speaks to the special bond the brothers shared. What's more, by working in this fashion, Olmsted would appear to all the world to be a literary juggernaut. He'd be able to churn out a second lengthy book in the space of a year!

While Olmsted's writing was going well, so well that it didn't even require his physical presence, things at *Putnam's* were going very poorly in his absence. Olmsted received a letter from Joshua Dix, his publishing partner. Apparently, the magazine's finances were much more precarious than anyone had suspected. Dix was in such a dither that he contacted John at Tosomock Farm, pressing him to write his brother as well. Immediately following Dix's letter, Olmsted received another letter from John, saying that *Putnam's* circulation had "fallen off alarmingly" and that he should return to the United States at once.

Then came another letter from Dix. This time, Olmsted's young partner said that everything at *Putnam's* was copacetic. He'd merely panicked. Ignore my earlier letter, Dix urged, and don't rush home on account of my overreaction. Stick around—enjoy England. The turnabout enraged Olmsted: "Write me in a fever of fear & trembling & what not one week—all going to the devil & no hot pitch to be had at any price unless I come home in my shirt tail to help you heat it up & then next day—all as smooth & jolly [as] a summer's sea of champagne and icebreezes. Damn you for a high pressure hypochondriac."

Olmsted had lost thirteen pounds from the anxiety caused by Dix's first letter, or so he claimed. He was getting very little accomplished. How could he enjoy England? He sailed for home. Back in New York, he quickly ascertained that Dix's initial dire account of *Putnam's* was more accurate than his second rosy one. The enterprise was losing $1,000 a month. Circulation had gone off a cliff, plummeting from a high near 20,000 to around 14,000. The falloff appeared to be due to a decrease in quality. There were whisperings that *Putnam's* had simply lost the magic of its earlier issues.

More bad news: John's health was getting worse. When it came to tuberculosis, one school of nineteenth-century medical thought urged sufferers—at least during the initial stages of the disease—to try to live a normal life, even engage in vigorous outdoor activity. The other school stressed the necessity of a quiet life in a suitable climate. John—himself a doctor by training—had alternated between these two approaches. He'd earlier tried living in Europe, but found that the invalid life sapped his spirit just as surely as the disease. He'd also taken a demanding trip through Texas. Now he was growing weaker. He was spitting up blood. Add to that, his wife, Mary, was now pregnant with a third child. Desperate, he chose to switch course once again. John set off from Staten Island along with his family, bound for Havana and a warmer climate. A renter was found for Tosomock Farm.

In a sad twist, John left just days before the publication of *A Journey Through Texas*. This was the account of the trip with his brother. It was also the book on which John had done much of the work. This latest Olmsted title was published by struggling Dix, Edwards & Company. It received great reviews but sold slowly—by now, an all too familiar pattern. Olmsted would always call *A Journey Through Texas* "my best book . . . because edited by my brother."

Putnam's continued to flail and was soon at the edge of bankruptcy. Dix, Edwards & Company was dissolved, and Olmsted's young partners scurried off. A new firm was formed, headed by George Curtis, *Putnam's* editor. Curtis borrowed $25,000 from his father-in-law. The magazine's printer, J. W. Miller, joined the venture for the purpose of protecting a large debt he was owed. He knew that if *Putnam's* went bankrupt, it would become almost impossible to collect the money. The new firm was called Miller & Company. Olmsted, stuck in a defensive position similar to the printer Miller, also stayed on. He'd already sunk $5,500 into *Putnam's*, money that he owed to his father. He needed some kind of bounce back.

The spring of 1857 found Olmsted writing an introduction to a book called *The Englishman in Kansas; or, Squatter Life and Border Warfare* by Thomas Gladstone. This was the lone British literary property that had come out of his abortive trip to England. It was the only book that Miller & Company had on its publishing calendar.

Olmsted's introduction contains some of the harshest sentiments he would ever voice about the South. He laid into Southerners as "ruffians" and "bullies" with a "special proneness to violence." Of the Kansas situation in particular he wrote, "The world should recognize the fact that the disgraceful condition of Kansas, the atrocious system which the federal government of the United States has been forced to countenance in Kansas, is the legitimate fruit of despotism, not of free government."

It's hard not to see Olmsted's heated and polemical writing as the product of his own grim turn of mind. Not only had he seen the country become increasingly divided, but his own life was in disarray. His two Southern titles were selling slowly; *Putnam's* had lost its literary luster; Olmsted's business venture, publisher of that magazine and a few stray books, was in financial trouble. Worst of all, his brother was growing sicker and had been forced to leave the country. "I much fear I shall never see him again," he wrote to a friend.

Olmsted was a man waiting on the next ill tiding. And when it came, it was no surprise. Olmsted was away from New York when he received a letter from Curtis. Apparently, Miller & Company had gone under. The plan was to sell *Putnam's* immediately.

Putnam's wound up being purchased by another publisher for $3,400 (a fire-sale price), and the magazine struggled on for another year before folding, a ghost of its former self. It had existed just four years in total. After such a promising beginning, *Putnam's* became just another casualty of the fast-changing new world of magazine publishing. Bankruptcy proceedings for Miller & Company would also drag on through the months ahead. Where Olmsted had once rubbed elbows with the likes of Ralph Waldo Emerson, he was now represented in bankruptcy by William Emerson, a New York lawyer and older brother of the celebrated philosopher and essayist. The final verdict found Olmsted liable to repay a debt of $8,000.

In his letter to Olmsted, Curtis spelled it out succinctly: "We failed today!"

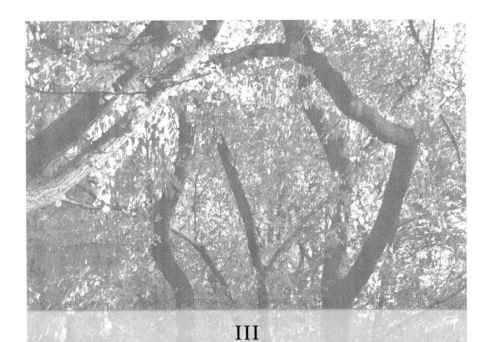

III

"A People's Pleasure-Ground"

CONCEIVING CENTRAL PARK, 1857–1861

CHAPTER 10

"Is New York Really Not
Rich Enough?"

IN EARLY AUGUST 1857, at a seaside inn in Morris Cove, Connecticut, Olmsted had a chance encounter that changed the course of his life. During afternoon tea, he struck up a conversation with Charles Elliott. Elliott was part of that tight nexus of interrelationships; he was a friend of Brace's, and he had once studied gardening under Andrew Jackson Downing. Elliott was also a board member on a project to create a large green space named, prosaically, for its location in Manhattan: Central Park. He told Olmsted that the board was looking to hire a superintendent.

Olmsted's interest was piqued. Never mind that the super's job, as Elliott detailed it, sounded pretty rough-hewn, overseeing teams of laborers, clearing brush, and smashing stones. The economy was in shambles, and Olmsted was in trouble. He had holed up at the Connecticut inn to finish *A Journey in the Back Country*, the final book in his Southern trilogy. The first two books, while critically acclaimed, had been financial failures, and he had no reason to think the latest installment would be any different. His prospects looked bleak.

Elliott encouraged Olmsted to apply for the job. Olmsted took the opportunity very seriously. That very evening, he boarded a steamer and returned to New York. To establish his credentials as a gentleman in good standing, Olmsted submitted a letter signed by his acquaintances, many from the literary world. It was written by James Alexander Hamilton, lawyer, politician, backer of Olmsted's abolitionist activities, and son of America's first treasury secretary. Among the signees was Washington Irving, at seventy-four the eminence grise of New York letters. Olmsted had met Irving at a dinner at the New York Press Club in 1855. Olmsted also circulated his own petition to such luminaries as George Putnam, banker Morris Jesup, and writer Bayard Taylor.

Olmsted submitted his formal application to the Central Park board. He enclosed Hamilton's letter and his own petition, nearly two hundred signatures strong—an act of supreme overkill. He included a covering note that highlighted his experience managing teams of laborers, though truth be told, he'd never overseen more than eight men on his Staten Island farm. But Olmsted needed the job. Besides his ever-growing tab with his father and his share in the failed publishing venture, he owed $75 for three months' lodging and $60 total to a pair of friends; his shoes were worn out, he didn't have a proper hat, and he was low on coal. "What else can I do for a living?" he lamented.

On September 11, 1857, the Central Park commission met in an office at 53 Liberty Street to consider Olmsted's application. While they deliberated, Olmsted—a nervous wreck—waited in the office of a friend who happened to practice law in the same building. The board seemed to take an unusually long time. To pass the time, he wrote a letter to John, who had made his way from Cuba to St. Thomas to Europe, still in search of that ideal climate. When Olmsted finally got the verdict, he added a postscript: "P.S. After a very long session, and much debate, I am elected: on the final vote, 8 of those present voting for me, one against me. . . . The strongest objection to me, that I am a literary man, not active."

Ironically, the mass of signatures Olmsted assembled from New York's leading lights gave the commissioners pause. The very person who had made the transition from farmer to writer was now viewed as too cerebral for such physically demanding work. Yet the signatures also convinced the commissioners that Olmsted was socially connected and reliable at least. He was hired for $1,500 a year and handed a job for which he was not ideally suited.

But Olmsted was nothing if not a canny opportunist. Through a twist, he was soon to be handed *the* vital role, as designer of the new park. Central Park stands as Olmsted's sublime achievement, a calm and lovely oasis in the frantic heart of Manhattan Island. This opportunity changed his life and transformed the practice of landscape architecture forever.

Most of all, Central Park represents a kind of bold assertion. Olmsted crafted beauty from a homely slice of land, drew light from enveloping darkness. In the course of creating his masterpiece, Olmsted would face three personal tragedies. And everything that happened between 1857 and 1861 (the crucial, formative years for Central Park) happened against the backdrop of rising tensions between the North and South, tensions that would ultimately erupt in a national calamity.

At the outset, however, Olmsted would act in a drastically more modest capacity, as superintendent. He was charged with the final cleanup necessary to ready the land for a park design. Olmsted stepped in during the final stages of a project that had been many, many years in the making.

The first call for a large park in New York City dates to 1785 and appears in an anonymous letter, signed "Veritas," that was sent to the mayor and alderman. Over time, the need became only more pronounced.

Between 1800 and 1850, New York's population increased fivefold to a half-million residents. Revolution in Germany and the Great Hunger in Ireland brought a flood of immigrants, and in some places 100,000 people were squeezed into a square mile.

As the city grew, its green space shrank. In Olmsted's time, New Yorkers still had fond memories of Niblo's Garden, a place for coffee and refreshments. It was located at the modern-day intersection of Prince and Broadway. That was the edge of town when it opened in 1828 on the old Bayard farm property. Within twenty years, the city had swallowed up Niblo's. The same fate befell Contoit's New York Garden, where people gathered for the rarefied pleasure of drinking lemonade chilled with ice, and Vauxhall Gardens, which featured summer concerts, fireworks, and an outdoor wax museum. The city, tight-packed and teeming, kept pushing relentlessly northward.

By midcentury, Manhattan Island had seventeen parks, all of them small and totaling a paltry 165 acres. Many of these parks were mere squares, oriented to their immediate neighborhoods. Meanwhile, places like Gramercy Park and St. John's Park were private, reserved for the exclusive use of the people who owned the surrounding properties. Ordinary New Yorkers who needed respite had taken to visiting Green-Wood Cemetery in Brooklyn. By the mid-1800s, hundreds of thousands of people each year recreated in this graveyard, ambling among the headstones, picnicking in the shade of mausoleums.

Enter Andrew Jackson Downing. Downing—America's preeminent arbiter of taste and editor of the influential *Horticulturist*, a journal to which Olmsted had contributed articles—sounded the one note guaranteed to get the burghers of New York exercised. London had Hyde Park and Berlin the Volkspark Friedrichshain, Vienna had the Prater, Paris its Jardin des Tuileries. But what about New York? If it had any hope of being a true world city, Downing argued in a series of essays, it needed a real park, a grand park, commensurate with its aspirations. "What are called parks in New-York," he chided, "are not even apologies for the thing; they are only squares or paddocks." And in another essay: "Is New York really not rich enough, or is there absolutely not land enough in America, to give our citizens public parks of more than ten acres?"

Downing hit the mark, and his call was soon taken up by other quarters, such as the popular press. William Cullen Bryant, editor of the *New York Post*, wrote a piece lamenting the existence of such a "very small space of open ground for an immense city." In the *New York Herald*, James Gordon Bennett voiced a conceit that was popular in the nineteenth century, comparing a park to a pair of lungs, capable of drawing in air and refreshment. "There are no lungs on the island," he wrote. "It is made up entirely of veins and arteries."

In 1850, both candidates for mayor of New York called for the establishment of a large park. There was a growing sense of urgency. The city's breakneck pace of development meant that soon enough, Manhattan would be filled in with buildings. Now was the time to set aside some land, while land was still to be had, and could still be had cheaply.

The first spot to receive serious consideration was Jones Wood, a 150-acre stretch along the East River. It was a fetching parcel of land, featuring gently rolling hills grown thick with trees that eased down to bluffs overlooking the water. Add a few paths, and it could be an instant park. The land belonged to a pair of old, established New York families, Jones and Schermerhorn. Neither was willing to sell. In 1851, a bill designed to take the property by eminent domain passed the state assembly and was signed into law. But the powerful families fought back, tying the eminent domain ruling up in court. Jones Woods was not to be.

New York's board of aldermen appointed a special committee to explore alternative park sites and options. Maybe a park could stretch across the island, east to west. How about a private, for-profit park? There was even a proposal for a serpentine park, winding through Manhattan. "Give us a park," demanded an editorial in the *New York Commercial Advertiser*, "be it sidelong, here, there, anywhere . . . a real park, a large park."

The special committee began to focus on a tract in the middle of Manhattan. It was in every way inferior to Jones Wood. The site consisted of a long, thin rectangle, a preposterously constraining shape for a park design. British troops had once camped here, denuding the area of trees. Post-Revolution, this had become a favored spot for New Yorkers in search of firewood or lumber for building, and there was scarcely a sapling to be found. Outcroppings of rock, bursts of 500 million-year-old mica schist, jutted through the turf at random intervals. If this wasn't enough, two separate large reservoirs disrupted the grounds. One was the old Croton receiving reservoir, which had handled New York City residents' water since 1842. The other was its replacement, just then getting under construction.

But at least the tract was central. The park would be convenient for visitors from different parts of New York. And the clincher was a fiscal advantage: Turn a rectangle of land into a park, and all the properties developed along the periphery would be valuable. Steep property taxes would flow into the city coffers. On July 21, 1853, the act that created Central Park passed, allotting 778 acres of land from 59th Street to 106th Street. Later the park would extend to 110th. (Most of these streets didn't even exist yet, but the city plan of 1811, in a kind of manifest destiny, laid a grid work of future streets all the way to 155th.)

While the site looked more like a moonscape than a parkscape, it was far from uninhabited. In the years before Olmsted was hired as superintendent and charged with clearing brush, the land had to be cleared of people. This was to be accomplished by eminent domain, the first time in U.S. history that this principle had been used to create a large park. The city earmarked money to pay off the land's occupants.

Some were business owners. The future Central Park was a center for "nuisance" industries, grim Dickensian operations that had been driven to the city's outskirts. Leather dressers and match manufacturers conducted their vocations amid a mélange of noisome odors and toxins. A pair of bone-boiling plants processed animal carcasses to create glue and charcoal filters used in things like sugar refining.

People also lived on the land. Impoverished immigrants, crowded into one-room cabins and rickety shanties, had formed communities with names like Dutch Hill and Dublin Corners. Residents tended small plots, growing vegetables like cabbage and corn to sell in pushcarts downtown. Following the 1849 cholera epidemic, livestock had been banned from the city proper, and anyone who wished to raise hogs, goats, or cattle had been pushed way up here. The animals roamed the land, foraging for feed.

There was also a predominantly black community called Seneca Village, occupying the western edge of the future park from roughly 81st Street to 89th Street. By the dawn of the nineteenth century, two-thirds of the city's blacks were free. Still, it wasn't until 1841 that slavery was completely abolished in New York State. Even so, only black *men* could vote and only if they owned $250 worth of property. Seneca Village had 264 residents, according to the 1855 census, many of them former slaves, now enfranchised due to home ownership. And many of them worked downtown as waiters and domestic helpers, pretty solid jobs for this era. The names of Seneca Village's churches, African Union Methodist and the African Methodist Episcopal Zion Church, showed a degree of ethnic pride that was rare in antebellum America.

Every one on the land had to go: bone boilers and hog farmers and waiters. Records show that the city paid $5,169,369.90 for 7,250 lots. Andrew Williams, one of Seneca Village's founders, received $2,335 for his house and property. He had purchased the land for $125 in 1825. Marshals forcibly evicted those who didn't go willingly. Supposedly, the great-great-grandfather of Yankee ballplayer Joe Pepitone was one of the marshals charged with clearing people so that work on Central Park could begin.

Andrew Jackson Downing would have been the natural choice to design the new park. Just a few years earlier, President Millard Fillmore had commissioned him to landscape the grounds between the Capitol and the White House. At the time, this would have been the largest park in the United States.

On July 28, 1852, Downing set off for New York City, aboard the steamship *Henry Clay*. He was en route to Washington, D.C., to work on his park commission. The *Henry Clay* got into a race with another craft, the *Armenia*. Opposite the town of Yonkers, fire broke out in the engine room of the overtaxed *Henry Clay*. Passengers began jumping overboard to escape the flames. First, Downing tossed deck chairs into the Hudson to serve as flotation devices. Then he jumped in himself.

Downing was a skillful swimmer. He ventured far out into the Hudson to help a woman with whom he'd once been romantically involved. In his younger days, Downing had swum this very river to meet up with this very woman. When he reached the woman, she threw her arms around his neck, in panic, and dragged him to his death.

His wife, Caroline, survived, clinging to a deck chair. Perhaps it was one he'd thrown overboard. At least, that's what people said in trying to console her. Downing was just thirty-six. The accident happened just one year after Olmsted's brief meeting with him in Newburgh. "There is no Downing among us," the *New York Herald* later declared, conjecturing about who should design Central Park.

For a time, it appeared certain that the job would go to Colonel Egbert Ludovicus Viele. Viele (pronounced Vee-Lay) was a West Point grad, engineer, and veteran of the Mexican War. He was surprisingly uncouth and was in the habit of swearing in the presence of women. He also had a strange fixation with the occult, centering on ancient symbols and their mystical powers. Most of all, he was ambitious. While working as a topographical engineer for the State of New Jersey, he'd repeatedly visited the land slated for Central Park. On his own time, sans pay, he had drawn up a park design.

Viele then managed to land the job as chief engineer of the park project. During its earliest days, there was a skeleton board of commissioners, consisting of just two members. Viele wrangled verbal okays from both of them. He then annotated his park plan with "adopted by the commissioners," dated it, and filed it as an official document. When a full eleven-person board was convened, Viele's plan was tabled for the time being. It was hoped that a better plan might emerge.

Olmsted began his work as superintendent in the autumn of 1857. It was his modest duty to cart away stones and drain swamps, clearing the way for a park design, perhaps even the one drawn up by his boss, the odious and grandiose Colonel Egbert Ludovicus Viele.

On his first day of work, Olmsted wore his finest suit. This appears to have provoked Viele. During their initial interview, the engineer had voiced concerns that Olmsted was too much the writer, not sufficiently "practical." Now Viele summoned a foreman to show Olmsted around the park. The foreman appeared wearing high wading boots and proceeded to lead Olmsted on a kind of hazing expedition, through thickets, over rock facings, and down into bogs, thickly congealed with the runoff from pig sties and bone-boiling works. It was a sweltering day, and Olmsted found the stench overpowering. The foreman spoke hardly a word, never smiled, but occasionally Olmsted detected the barest flicker in the man's eyes. Clearly, he was enjoying this march, as Olmsted recalled it, "through the midst of a number of vile sloughs in the black and unctuous slime of which I sometimes sank nearly half leg deep."

Olmsted set to work. There were 700 laborers in his charge, and he had something to prove. During his first days on the job, he supervised the draining of swamps and the demolition of hundreds of abandoned structures.

It was treacherous work. A team of men assigned to clear underbrush fell ill, fevered and itching terribly. Turns out, they had mistakenly set poison ivy vines ablaze. During a particularly grim week, Olmsted estimated that 100 of his workers came down with remittent fever, the old-fashioned name for malaria. In the mid-1800s, no one knew that malaria was caused by mosquitoes that bred in brackish water. But Olmsted certainly made the general connection between disease and the squalid park site.

Olmsted received his first paycheck, $80, and was starting to feel a bit easier about his prospects. But just one month into his new job, the economy, already shaky, took a nosedive. Ominous signs had been piling up for quite some time. Ever since 1849, the steady flow of Gold Rush gold had caused inflation to steadily climb. With the end of the Crimean War, Russia had reentered international markets, and demand for U.S. agricultural exports had dropped precipitously. Now, the Ohio Life Insurance and Trust Company collapsed due to rampant embezzlement.

In an earlier time, this latest event might have been containable. But thanks to the telegraph, news of the company's failure quickly spread across the United States, sparking panic selling in the stock market. It was a full-scale "revulsion" in the financial parlance of the day. Later, this event would come to be known as the panic of 1857, a frighteningly precipitous economic downturn.

The city comptroller had just floated a fresh round of Central Park bonds, but now the issues found no takers. With money short, work on the site ground to a halt. Olmsted was forced to furlough most of his 700 employees. Throughout the city, jobs were scarce, and the laid-off workers faced impending winter and grim futures: frigid tenement rooms, bread lines, eviction, starvation. "Everything is black & blacker in New York," observed Olmsted. The clearing of Central Park had been the single largest public works project in the city. Now, ill-clad men milled about the partially cleared grounds. They kept warm by burning scrap lumber and waited to be called back to their jobs.

Olmsted continued to show up at Wagstaff House, an old farmhouse that served as the superintendent's office. Wagstaff House was at the eastern edge of the future park, on 79th Street, one of the few uptown New York streets then in existence, as opposed to merely appearing on the grid plan. As days dragged on, as the crisis deepened, mobs of the unemployed, sometimes 5,000 strong, surrounded Wagstaff House.

Many of the desperate job seekers were German, and Olmsted saw placards that read "Work-Arbeit" (the second word being the German translation of the first). More ominously, he spotted a sign bearing the slogan "Bread or Blood." Politicians representing the hardest-hit wards delivered speeches, stirring up chants of "soup, soup, soup." On one occasion, Olmsted even feared for his safety. A candidate for a magistrate's post stood upon a wagon bed, urging the assembled crowd to demand work. The man produced a prop, a short piece of rope, which he fashioned into a noose. He then pointed to a tree. That would be the fate, the man suggested, of anyone who stood in the way of gainful employment.

Fortunately, the revulsion of 1857 was V-shaped, its rapid onset matched by an equally swift recovery—a common pattern for economic crises. It was over in a matter of weeks. The city aldermen were soon able to authorize $250,000 for park construction. Olmsted rehired many of the laid-off workers, even adding new hands for a total force of 1,000.

The main job was now breaking stones, taking sledgehammers to outcroppings of schist. Larger pieces were carted to the edges of the park and then piled up for what was to be a six-mile retaining wall. Small pieces were gathered to pave future paths.

Fresh hires earned as little as 3¢ an hour for working 6:00 a.m. to 5:00 p.m., six days a week. Olmsted proved a taskmaster: Employees who missed two days were summarily fired. But there was a ready pool of men willing to work a punishingly long day for less than a dollar. Those who rose to the position of foreman, overseeing a team of roughly a dozen men, could make $1.50. Anyone willing to work Sundays—disguised on time sheets as "unusual times" so as to avoid the ire of Sabbatarians—could earn time and a half. Olmsted boasted that he had whipped his charges "into a capital discipline, a perfect system, working like a machine." Things were going well.

But then came news of Olmsted's brother, and it was devastating. All through 1857, John and his family had been traveling, in an effort to find a climate where he might convalesce. They had tried Cuba, St. Thomas, Rome, and Switzerland. Now he was in Nice, on the French Riviera. But this desperate search was taking its toll, and he arrived at this latest locale completely worn out. He checked into a flea-ridden hotel and consulted with a doctor who told him that the resort's winter climate might prove colder and damper than is ideal for a tuberculosis sufferer.

John was failing fast. His weight had fallen to one hundred pounds. He was short of breath and terribly weak. Excruciating cramps shot up and down his back and sides. "Dear dear Fred," begins a letter from Nice, "it appears we are not to see one another any more. . . . I never have known a better friendship than ours has been & there can't be a greater happiness than to think of that—how dear we have been & how long we have held out such tenderness." John urged Fred to hold on to one of his possessions, as a memento: "I want you to keep something of mine— my watch or cane or something."

To treat the pain, John was administered progressively heavier doses of opium, and he slipped into a stupor. Olmsted's father raced to be at his son's bedside. On November 24, 1857, John died. He was just thirty-two. He left behind a wife, Mary, and three young children.

Olmsted received the news in a letter from his father. "In his death I have lost not only a son but a very dear friend," his father wrote, adding: "You almost your only friend."

It was true. If not his only friend, John had certainly been Fred's best friend. Even as adults, the two brothers had lived together on the Staten Island farm. They had traveled through Texas on a rugged horseback adventure.

Olmsted read and reread his brother's letter from Nice. Hard to fathom, painful, but these really had turned out to be John's final words to him, a deathbed letter. The very last line was striking. Here, John delivered an imploring message to his brother: "Don't let Mary suffer while you are alive."

CHAPTER 11

Right Man, Right Place

JOHN'S DEATH STILLED something in Olmsted. Before, there had often been a lightness about him, an exuberance even, but such displays would become rare going forward. In the months following John's death, he fell back on what would become a pattern in his life when dealing with grief. He threw himself into work.

Olmsted continued to clear Central Park, breaking stone, demolishing shanties, draining swamps. In what spare moments he could find, he worked to complete *A Journey in the Back Country*, the final book in his Southern trilogy.

While Olmsted toiled, completely unbeknownst to him, a sequence of behind-the-scenes machinations was nearing completion, and soon his relationship to the Central Park project would be drastically altered. The unlikely agent of this change was Calvert Vaux.

Vaux was an architect, a profession in scant supply in nineteenth-century America. He was also the onetime business associate of dearly departed Andrew Jackson Downing. Olmsted had met Vaux briefly and unmemorably during his own pilgrimage to Newburgh.

Vaux was born in England to a surgeon father who died young. As a teenager, he set out on his own, becoming an apprentice to Lewis Cottingham, a Gothic Revival architect. It soon became clear that Vaux was a superb draftsman. He traveled on the Continent, making a series of sketches of royal gardens. In 1850, his work was exhibited in a London gallery. As luck would have it, Downing was visiting England at this time. And he was on a mission. His landscape gardening practice was flourishing, and he was increasingly being called upon to design houses, too. The time was right, he realized, to bring a trained architect into his practice.

Downing saw the exhibit and was enchanted by Vaux's sketches. He asked Vaux, then twenty-five, to join his firm, and Vaux immediately accepted. Three weeks later, Vaux had relocated to Newburgh, New York.

For the Newburgh practice, Vaux combined Gothic architecture, then in vogue in England, with Downing's scrupulously honed rural aesthetic. It was a compelling mix. Signature touches included rustic stonework, severely pitched roofs, and jutting eves that fostered a play of light and shadow. The pair preached the value of asymmetry in house design and the need to bring a home into harmony with the surrounding landscape.

One of their first commissions was to renovate a house near Newburgh owned by Warren Delano II, a wealthy merchant. Shortly after, a daughter, Sara Delano, was born into the household. Sara Delano, in turn, was the mother of FDR.

Downing and Vaux began to receive increasingly prestigious jobs, such as a commission to design a house in Newport, Rhode Island. The client was Daniel Parish, a clothing magnate-turned-financial speculator and one of the richest men in America. There was even a commission from President Millard Fillmore, who called upon Downing's firm to design a park in Washington, D.C. For this, Vaux appears to have helped design a suspension bridge (never built) and an arch (same fate). One cannot be sure, as the architectural sketches are signed only by Downing. It is also believed that Vaux suggested modifications (ignored) to Robert Mills's Washington Monument, then under construction. Neither he nor Downing liked this obelisk. They didn't appreciate having to work around it in their park plan. When Downing drowned, a shaken Vaux identified the body. Following his mentor's death, Vaux carried on the architectural practice and remained in Newburgh.

Mid-nineteenth century, Newburgh was a seat for painters of the so-called Hudson River School. These painters had taken up Ralph Waldo Emerson's call to "ignore the courtly Muses of Europe." Rather than city scenes or royal portraits, they made the landscape of America—verdant, untrammeled, awe-inspiring—the central subject of their paintings. Figures of people, when they appear at all, are dwarfed by the scenery, an assertion of egalitarianism: *We are mere specks, and our best selves are found in an outward-looking apprehension of nature's grandeur.*

Vaux became friendly with a number of Hudson School painters, including Worthington Whittredge, Frederic Church, and, most especially, Jervis McEntee. McEntee favored a melancholic palate, creating hushed hymns of brown and gray and tan. He was renowned as a master at depicting autumnal scenes. In exchange for a painting, Vaux designed a little board-and-batten studio for McEntee. Then Vaux married the artist's sister, Mary Swan McEntee.

In 1856, Vaux moved to New York, source of an increasing number of his commissions. Shortly after arriving, he helped found the American Institute of Architects. There were no architecture schools then in the United States. Neither was there any form of licensing or accreditation. Owning a hammer was about the only prerequisite for designing a house or building, and that's pretty much how it went. Vaux was aiming to create some standards for his upstart profession.

Vaux was a tiny man—standing four feet ten inches tall—and anxious, too. He constantly pushed his spectacles up on his nose. He was easily flustered, stumbling and stammering, losing his train of thought. In spite of this manner, Vaux managed to communicate one thing loud and clear: He burned with a white flame for pure art.

Summer of 1857 found Vaux in a state of agitation. At this juncture, Viele's plan was still the plan for Central Park, and Vaux couldn't believe it. Why, Vaux wondered, on a civic undertaking of such vital import, was the plan to go with a design, never debated, never discussed, simply rubber-stamped years back by two provisional park commissioners who had since moved on? "Being thoroughly disgusted with the manifest defects of Viele's plan," Vaux later recalled, "I pointed out whenever I had a chance, that it would be a disgrace to the City and to the memory of Mr. Downing."

Vaux voiced his concerns to a couple of members of the Central Park board, urging them not to be so hasty. He had made inroads into this powerful body, having recently designed the Fifth Avenue mansion of one of its members, John Gray. What's more, Vaux was the living emissary of Downing, America's Apostle of Taste. Vaux even had a little son named Downing Vaux. Utterly persuaded, the commissioners agreed to table Viele's plan. He continued to lobby the park commissioners in his bumbling, but strangely effective, way. How about a design competition? In England, where he had received his training, competitions were a well-established method for ensuring that architectural jobs were doled out on merit. Once again, the commission took up Vaux's suggestion.

In the autumn of 1857, the board announced a competition for the design of Central Park, open to the general public. Though Viele's plan had been tabled, he was welcome to submit it for consideration against the other plans. He was also given the option of making changes to it or drawing up an entirely new design.

For all submissions, the following design elements were mandatory: a prospect tower, exhibition hall, formal garden, large fountain, and three playgrounds. Contestants were required to include at least four separate roads crossing the park. They would also need to provide for a parade ground, 20 to 40 acres in expanse. Not only did all plans need to include these elements, but all plans had to be executable within a budget, set at $1.5 million.

The contest participants would have access to a topographic map, executed by Viele, to aid them in their work. Designs were to be done in a scale of one hundred feet to an inch. That meant contestants would need to execute large and detailed plans that were roughly ten feet long by two feet wide. It was an odd shape, awkward and unwieldy, just like the park. First prize was $2,000, and there would be prize money for second through fourth places, as well. The due date was March 31, 1858.

Vaux approached Olmsted about teaming up for the competition. It wasn't the Downing association—that forgettable encounter in Newburgh years earlier—that drew Vaux to Olmsted. Neither was it his profile as a journalist, though Vaux had read Olmsted's work and admired it. No, Vaux's main reason for seeking out Olmsted was this: Viele's topographic map was rumored to be highly inaccurate. As superintendent, Olmsted was intimately familiar with the terrain of the park, and that might just provide an edge in the competition.

Olmsted was hesitant. He worried about the consequences if he entered a design contest that pitted him against Viele, his boss. Olmsted decided to consult him first. Viele merely shrugged. With that small, dismissive gesture, the partnership of Olmsted and Vaux was launched.

For now, Olmsted kept his job as superintendent, and Vaux maintained his architectural practice downtown, at 358 Broadway. After the day was over, the pair worked into the night, frequently riding on horseback over acre upon acre of parkland. The grounds looked especially barren by moonlight. It was clear that they weren't working with a proverbial blank canvas. No, this was something vastly inferior, a scarred and scraggly landscape that posed quandaries at every turn. "It would have been difficult to find another body of land," Olmsted later recalled, " . . . which possessed less of what we have seen to be the most desirable characteristics of a park."

Olmsted and Vaux began to puzzle out the first inklings of a design. Often, in what was to be a pattern throughout their long association, their discussions slid into heated argument. They made quite a team, a kind of diminutive duo: Vaux under five feet and Olmsted at five feet six inches (according to the crew manifest of the *Ronaldson*, the ship he sailed to China). Vaux was the trained architect (specializing in structures rather than landscapes). Olmsted was a jack of many, many trades.

Though Olmsted hadn't been aware of it, hadn't had the ghost of a plan, his whole life to this point had been a sort of apprenticeship, preparation for this grand act. As a small boy, Olmsted had perched on his father's saddle, enjoying "loitering journeys" through the Connecticut countryside. He had read the work of esoteric landscape theorists like William Gilpin and Uvedale Price at the tender age of nine. As a farmer, Olmsted had imported thousands of trees from Europe and developed an appreciation for plants in all their variety. His book *Walks and Talks* had shown him to be a keen observer of English parks, especially from the perspective of a visitor, a *user* of parks, if you will.

Even his experience traveling through the South would inform his approach to the design contest. He'd concluded, as mentioned earlier, that an almost perfect correlation existed between slavery and cultural atrophy. Seeing the decrepitude of the South had prompted Olmsted to write the prescient letter, urging his friend Brace to "go ahead with

the Children's Aid and get up parks, gardens, music, dancing schools."
Now Olmsted was actually trying to "get up" a park. At a time of increased tension with the South, a park could showcase the superiority
of the North.

Most of all, Olmsted would approach this task as a social reformer.
Park making was another opportunity for the activism that Olmsted had
earlier applied to scientific farming or writing about the South. From the
outset, he saw Central Park as a place of tranquillity for all the residents
of the crowded metropolis. "The Park is intended to furnish healthful
recreation," he asserted, "for the poor and the rich, the young and the
old, the vicious and the virtuous."

Olmsted had proved surprisingly able at the job for which he'd originally been hired—park superintendent. But designing a park was where
his deepest talents lay.

A large improvised table sat in the parlor of Vaux's home at 136 East 18th
Street. The table had been created by sliding several smaller tables together. When Olmsted and Vaux weren't out surveying the real park, a
proxy awaited them here, a ten-foot-long plan in progress. Deep into the
night, Olmsted and Vaux pored over this plan obsessively, thinking about
where to place certain features and details.

Because of Central Park's unfortunate shape, a rigid rectangle, it was
desirable to convey visitors away from its sides. For their design, Olmsted and Vaux decided on a main entrance running from Fifth Avenue
diagonally toward the middle of the park. They placed the promenade,
the main stretch for strolling, on a further diagonal. Such touches were
meant to subtly but firmly push visitors into the heart of the park as
quickly as possible.

Olmsted and Vaux also proposed to make the promenade really short,
just one-quarter of a mile long. The pair wanted to avoid a classic grand
promenade, stretching past formal gardens and traveling under marble
archways. Such opulent touches smacked of European-style royalty. A
short walkway would achieve an intimate scale, proper to the common
person "who in the best sense is the true owner" of the park, as Olmsted
put it.

Olmsted and Vaux also planned a distinctly rural treatment for Central Park, a massive challenge. It meant utterly transforming this battered piece of land. Everywhere their plan called for trees, trees, and more trees. The short promenade was to be overhung by a canopy of elms. On the tops of hills, thick groves would stand. A screen of trees was to be planted around the entire periphery of the park. Tiny individual trees were drawn on the ten-foot plan in order to communicate this rural feel. These trees were generic, of no discernible breed, but thousands of them had to be sketched to fill up the blueprint, just as thousands would need to be planted to fill up the park.

Whenever Vaux's friends dropped by his home, they were invariably drafted into tree-drawing service. One of these was Jacob Wrey Mould, a fellow English-born architect. Mould was a flamboyant figure who managed to scandalize many in his circle by living with a woman out of wedlock. As an architect, he described himself as "Hell on Color." His bold design for New York's All Souls Church, featuring alternating stripes of red and yellow brick, earned his creation the sniggering nickname "Church of the Holy Zebra." After Vaux designed the Fifth Avenue mansion of park commissioner John Gray, Mould had done the interior in a riot of color. In the future, Mould would play a huge role in the creation of Central Park. But at this juncture, he wasn't sold on Olmsted and Vaux's prospects for winning and confined his involvement mostly to sketching little trees.

Along with Viele's topographic map, every design contestant had been furnished with photographs of various points in the park to use for reference. These came from the studio of Mathew Brady, renowned for his photos of such American icons as John Audubon and Daniel Webster and later for his Civil War portraits.

Olmsted and Vaux had a great idea. Why not include before and after images as part of their submission? The Brady photos, washed-out daguerreotypes of unlovely little tufts of land, perfectly captured the grim look of the current park. Vaux, in turn, did some studies in pencil and watercolor, suggesting what the same views would look like in the future if his and Olmsted's plan was executed. Jervis McEntee—the notable painter and Vaux's brother-in-law—also did some works in oil under

Olmsted and Vaux's direction. Mould created some images as well for the submission.

The highlight of Olmsted and Vaux's design was the treatment of the four mandatory roads that cut across the park. Supposedly, inspiration struck as the pair witnessed a horse-drawn ambulance cart, racing across Manhattan, bell furiously ringing. An innovation was needed, they realized, that would allow people to amble through the park without constant intrusion from the city in the form of traffic. Olmsted and Vaux proposed to sink the roads below ground level in eight-foot-deep channels. Fences would prevent pedestrians from falling into the channels, and scrims of hedges could, in turn, hide the fences. The upshot: Traffic could cross the park via invisible subterranean routes.

In certain places, Olmsted and Vaux's plan called for bridges of land across the roadway channels. This ensured that Central Park—already disrupted by two reservoirs and countless bursts of mica schist—wouldn't be further carved up by roads. The sunken transverses were a brilliant solution, providing Olmsted and Vaux's design with a sense of flow. Long stretches of meadow and broad vistas were now possible. Visitors could circulate more easily through the park, without having their view disrupted or mood punctured by a clattering dung cart. On top of everything, there was a practical benefit. The park could be closed at night, yet traffic could continue to use the sunken transverse roads.

Olmsted and Vaux called their design the Greensward plan, *greensward* being an English term for an unbroken swath of land. They wrote an accompanying text, featuring detailed descriptions of the various design touches and discussion even of the philosophy underlying their choices.

Whereas fellow contestants frequently accompanied their ten-foot blueprints with the barest annotations, Olmsted and Vaux crafted a kind of park maker's manifesto. A particular theme, one that they sounded again and again in the Greensward text, was the necessity of delivering a design that would hold up for posterity. "Only twenty years ago Union Square was 'out of town'; twenty years hence, the town will have enclosed the Central Park," they wrote. "Let us consider, therefore, what will at that time be satisfactory, for it is then that the design will have to be really judged."

By late in the afternoon of March 31, 1858, the due date, Olmsted and Vaux were still putting the finishing touches on their submission. They rushed to the Arsenal, an old munitions depot on the park grounds being used as an office by the commissioners. The doors were locked. But they were able to get the attention of a janitor by pounding on the door. Olmsted and Vaux left their entry with the janitor. The board had already received the other thirty-two submissions but wouldn't receive theirs until the next day. Technically, they had missed the deadline.

Olmsted and Vaux still won. Their plan, logged in as entry number 33, received first-place votes from seven of the eleven commissioners.

Among historians, a convention holds that Olmsted and Vaux came out of nowhere to win a public design competition. This is far from the truth. Obviously, they were already an extremely accomplished team, even if—in Olmsted's case—the accomplishments were in completely different fields. Clearly, they devised a unique and compelling design. But they helped their cause still further with a highly polished submission.

In the ten-foot blueprint, Vaux's skill as a draftsman shines through. Then there are the before and after images, something no other contestant thought to do. Here, they enlisted the aid of McEntee, the Hudson River School painter, and the talented Jacob Wrey Mould. There's also the rich and descriptive text, accompanying the Greensward plan. Olmsted and Vaux even went so far as to have this document professionally printed by Wm. C. Bryant & Company, a press owned by the *New York Post* editor.

Olmsted and Vaux had the best plan and the best presentation by far. Their rivals didn't stand a chance. One of the competing plans proposed to turn Central Park into a living map, composed of meadows shaped like the world's continents. The problem of representing the vast oceans would be solved by filling in a few swamps and dubbing them "Atlantic," "Pacific," and so on. Another plan was a collection of little green spaces named after founding fathers, including Washington, Jefferson, Franklin, and Adams.

There was a heavy emphasis on fountainry among the competing entries. The centerpiece of a plan dubbed "The Eagle" was a stack of thirteen star-shaped basins, representing the original U.S. colonies. On top perched a huge statuary eagle, water ushering from its beak and cascading from basin to basin, like a tower of champagne glasses at a wedding. Another plan proposed a grand fountain spewing a jet of water 125 feet into the air.

Viele simply resubmitted his existing plan without making a single change. "Commonplace and tasteless" is how Clarence Cook, a critic for the *New York Times*, described it at the time. There was also a mysterious submission, logged as entry number 2. Tucked inside an envelope was a single piece of paper, unsigned and featuring a drawing of a pyramid. Almost certainly, this was a second, anonymous, submission by Viele. After Viele died, he was laid to rest in the graveyard at West Point inside a large pyramid-shaped mausoleum of his own design.

The contest guidelines contained a laundry list of mandatory features: the prospect tower, exhibition hall, three separate playgrounds, and so on. Another mistake, made by most of the contestants, was following this prescription to the letter. This resulted in frenetic park plans, with the grounds chopped up into many different sections for discrete activities. Olmsted and Vaux simply ignored elements they didn't wish to include in their plan. As a result, they achieved a cleanness and continuity of design utterly lacking in the competing submissions. The pair found all kinds of creative ways to excuse their omissions.

For example, they didn't want a prospect tower. In the Greensward plan's text, they proposed tabling the design of any such feature until some grand historic event presented a tie-in opportunity. "If, as is not improbable, the transatlantic telegraph is brought to a favorable issue while the park is in an early stage of construction," they wrote, "many reasons could, we think, be urged for commemorating the event by some such monument." Olmsted and Vaux's refusal to include all the mandatory elements had zero consequences. And a prospect tower was never built in Central Park.

The contest rules also called for a parade ground of 20 to 40 acres. The Greensward plan included one that occupied just 25 acres, near the minimum. For this feature, some of the competitors—particularly those with a military background—set aside the maximum 40 acres. Viele went above and beyond, allotting roughly 50. Among other things, a parade ground would furnish a place where soldiers might drill. Olmsted felt strongly that a park would be a great showcase for the civility that prevailed in the nonslaveholding North. But if tensions continued, if war broke out, as was looking increasingly likely, he resolutely did not want the park to be a training ground for troops.

Olmsted and Vaux split the $2,000 purse. They had won the competition by laying out an uncompromising vision, and now they were ready to bring that vision to life.

But this was New York, and in New York nothing ever gets done easily. Just one week after Olmsted and Vaux were declared the winners, they encountered serious objections from two members of the Central Park board. Robert Dillon was a politician who had recently served two terms as New York City's corporation counsel. August Belmont, the newest member of the board, had earlier served as American representative of the Rothschild banking empire and had built a vast fortune in his own right. Both men were Democrats, and per the party's political leanings in this era, both were deeply conservative.

Dillon and Belmont proposed seventeen separate amendments to the Greensward plan. The pair proposed scrapping Olmsted and Vaux's masterstroke, the sunken transverses, on the grounds that they might fill up with snow during the winter. They also demanded that more ample equestrian paths be added to the design. This was at the behest of Belmont, in particular, as he was a horse racing aficionado. The Belmont Stakes, the third leg of thoroughbred racing's Triple Crown, is named after him.

Dillon and Belmont's most far-reaching suggestion was replacing Olmsted and Vaux's modest walkway with a truly grand promenade, running nearly the entire length of the park. Along the way, a wire suspension bridge would connect the tops of the two receiving reservoirs, features Dillon and Belmont described as "jewels of the Park." In their conception, the reservoirs, as engineering marvels, would become the focal point.

A full-on aesthetic clash was under way. Olmsted and Vaux had designed a rural-style park, in keeping with enduring notions that extended from the founding fathers to Emerson to Andrew Jackson Downing to the Hudson School painters, namely, that the countryside was the source of the soul's replenishment. By contrast, cities were morally suspect. "Cities are great sores," Thomas Jefferson once said. A proper city park, then, should provide escape from the city.

"It is one great purpose of the Park," declared Olmsted, defending the Greensward plan before the board, "to supply to the hundreds of thousands of tired workers, who have no opportunity to spend their summers in the country, a specimen of God's handiwork that shall be to them, inexpensively, what a month or two in the White Mountains or the Adirondacks is, at great cost, to those in easier circumstances."

Dillon and Belmont had very different ideas. They thought that a city park should celebrate the wonders of city life. What's more, they worried that the transition from urban New York to a rural-style park would be jarring. "The contrast will be sudden and violent," they argued, "—the effect, we apprehend, will be grotesque." Dillon and Belmont were powerful men, used to getting their way. They purchased "cards"—a forerunner of the advertorial—in papers such as the *New York Post*. They used their space to take swipes at the Greensward plan.

Olmsted fought back. His journalism experience may have rendered him too impractical for an ideal park super, but as a park designer it came in handy. Olmsted had influential friends. Olmsted invited Henry Raymond (his *Times* editor for the Southern dispatches) and Charles Dana (a *Tribune* editor who had been one of *Putnam's* secret staffers) to meet him at a large boulder in the southern end of the park. The two editors fired up cigars. Olmsted then proceeded to point out elements of his and Vaux's design that would be damaged by Dillon and Belmont's plan. Both papers ran articles sympathetic to Olmsted's point of view.

Olmsted gave a personal park tour to Richard Grant White, another onetime *Putnam's* employee, now editor of the *New York Courier and Enquirer*. Afterward, White wrote a staunch defense of the Greensward plan: "It is not only so beautiful in its grand outlines and its details, but so complete, symmetrical, and consistent with itself, that it can hardly be changed in any essential point." And he added a word in Olmsted's defense: "Once a practical farmer, he has traveled extensively . . . and has seen and carefully studied all the great parks in the world. He presents the rare spectacle of the right man in the right place."

When the article ran, Olmsted dashed off a letter to White, thanking him for the help. This article, along with many others Olmsted placed with his contacts in the "literary republic," convinced the board—seven of whom had voted for the Greensward plan anyway—that it was time to move forward. Olmsted had won this nineteenth-century public relations battle, besting Dillon and Belmont. The park plan could now proceed.

Olmsted was hired at $2,500 a year and was handed the title architect in chief, despite the fact that he had no training as an architect. The press battle appears to have fixed the idea that he was the prime mover behind the park.

Vaux—advocate of standards for the nascent architecture profession in America—was named Olmsted's assistant at $5 per day. But Vaux didn't mind, or at least he didn't let it show . . . yet. His goal was to get art done, and he had obviously chosen a ramrod for a partner.

Viele was fired.

CHAPTER 12

A Park Is Born

ONCE OLMSTED AND Vaux received the nod to proceed with their design for Central Park, the commissioners pressed them to move quickly. By 1858, the issue of a large park in New York had dragged on for many years. Millions had been spent obtaining the land; thousands more had been spent clearing it. To justify all this expenditure, some progress needed to be shown.

The plan was to open the park to the public in stages. The board asked Olmsted and Vaux to have certain sections ready by winter so the park could receive its very first visitors, ice skaters.

There was a vast amount to be done. Olmsted hired another 1,000 men, and Central Park, already the largest public works project in New York, instantly doubled in size. While designing the Greensward plan involved careful thought and drafting skills, bringing it to life would prove a rawer task, centering on things like detonation and drainage. Huge amounts of rock had to be blown to smithereens. This was Manhattan bedrock, the source of unshakable foundations for future Midtown skyscrapers. By a quirk of geology, the rock didn't lie deep underground in the park, as in other parts of the city. A stratum ran just beneath the surface of the ground.

Roughly 250 tons of gunpowder were used in the making of Central Park, more than would be used at the battle of Gettysburg. This was dangerous work, earning blast foremen an extra 25¢ a day. A red flag flying from a tower was the signal that a blast was imminent. Workers were given two full hours to clear the area. Even so, during the first year of construction, a blast caused the very first fatality. Four more men would die, from other types of accidents, during the construction of Central Park.

Massive rock outcroppings were reduced to rubble. Channels and tunnels were blasted to create the sunken transverse roads—and still the rock, so much rock, burst through the turf. Olmsted and Vaux chose to keep some of the more striking rock formations, appropriating them into their design. Sometimes they even excavated farther, removing soil from the base of a formation to increase its size. Bold crags of stone became architectural touches, looming above gentle man-made glades.

Thousands of trees were planted. Tons of grass seed were scattered. To ensure proper drainage, a series of trenches were dug at forty-foot intervals throughout the park. The trenches were laid with clay pipes.

Carts rattled to and fro, bearing loads of dirt and rock. Virtually none of this material was removed from the grounds. Instead, it was simply shifted from one place to another. Enough earth was moved, Olmsted later estimated, to fill 10 million "one-horse cart loads," and if said carts were lined up, the procession would stretch for 30,000 miles. Marshes were filled in with soil in order to create meadows. Low-lying areas were bulked up into rolling hillocks. The natural look of Central Park was thus achieved in no small measure through artifice. The park was full of "undignified tricks of disguise," as Olmsted called them, used in the service of "simplicity, tranquility, and unsophisticated naturalness."

The Lake, the site of future ice skating, was in reality a low-lying piece of swampy ground. Before park construction began, it existed only on Olmsted and Vaux's ten-foot blueprint, where the squiggly, naturalistic contours of its shoreline were rendered in india ink. To fill it, clay pipes carried rain runoff from the carriage paths and other spots in the park. To drain it, a series of sluices could be opened. Some of the sluices fed into natural springs running under the parkland, and certain springs, in turn, emptied into New York's East River.

This ingenious system, created in collaboration with a talented drainage specialist hired by Olmsted, made it possible to raise and lower the water level in the Lake. Rustic Central Park was also a triumph of the latest technology. The plan was to keep the water seven feet deep during the summer for rowboats, but to lower it to four feet in winter for iceskating. Shallower water would pose less danger if someone fell through the ice.

The Lake's design even included concrete steps built into the naturallooking shoreline. During summer, the steps were covered in water. But in winter, the steps could be used to walk down to the frozen surface.

During these early months of park making, Olmsted and Vaux's partnership was still very new. But they quickly fell into the roles that would define all their future collaborations. Vaux, being an architect, was responsible for designing structures such as bridges and archways. Olmsted took the lead on designing the landscape elements themselves, though often with considerable input from Vaux. In an extension of his earlier role as superintendent, he oversaw the construction, giving orders to crews of workmen. As their work progressed, Olmsted would become more involved in administration, developing rules for park use and figuring out policing strategies. As a pure artist, this held no interest for Vaux.

Vaux's training ensured a certain polish for anything the pair undertook. Olmsted compensated for his lack of training with an agile mind and an intuitive sense of design, drawing on his varied life experiences. He brought a fine sense of narrative to these park creations and a flair for the dramatic.

Together, Olmsted and Vaux were the American pioneers of a profession, landscape architecture, that to this point had barely existed in the world in either name or deed. This was a quantum step up from humble landscape *gardening*, which centered on planting flowers and terracing lawns. And while it incorporated the practice of architecture, it was so much more. Landscape architecture was the sum of Olmsted's and Vaux's parts, quite literally. It might best be described as the art of applying rigorous design to large pieces of land. To this point in history, there had been a tiny number of practitioners, mostly in Europe but also in Asia, who might rightly be described as landscape architects, though fewer still used the designation. In the United States, it was a novel field.

Oh, and there's one last useful way of breaking down the division of labor between Olmsted and Vaux. Vaux was supremely gifted; Olmsted quite simply was in another realm.

Olmsted's extraordinary gifts were nowhere more evident than in Central Park's meadows, as originally conceived. For these, Olmsted developed a signature hourglass shape, narrow in the middle and flaring out at each end. This shape was achieved by planting trees around the edge of the meadow. Someone standing in such a meadow, Olmsted surmised, would naturally be drawn toward the narrow middle. It presented an allure and a mystery. What was on the other side? After walking through the passage, there was a release, like walking through a tunnel into a stadium. Or like a city street that spills suddenly into an open field. "Passages of scenery" Olmsted called these set pieces of tree and turf.

At certain key spots, Olmsted planted so-called specimen trees. These might be solitary oaks or maples that would grow to awesome height, limbs stretching dramatically, exploding in color during autumn. Such a specimen was sure to grab the attention of someone who had just entered the open portion of a meadow. It was an ideal focal point for a vista.

Olmsted varied his plantings by color, planting trees with dark foliage such as evergreens in the foreground of a vista and lighter tones such as beeches more distantly. This trick of light and shadow made his meadows appear larger than they actually were. In cramped Central Park, creating a sense of boundless space was desirable, even if it was just an illusion.

Of course, time was needed for the trees to grow and for Olmsted's hourglass planting pattern to emerge. The Greensward plan had contained the argument that the passage of twenty years was required before Central Park's design could be properly judged. And so it would be with the meadows. Year upon year, visitors to the park would delight as Olmsted's grand tree plan unfurled. (Today, sadly, the park's meadows no longer hold to this imaginative scheme.)

Other brilliant touches were more rapid to reveal themselves. The Lake, for example, opened right on schedule. On December 11, 1858, Central Park welcomed its first official visitors, the ice skaters. Roughly 300 people showed up on that first Sunday. A week later, 10,000 descended on the park. New York, suffering through the latest in a series of unseasonably cold winters, fell quickly into an ice-skating swoon.

Diocletian Lewis, one of America's first physical fitness gurus, had created a recent stir, lecturing about the healthful benefits of outdoor activity. Here at last was an opportunity for cooped-up city dwellers to get outside during this harsh winter, visit the new park, breathe in the crisp air.

Soon all kinds of makeshift concessions sprang up to serve this ice-skating craze. Skates could be rented for 10¢ an hour with a $1 deposit. Enterprising little boys wandered the ice, helping people affix skates to their boots for a 3¢ fee. This service was aimed especially at women, frequently decked out in so much finery that they had trouble bending over. For those too skittish to skate, armchairs for sliding over the ice could be rented for 15¢ an hour. The ideal configuration for this activity was an eligible gentleman pushing a seated young lovely over the ice. Yes, a yen for physical fitness may have been the original purpose for visiting the park, but something more basic turned this into a full-on frenzy.

In Victorian New York, ice skating was one of the few activities where unmarried men and women could mingle without chaperones. It was even possible for a woman to get ever so slightly coquettish, perhaps showing a hint of ankle as she glided past. "Many a young fellow has lost his heart, and skated himself into matrimony, on the Central Park pond," a guidebook would note some years later. For the demure, or for those who wished to skate in peace without constant male attention, there was a separate ladies' section of the Lake.

As the winter drew on, sometimes as many as 100,000 people a day visited the park. Skating proved so popular that the park was kept open well into the night. The Lake's icy surface reflected the glow of newly installed calcium lamps. Vaux went skating. There is no record that Olmsted did.

Anytime the ice was thick enough for skating, a red ball was hoisted from the same tower used to signal that an explosion was imminent. The ball could be seen from quite a distance. This little touch was meant to save someone who had come all the way uptown the further trouble of trekking into the park if there was no skating to be done.

By the standards of nineteenth-century New York, skating was an unusually egalitarian activity, available to many, though by no means all, of the city's residents. The frenzy was a huge sensation, covered by every paper, and writers couldn't resist commenting on the atypical mix of people they saw on the ice. The *New York Herald* reported that the Lake contained "members of the homo genus of every age, and probably every country that constitutes our nationality." The *Times* encountered skaters from "all ages, sexes and conditions in life, from the ragged urchin with one broken skate, to the millionaire." And again from the *Herald*: "Masters Richard and William from Fifth Avenue, in their furs, and plain Dick and Bill from the avenues nearer the rivers, with bunting flying from joints and middle seams, were all mingled in joyful unity." Breathless as they are, these newspaper accounts were a heartening sign about Central Park. As Olmsted stated proudly, the park was turning out to be "a democratic development of the highest significance."

In the summer of 1859, a second feature in Central Park was opened to the public. This was the Ramble, a wild garden, densely planted and laced with intricate pathways that crossed and then recrossed, switched and then switched back, until a person was hopelessly lost, and that was the fun of it.

The Ramble had been conceived as a way to disguise a bald hillside leading up to the embankment of the old Croton reservoir. Here—in stark contrast to his eons-to-unfold meadows—Olmsted planted fast-growing shrubs and flowers such as columbine, kalmia, and azalea. Vaux added a rustic arch, hidden away, spanning a path that had meandered deep into the Ramble. There was also a little stream that trickled down the hillside, spilled into a waterfall—and was totally engineered. It could be turned on and off with a spigot, and for its source it drew on the old reservoir, the one that had provided the city's drinking water. A natural-looking "grotto" was built to hide the pipes.

Olmsted considered the Ramble his greatest work in the park. It was—and would remain—very much a work in progress. He worried ceaselessly over the plantings, constantly changing out one plant for another. With the Ramble, Olmsted was like a mad scientist, endlessly tinkering with the botanical formula, aiming for just the right mix of color and texture on that once-homely hillside.

New Yorkers by the thousands flocked to the Ramble, eager to enjoy a piece of countryside right in the city, just as Olmsted and Vaux had envisioned. In these times, the only hint of the rural for many city dwellers was a few stray flowers grown in window boxes. One of the great pleasures of the Ramble was vast beds of flowers, growing without limit. Visitors were particularly taken with the dandelions, not yet viewed as a nuisance plant. One account waxed rhapsodic about the "blessed dandelions, in such beautiful profusion as we have never seen elsewhere, making the lawns, in places, like green lakes reflecting a heaven sown with stars."

But the most striking feature of the Ramble was a cave. It had been discovered, partially obscured by stone, when work on the hillside got under way. The stones were cleared, and the cave was wholly integrated into the park plan. The man-made Lake was extended so that it was possible to row a boat right into the entrance of the cave. The paths of the Ramble were construed so that just when visitors had tarried a bit overlong, they were suddenly confronted with this fearsome natural wonder.

The cave set people's hearts palpitating. And if a man played it just right, a woman might faint into his arms. As ever with the adoption of new things—those first dime-store movie reels, VCRs, and the Internet come to mind—Central Park's growing popularity was helped by having some racy content.

Walking through the Ramble, on a balmy Saturday, a person might also catch the strains of a Verdi aria, wafting through the air. During the summer of 1859, the first concerts were held in Central Park.

Harvey Dodworth was the versatile conductor of an orchestra that played everything from Strauss waltzes to Rossini marches to a song called "The Moorish Minstrel." The free performances, dubbed "citizens' concerts," were designed to appeal to a broad spectrum of New Yorkers. In fact, Dodworth had to get his programs preapproved by Olmsted and the Central Park board. For those first concerts, a bandstand had not yet been built in the park. The orchestra set up along the edge of the Lake. While they played, visitors often went about other park activities, sunbathing or rowing in boats.

Olmsted loved music. He was aware of a distinct consonance between his creations and the flow of a symphony. "Landscape moves us in a manner more nearly analogous to the action of music than anything else," he once wrote. Keen to heighten the interplay between music and the park, he obsessively paced over the grounds during Dodworth's concerts. Acoustics was still a casual science then, but Olmsted noted how sounds were amplified when they bounced off rock faces and other surfaces. He was struck by how sound traveled across water, making the orchestra seem closer to the listener than it actually was.

Olmsted drove poor patient Dodworth to distraction, asking him to arrange the orchestra at different points along the Lake, seeking that elusive sonic sweet spot. He even tried having the orchestra play from the middle of the Lake, aboard boats. That innovation didn't take.

At times when Dodworth's orchestra performed, the laborers who were building Central Park paused for a moment to listen. More often, they kept right on working, but as onlookers noted, their hammer thuds and clangs seemed to meld with the rhythm of the music.

The summer of 1859 was *the* intense stretch in park construction, the period when the most got done. Olmsted had nearly to double the workforce once again to 3,600 men. Men worked seven days a week, week in, week out. Olmsted drove his charges hard and jokingly referred to himself as a "Sabbath cracker."

As Central Park progressed, being a vast public work, it also began to deviate from Olmsted and Vaux's original plan. Olmsted despised the idea of the statues in Central Park, for example, referring to them scornfully as "incidents." In his view, objects so very temporal—a statue of a politician recently deceased, the bust of a poet currently in vogue—had no place in a landscape meant to be timeless. But New York is a big city, and plenty of people disagreed with him.

In 1859, a group of German Americans erected a statue in Central Park of one of their cultural heroes, Johann Christoph Friedrich von

Schiller. The statue of Schiller begot a statue of poet Fitz-Greene Halleck, which in turn begot John Quincy Adams Ward's masterful *Indian
Hunter*, until before too long the park was full of statues, Olmsted be
damned.

Olmsted and Vaux were also forced to make accommodations to Dillon and Belmont. Though the seventeen amendments had been shot
down in a highly public battle, the fact was that a few of the ideas demanded consideration, particularly Belmont's request for more ample
horseback riding trails. The board told Olmsted and Vaux that they had
to address this deficiency. So they went back to the drawing board and re-
designed the paths. What they came up with is known as the separation
of ways. As an innovation, it's second only to their sunken transverses
and can be seen as the logical extension of that idea. The sunken transverses moved commercial traffic through the park without disturbing visitors. The separation of ways was meant to divvy up the different kinds
of traffic *within* the park. There were pedestrians, horseback riders, and
carriage passengers—and never the trine shall meet.

To achieve this involved radically rethinking Central Park's circulation system. Olmsted and Vaux laid out intricate exchanges where riding
paths swung clear of carriage roads, and pedestrian walkways traveled
over and underneath them both. This system benefited all visitors, but especially pedestrians. It meant a person could meander through the park,
absentmindedly or caught up in an idyll, without any possibility of coming upon a horse.

To create this separation of ways, Vaux had to design a slew of new
structures. The original Greensward plan called for just nine bridges.
Now he embarked on a series of thirty-four bridges and archways, completed between 1859 and 1865. Vaux's designs were stunning and stunningly varied: Some were rustic and some classical; some used cast iron
and others marble. He gave particular consideration to the way pedestrians might experience these creations.

Walking underneath a bridge, a person is in a dark tunnel looking out
into a lighted area. Ahead, the opening forms a kind of frame. Vaux oriented his bridges and shaped their arches to play off the surrounding
scenery. Many of the framed views were designed to be reminiscent of

vivid Hudson River School landscapes, only fitting, given Vaux's personal credo: "Nature first, second, and third—architecture after a while."

The Central Park board also demanded that a bridge be built across the Lake. To cross this body of water required a long bridge, a suspension bridge, though nothing like the wire behemoth that Dillon and Belmont had proposed. Vaux created his Bow Bridge, so gloriously low-slung that it nearly kisses its own reflection in the water below.

Around this time, Central Park began to receive its first reviews. The press treated the project like the debut of a symphony or the unveiling of a painting. This was a major artwork, and the reviews, as they began to roll in, tended to be unqualified raves. "Vast and beautiful . . . majestic," said the *New York Times*. "A royal work . . . the beau-ideal of a people's pleasure ground," announced the *Atlantic*. But Olmsted and Vaux felt that the most satisfying assessment was contained in a comment by Horace Greeley, editor of the *New York Tribune*. On first visiting Central Park, he took one look around and pronounced: "Well, they have let it alone a good deal more than I thought they would."

As Central Park evolved, people besides Olmsted and Vaux became intimately involved. Ignaz Pilat was the park's head gardener. Born in Austria, Pilat had served as director of Vienna's botanical gardens and worked in Venice as a gardener before fleeing to the United States during the political troubles of 1848. Olmsted had a great eye for picking what tree or flower should go where. He was a master at foliage composition. But Pilat's talent was the actual planting. Pilat was skilled at maintaining soil and pruning limbs and killing weeds, everything necessary to ensure these trees and flowers grew. Incredibly, between 1859 and 1863, Pilat oversaw the planting of an estimated 240,000 trees in Central Park.

Anton Gerster was a Hungarian carpenter who executed Vaux's designs for wooden structures in the park. Vaux sketched these by the dozen: fences, birdhouses, boat landings, and pergolas. Gerster gave these a raw and rustic treatment, selecting gnarly pieces of wood, only partially stripping away the bark. But there was intent behind everything this master carpenter did. Many of the designs featured trellises, and soon Vaux and Gerster's structures were hung thickly with vines—wisteria, honeysuckle, and wild grape.

Jacob Wrey Mould, who drew trees and contributed some images to the original Greensward submission, signed on as Vaux's assistant once the park got under way. Like Olmsted, Mould was multitalented. He was an organist, spoke several languages, and translated a number of opera librettos into English.

Where Vaux was a study in understatement, Mould was like an unchecked id, and in select parts of the park's design, he was allowed to run free. Mould designed a bandstand for Dodworth's orchestra that was so maniacally polychromatic that a contemporary guidebook's attempt to recount his color choices—"red-brown line; indigo-blue moulding; gilt moulding; red-brown line; green line"—drags on for a full fat paragraph. (The bandstand was torn down in 1922.)

Mould's greatest work in Central Park would come a couple years hence, during the early 1860s, when he contributed a set of stone carvings to the terrace that leads down to the Bethesda fountain. The carvings are seemingly boundless in their variety—an open Bible, a sheath of wheat, pine cones, a witch on a broomstick—and each renders a little story in stone that is, by turn, naturalistic, allegorical, or merely whimsical. A rooster on the east side of the terrace corresponds to an owl on the west, an allegory of day and night. A pair of ice skates hidden among the carvings alludes to the skating frenzy.

And then, there's Andrew Green. Unlike Pilat, Gerster, and Mould, Green was neither an artist nor an artisan. But his influence on the park's creation would prove equally profound. Green was a prominent New York lawyer and member of the Central Park board. He was also an unmarried teetotaler who loved Milton and read the Bible every day. Despite being one of the more conservative commissioners, Green had pushed hard for the adoption of the Greensward plan. Olmsted and Green had even developed a kind of uneasy friendship. Every other week, bachelor Green was in the habit of joining Olmsted for Sunday-evening dinner. Secretly, Olmsted thought Green something of a ponderous windbag. Green liked to hold forth on politics, a subject on which he and Olmsted couldn't be further apart. Olmsted had the distinct sense that Green was schooling him, spooling out political discourse meant to instruct him on how the world really worked. First Viele, now Green:

Olmsted was ever on the alert for the mere hint that someone thought him too much the aesthete, not sufficiently a pragmatist.

Over time, the tension between these two would only grow. Green began to have serious issues with how the project was taking shape. Olmsted's unslakable demand for trees, Vaux's twenty-five extra bridges, a color-crazed bandstand—all of this cost money, and by the summer of 1859, the construction of Central Park had already run double the original $1.5 million budget. By some estimates, the project was going to come in at upwards of $8 million.

What of Mary? What about Mary Perkins Olmsted, brother John's widow? In the years since John's death, she had been traveling in a vast geographic spiral, slow and sad, stretching across two continents and an ocean. That first winter, Mary and her three small children had gone to Switzerland. Then it was on to Boston for a while, to live with her relatives, and to Hartford, visiting Olmsted's father. From there, she moved to Staten Island, returning to Tosomock Farm, where she had spent her years as a newlywed. But there were too many old memories and ahead loomed another winter and the possibility of being stranded on a farm, so Mary just kept on moving, her spiral growing ever tighter.

Mary was a tiny woman, less than five feet. She was sharp-witted, per the knives poem, and there was also a marked toughness about her. Mary had dealt with great loss before—she had been orphaned as a child—and she was nothing if not a survivor.

She moved to Manhattan and took a place on 79th Street, one of the only paved streets that far uptown back then. It was right down the way from Wagstaff House, where Olmsted worked. Mary signed a lease agreement, and Olmsted served as a witness.

Olmsted had had a curious quasi flirtation with Mary before she had married his brother. "Just the thing for a rainy day" is how he once described her to Kingsbury, "not to fall in love with, but to talk with." After a string of youthful setbacks, Olmsted had resigned himself to never getting married.

But things had a way of coming to Olmsted. Now came Mary, borne on sadness. John's dying words to him had been: "Don't let Mary suffer while you are alive."

On June 13, 1859, Frederick Law Olmsted and Mary Perkins Olmsted were married in Central Park. The small ceremony took place in a house on Bogardus Hill. She brought three children to the marriage, John Charles (age six), Charlotte (age four), and Owen (nearly two). Olmsted would adopt his brother's children and raise them as his own.

Olmsted asked the board to allow him and his new family to move into Mount St. Vincent, a recently vacated Catholic convent at roughly 109th Street, in what then as now was the northern less-developed section of Central Park. Vaux and his family planned to move in, too. The convent had several large, glass-enclosed galleries where the children could play, even on a chilly day. There were so many children now: Mary's three and Vaux's three, Downing, Bowyer, and the infant, Julia.

Olmsted and Vaux had created Central Park, and now they intended to live in their own majestic creation.

CHAPTER 13

Growling Green

FOR OLMSTED, EVEN *newly*wed bliss proved fleeting. He was thirty-seven years old, and Mary twenty-nine, with the weight of recent sorrow and children thrown into the bargain, so even at the outset their union was no frolic. They didn't take a honeymoon—a tradition that was only just beginning at this time. Instead, they spent their first months together tending their brood through constant illness. "There is not one of us in moderate health," Olmsted wrote his father, "and never less than three that need careful nursing & bolstering." Charley (Olmsted's nickname for little John Charles) was suffering from some kind of eye condition. Charlotte developed a rash and was covered in sores. Mary, he reported, was distracted by a "multitude of anxieties." But he tried to put the best face on his account, adding: "We have a good deal of happiness between the drops; that's a fact."

By September 1859, Olmsted had fallen ill as well, suffering from a crushing bout of insomnia and depression. Two years of ceaseless effort on Central Park, and he had worked himself into a state. "I feel just thoroughly worn-out, used up, fatigued beyond recovery, an older man than you," he wrote his father. He went to Saratoga Springs for a week of recuperation but returned feeling no better. For another week, he simply lay on a sofa, doing nothing. Mary read to him. And he ingested a variety of substances including mercury, quinine, "bitters," and "effervescents"—the last two items being lingo of the day for medicinal spirits.

It's curious—perhaps telling—that Olmsted suffered this breakdown only months into his marriage. It's also tempting to tag Olmsted with a mental-illness diagnosis. The periods of frantic activity followed by stuporous lows are in keeping with the condition now known as bipolar disorder. Then again, he suffered from so many different conditions during his lifetime: chronic insomnia, hypochondria, crippling anxiety, a periodic and unexplained ringing in his ears. There's also the puzzling poison-sumac blindness incident from age fourteen, which would be echoed later in his life. Taken together, Olmsted was a bouillabaisse of symptoms.

Because notions about mental health were so different, Olmsted is best understood in the context of his times. He was a person who periodically slipped into a variety of tumultuous emotional states. During the nineteenth century, this was understood as the wages of life, especially for people of a sensitive, artistic temperament. There were even conventions in place for managing such tumult. Society allowed people to have full-on breakdowns in which they temporarily retreated from life (to a sanitarium, if they had the means) and then returned to the world, renewed.

The Central Park commissioners voted to send Olmsted on a trip to Europe and even advanced him $500 for expenses. The board's motive was hydra-headed. The trip was meant as a rest cure to ensure that Olmsted could complete Central Park. It was also a bonus, a reward for the excellent job he had done so far. Officially, the trip was billed as an idea-gathering mission, a chance for Olmsted to visit various European parks and collect insights for use back home. Of course, the construction of Central Park was well along, and what hadn't been done had been planned. The time for gathering design inspiration was long past.

In addition to all that, a lengthy trip furnished the opportunity for a palace coup. The board was considering some changes in the way the park project was managed. They were the final authority: They could do as they pleased, when they pleased. Still, the planned changes would be easier to accomplish while Olmsted was deposed from Central Park, even if only temporarily.

On September 28, 1859, Olmsted set sail from New York for Liverpool aboard the *Persia*. Three people—Mary, Vaux, and Olmsted's father—accompanied him to the pier. After seeing him off, the three boarded a

Staten Island-bound ferry, and Mary convinced the captain to break from his usual course, instead steering the ferry in a wide arc around Olmsted's ship as it headed out to sea. Mary could see passengers arranged along the ship's railing, tiny specks, and she spotted one she thought might be Olmsted. She waved.

During the voyage, Olmsted was bemused by the mundane way passengers passed their time, mostly playing cards. He remained in his cabin, working on the index of his book *A Journey in the Back Country*. But he did go above deck occasionally to study the sea and to watch the sailors at work. This was work with which he was quite familiar.

Olmsted sent Mary a letter from the *Persia*, addressed "Dear little woman at home," and included an account, meant for Charley's benefit, of the ocean life he'd spotted: "Tell Charly [*sic*] I saw five whales, altogether, snorting and turning somersets (so it looked) in the water. Lots of birds, floating and flying, and once, a little sparrow, several hundred miles from land, too tired to move more, dropped on deck and allowed itself to be caught. It is alive—and the sailors keeping it."

On October 11, Olmsted arrived at Liverpool. He visited Birkenhead Park, a place he had first seen during his 1850 walking tour of England and one that influenced the design of Central Park.

Then Olmsted, so recently languishing on a sofa, went off like a slingshot. He visited the Derby Arboretum, the gardens at Chatsworth, the Forest of Windsor. He went to Aston Park and the Birmingham Botanical Gardens. Over the next few weeks, he would visit dozens of parks and gardens in six different countries, taking in some of Europe's finest examples of landscaping.

Olmsted didn't confine his activities to mere grounds walking. In Birmingham, he met with an engineer and arranged for a tour of the sewerage and filtering works. Birmingham's mayor furnished Olmsted with details and statistics on policing the city's parks. In London, he conducted a lengthy interview with Sir Richard Mayne, commissioner of the police force. Once again, Olmsted obtained details on the methods for policing a large city park.

Word of Olmsted's Central Park feat had reached England. As a consequence, the superintendents of all of London's public parks were placed at his disposal. He visited Hyde Park, St. James's Park, and the other West End parks, some of them again and again. He obtained the plans for all of them.

The weather was terrible; it rained virtually nonstop. After a day's delay, waiting for gale-force winds to subside, Olmsted crossed the Channel to France, where rain continued unabated. He visited parks in Versailles and Saint-Cloud, along with the Jardin du Luxembourg. He met with Jean-Charles Adolphe Alphand, an engineer playing a crucial role in Napoléon III's renovation of Paris. Among other things, Alphand had overseen the recent transformation of the Bois de Boulogne from a forest into a landscaped park. During two weeks in Paris, Olmsted visited the Bois de Boulogne on eight separate occasions. He then went to Brussels and Munich and Lille, an industrial town in northern France, known for it boulevards and squares.

Then it was back to England, where news of Central Park awaited. While Olmsted was abroad, Mary had completed the planned move, and his new family was now living at Mount St. Vincent. Something else had happened during his trip: On October 6, while Olmsted was traveling on the *Persia*, the board had elected Andrew Green to the newly created position of comptroller. It would fall to Green to get the park's runaway budget under control.

Even in Olmsted's absence, bachelor Green had continued his practice of fortnightly dining at the Olmsted household. With his recent promotion, Mary found him more insufferable than ever. "I must confess he frets me with his manner of thinking himself so much more efficient than you or anybody else," she wrote in a letter that reached Olmsted in England. Another letter from Mary, dated exactly two weeks later and following another Green dinner, stated simply, "Green here. . . . He growled a great deal."

Olmsted also received a letter from Vaux. "Upon my word Olmsted," wrote Vaux, "I will *not* forgive you if you do not make a better show." He chided Olmsted for lately cutting such a "lugubrious sallow bloodless figure," before adding a curious line: "I consider that the only thing to be really regretted in our last two years operations is the absence of jollity."

Absence of jollity. While creating something of beauty, Vaux seemed to imply, Olmsted hadn't experienced any joy himself. Why, he hadn't even gone ice skating on the Lake. But now matters were spinning out of control. Green was ascending, and Olmsted would need to be focused for a possible battle ahead. *Buck up* was the message of Olmsted's worried partner.

News of Green's power grab disturbed Olmsted. But there was nothing to be done at 3,500 miles' remove, so he continued his tour full-tilt, visiting Biddulph Grange, Elvaston Castle, and Stoneleigh Abbey, followed by the Crystal Palace, Charlecote Park, and Trentham, which featured what he deemed the "best private garden in England."

Olmsted met with Samuel Parsons, a Queens, New York, nurseryman who was in England on a tree-buying mission for Central Park. He dropped by a bookseller and purchased four titles: *Forest Planter, Parks of London, Sowerby's Farms and Farm Allies*, and John Ruskin's *The Two Paths: Being Lectures on Art and Its Application to Decoration and Manufacture*. As an ardent admirer of Ruskin, the celebrated British social critic, Olmsted was pleased to get a copy of *The Two Paths*, hot off the presses, and based on lectures Ruskin had delivered during the previous two years.

Olmsted also commissioned pioneering photographer Roger Fenton to take some pictures. Fenton's images of the recent Crimean War had shocked the British public, just as Mathew Brady's of the Civil War would shock Americans. Fenton's spare *Valley of the Shadow of Death*—featuring no soldiers, only spent cannonballs in the aftermath of battle—is considered *the* seminal war photo. For Olmsted, Fenton took forty-eight pictures of Regent's Park.

After a visit to Dublin for one last flash of green, Phoenix Park, Olmsted traveled to Cork, where he boarded a Cunard liner headed home.

During his earlier 1850 trip, Olmsted had been a rambling farmer. He had returned as a park maker, viewing the landscape through fresh eyes. The mass of ideas he gathered would swirl around in his fertile brain for years to come, furnishing creative sparks for future designs.

Olmsted arrived home just before Christmas, 1859. He brought a dress from Paris for Mary and a silver spoon for Vaux's infant daughter, Julia—a

gift from Vaux's sister, who lived in London. "I return with greatly improved health," announced Olmsted.

Back at Central Park, Olmsted waited for the other shoe to fall. Green
was the new comptroller, but that didn't seem to have any consequences
just yet. Olmsted returned to work, drawing on the one part of his new
store of park knowledge that had immediate application—policing. This
had long been an area of focus—some would say obsession—for Olmsted.
As he had once told the board: "A large part of the people of New York are
ignorant of a park, properly so-called. They will need to be trained in the
proper use of it, to be restrained in the abuse of it." Olmsted may have envisioned Central Park as a haven of democracy. But a public park, as he
was keenly aware, also needed to be protected against the public.

Before his Europe trip, Olmsted had organized a security detail known
as the park keepers. More than fifty of them were hired, and their $1.50-
a-day salaries were paid directly out of the Central Park budget. Olmsted's force, derisively called "sparrow cops," wore gray uniforms with
brass buttons and gloves, distinguishing them from New York City police
officers, who wore blue. The keepers maintained strict discipline, not
speaking to the public unless spoken to first.

During 1859, Central Park had an estimated 2 million visitors. The
park keepers made 228 arrests for infractions ranging from drunkenness
to loitering to assault. No murders happened in the park in 1859; there
would be only a couple during the first three decades of the park's history.
Still, despite crime's relative rarity, anyone apprehended by a park keeper
faced severe punishment. One of the first arrests was a man who had
stolen a pair of ice skates. To make an example of him, a judge sentenced
the man to thirty days in jail.

After conferring with an assortment of English constables during his
trip, Olmsted appears to have opted for a complete turnabout to a more
passive policing strategy. He returned to America convinced that the
keepers' hostile demeanor toward the public had actually been counterproductive. The mere presence of the keepers in the park should serve as
a crime deterrent. Beyond that, Olmsted concluded, it probably made
more sense for the keepers to concentrate on something like community
outreach—call it park outreach. The force's new responsibilities, as

spelled out in a notice Olmsted posted, were to "direct strangers to different parts of the park, to instruct them as to distances, size, purposes, costs &c. of different objects in the park."

Making arrests was downplayed; there would be fewer than 100 in each of the next five years. Park keepers were now closer to park rangers. Olmsted even devised quizzes for his force to make sure they were properly versed in the park's latest features and aware of arcane trivia—just in case they were asked.

How, then, to make sure rules were enforced? Signs. Olmsted installed signs, hundreds of signs. One of the most ubiquitous was the following:

Central Park Visitors are Warned
Not to walk upon the grass; (except of the Commons)
Not to pick any flowers, leaves, twigs, fruits or nuts;
Not to deface, scratch or mark the seats or other constructions;
Not to throw stones or other missiles;
Not to annoy the birds;
Not to publicly use provoking or indecent language;
Not to offer any articles for sale.

Disregard of the above warnings, or any acts of disorder, subject the offender to arrest and fine or imprisonment.

Olmsted was finding that he had a knack for park administration just as much as park making. He posted speed limits: five miles per hour for carriages, six for horses. And he also set aside designated spots where visitors could leave carriages, an innovation that he was among the first to employ. In fact, the innovation was so cutting-edge that no term for it yet existed, so Olmsted called these spots "carriage rests." During the twentieth century, planners would also need a place where an automobile could be left, and some anonymous wordsmith finally dreamed up a suitable term—*parking space.*

Green began to growl again. Olmsted had known that it would be only a matter of time, and soon enough his nemesis was all over him. Green

stripped Olmsted of his $200 a week in discretionary spending and in-
stituted a new rule that any proposed expenditures had to first be run
past him.

When Olmsted requested $28 for a new red signal ball for ice skat-
ing, Green questioned the expense. When Olmsted requested money
for some additional rock blastings, Green asked whether such work
was necessary or "merely desirable." Soon their never-easy friendship
had devolved into a series of petty memo battles, such as the following
exchange.

Green composed a memo, complaining that some willow trees had
been cut down without his approval: "It is quite expensive to get trees
on the Park, and I hope nothing in shape of a tree will be cut."

"None were cut except as I had designated—worthless of course,"
wrote Olmsted.

Then Green again: "I recollect the willows very well, and do not
agree with you that they were worthless. I think they should have been
preserved."

Green was actually a very able administrator. Years in the future, he
would serve as comptroller for the City of New York, helping untangle
the financial mess left behind by the notorious Tweed administration.
He was also a tireless advocate for consolidating outlying communities
such as Brooklyn and Staten Island into New York City proper, something that happened in 1898. Green had also backed up Olmsted in his
fight against Dillon and Belmont. Though Olmsted refused to see it,
Green truly had in mind the best interests of the park, an undertaking
currently headed for a budget cliff. But it was Green's manner that irritated Olmsted mightily.

Olmsted was aware that he was creating something grand—the reviews were rolling in, and the park was packed with visitors—and he
didn't appreciate having some bureaucrat pinching pennies. Green, in
turn, picked up on this attitude and was bent on teaching Olmsted a
real-world lesson. Green was all for art. Run out of money, though, and
you could say good-bye to art.

When a paycheck was erroneously issued to a Central Park employee
who had actually been absent from work, Green dashed off yet another

memo: "Although an error is not a crime, yet in money matters it is a very serious affair." To Olmsted, this was just one more piece of galling Green pedantry.

A welcome diversion arrived on June 14, 1860. "Just in the earliest flush of dawn," Olmsted wrote his father, "—the birds all singing—the boy came, with a great cry."

Although Mary already had a child named John Charles (Charley), the newborn was christened John Theodore, after Olmsted's brother. He weighed ten and a half pounds, huge for a tiny woman like Mary. This was Fred's first child, and he was delighted that the baby had "a three cornered nose and other 'Olmsted' marks, which Mary sees better than I do."

John Theodore was delivered at home with a doctor in attendance. The extended family at Mount St. Vincent—Vaux's children, too— were delighted by the new addition, well, all except Charlotte, who had been counting on a baby sister. It had been far and away Mary's hardest labor. She rested comfortably now. She described her newborn as a "young pugilist."

With a new baby in the household, Olmsted began casting about for additional work besides Central Park. He had another mouth to feed, but the far greater motivator seems to have been his innate restlessness. Even in the midst of a vast undertaking, even with a newborn, Olmsted had a surfeit of capacity, and he simply had to find an outlet. What's more, he was drawn to the prospect of working with someone, anyone, besides Green.

Vaux joined Olmsted in looking for extra work. Throughout the Central Park project, he had maintained his architectural office on Broadway, though his practice had gone moribund. In pursuing new commissions, the pair worked out of this office rather than the Central Park office so as to avoid any impropriety. As a moonlighting job, Olmsted and Vaux designed the grounds of the Hillside Cemetery in Middletown, New York. They also did some work for a government commission, providing recommendations on how the streets above 155th (a part of Manhattan left off the 1811 grid) should be laid out. Their report was never even published. But the project is notable because in correspondence the client refers to Olmsted and Vaux as "landscape architects."

Working on Central Park, they had certainly acted in this capacity. But so far—during a two-year association featuring thousands of pieces of correspondence and thousands of newspaper articles—Olmsted and Vaux had never once been referred to as "landscape architects." This was a first. Several more years would pass—and there would be some serious convolutions along the way—before the two settled into a formal partnership working in this capacity.

There was also the prospect of park work in Brooklyn. Vaux accompanied James Stranahan, a businessman and civic booster, to look at sites. New York City had its Central Park, and Stranahan was keen on keeping pace in the nearby but separate city of Brooklyn. He and Vaux visited a number of potential sites, but Vaux didn't find any of them suitable for a park.

Yet another sideline was designing the grounds surrounding a couple of mental institutions, the Retreat for the Insane in Hartford, Connecticut, and the Bloomingdale Asylum in New York City, on the current site of Columbia University. Olmsted and Vaux partnered on both these, but the designs reflect Olmsted's singular vision. This was an area of special interest for him.

As a boy, Olmsted had read *Solitude,* a book by Swiss physician Johann Georg Zimmermann that discussed the powerful ability of scenery to ease a person's melancholy. Growing up in Hartford, Olmsted had also been exposed to the ideas of the Reverend Horace Bushnell. Bushnell frequently preached about something called "unconscious influence." This was the reverend's term for the striking ways that people's spiritual states can be shaped by their environments. Bushnell had been the Brace family's minister, though not the Olmsteds'—stepmother Mary Ann Olmsted considered his views too radical. But Olmsted was familiar with Bushnell and even once asked Brace to send him some of the minister's writings on "unconscious influence."

Now, called upon to landscape a couple of mental institutions, Olmsted drew on the ideas he'd been exposed to in youth. The Hartford Retreat had been just the third asylum in the United States when it opened in 1824. John Olmsted had donated money to help get it started. Over the years, the grounds had become overgrown with trees and shrubbery.

Olmsted's plan called for clearing the grounds to create a wide-open meadow that rolled gently down toward the Connecticut River in the distance. Unlike Central Park, he aimed for a minimum of drama—no passages of scenery, no hulking specimen trees, branches snaking out, leaves vibrating with color. To enclose the meadow, he proposed a simple scrim of trees. This would shut out sights and sounds from the nearby city.

John Butler, the Hartford Retreat's superintendent, was thrilled when he received the plan. He grasped immediately that the design was meant to, as Butler put it, "Kill out the Lunatic Hospital and develop the Home."

As an avowed social reformer, Olmsted took the plight of the mentally ill very seriously, a stark contrast to many of his nineteenth-century contemporaries. And as a person who suffered a variety of torturous mental states, Olmsted had a deep empathy for fellow sufferers. This, in turn, lent him preternatural insight when designing asylum grounds.

In the years ahead, Olmsted would frequently take on mental-institution commissions. Invariably, his designs would seek to provide a sense of calm, a feeling so sorely lacking in his own life.

CHAPTER 14

Swans

ON AUGUST 6, 1860, Olmsted took a ride in an open buggy through upper Manhattan, accompanied by Mary and the baby, John Theodore. His buggy was harnessed to a horse that he was looking to buy.

Exhausted from overwork, per usual, Olmsted fell asleep. The reins slipped from his hands. The horse bolted. Olmsted snapped to and seized the reins, but as the buggy whipped around a corner, one of its wheels rolled over the base of a lamppost. The buggy upended, and all three passengers were thrown clear. Mary landed on her back, clutching the baby to her chest. Miraculously, both were unharmed. But Olmsted was dashed against an outcropping of rock.

He lay in the road, writhing in pain, his shattered left thighbone jutting through a tear in his pants. Mary raced to a nearby house for help. In a bizarre coincidence, the house belonged to Charles Trask, fifth wheel of the "uncommon set." Olmsted hadn't seen him in years. Trask's wife removed a large shutter from her house's window, and the shutter was carried out to the street where Olmsted lay. Bystanders lifted him onto the shutter, an improvised stretcher, and carried him into the Trask house.

Doctors were summoned, among them Willard Parker, a onetime teacher of Olmsted's brother John, yet another coincidence. It quickly became clear that this was a very serious injury. Olmsted's left thigh was broken in three places. Amputation was an option, but after conferring, the doctors agreed that his condition was too precarious. The procedure would surely kill him. Left alone, he might live for a week. The next morning, Olmsted, carried into the Trask house on a shutter, was carried out on a bier and back to Mount St. Vincent to die. Dr. Parker put Olmsted's odds of survival at one in one hundred.

But he lived through a day. Then another and another. On the eighth day following the accident, little John Theodore died. The date—August 14, 1860—was his three-month birthday. The official cause was infant cholera. In Fred's and Mary's minds, these two events—the carriage crash and the death of their baby—would forever be linked. How could they not be? Mary was inconsolable. She took to her bed and remained there for days, racked by excruciating headaches and incalculable grief.

Within ten days of his accident, just two days after John Theodore's death, Olmsted was back on the job. Following the loss of his brother, work had proved a balm for Olmsted, and so it would again, following the loss of his brother's namesake. Slowly, painfully, he arranged himself into a sitting position on the floor of his bedroom. Then he pored over a set of Central Park maps, arrayed before him.

Very soon, Olmsted was moving around in the world again. His left leg—so severely damaged that it would remain two inches shorter for the rest of his life—was set with a splint and bandaged tightly from hip to toe. Employees carried him from place to place in Central Park on a makeshift litter. Sometimes it was necessary for Olmsted to examine a park feature not so easily accessed in a litter. The attendants would lower him to the ground. Then Olmsted would use his hands and his one good leg to propel himself awkwardly through the underbrush, his wounded and bandaged leg outstretched and dragging behind. It was an arduous, excruciating form of locomotion.

Olmsted was doubly anxious to get back to work because Green had assumed his responsibilities following the accident. Olmsted didn't want to lose control of Central Park. Green, for his part, was remarkably unsympathetic to everything Olmsted had just endured. Friends sent Olmsted bottles of wine and books and awkward notes of condolence. "Whilst expressing my deep regret for the Calamity which has again befallen you," begins a note from an engineer employed at the park.

There is no record of Green sending anything. By now, thanks to the memo battles, the park's precarious finances, and the ceaseless sniping, their friendship had simply imploded, and grace and civility were no longer possible. Olmsted and Green had each lost all sense of perspective where the other was concerned. As winter came on, Green refused to honor a requisition for coal to keep Olmsted's office warm. Green insisted on several separate meetings before he agreed to reimburse an outlay of twelve and a half cents! To Vaux, Olmsted later described Green's manner as "a systematic small tyranny, measured exactly to the limit of my endurance." To a friend, Olmsted wrote, "Not a cent is got from under his paw that is not wet with his blood & sweat."

As 1860 came to an end, things came to a head. Going into the year, the board had asked Olmsted to prepare careful estimates for the cost of park construction. Now, at year's end, it became clear that actual costs had drastically outstripped the estimates. At Green's urging, Olmsted went over and over the numbers, but try as he might, he was unable to arrive at an exact number for the cost overrun. (For the record, the main period of construction in Central Park cost $8 million, more than five times the original appropriation.)

Green's goading was maddening, but deep down what really smarted for Olmsted was the inability to arrive at a precise number. He prided himself on achieving a rare combination, both artist and administrator. This required a grasp of the data: 288 park keeper arrests in 1859, $30 to be paid to a contractor for each transplanted elm that survives three years. Numbers are the currency of the practical realm, and with Green as his witness, Olmsted had busted an annual budget and couldn't even account for the discrepancy.

Given the situation, Olmsted opted for the only suitable course. He decided to resign. He didn't want to go, but he took comfort at least in the fact that the bulk of the work was complete. Of course, Central Park wasn't finished, never really would be in the final way of a Vermeer or the Beatles' *Sgt. Pepper*. It is, after all, a kind of living artwork. But by the end of 1860, Olmsted and Vaux had placed their stamp on Central Park, inexorably. As Olmsted had recently written to his father, "I have fixed what I most cared for on the park beyond reconsideration."

Olmsted's resignation letter was forty-one pages long, full of self-laceration, grand claims, petty excuses, and digressions about art, finance, and god-knows-what. Although the letter was meant for the entire board, it repeatedly employed the salutation "Sir," as in: "It is humiliating to me, Sir, to be dealt with in this way." Perhaps this was a rhetorical device, intended by Olmsted to create a sense of intimacy, as if he was addressing a single person rather than an entire board. Maybe Olmsted was addressing a single person—Green.

Olmsted's resignation is a wild and woolly document. Just as Vaux's bumbling manner somehow managed to convey a passion for art, something also shone through these forty-one rambling pages. "I love the park," Olmsted wrote. "I rejoice in it and am too much fastened to it in every fibre of my character to give up. . . . I don't care a copper for myself, Sir, or for what becomes of me, but I do care for the park, which will last long after I'm dead and gone, years & years, I hope."

The board talked Olmsted down. Even Green appears to have been moved. Olmsted was persuaded to stay on, and it was even agreed that his resignation letter would be stricken from the minutes of the meeting at which it was considered. The board needed this man who had designed and then executed a masterpiece out of stone and turf and trees.

The winter of 1860–1861 was another severe one for New York City. When the snow finally melted, a reporter for the *New York World* decided to visit Central Park. The reporter was surprised to see virtually no one there.

It was the middle of the week in a kind of in-between season. The skaters, the people who came by the thousands to ride horse-drawn sleighs, the Scottish immigrants who enjoyed the sport of curling on a frozen corner of the Lake—all had departed with the first thaw. The horseback riders, Dodworth concertgoers, Ramble perambulators, and baseball players were yet to arrive.

The previous summer, Central Park had already seen its first baseball games, and there's even a newspaper account of a game where the Atlantic, a team from Brooklyn, bested the Liberty, hailing from New Brunswick, New Jersey. "The pitching appeared to get the best of the batting," laments the account. The final score: 15–10.

On this particular day, however, the reporter from the *World* noted only the first crocuses poking up out of the ground. And he saw that there were swans on the Lake. There had been swans the previous year, though they had died, perhaps victims of foul play. Many people suspected that they had been poisoned. But now there were new ones. The reporter counted about forty.

Over the same lake so recently a glaze of ice, tracing and retracing the same paths where the skaters had glided and tumbled and laughed, the swans now traveled . . . silent, intent.

IV
"Heroes Along with the Rest"

CIVIL WAR SERVICE,

1861–1863

CHAPTER 15

In Search of a Mission

APRIL 12, 1861, 4:30 a.m.: Rebels open fire on Fort Sumter in Charleston Harbor. Civil war, long a threat hanging over the nation, has broken out.

Olmsted immediately started searching for a way to contribute. Because his leg was still terribly damaged from the carriage accident the previous year, because he was still on crutches, Olmsted watched in frustration as his underlings at Central Park enlisted and headed down to Washington.

Olmsted hungered to be involved, even though this was such a turnabout from the task he was just then completing. Central Park was a rarefied artwork of utmost majesty; war promised to be brutal and soul-scarring. Yet for Olmsted, the two were strangely similar. Olmsted viewed the world as a social reformer, first and foremost. Designing a pleasure ground to edify the citizens of a growing metropolis was a noble cause in peacetime. Now it was war. Pleasure grounds were soon to give way to battlegrounds, and joining the cause was the proper course.

He considered joining the navy, something that would allow him to draw on his experience of sailing to China as a young man. He sent a letter urging his sixty-nine-year-old father to join the navy, too. Olmsted also assembled some members of the park police into a home guard. He led them in military drills, but it felt like mere pageantry in the face of a mounting crisis.

Ultimately, Olmsted would find the sense of purpose he so keenly desired with the United States Sanitary Commission, a battlefield-relief outfit. The USSC is now largely forgotten but was of incalculable importance in its day. Over the course of the Civil War, under Olmsted's leadership, the USSC—in the assessment of distinguished historian Allan Nevins—grew into "the most powerful organization for lessening the horrors and reducing the losses of war which mankind had thus far produced."

But first the USSC would get off to a terribly choppy start, and its survival would be uncertain. Olmsted's tenure in the capital would be marked by extreme impatience, particularly at the outset. He'd grown used to making rapid-fire change in his own life. Washington felt so sluggish by contrast. Seven decades after its founding, the city remained a work in progress, in many ways less complete than Central Park. And the leadership in Washington struck Olmsted as terribly ineffectual. At times, it would fill him with disgust.

This was an earnest stance, naive even, but terribly useful in wartime. The stakes were truly high. Olmsted was someone who genuinely *believed* that big things could be done quickly.

While Olmsted would become the recognized public face of the USSC (the "famous Olmsted," said an awestruck soldier ministered to by FLO himself), it was not his brainchild. In fact, the USSC has its origins in one of those uniquely American grassroots movements.

Eight days after Sumter, a patriotic rally was held in New York City's Union Square (named for the union of two main streets, though the choice of venue seems apropos). An estimated 100,000 people were present, at the time the largest gathering in U.S. history. Major Robert Anderson was the big draw and he arrived bearing the very flag—thirty-three stars representing the thirty-three states in the now dissolved Union—that had been lowered when he surrendered Fort Sumter to General Beauregard. Major Anderson placed the flag in the stony grip of a statue of George Washington on horseback. The crowd went wild.

After the Union Square rally, Major Anderson continued to travel through the North with his Sumter flag on a kind of fire-up-the-Union tour. The results were stunning. Men enlisted in droves. Women formed relief societies in places like Lowell, Massachusetts, and Newport, Rhode

Island. They busied themselves sewing blankets, preserving fruit, gathering lint for dressing wounds—all to aid the soldiers who would soon be heading off to battle.

One of these outfits was the Women's Central Association of Relief, a group of New York City society women. They contacted the Reverend Henry Bellows, an Olmsted acquaintance, and asked the reverend to lend focus to their work. Apparently, the relief group approached Bellows because of a nineteenth-century convention holding that women required male oversight when participating in heady civic matters. According to an old history of the USSC, "Without concert of effort and a clear idea of common goals these devoted women might waste their zeal and produce as much harm as good from their excitement."

The women could not have lit on a better choice than Bellows, though. A transplanted New Englander and graduate of the Harvard Divinity School, Bellows was known for his urbane sermons, generously laced with progressive social ideas. His congregation at the All Souls Church included some of New York's most influential citizens, such as William Cullen Bryant, industrialist Peter Cooper, and Moses Grinnell, a prominent merchant. Like Olmsted, like so many Americans at the onset of the Civil War, Bellows was searching about for a way to be meaningfully involved. He seized on the women's war relief group. As it happens, he had his own brilliant notions about expanding its mission and making it much more than a local New York City aid society.

Bellows envisioned a central organization that could coordinate the activities of all the various women's relief outfits—Hartford, Cleveland, and Lowell—lately cropping up across the Union. Items such as blankets the women made, supplies like shoes that were donated, and money that was raised—all of it could be so much better used if it were funneled from the local relief societies into some kind of national clearinghouse.

Bellows had an ambitious vision for this new organization. Besides acting as a central supply depot, the relief outfit, as Bellows saw it, could act as an adviser to the woefully shorthanded Medical Bureau, still staffed for a peacetime army. Surgeons at the front were likely to be poorly trained and overwhelmed by the sheer scale of the carnage. Maybe Bellow's group could circulate monographs filled with sanitary advice, *sanitary*—in nineteenth-century parlance—meaning hygiene and cleanliness practices that could prevent disease. Perhaps it could also disseminate medical best practices, gleaned during recent Continental wars.

During the 1850s, Britain and its allies had fought Russia in the Crimean War, a punishing conflict for control of a Black Sea peninsula. Within months of the war's outbreak, the death rate among British troops had climbed to a startling annualized clip of more than 100 percent. Statistically speaking, that meant the entire army was on track to be dead within less than a year!

Still more disturbing, 97 percent of the deaths happened not on the battlefield but in makeshift barracks hospitals from diseases such as typhus, cholera, and dysentery. The cause was obvious: The hospitals in Crimea were grossly overcrowded and relied on Dark Ages hygienic practices. In response, the British Sanitary Commission was created to clean up the pestilent barracks hospitals and change the military's medical culture. Within a year, mortality had plummeted to an annualized rate of 25 out of 1,000 men.

Now, as the Civil War began, Bellows proposed a similar outfit, dubbed the United States Sanitary Commission. Bellows assembled a board of notable men. Among them were prominent citizens such as George Templeton Strong, a New York City lawyer, and distinguished doctors such as Elisha Harris, chief physician of the quarantine hospital on Staten Island. There were career military officers and members of the government, such as Alexander Bache, superintendent of the U.S. Coast Survey and a great-grandson of Ben Franklin. Bellows rounded out his board with Oliver Wolcott Gibbs, America's most accomplished chemist.

The reverend went to Washington to lobby for the USSC. Thanks to his intense commitment, he was able to get his idea up for consideration very quickly. The army's Medical Bureau did not like the notion of an outside body meddling in its affairs. But the bureau was willing to countenance the USSC so long as it confined its activities to providing supplies and the occasional piece of advice. Lincoln was also less than enamored of the idea; a sanitary commission struck him as unnecessary. But the enterprise slipped past as he settled into the vast, thorny business of executing a war. On June 13, he signed an executive order launching the USSC. "I approve the above. A. Lincoln," he wrote.

Bellows immediately turned his attention to finding a general secretary, essentially a chief executive officer to run this new outfit. The reverend had in mind Olmsted, who at thirty-nine was eight years his junior. Bellows was familiar with Olmsted's work because, as a sometime journalist himself, he had written an article about Central Park for the *Atlantic*. Olmsted, in turn, had once approached Bellows about contributing to *Putnam's Magazine*. The reverend was also a founder of the Century Club, which counted Olmsted as a member. Bellows described Olmsted as "long-headed," a high compliment that implied prescience and foresight.

A lot had changed in a few short years. When he landed the initial job as Central Park superintendent, there had been doubts about Olmsted's administrative experience. At the time, he'd never managed more than eight people. Viele had questioned his pragmatism. But Olmsted's work had gained him a national reputation as a talented administrator.

Still, nothing in Olmsted's background really qualified him to run a medical commission. Then again, nothing had prepared him to design a park. America was still in the grip of a pioneer spirit that valued derring-do over narrow specialization. This was doubly so with the outbreak of war; a kind of all-hands-on-deck attitude was now in sway.

On June 20, 1861, Olmsted was offered the job and immediately accepted. In a letter to his half-sister Bertha, he described his new post: "It is a good big work I have in hand, giving me absorbing occupation and the sort of connection with the work of the nation without which I should be very uncomfortable." He was granted a leave of absence from Central Park with the understanding that he would return periodically from Washington to continue work on the project. It was nearing completion, in any case. There would be other reasons to return, too. His wife planned to stay in New York. She was pregnant.

Olmsted traveled to Washington by train. While making this same journey a decade before, he'd had his first glimpses of slavery. Now he witnessed his first evidence of a nation at war. Outside Havre de Grace,

Maryland, he spotted a sign scratched in charcoal: "Bloody 11th Camp C." As the train rolled on, he began to see scattered encampments with little groups of soldiers, squatting in front of tents, tending fires, muskets leaned together.

Olmsted arrived in Washington at sundown and took a carriage to his hotel. The first sight that greeted him was the Capitol building, sitting on a low hill in an arrested state of repair. Its marble wings were unfinished; scaffolding surrounded a new, larger dome then under construction. The Washington Monument, half built, rose above a scruffy mall. Landscaping efforts had stalled in the aftermath of Downing's death; the ambitious park that Downing and Vaux had been commissioned to design had never been realized.

This was not the seat of a mighty war machine . . . not yet. It was really nothing more than a large town, population 75,000, according to the 1860 census. Even the major thoroughfares were largely unpaved and lined with stables and saloons, boardinghouses and little shops. Official Washington was represented by just a scattering of structures, including the redbrick headquarters of the Navy, State, and War departments and the Greek Revival building where Treasury resided. The White House, circa 1861, opened onto a small park where anyone could amble, right up to the front door.

Still, this was the capital. In fact, Southerners had until recently held designs on making Washington capital of the Confederacy. They might have succeeded had they not been driven off by the small fighting force that trickled into Washington during the first days of the war. The rebels soon took up in Richmond instead. Washington was guarded by a single fort, twelve miles to the south.

Olmsted checked into the Willard, the only halfway respectable hotel in town. It featured bathrooms on every floor, a rare luxury. Until recently, both Union supporters and secessionists had continued to stay at the Willard. To minimize friction, a convention had grown up: Northerners used the Pennsylvania Avenue door, while Southerners used the door on F Street. Now, this was Union territory. While covering the Civil War for the *Atlantic*, Nathaniel Hawthorne would use the Willard as his base.

On his first night, Olmsted undertook his first official duty. He visited one of the camps on the outskirts of Washington. He was issued an official pass, inscribed with an ominous warning: If Olmsted fought against the Union or gave aid to the enemy, he would be subject to the death penalty. After drinking a brandy with a group of officers, he bedded down in a tent but had trouble sleeping due to strange noises such as sentinels making their rounds. Next morning, in the light of day, Olmsted was shocked by what he saw. Olmsted visited another nineteen camps in the days ahead, encountering endless variations on the same unsettling themes.

Camps were crowded and filthy, with enlisted men packed five deep into stuffy little wedge tents. Many preferred to sleep outside on the hard ground. Each camp was supposed to have an eight-foot trench that served as a makeshift toilet. It was supposed to be covered once a day with six inches of fresh dirt. This regulation was routinely ignored. The men were in the habit of relieving themselves wherever they could find a free spot. Reaching the edge of camp was a bother at night, a luxury by day.

This was largely a volunteer army, so the enlistees wore whatever they could piece together. Often uniforms were poorly made, and they were anything but *uniform*. Where items were missing the soldiers improvised, going barefoot in boots if they lacked socks, substituting straw hats for caps.

Some took the improvisation to great lengths. Entire regiments were outfitted for a kind of wartime fantasia. In the preceding years, magazines had carried numerous stories about Zouaves, fierce battalions of Algerian soldiers who had sided with the French in North Africa. The exploits of these legendary fighters had captured the popular imagination. As a consequence, a number of so-called Zouave regiments were formed. Fresh-faced Northern recruits emulated the dress of the Algerians, right down to the billowing trousers, wool turbans, and sashes, items appropriate for desert warfare but ridiculous for doing battle along the Atlantic seaboard.

The rations were terrible, the cooks careless. Hardly any fruit or vegetables were available, and scurvy was an ever-present threat. The mainstay was salted beef, foul tasting and leather tough. Though designed to withstand summer heat, by the time it was consumed, it had often gone rancid anyway. Another staple was hardtack: thick, flavorless crackers that had to be soaked in water before one could manage a bite.

But perhaps the most discouraging sign: As Olmsted visited the various camps, he encountered almost no one who could make even the vaguest claim to medical knowledge. Precious little medicine had been stockpiled.

Taken together, Olmsted's camp inspections offer a snapshot of the Union army before it had fought its first major battle. He drew up a report full of dire warnings, such as: "It is now hardly possible to place the volunteer army in a good defensive condition against the pestilential influences by which it must soon be surrounded." In his report, Olmsted offered a series of recommendations. Some were self-evident: Hire better cooks! And some were novel: Maybe a depot could be set up in Washington to greet incoming volunteers. That way, soldiers who arrived ill could be quarantined and kept separate from the crowded camps.

Olmsted's report fell on deaf ears; his recommendations went straight to the dustbin. The army's job was to prepare legions of men for battle, period, and military convention held that privation was a natural state and perhaps a desirable one, too, as it kept the troops focused. The matters Olmsted had raised—diet, hygiene, availability of medicine—were so very soft and secondary.

During his first weeks in Washington, Olmsted was struck by how tawdry and makeshift everything appeared, right down to the USSC's temporary offices in the Treasury building. He was constantly battling the flies—worse than on his Staten Island farm, he noted. Most nights, he worked past midnight before retiring to his stuffy room at the Willard, where he'd lie down still in his clothes, tossing and turning, worrying about money.

Olmsted had accepted the job at the USSC without settling on a salary. He assumed he'd be making something like $2,000 per year. At the same time, he expected to lose something like $2,000 over the next year due to his diminished role with Central Park. Again, nothing definite had been arranged.

While walking to the USSC offices, Olmsted caught his first glimpse of Abraham Lincoln. The president was moving at a brisk clip, headed to the War Department, accompanied by three other men. Olmsted thought the president looked younger than expected. He was put off by the president's style of dress, describing Lincoln as wearing a "cheap & nasty French black cloth suit just out of a tight carpet bag. Looked as if he would be an applicant for a Broadway squad policemanship, but a little too smart and careless."

On another occasion, he spotted Mary Todd Lincoln. Again, his first impression was not favorable. While taking an after-dinner stroll, Olmsted wandered over to the little park in front of the White House. A German marine band was playing Verdi's opera *Nabucco*. Mary Lincoln was standing on the White House's grand portico looking down at the performance. Nearby was Henry Wikoff, an American notorious for his foreign adventures such as advising European royalty, perhaps spying, even—according to rumor—abducting an American heiress in Italy. Wikoff had written an *anti*abolition pamphlet, *A Letter to Viscount Palmerston, K.G., Prime Minister of England, on American Slavery*. Olmsted was troubled that Mary Lincoln appeared so solicitous of Wikoff. During the opera, she smiled at him and followed his conversation with apparent interest. How could the first lady be in the thrall of this "insufferable beast," as Olmsted termed him?

All seemed folly to Olmsted: the fragile Union, its clay-foot leaders, the ragtag army, the toothless USSC. His letters of the time show a growing despondency. "Lincoln has no element of dignity; no tact, not a spark of genius," he writes in one, and in another: "The official machinery is utterly and absurdly inadequate for the emergency & there is no time to think of enlarging it. I feel the whole business is exceedingly uncertain & should not be much surprised to get up & find Jeff Davis in the White House." To Mary, he struck this plaintive note: "Give me some good news of yourself, please, and of the park. I can not get on long without you here."

July 21, 1861: The day had finally arrived for the Union army to be tested by a major battle. Roughly 35,000 troops arrived at Manassas, Virginia, thirty miles southwest of the capital. If they could capture the railroad junction there, then it would be on to Richmond unimpeded. The ninety-day enlistment period for the volunteers was about to end, and as Lincoln well knew, progress was needed.

Because it was a summer Sunday, many of Washington's haut monde, including several congressmen, set out in carriages carrying picnic baskets and wine. The revelers expected to witness a decisive victory, perhaps one that would instantly quell the rebellion.

The two sides engaged near a small creek named Bull Run. By afternoon, they were seesawing back and forth, trying to seize control of Henry House Hill. About four o'clock, reinforcements arrived to help Beauregard's army. They proceeded to break the Union right flank. As wave upon wave of fresh troops poured down Henry House Hill, the Confederates debuted a blood-chilling banshee shriek, what came to be known as the rebel yell.

The Union fell back. Arriving at the main road, the retreating troops were forced to spill around a clot of carriages; the picnickers now headed north. It was then that panic set in.

Olmsted was in New York during Bull Run, but news of the battle reached him quickly. It was a time of high anxiety, as many feared the South would storm the capital. But Confederate troops were also exhausted, so much so that they were unable to take advantage of their victory. Olmsted boarded the next train and returned to a Washington in pandemonium.

Wild-eyed Union soldiers milled in the streets, filthy and unshaven, caps gone, muskets gone, uniforms shredded, many of them barefoot. Some busied themselves tearing up citizens' wooden fence posts to build fires. Others wandered door to door begging for food. Still others lay asleep, heads resting on lampposts, or lay passed out full-length in gutters. "A large portion of our forces were stricken with a most terrible mental disease," Olmsted wrote, "under which all manliness was lost and utmost cowardice, unreasonableness and fiendish inhumanity were developed."

What about the officers? Where were the men who were supposed to be in command? The officers were nowhere to be seen—that is, until Olmsted arrived at the Willard. The hotel's bar and lobby fairly crawled with them. "They, too, were dirty and in an ill-condition," he observed, "but appeared indifferent, reckless, and shameless, rather than dejected and morose. They were talking of the battle, laughing at the incidents of the retreat, and there was an evident inclination among them to exaggerate everything that was disgraceful." Olmsted even recorded a telling snatch of dialogue that he overheard.

Where is your regiment? an officer was asked.

"Completely demoralized, sir; completely demoralized."

But where could it be now? the questioner persisted.

"All disorganized—all disorganized."

But your men simply have to be somewhere?

"I'm told that there are two or three hundred of them together somewhere near the Capitol," said the officer, "but I have not seen them yet since the battle."

Just four days after Bull Run, in his capacity as USSC head, Olmsted launched an inquiry into the causes of the defeat. He drew up a list of seventy-five questions. *How much sleep did you get the night before the battle? What was your most recent meal? How far did you march on the day of July 21?*

Olmsted dispatched seven inspectors, including his friend Brace, to track down the dispersed battle participants and pose the questions. The data were then tabulated by Ezekiel Elliott, a USSC employee who had worked before the war as an actuary for a Boston life insurance firm. To make sense of the first major battle of the Civil War, Olmsted was relying on empirical methods and drawing on his earlier experience as a scientific farmer.

The data was stark. Of twenty-nine regiments surveyed, ten reported that at least a third of their number had simply collapsed from exhaustion before the battle even started. For many of these soldiers, the cause of such breakdown was want of water, food, or sleep. Others had been worn out by the need to march the final miles to battle at a punishing pace known as "double-quick." Combining the march and the retreat, Olmsted determined that the average soldier traveled forty-four miles on foot the day of the battle.

He was even able to provide a side-by-side comparison of two regiments that experienced vastly different outcomes at Bull Run. The 2nd Rhode Island was well rested and well fed, enjoying soft bread, butter, and fresh fruit. To keep up morale, they had a chaplain and even a crack marching band. At Bull Run, the 2nd Rhode Island was first to engage, lost 16 percent of its ranks, but the regiment stood firm while others panicked.

A study in contrast was the Fire Zouaves, a regiment that favored garish desert garb and was composed mostly of New York City firemen. For several nights prior to Bull Run, the soldiers had slept on the ground without tents or blankets. The regiment hadn't been paid, either, leaving many of its members agitated. (Soldiers that volunteered to serve still got paid—$11 a month for an infantry private at the beginning of the war.) The Fire Zouaves were routed at Bull Run.

Olmsted wrote up the findings in the USSC's *Report on the Demoralization of the Volunteers*. His conclusion: The prevailing wisdom about Bull Run was completely backward. The soldiers wandering around Washington weren't demoralized because they had lost in battle. Rather, the *demoralized* Union army had already lost Bull Run before the first shot was fired. This was a provocative idea. To assign a battlefield loss not to botched strategy but to such seemingly ancillary variables as bad diet and lack of sleep was utterly out of step with then-current thinking. Olmsted even called this demoralization a *mental disease*. He was now so far ahead of his time that understanding from his contemporaries was inconceivable. When it came to naming a culprit for the debacle, Olmsted did not flinch. He placed the blame squarely on a government that would send woefully unprepared soldiers to certain death.

The first draft of Olmsted's report hasn't survived. Something of its flavor can be found in a letter to Mary, where he refers to the "imbecility of the government."

Olmsted read the report to an assembled group of USSC colleagues. It was not well received. Board members with government ties, especially, worried about Olmsted's controversial conclusions. The USSC had been created by executive order and could easily be uncreated. The board asked Olmsted to revise his report, a task he did over a weekend. But even in the new draft, Olmsted could not contain his reformer's fire. "Did the government really care at all for the 'brave volunteer?'" writes Olmsted. "If so, why did he sometimes have food that he could not eat, and sometimes none at all, for days together? Why should he be left to sleep in rotten straw and shoddy blankets, and sometimes for months with nothing at all, on the bare ground?"

The board's solution was that Olmsted's report would receive a private printing. In other words, it was to be circulated only within the USSC. A few copies were printed, "Confidential" was stamped on the cover, and that was that. "So it will become a historical document," Olmsted observed wryly in a letter to his father.

After Bull Run, it was clear that the Union was in for a prolonged conflict, not the one-big-battle-and-done that many had envisioned at the outset. Olmsted now predicted the war would last two or three years. The USSC moved into more permanent headquarters, a three-story townhouse at 244 F Street, once owned by John Quincy Adams. It was also clear that certain things stood in the USSC's way, preventing it from being truly effective.

The major hindrance was the Medical Bureau, composed for the peacetime needs of 15,000 soldiers and adjusting ever so slowly to the new realities. Remarkably, the bureau had begun the Civil War with just twenty-six surgeons and eighty assistants. Most of them had spent recent years at isolated frontier outposts, and as a consequence their skills were dangerously outdated.

The Medical Bureau was headed by the surgeon general, a man named Clement Alexander Finley. Ramrod stiff, with a fondness for capes, the sixty-four-year-old Finley was a career army doctor with a reputation for extreme parsimony. He was routinely suspicious of new medical practices. As a military man, and a pompous one at that, Finley reminded Olmsted of no one so much as Egbert Viele. From the outset, he and Finley clashed repeatedly. Olmsted had suggested that soldiers be given quinine to fight malaria. Finley pronounced this an experimental treatment and resisted. Olmsted had suggested smallpox vaccines for the troops. Unnecessary, said Finley. So the USSC spent money raised by its network of women's aid groups to buy 5,000 vaccines and distributed the doses itself.

Privately, Olmsted described Finley as "a self-satisfied, supercilious, bigoted blockhead," adding, "He knows nothing and does nothing and is capable of knowing nothing and doing nothing." How could the USSC offer any kind of support or counsel if it was forced to work with a retrograde outfit like the Medical Bureau? Finley had to go.

Hoping to accomplish this, Olmsted arranged to meet with General George McClellan, commander of the Army of the Potomac. The meeting was held on September 12, 1861, at McClellan's private quarters in Washington. The general adopted a surprisingly confidential manner, telling Olmsted the estimated size of the Confederate army. He also told him how large the Confederates estimated the Union force to be. Olmsted returned that same Friday evening to further their business. Now he broached the subject of replacing the surgeon general, and McClellan appeared receptive. The two men enjoyed glasses of Pennsylvania whiskey, and Olmsted left at midnight feeling confident.

But McClellan reneged. Looking back, Olmsted reflected that he'd have to credit McClellan with a political subtlety that hadn't registered during their meeting. After all, the general had speculated on the size of the Confederate force. He'd provided a Confederate estimate of the Union force. What he'd held close was the one fact he knew cold: the actual size of the Union army.

Olmsted kept at it, camping out in the lobbies and anterooms of the Washington power elite. Bellows was forever impressed by Olmsted's drive: "His mind is patient in meditation, capable & acute, his will inflexible, his devotion to his principles & methods, confident and unflinching." On another occasion, the reverend offered a telling backhand assessment, describing Olmsted as "a severe judge, seldom pleased & whose presence I dread more than every body else's."

Olmsted even managed to gain an audience with Lincoln. On October 17, 1861, he and several other USSC commissioners visited the White House from nine to eleven in the morning. Lincoln not only refused to remove Surgeon General Finley but also suggested that the USSC was trying to "run the machine."

Following the meeting, Olmsted composed a letter to his nine-year-old stepson, John Charles. Ordinarily, Olmsted wrote at tremendous speed in a dense scrawl. This time, he wrote slowly, forming his letters with great care. Given that his recipient was a child, Olmsted was more charitable toward Lincoln than in earlier impressions, but still it's possible to read between the lines. "Dear Charley," Olmsted wrote. "I went to the White House to-day and saw the President. He is a very tall man. He is not a handsome man. He is not graceful. But he is good. He speaks frankly and truly and straight out just what he is thinking. Commonly he is very sober but sometimes he laughs. And when he laughs he laughs very much and opens his mouth very deep."

Olmsted had gone to the top of the chain of command without success, but he wasn't done. He convinced Henry Wilson, a Massachusetts senator, to introduce a bill calling for the reorganization of the Medical Bureau. The bill got off to an extremely unpromising start, kicking around in various committees. But soon this bill would change everything for the USSC.

Olmsted was driving himself hard. It wasn't until six months into the USSC job that he spent a night at the Willard without sleeping in his clothes. He crowed in a letter, "I have discovered that pale ale is an admirable prophylactic of nervous exhaustion." A friend had brewed him a number of bottles.

Mary had the baby, a girl. This was Olmsted's second child. Little John Theodore had died just over a year earlier. Olmsted rushed back to New York. He'd been so busy that he wasn't clear on the child's birth date. It was October 28, 1861.

"We have a girl," Olmsted wrote to Brace, "which though not what the country wants right now is to me personally more agreeable than a man-child would have been." He added that he and Mary were considering the name: "ThankGodthingscan'tbemuchmeanerinmytimes." Although that was a grim joke, there was serious discussion about naming the baby Content. Content Pitkin Olmsted was the paternal grandmother whose books had given FLO so much precocious enjoyment. While the name was hopeful, it just didn't feel right. They named her Marion instead.

Returning to Washington, Olmsted began contemplating an enticing possibility. A joint army-navy expedition, led by General Thomas Sherman, had recently captured the Sea Islands, a plantation region in the Port Royal

Sound off the coast of South Carolina. The slave masters, foremen, and other whites had all fled the region. But the slaves had stayed behind and were, in effect, living as a free community. Olmsted began thinking about leaving the USSC to work with these former slaves instead.

The war was only a few months old, and everything about his current post remained distressingly undefined. Could the USSC make a difference in the lives of soldiers? Would the USSC even survive? Meanwhile, working with freed slaves seemed uniquely designed for him, something where he might be able to put to good use his very specific knowledge about the South and slavery.

Olmsted was familiar with the Sea Islands from his travels while writing his Southern books. He knew that Port Royal contained roughly one hundred of the richest cotton plantations in the Confederacy. He also knew that it was an incredibly isolated place, due in part to widespread diseases such as malaria and yellow fever. The Port Royal plantations were worked by the Gullah, blacks brought as slaves from West Africa, from areas that are now such countries as Gambia, Senegal, and Guinea-Bissau. In the New World, the Gullah proved immune to the diseases that periodically swept the Carolina lowlands. This was probably due to some kind of inherited resistance built up over generations in West Africa, where the same diseases were prevalent.

A unique master-slave relationship had grown up in the Port Royal plantations. Here, the white masters were in the habit of keeping their distance from the slaves. Even a vast plantation might have only a few white overseers. During the rainy season, when disease was rampant, the whites simply retreated inland. As a result, the Gullah didn't have the kind of contact with whites found elsewhere in Southern plantation culture. Many of the Gullahs' African cultural traditions remained intact. They even spoke their own dialect, as some of their descendants continue to do today. *Goober*, meaning *peanut*, is a Gullah word derived from *n'guba*, a word in the Kikongo language spoken in West Africa. *Gumbo* is another Gullah word, this one from Umbundu, another West African language.

When Sherman invaded Port Royal, the handful of whites had turned tail. But the Gullah had not joined them. This circumstance, Olmsted recognized, gave the lie to a favorite Southern notion, namely, that slaves enjoyed a beneficial relationship with masters and would voluntarily join them in all situations. In this most isolated patch of the Confederacy, where slaves could easily be misinformed about the motives of the Union army, the Gullah chose not to join their fleeing masters.

To Olmsted, Port Royal presented an opportunity for a worthy experiment. He envisioned the former slaves still working the cotton plantations, but for their own profit and livelihood. With the Civil War in progress, this could be quite an object lesson, showing that blacks were capable of being moral, vital, productive members of society. In his books, Olmsted had argued that free labor trumped slave labor because it was a natural state, governed by practical self-interest and incentives. Now Olmsted saw a unique chance to prove his ideas. Perhaps Southerners would at last see slavery for the corrupt institution it was.

Olmsted had grown adept at moving between one situation and another, going from farmer to writer to park maker to head of the USSC. Constant change had become his personal status quo. Enticed by what he saw as a perfect opportunity, he began approaching power brokers in Washington, such as Salmon Chase, the treasury secretary. He proposed himself as "commissioner of contrabands" for the Port Royal plantations. *Contrabands* was a term then commonly in use, with overtones of property law, applied to blacks who were no longer slaves but not yet free, either.

Olmsted described his proposed new role as an "ambition with which I am fired," adding, "I have, I suppose, given more thought to the special question of the proper management of negroes in a state of limbo between slavery & freedom than anyone else in the country. I think, in fact, that I should find here my 'mission' which is really something I am pining to find, in this war." In a letter to his father, he added, "I shall go to Port Royal, if I can, and work out practically every solution of the slavery question—long ago advocated in my book. I have talked it over with Mary and she agrees."

As an experienced farmer, Olmsted knew that it was necessary to act immediately. Already it was autumn, and by February the fields would need to be listed (shaped with hoes so cotton seeds could take root), and planting loomed in April. A delay would mean a missed growing season, and, rather than a noble experiment, the Union would be stuck with 12,000 paupers on its hands.

Olmsted launched a kind of all-fronts campaign. He dashed off a letter to Lincoln, outlining his "thoughts about the management of the negroes at Port Royal." He hoped the president would support his bid to be commissioner of contrabands. He revived the pseudonym "Yeoman" and wrote an editorial for the *New York Times*, arguing that Port Royal could be the prototype for an experiment repeated across the South. Whenever a region was captured, the former slaves could work the plantation lands themselves, for their own livelihood. Over time, pockets of free blacks would be found everywhere across the South, and escaped slaves could be expected to rush to these beacon communities. "A hostile force would thus invade the enemy in his very stronghold," he wrote.

Olmsted even teamed up with another congressman for another bill, to create a commissioner of contrabands post for Port Royal. This time, he worked with Lafayette Foster, a senator from Connecticut. Apparently, Olmsted drafted the bill, and Senator Foster didn't change a single word.

Knowing that time was crucial with the cotton crop, the bill was constructed broadly. Olmsted was careful to avoid any controversial provisions. For example, the bill didn't delve into the legal status of blacks in Port Royal, referring to them simply as "indigents" and "vagrants." As for what department would oversee this project (War and Treasury were the natural candidates), those details were left to be worked out later. Olmsted lobbied hard. He drew up a petition and sent it to his father, who in turn got seventy-five signatures from citizens in Hartford. He circulated similar petitions in Boston, Chicago, New Haven, and New York, which were then used to drum up support for the bill in the House of Representatives. Olmsted intended to force action and quickly; he resolved to "keep up a steady hard fire without rest or intermission for a single day."

CHAPTER 16

In the Republic of Suffering

OLMSTED APPEARED TO be headed for Port Royal to become commissioner of contrabands. Then everything changed. Olmsted became aware that he had misread the political winds in Washington. He had been counting on Treasury Secretary Salmon Chase to act as his sponsor for the Port Royal post. But it became clear that the secretary had no real authority to appoint Olmsted, and, further, Chase had not even bothered to read Senator Foster's bill.

Olmsted withdrew his name from Chase's consideration. He refocused all his efforts on lobbying Edwin Stanton, the secretary of war, and apparently the person with the authority to appoint someone to Port Royal. Foster's bill passed quickly, but Olmsted was not Stanton's choice. Instead, the secretary picked a brigadier general to act as commissioner of contrabands. Port Royal wouldn't wind up being a disaster; the government didn't get stuck with 12,000 paupers. Neither did it become the noble experiment, the beacon to slaves throughout the South, that Olmsted had envisioned.

But at the exact moment the Port Royal post fell through, the bill to reorganize the Medical Bureau passed Congress. Olmsted wrote an exultant letter to his father, in which he also showed himself to be a sly observer of the Washington legislative process: "As for the Sanitary Commission, our success is suddenly wonderfully complete. The Medical Bill after having been kicked about like a football, from House to Committee & Committee to House & over & over again, at each kick losing on one side & gaining on another, until it was so thoroughly flabber-

196

gasted that nobody knew where or what it was, and a new one had to be started—this process repeated several times—all of sudden a bill which is just the thing we wanted quietly passes thro' both houses the same day and before we know it is a law."

Victory was made still sweeter by a coincidence. Clement Finley, the hidebound surgeon general, got into a personal scrape with Secretary of War Stanton and was immediately relieved of his duties. He was replaced by William Hammond, an energetic reformer half Finley's age. Just like that, there was a reorganized Medical Bureau headed by a new surgeon general. The response to this improved circumstance was almost instantaneous. It's incredible how quickly things moved. With a war on, facing a desperate need for medical aid, Olmsted recommitted to the USSC and mobilized the outfit at dizzying speed.

A new military campaign was just getting under way, directed by General McClellan. The goal was to move up the Virginia peninsula, through an area girded by the York River to the east and the James River to the west, and to take Richmond, the Confederate capital. This would be the largest military mobilization the United States had ever undertaken, featuring 121,500 troops, 1,150 wagons, 15,000 horses, and untold tons of equipment and supplies.

Such a huge mobilization was sure to generate enormous casualties. To support the campaign, the army's Medical Bureau was ramping up fast, adding hundreds of new surgeons and nurses to attend the injured on the battlefield. But backup would be needed. Per its original mandate, the USSC might be called upon to furnish the surgeons with information on the latest medical practices. And the USSC certainly would need to provide supplies gathered from its network of women's aids societies, items like bandages for the surgeons' use and socks and blankets for the soldiers. The USSC might even need to go beyond its official duties. Be prepared, Olmsted was told by the military brass: If there was an overflow of sick and wounded, the USSC might not only be called on for advice and supplies but also have to provide actual medical treatment. With a war on, the lines were blurring. The military's plan was to furnish the

USSC with unused ships that could be converted into floating hospitals stationed along the rivers of the Virginia peninsula. As to how such care was delivered—that was the USSC's concern.

As the USSC's general secretary, Olmsted opted to oversee this endeavor himself. On April 27, 1862—exactly eleven days after the medical bill was signed into law—he set out aboard the *Daniel Webster*, a small steamer. Accompanying him were some medical personnel he'd drummed up, including four surgeons and twenty male nurses. There were also three carpenters and four female volunteers: Katharine Prescott Wormeley, Christine Kean Griffin, Laura Trotter, and a woman who appears in records only by her last name—Mrs. Blatchford. It was a stunning Sunday afternoon, and the four women sat above deck singing hymns and sewing a red-and-white USSC hospital flag. These were society ladies, drawn from the aid groups that funneled into the USSC. Katharine Wormeley, for instance, was a resident of Newport, Rhode Island, and a French scholar, who became well known after the war for her translations of authors such as Balzac.

During the voyage, Olmsted oversaw a complete retrofit of the *Webster*. He ordered an apothecary's shop built along with bunks to accommodate 250 patients. The entire boat was scrubbed, and various bulkheads were knocked out to open up the circulation of fresh air. It was still a few years before the breakthrough findings of Louis Pasteur and Joseph Lister and the existence of microbes remained unknown, but there was a convention that cleanliness—for whatever reason, perhaps its proximity to godliness—could arrest the spread of disease.

The *Webster* arrived on the peninsula while the siege of Yorktown was under way. The ship traveled up Cheeseman's Creek, a tributary of the York River, and weighed anchor. The creek was crowded with military transports and battle ships. On either bank, Olmsted could see the forest, full of tents and thrumming with the activity of thousands of soldiers. As night fell, campfires illuminated this vast temporary city. Soldiers sang and played bugles, and occasionally the sound of big guns roared in the distance.

Soon, the USSC had its first patients of the peninsula campaign, a group of Union soldiers desperately ill with typhoid fever. By necessity, the overstretched surgeons of the Medical Bureau focused on the battle-field wounded; those who succumbed to illness were given low priority. The sick soldiers had been left unattended in abandoned Confederate barracks that were really nothing more than crude huts. They had been alternately pelted by rain and baked by the sun. Olmsted described the squalid quarters as "a death-place for scores of our men who are piled in there, covered in vermin, dying with their uniforms on and collars up—dying of fever."

The soldiers were placed on stretchers and carried onto the *Webster*. First order was giving them stimulants, the Civil War medicinal description of whiskey and other liquors. Doctors had noticed you could revive someone with a stiff drink, so alcohol was viewed as a stimulant rather than a depressant. The soldiers were also given beef tea with muriatic acid, the oldfangled name for hydrochloric acid. It was considered a tonic when small doses were mixed into a hot drink. The volunteer women used damp sponges to dab the foreheads of those suffering from high fevers. That was about all the medical help then available to typhoid-fever victims. Soon the *Webster* was filled with 182 soldiers, and it set sail for New York, where the sick were transferred to hospitals to convalesce.

To replace the *Webster*, the quartermaster department (the army outfit in charge of transporting soldiers) issued Olmsted a new boat, the *Ocean Queen*. This was a 2,800-ton side-wheel steamship that had once belonged to Cornelius Vanderbilt. Olmsted assembled a fresh crew of USSC workers and ordered them to retrofit it for floating-hospital duty. Then he went ashore to bury a dead soldier.

When Olmsted returned, he saw two small boats pulled up alongside the *Ocean Queen*. Both were packed with soldiers who had fallen ill with typhoid fever. Olmsted protested that the *Ocean Queen* wasn't yet outfitted for patients; there wasn't a single doctor among his new crew. Too late: Sick soldiers began staggering onto the *Ocean Queen,* and soon there were 900 onboard. Olmsted went onshore and after considerable searching located a single doctor willing to help out with this deluge of the infirm.

Meanwhile, the female volunteers discovered a barrel of Indian meal tucked away in some forgotten corner of the *Ocean Queen*. When Olmsted returned after nightfall, they were ladling it out of buckets to the soldiers. Here's his description of the scene: "Poor, pale, emaciated, shivering wretches were lying anywhere, on the cabin floors, crying with sobbing, trembling voices, 'God bless you, Miss! God bless you!' . . . I never saw such misery or such gratitude."

Olmsted made the rounds cautiously, favoring his shattered left leg, careful not to step on the soldiers crowded everywhere on the decks of the *Ocean Queen*. The men lay head-to-head, taking up every available bit of space. Casting his lantern light across the ailing masses, he was pained to see how many of the soldiers had died. Olmsted limped back to his bunk and collapsed into exhausted sleep.

Olmsted proved to be a talented administrator. As much as he was a writer or park maker, this was starting to be an important part of how he defined himself. He drew up rules on the chain of command, time of meals, and how to process patients. He divided work into two watches—"sea fashion"—based on his long-ago voyage to China. Upon receiving a new ship, he'd divide it into wards, segregating those with communicable diseases from those with other ailments. For many of his patients, the problem was simple exhaustion. These soldiers needed a few days free from combat duty, he figured, and it was imperative not to expose them to disease while they recuperated.

Many of the troops were shockingly young, some just thirteen. So there was also the problem of soldiers who faked illness but were merely homesick. Upon learning that one of his ships had a large number of patients angling to return to New York City and its environs, Olmsted diverted the ship to Boston instead. He figured this would send a message: *Don't rely on hospital transports to desert the army.*

Whenever the ships returned from various ports, Olmsted always tried to arrange for them to carry fresh USSC supplies along with female volunteers—and more surgeons, always more surgeons.

For the first part of the peninsula campaign, the USSC dealt mostly with disease victims. It aided relatively few soldiers who had been wounded in battle. All that changed with the battle of Williamsburg. The Medical Bureau surgeons were totally overwhelmed by the sheer volume of injuries. For days after the battle, wounded soldiers lay where they had fallen, suffering and starving.

Those who survived were often carried to the USSC's hospital transports anchored along the York River and its tributaries. Once aboard, surgeons would begin by rubbing a little powdered opium into a soldier's wounds. Syringes for injecting morphine didn't become available until later in the war. Once the pain had deadened, it was possible to extract the bullet. For amputations, necessary on almost any wound to an extremity, chloroform was available as a general anesthetic—if one was lucky. Next, a dresser would pack lint around a soldier's wound and apply bandages. Aftercare fell to the female volunteers; it consisted of washing the wounds with soapy water and putting on fresh lint and bandages.

This was so much more than the good ladies of Hartford and Cleveland had signed on for. And it was thrilling! The female volunteers had expected to be charged with domestic duties aboard the hospital transports—cooking, cleaning, laundry—similar to what they did in their own households. Instead, they were helping soldiers in dire need, cleaning wounds and doling out medicine.

Olmsted was a stickler about proper registration of any soldier who came onboard a hospital transport. He wanted to know a soldier's company and regiment, for when he returned to combat, and next of kin, in case he died. For the female volunteers, one of the most poignant duties involved recording a soldier's last words or, as Olmsted described it, "catching for mother or wife the priceless, last faint whispers of the dying."

The volunteers sent letters to loved ones with details about how the soldier died, the cause, and his final wishes. One bereaved wife wrote back, deeply pained that she hadn't gotten to see her husband's corpse. "Give him back to me dead *if* he is dead," she begged, "*for I must see him.*" The soldier had been buried under an elm tree in an unmarked grave. In an effort to provide some comfort, one of the volunteers drew a sketch of his final resting place and sent it to the widow.

Some of the women who worked on the hospital transports kept diaries or wrote letters that have survived. From these, it's clear that service aboard the ships was harrowing but also strangely rewarding. It's also clear that the female volunteers held Olmsted in special reverence. They called him "Chief" and were deeply appreciative of the trust and responsibility he granted them. Katharine Wormeley's diary includes a vivid observation about Olmsted's appearance and countenance:

> He is small, and lame . . . but though the lameness is decided, it is scarcely observable, for he gives you a sense that he triumphs over it by doing as if it did not exist. His face is generally very placid, with all the expressive delicacy of a woman's, and would be beautiful were it not for an expression which I cannot fathom,—something which is, perhaps, a little too severe about it. . . . He has great variety of expression: sometimes stern, thoughtful, and haggard; at other times observing and slightly satirical (I believe he sees out of the back of his head occasionally); and then again, and not seldom, his face wears an inspired look, full of goodness and power. I think he is a man of the most resolute self-will,—generally a very wise will, I should think; born an autocrat, however, and, as such, very satisfactory to be under. His reticence is one of his strong points: he directs everything in the fewest possible words; there is a deep, calm thoughtfulness about him which is always attractive and sometimes—provoking.

Every moment on the peninsula seemed to bring a fresh challenge for the USSC. One Sunday in late May, Olmsted received an order from the quartermaster department to convert the *Spaulding*, a boat he'd been using, from a floating hospital back into a boat for transporting soldiers. He was given a new boat, the *Elm City*. Olmsted launched into what by now had become a familiar drill: Remove patients, medical supplies, and bedding from the old boat; scrub down the new boat. He and a crew of thirty surgeons, nurses, and volunteers worked all day. That evening, the quartermaster department issued a new order. Keep the *Spaulding*, Olmsted was told. The *Elm City* was the boat the army wanted. Oh, and please load it with sufficient coal for an eighteen-hour journey.

Now, an entire day's work—on a Sunday no less—by Olmsted and his crew had to be reversed. It was also necessary to locate twenty tons of coal and load it onto the *Elm City*. Olmsted made the rounds of other hospital ships currently in his possession, scrounging coal. Meanwhile, two soldiers died during the shuttling back and forth. By four in the morning, the task was complete. The *Spaulding* was back to being a hospital ship. The *Elm City* was ready to transport troops.

Such work was wearying. Such work could make one insane. "Will you please engage a pleasant room for me in Brown's Bloomingdale Hotel," joked Olmsted. This was a reference to David Brown, a doctor at Bloomingdale's Asylum, where he and Vaux had recently done a landscaping job.

As spring gave way to summer, the fighting along the peninsula grew more desperate and merciless. General McClellan and the Union army pushed to the outskirts of Richmond. There, they fought the battle of Fair Oaks, the largest conflict so far in the Civil War's eastern theater and second only to Shiloh in terms of casualties. Stationed at a distance, Olmsted was aware of Fair Oaks and gleaned from reports that it had been a bloodbath, but the battle was followed by an eerie calm for the USSC. It was a full day before the injured began to pour in.

And pour in they did. The wounded arrived by train, and there were so many that Olmsted set up a processing station between the rail depot and his hospital ships. Many arrived at night, so Olmsted used candles to mark a path to guide the soldiers. The processing station consisted of a long trench filled with burning wood, above which hung big iron kettles suspended on forked stakes. Olmsted instructed that the soldiers be given warm gruel and hot coffee, with as much condensed milk as they desired. Those who arrived feverish received brandy and other "stimulants." The wounded were given lemonade with ice, a luxury. This lemonade treatment was based on the odd notion that someone who had taken a bullet could derive great benefit from a cool drink.

As the casualties stumbled by, or were carried past on stretchers, the female volunteers tried to determine their ailments and triaged them accordingly. Critical cases went straight to the ships. An overflow hospital, consisting of twenty tents, was set up for the others.

In the midst of all of this, Olmsted lost contact with Mary. He sent her eight unanswered letters. "I need not say that my anxiety has become painful almost beyond endurance," he wrote in his ninth missive. "It is useless to speculate on the cause of my not getting letters from you." As it turned out, Mary had recently moved to a new address. Their home at Mount St. Vincent was being turned into Central Park Hospital, a facility for the Union wounded. These were chaotic times, and with all that was going on, it appears that the couple had failed to communicate on this simple matter.

For days after Fair Oaks, the trains kept rolling in, at all hours day and night. Sometimes there were several hundred soldiers packed into a single car. Typically, they hadn't had a drink or a single morsel of food since before the battle. The soldiers showed up, Olmsted observed, "without beds, without straw, at most with a wisp of hay under their heads. They arrived, dead and alive together, in the same close box, many with awful wounds festering."

Union and Confederate soldiers often arrived together. Olmsted estimated that about a quarter of the troops treated by the USSC after the battle of Fair Oaks were enemy combatants. While their treatment was the same, he also couldn't resist some patriotic bias, observing that the rebel wounded were prone to "not only more whimpering, but more fretfulness and bitterness of spirit."

The USSC converted boat after boat into floating hospitals. Sometimes as many as five were anchored abreast, and the USSC staff scrambled from one to another using gangplanks. Horrible, inhuman shrieks and howls issued from the *State of Maine*, designated as the vessel where operations were performed. Whenever a boat filled up, it set off for New York or Boston to deliver patients to hospitals. When things worked out, a USSC hospital transport returned in time to relieve the one that had just left.

So great was the emergency that Olmsted's system for registering patients broke down entirely. Throngs of soldiers piled onto the boats. "In this republic of suffering," Olmsted had recently written, coining an apt phrase for wartime, "individuals do not often become very strongly marked in one's mind." Now, this was truer still. Everything had been reduced by the scope of the carnage, leaving only harried USSC workers aiding anonymous soldiers, doing what little was possible.

Fair Oaks was the pivotal moment of the peninsula campaign. General McClellan had managed to push to within striking range of Richmond. But just when a decisive blow was possible, he held off. This was partly due to McClellan's innate caution, a trait that earned him the unflattering nickname "Mac the Unready." He was forever overestimating the number of Confederate troops he faced. His decision also stemmed from his depleted army, badly in need of reinforcements. The peninsula campaign had taken its toll.

On July 4, 1862, Olmsted sailed up Chesapeake Bay, en route to Washington, aboard the *Wilson Small*, a steamer that had become his floating headquarters. As he moved north, he was distressed to see that not a single boat bearing soldiers was headed south. Why weren't reinforcements being sent?

Next day, Olmsted arrived in Washington. He went to the White House hoping for an audience with Lincoln. But the president was indisposed. He had taken to his bed in the middle of the day, apparently worn out by the demands of the war. Sailing back south, Olmsted composed a letter to Lincoln. He begged the president for 50,000 fresh troops. "Without these," he wrote, "the best army the world ever saw must lie idle, and, in discouragement and dejection, be wasted by disease."

Olmsted sent the letter to a fellow USSC commissioner and instructed him to deliver it. But it was no use. Soon McClellan was retreating back down the Virginia peninsula. Where only weeks before the USSC had been overwhelmed, the flow of soldiers in need of help now slowed to a trickle. Olmsted and some of the USSC volunteers sat out on the deck of a boat for a whole night, reminiscing about the intense experience they had shared together. Every so often, way in the distance, they could see a flash, hear a vague rumble, as a shell exploded. The military campaign itself seemed to be fading away.

By mid-July 1862, Olmsted's work on the peninsula was done. He sailed to New York aboard the *Daniel Webster*. Katharine Wormeley watched as the Chief disembarked. Olmsted appeared haggard, but she also thought she noticed something triumphant in his manner. The peninsula campaign may have been a tactical failure for McClellan, but for Olmsted, achievement was measured by a different yardstick. He estimated that USSC hospital transports had cared for perhaps 10,000 soldiers. Back in New York, the first thing he did was arrange for the USSC to send a boatload of vegetables to the retreating troops to stave off scurvy. "The summer's work has paid splendidly in lives saved and pain alleviated," he told the Reverend Henry Bellows.

Olmsted spent the first years of the Civil War in a kind of heightened state of awareness, agonized by the human misery he witnessed, exultant when he was able to provide some measure of relief. His energy level was staggering, but the exertion came at a price. As the war dragged on, he would become increasingly prone to both despondency and panic. Still, the amount he accomplished is quite simply amazing. It's almost as if Olmsted was in two places at once.

Sometimes he was. While Olmsted was on the Virginia peninsula, making a difference with his hospital transports, he was also making an impact across the Atlantic, with a just-published literary effort.

Right before the Civil War started, Olmsted had been approached by a London publishing house, Sampson Low, Son & Company. The firm had done the English editions of Olmsted's Southern trilogy. They had asked whether Olmsted would be willing to abridge those books into a single volume that might find a fresh audience.

All together, Olmsted's Southern trilogy had sold maybe 25,000 copies. Commercially, the series had been underwhelming. But the books had achieved an outsized influence. Not so many people read Olmsted, but the right people read him—politicians, professors, and journalists. While numerous abolitionist titles were available, many of them full of fervent moralizing, Olmsted's readers valued his nuanced firsthand accounts of plantation life and his sophisticated critique of slavery on economic grounds. Charles Eliot Norton, the noted critic who would later become a friend of Olmsted's, described the books as "the most important contribution to an exact acquaintance with the conditions and result of slavery in this country that have ever been published. They have permanent value, and will be chief material for our social history, whenever it is written."

Olmsted's books had also found a small but influential audience in England. Charles Dickens, who had traveled widely in the American

South, was impressed with the accuracy of Olmsted's reporting. Karl Marx, who lived in London from 1849 onward, cited Olmsted's writings in *Capital*, his monumental three-volume work. Charles Darwin was so horrified by some of the incidents described in Olmsted's *A Journey in the Seaboard Slave States* that he couldn't sleep at night. This was at the time when Darwin was writing *Origin of Species*, so Olmsted's work had special resonance. Given Darwin's thesis that all humans shared common ancestry, the idea that one person could enslave another seemed grotesquely contrary to nature.

Olmsted had jumped at the opportunity to publish a new work for English readers, even though Sampson Low offered no payment. Olmsted teamed up with Daniel Goodloe to prepare the new edition. Goodloe was a wise choice. A onetime clerk for President Zachary Taylor, he had lost his job due to a letter he wrote in praise of *Uncle Tom's Cabin*. He had become editor of the abolitionist *National Era*, where he wrote frequently on the economics of slavery, a topic of special Olmsted expertise.

Olmsted well knew that editing one's own work is like digging one's own grave, so he gladly handed that task off to Goodloe. Time was tight, so he gave Goodloe latitude to cut as he saw fit. Goodloe pared three volumes, 606,000 words, down to a single work of 276,500 words. Meanwhile, Olmsted updated the data used in the earlier volumes. He changed the average price of a slave to $1,400, adjusted for inflation from $1,000, the figure he'd used a few years before.

While work on the volume was under way, the Civil War had broken out. Early in the summer of 1861, just as Olmsted began his tenure with the USSC, he had finished the book. He added a new introduction, "The Present Crisis," that covered events right up to the first shots at Fort Sumter. Now, he stated, his "impression" about the South had hardened into a "conviction." He also framed this new introduction so as to specifically address British readers: "It is said that the South can never be subjugated. It must be, or we must. It must be, or not only our American republic is a failure, but our English justice and our English law and our English freedom are failures." As a final touch, Olmsted repositioned a particularly brutal episode he'd witnessed during his Southern travels, the whipping of the slave Sall. He placed it at the end of the new volume, making it the dramatic climax. Olmsted titled his book *The Cotton Kingdom*.

Olmsted's timing was perfect. In *A Journey in the Back Country*, published in 1860, he had warned that Southern secession would bring war. That prediction had borne out. Just as the Civil War began, Olmsted had a brand-new volume, full of his unique observations about the South and aimed at an English audience.

Early on, Great Britain was surprisingly ambivalent about the Union. The Trent Affair, where Northerners boarded a British ship to seize two Confederate diplomats, had actually brought England and the Union to the brink of war. The influential *Times of London* provided sympathetic coverage to the Southern cause. In some British circles, Jefferson Davis was viewed as a superior, more experienced executive than Abraham Lincoln. British companies would even manufacture two battleships for the Confederacy, the *CSS Alabama* and *CSS Florida*.

The Confederacy, in turn, was banking on Britain coming to its aid. *England can't live without our cotton* was the Southern refrain. "What would happen if no cotton was furnished for three years?" demanded South Carolina senator James Hammond in a famous speech, shortly before the Civil War. "England would topple headlong and carry the whole civilized world with her save the South. No! You dare not make war upon cotton; no power on earth dare make war upon it. Cotton is king." Olmsted had taken his book's title from Senator Hammond's famous speech.

The Cotton Kingdom was no best-seller. But once again, Olmsted managed to reach the opinion leaders in English society. Emma Darwin, wife of Charles, wrote the following in a letter to J. D. Hooker, the celebrated British botanist: "About America I think the slaves are gradually getting freed & that is what I chiefly care for. *The Times* evidently thinks that is to be deplored, but I think all England has to read up Olmsted's works— again & get up its Uncle Tom again."

The Cotton Kingdom received favorable notices in such high-tone British publications as the *Athenaeum* and the *Westminster Review*. In an essay in *Fraser's*, John Stuart Mill argued that Britain and the Confederacy were at odds—cotton be damned—and if the South was victorious in its current conflict, he predicted war with England within five years. As to what had led him to such conclusions, Mill credited the "calm and dispassionate Mr. Olmsted."

England would undergo a shift on the question of its loyalties in the conflict. In the end, not only would Britain withhold its military support from the South, but it also refused even to recognize the Confederacy as a legitimate government. It's difficult to assess the precise extent of Olmsted's influence on British public opinion. Crediting him with convincing England not to side with the South would surely be going too far. But it's clear that he helped shape the debate. And the truly remarkable thing: He did so by means of a book, *The Cotton Kingdom*, published at the same time that he was busy—crazily busy—running the USSC.

Small wonder that by August 1862, Olmsted was exhausted. His Civil War service had been harrowing. This, on the heels of several years filled with traumatic events: the death of his brother, a carriage accident, the death of a child. Shortly after Olmsted returned from the Virginia peninsula, he experienced another of his breakdowns. This time it appears that he was suffering from something akin to what's now known as post-traumatic stress syndrome.

Olmsted spent a week recuperating on Staten Island with his family. Upon returning to Washington, his condition grew worse. He was nauseous and had a perpetual ringing headache. To combat his symptoms, he was given mercury. Mercury was used as a purgative to flush toxins from the body. Typically, it was administered in the form of tiny blue pills. By the 1860s, the medicinal use of mercury was in decline. People were becoming aware that it was a toxin in its own right.

The phrase *mad as a hatter* is based on the observation that there was a high incidence of insanity among people who made hats for a living. Mercury nitrate used to be the favored compound for removing fur from pelts to create felt for hats. Eventually, the connection was made between mercury and insanity. For someone such as Olmsted, given to fragile emotional states, probably nothing could be more counterproductive than taking those tiny blue pills.

Olmsted soon developed jaundice along with a bizarre skin irritation. "I itched furiously," he wrote his wife, "and where I plowed the surface with my fingerends, it presently became purple, and a purple maculation began to grow on my arms. A little exertion or excitement shook me so that my voice trembled."

After another round of recuperation in Saratoga Springs, he headed back to Washington, stopping in New York again for more family time and a visit with Vaux. His partner had been diagnosed with malaria. Fever had caused Vaux to have wild hallucinations, and he had been acting so rashly that a nurse sometimes needed to restrain him. Andrew Green had tried to visit, and Vaux had demanded that Green leave. "He has said, of course, some very clever and sensible things," quipped Olmsted.

During Olmsted's visit, Vaux babbled about glass and colors and drapery and seemed to believe he could float in the air. Olmsted departed, terribly distressed by Vaux's condition. The pair had worked out an arrangement where they shared the annual proceeds from their position with Central Park, with Olmsted taking $2,000 and Vaux receiving $2,500, since he did more work. After seeing Vaux, Olmsted reduced his own share to $1,200. He borrowed $300 from his father to help out the Vaux household.

Olmsted hoped to stay in New York—even for one more day—to supervise a planting of trees in Central Park. But events were calling him away.

John Olmsted was a kind father and extremely indulgent, allowing Fred to enjoy a kind of extended adolescence. He bankrolled many of his eldest son's speculative schemes.

During his early twenties, Olmsted hung out in New Haven and became friends with his brother John's Yale circle. This 1846 daguerreotype features (l. to r.) Charles Trask, Charles Brace, Fred Kingsbury, Frederick Law Olmsted, and John Hull Olmsted.

John Olmsted,
Fred's brother.

Mary Perkins Olmsted,
who was first John's wife
and later Fred's wife.

FLO in cap and cape, circa 1860.

Olmsted and Vaux's inspired Greensward plan beat out thirty-two other entries to become the design for Central Park. The Ramble, originally an untamed garden, was Olmsted's favorite feature. The Cave added a sense of mystery during the early years of the park. (Its opening was later covered over.)

Central Park's creators (l. to r.): Andrew Green, George Waring Jr. (probably), Calvert Vaux, Ignaz Pilat, Jacob Wrey Mould, and Olmsted.

The partners: Calvert Vaux (left),
a trained architect of immense
talent, and Olmsted (below),
self-taught and sublimely
intuitive, had a strained
working relationship.

During the Civil War, Olmsted headed the U.S. Sanitary Commission, forerunner of the Red Cross and a vital source of aid to wounded soldiers. Olmsted raised money and purchased this cannon, which was placed in front of the Free State Hotel in Lawrence during the Bloody Kansas struggles.

Early environmentalist: Before this gathering of influential journalists, Olmsted delivered a seminal 1865 speech that stepped up efforts to preserve Yosemite, even helped set in motion the idea of a national park system. The photo was taken by Carleton Watkins, renowned for his images of Yosemite. Olmsted is in the front row (second from left).

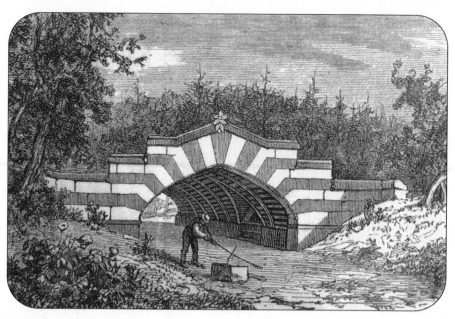

The Endale Arch—a beloved feature of Prospect Park, Olmsted and Vaux's Brooklyn masterpiece.

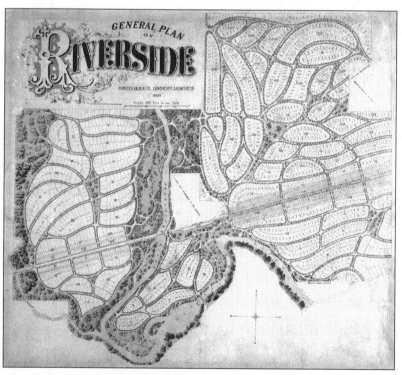

The plan for Riverside, Illinois, a model suburb featuring many innovative ideas that continue to influence modern suburbs.

Nature ruled at Fairsted, Olmsted's home in Brookline, Massachusetts.

The 99 Steps
in Boston's
Franklin Park.

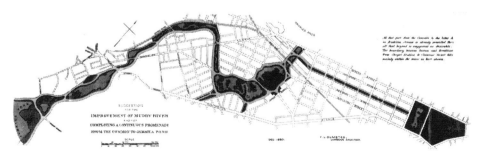

The Muddy River Improvement is just one portion of Olmsted's ambitious park system for Boston—what came to be known as the Emerald Necklace.

To achieve his vision for the U.S. capitol grounds, Olmsted had to battle Congress for decades. He won. This modern aerial view shows how faithful the capitol grounds have remained to Olmsted's original plan.

Olmsted (right) and three of his children, John, Marion, and Frederick Law Olmsted Jr. Not pictured here: Charlotte, who had to be institutionalized, and the three children he lost.

Olmsted's design for the 1893 World's Fair in Chicago was one of his greatest, featuring winding waterways, a wooded island, and brightly colored boats with quiet electric engines (all visible in this photo).

Olmsted and daughter Marion on the grounds of North Carolina's Biltmore Estate.

Changing of the guard: Olmsted was present for the initial sessions with painter John Singer Sargent. But by 1895, Olmsted was frail and failing fast. Frederick Law Olmsted Jr. stood in, even wore his father's clothes, so that Sargent could finish the portrait.

The Biltmore Estate near Asheville, North Carolina, is Olmsted's swan song.

He spent his final years at McLean, an asylum for which he'd earlier provided a landscape design. Proctor House (pictured here) is the residence hall where Olmsted likely lived.

CHAPTER 17

Antietam to Gettysburg

Soon Olmsted was back in Washington, contending with fresh emergencies. A large Confederate force, commanded by General Robert E. Lee, had crossed into Maryland, where a number of battles had been fought, leaving Union troops exhausted and supplies depleted. By taking the war to Northern soil, Lee hoped to influence the midterm elections, maybe force Lincoln to sue for peace. By entering Maryland, a slave-holding border state that hadn't seceded, he hoped to fracture the fragile Union. On September 17, 1862, the two armies clashed in bucolic farm country near Antietam Creek. The soldiers soon found themselves boxed in tight in a cornfield, forced into close-range combat.

It was a balmy day, the sun was brilliant. As the battle wore on, the soldiers' faces turned black with powder from repeated musket firings, a surreal contrast to the blue sky overhead. Soon the stubble of the new autumn corn was splattered red with blood. And a peculiar smell hung over the battlefield, a mix of gunpowder, trampled vegetation, and human sweat. Forever after, among survivors of Antietam, this odor would be remembered as the very essence of terror.

Antietam—a battle in which 3,654 soldiers lost their lives—is the single bloodiest day in American military history. It also proved to be a logistical nightmare; Antietam is probably the Civil War battle in which medical supplies were most a problem.

The USSC did what it could. It had become a well-prepared outfit. Under Olmsted's leadership, the Sanitary Commission had grown into a formidable force at remarkable speed. The hospital transports used during the peninsula campaign had been a serious boon. While docked in various Northern ports, boats flying the red-and-white USSC flag had been seen by countless people, a tangible symbol of wartime relief and one that made soliciting support or funds all the easier.

Olmsted had managed to set up twelve supply depots behind Union lines. Drawing on its network of women's aid societies, the USSC had ready stores of dried fruit, onions, pickles, sauerkraut, and brandy. Books and Bibles were donated for wounded soldiers, along with games like dominoes and backgammon. Money raised by the aid societies was used to buy medical supplies such as bandages, quinine, and opium.

The women provided an unending supply of home-sewn clothing. There was woolen underwear for winter, flannel for summer—and shirts, always more shirts. "Most of our ladies," quipped Bellows, "have so magnified our soldiers in their hearts that the shirts and drawers they send us would fit the Anakims." With *Anakims*, the good reverend was making a biblical reference to a race of giants mentioned in the book of Deuteronomy. Bellow's advice to the women's aid societies: *If you make a piece of clothing, use your own husband's actual dimensions as a guide.* The USSC was forever providing directives. For a while, there was a mania for lint, and women gathered it by the barrelful until word came down from Washington that enough was enough.

The USSC held regular sanitary fairs in various Northern cities to raise money, awareness, and whatever items were most needed at the time. Olmsted even arranged for notable people to go town to town, touting the organization in speeches. Horace Howard Furness, an eminent Shakespearean scholar, traveled through New York and Connecticut in service to the USSC and sent the following note to Olmsted: "I have addressed large bodies and little bodies, and nobodies and somebodies. I have spoken in Town Halls, in Concert Halls and in Court Rooms, in Presbyterian, Methodist, Baptist, Lutheran and Episcopalian Churches, from pulpits and from judicial benches, before communion tables and baptismal fonts. I have seen before me eyes glistening with interest and eyes drowsy with sleep."

Following the battle of Antietam, barns and churches for miles around were converted into makeshift hospitals. A railroad bridge over the

Monocacy River had been destroyed during the battle, cutting off a vital supply route. Olmsted dispatched USSC agents to Philadelphia with $3,500 to buy supplies. Under no circumstances, he instructed them, were they to place these items on trains, as that would leave desperately needed goods choked in the rail jam caused by the bridge outage. Instead, the agents scared up as many wagons as they could. USSC supplies arrived at Antietam a full day before those of the Medical Bureau.

According to its records, during the week following Antietam, the USSC provided 28,763 dry goods, including shirts, towels, pillows, and tin cups; 30 barrels of linen bandages and lint; chloroform, opiates, and bedpans; 2,620 pounds of condensed milk; 5,000 pounds of beef stock and canned meats; 3,000 bottles of "wine and cordials"; and assorted tons of lemons, crackers, tea, and sugar. Olmsted traveled to Antietam to oversee the relief effort. "It was very squalid," he reported, "but everywhere I saw the great value of our work."

At Antietam, once again, General McClellan demonstrated his hesitancy. He allowed Lee's army to slip back across the Potomac. Lincoln was furious, and McClellan was relieved of his command soon after. Still, Antietam was a Union victory. Lee's Army of Northern Virginia had been driven back to the South.

Lincoln had been holding out for a battlefield win, however slight, because he had a gambit planned. Five days after Antietam, on September 22, 1862, the president issued a preliminary Emancipation Proclamation, promising freedom to the slaves in any Confederate state that did not return to the Union by January 1. For states in rebellion that didn't respond by the deadline, Lincoln planned to follow through by decreeing their slaves free.

Up to this point, the Civil War had enjoyed the support of abolitionists in the North, but its official purpose had been to prevent Southern secession. With the Emancipation Proclamation, Lincoln invested the Union's efforts with a new, higher, almost mystical mandate. No longer was this merely a war to preserve the republic; this was about ending slavery. His timing was perfect. The soldiers and citizens of the North were growing weary of ceaseless war, but now with a fresh purpose, they were galvanized.

Throughout the war, Olmsted—like so many Northern opponents of slavery—had been frustrated by Lincoln's gradualism. It was a stance Olmsted himself had once held, before traveling the South in the 1850s. Now, Lincoln had made the same transition to red-hot abolitionist. Olmsted revised his estimate of the man: "The Proclamation of Emancipation by President Lincoln, looking at its possible economical and moral results in the future, is undoubtedly one of the great events of the century," he declared in a *New York Times* editorial on September 28, 1862. Privately, in a letter to a fellow USSC commissioner, Olmsted wrote: "I shall stand by it [the proclamation] now as long as I live, and I shall try to bring up my children to make it good. I shall be for continual war, or for Southern independence rather than go back one step from it."

Olmsted sent a package to John Nicolay, Lincoln's private secretary. The package contained several books, presumably a sampling of Olmsted's Southern works. There's no record of the titles sent, nor is there anything to indicate that Lincoln read them. An accompanying letter contained all kinds of suggestions on how the Emancipation Proclamation might be publicized—printed on linen, drawn up in handbills, distributed to slaves whenever the Union army encountered them. As with Port Royal, Olmsted liked the idea of enlisting Southern blacks to undercut the Confederacy. "Each would then become a centre of more correct rumors of the purposes and offers of the President," he wrote to Lincoln, "and knowledge of the true designs of the government would thus be disseminated among those now so generally grossly deceived in this respect."

Beneath the charge of big events—the battles, the relief efforts, the political intrigue—Olmsted's personal angst continued. "You are too near the machinery," a friend wrote him right after Antietam. "You smell the grease and feel the thick air, and it makes you sick."

Olmsted was increasingly lonely in Washington, separated from Mary and his children. Mary sent him some photographs of herself. He commented on one he liked in particular and said that the photographs would have benefited if they had been taken in a garden. He ended the letter with, "Kiss all the young ones. I thought of them when I saw hundreds of men dying for them." This was followed by a series of letters in which husband and wife grew testy from their long separation. Mary recited the stresses of raising children by herself. She asked to move to Washington. Olmsted resisted, citing financial woes. He'd already moved a couple of times, from the Willard to a cheaper place, then cheaper still. But then Olmsted relented. "Thank you for encouraging me," he wrote to Mary as a kind of mea culpa. "That I suppose is what I need."

In November 1862, Olmsted moved his family to a furnished house in Washington at a very modest address, 332 G Street. "We will be as frugal as we can," he told Mary. The owner was the retired captain of a potato steamer, and the house was filled with items taken from the boat. There was sticky mahogany furniture that plastered to one's backside and a hideous ottoman with a pattern that Olmsted likened to a spider's eye. But there were five hens, providing fresh eggs, and a cow for milk. Olmsted signed a six-month lease for $750. Six months was his estimate of how much longer the Civil War would last.

Half a year later, the conflict still raged. In the spring of 1863, in his official capacity as general secretary of the USSC, Olmsted took a six-week trip. His itinerary included stops in Cleveland, Cincinnati, Chicago, St. Louis, Louisville, and Young's Point, Louisiana. Mary balked at another separation. But Olmsted had told her, "It is a day for heroes, and we must be heroes along with the rest." It was his way of saying that the war was bigger than the both of them and demanded sacrifice.

The main purpose of the trip was to repair a schism that had grown up between the USSC in Washington and its western operations. The Louisiana leg was to meet with General Ulysses Grant. Olmsted planned to gauge the medical needs of Grant's Army of the Tennessee, then involved in a protracted and unsuccessful siege of Vicksburg. The trip also held personal interest for Olmsted because, while he had traveled extensively in the South, he had never been to such northern cities as Cleveland and Chicago.

In a stunningly short time, the USSC had grown into an institution renowned for its aid to wounded soldiers. There was even a song, "Sanitary Fair Quadrille"; it was no "Battle Cry of Freedom," but popular nonetheless. The USSC was also becoming increasingly complex and far-flung. It now had branches in places such as Pittsburgh and Cincinnati. The branches connected with the women's aid groups in that region. The aim, for Olmsted, was an efficient system that funneled goods and money from the tiniest hamlet to the vast Union army.

But there were hitches, especially out West. This had everything to do with the way the army was structured. Soldiers tended to enlist in the town nearest to where they lived. Once in the army, they remained together in companies organized by common geography. This fostered cohesion on the battlefield. With medical relief efforts, the result could be just the opposite. As the USSC branches had learned, it was possible to solicit supplies earmarked for soldiers from a particular locale. Thus, Cincinnati could channel goods to Ohio soldiers, and Iowa could likewise take care of its own.

To Olmsted, this was anathema. Such localism, as he saw it, was akin to the secessionist impulses that had led to the Civil War in the first place. This was the *United States* Sanitary Commission. It aided the *Union* army. Of course, he was also rankled by the personal affront. Individual branches were undercutting a national organization that he had built.

Thomas Starr King, a Unitarian minister and friend of Bellows, had recently pledged $200,000 to the USSC. This upped the separatist tensions still further. The Cincinnati branch demanded $15,000 of that sum for its own coffers. Olmsted composed a 138-page treatise, spelling out in minute detail the organization and mission of the USSC, and circulated it to the branches. It was ignored.

Obviously, Olmsted would need to engage in some delicate diplomacy. Bellows had the highest respect for Olmsted's abilities, but he knew his colleague could be difficult. Trying to smooth the waters in advance of the trip, Bellows wrote a letter to a USSC operative in Louisville: "You understand . . . the glorious and invaluable qualities of our General Secretary, his integrity, disinterestedness and talent for organization, his patriotism. You also understand his impracticable temper, his irritable brain, his unappreciation of human nature in its undivided form and his very imperfect sympathies to weak, mixed, and inconsequent people."

Judging from his memos, Olmsted was able to keep this harshness, the dark side of his reformer's zeal, in check during his trip. He attended

sanitary conferences and had tea with various USSC functionaries—
all very civilized. In a letter to Bellows, Olmsted described his role as
cultivating "a friendly feeling amongst all concerned by a little white
lying." He also gained no real concessions from the USSC's western
branches.

The inspection of General Grant's operation was more successful. On
March 23, 1863, Olmsted arrived in Young's Point, a small Louisiana
town, and from there traveled to a nearby army outpost, along the western bank of the Mississippi. Grant had a vast force under his command.
Anchored alongside his floating headquarters, the steamship *Magnolia*,
were scores of craft: supply boats, coal barges, and ironclads, a new type
of armored warship. At this point, nearly 30,000 troops were assembled.
Because the surrounding land was swampy and impenetrable, they were
camped on terraces cut into a levee.

Across the top of the levee, Olmsted could see two long rows of graves
stretching into the distance. These were for soldiers who had died of disease. Forcing an army to wait, as Olmsted knew, was always a bad thing.
So far, Grant had not been able to figure out how to take Vicksburg, a
Confederate fortress city on the Mississippi. Many thought Grant's days
were numbered and that he would soon be relieved.

Olmsted toured the camps. And he met with William Le Baron Jenney, an engineer and senior member of William Sherman's staff. (Sherman was then serving under Grant.) Jenney was involved in an elaborate
and somewhat fanciful plan. He was overseeing an effort to carve a canal
through the equally swampy terrain east of the Mississippi. Then Grant's
troops could be transported by boat to the other side of Vicksburg. They
could take the city by land.

Olmsted doubted this plan would work. But Olmsted liked Jenney,
especially after he learned that they shared a passion for architecture and
gardening. The two had lunch in a tent on the grounds of an abandoned
plantation house that served as Sherman's headquarters. To Olmsted's delight, Jenney reminisced about his student days in Paris, studying at the
École Polytechnique and visiting the Louvre and the Palace of
Fontainebleau. As they talked, the view across the Mississippi was of tree-
tops hung with Spanish moss, vultures circling lazily above. A group of

blacks was hard at work, tearing down an old gin house. Olmsted could hear drum beats and bugle calls and, way in the distance, the boom of big guns pitching shells at a rebel position. The conversation was a welcome respite from war. Olmsted recorded the meeting with Jenney as having a "peculiar zest in the midst of raw upper Louisiana plantation, where nature's usual work is but half-done."

That evening, Olmsted had an appointment with Grant. But the general was distracted. He was dealing with a fresh slate of setbacks, as per usual. Grant pored over various reports, leaving Olmsted waiting. "I am not always as much occupied, as I am tonight," said Grant, as Olmsted rose to go, "and whenever you see that I am not, understand that I shall be glad to talk with you."

The next evening they spent an hour together. The two were almost exact contemporaries; Olmsted was born the day before Grant in April 1822. But where Olmsted was a light drinker, Grant was known for prodigious alcohol consumption. According to the account of someone who walked in midmeeting, Grant was imbibing heavily that very night and had to cling to the back of a chair to remain standing. Maybe it was discretion, but Olmsted didn't record any impressions of Grant's drinking. He tended to be temperate in his view of excessive drinking and once described alcoholism as "a disease" that needed to be "cautiously and delicately helped"—an atypical view in his times.

At any rate, Olmsted found Grant disarmingly candid, especially in detailing the annoyances of his job. The general was put off by governors who were forever demanding special considerations for soldiers from their states. This struck a nerve with Olmsted. He'd been dealing with the scourge of localism, too. But Olmsted truly warmed to Grant when the general declared the USSC indispensable and requested its help. Grant wanted the USSC to convert transport steamers to hospitals, as it had on the Virginia peninsula, but this time in support of his Vicksburg campaign. Olmsted, in turn, requisitioned two hundred barrels of potatoes and onions for immediate delivery to Grant's army to ward off scurvy.

For a normal person, possessed of normal ambition, fulfilling a demanding schedule of meetings and obligations would have been sufficient. Not Olmsted. Throughout his whole six-week journey to the various western USSC branches and to Grant's Louisiana headquarters, he took copious notes.

Apparently, on this trip, he once again saw the potential of shaping his observations into a book. Anthony Trollope had recently published *North America*, a much-acclaimed travelogue laced with trenchant social criticism. William Howard Russell's *My Diary North and South* was hot off the presses, published in 1863. Both authors were British, and Olmsted didn't feel either had succeeded in laying bare the American psyche. But he had been credited with doing exactly this, for one region of the country at least, with his Southern trilogy.

While taking notes on his travels, Olmsted even adopted a new pseudonym, "Carl." It was akin to "Yeoman," which he'd used in his *Times* dispatches. *Carl* is a play on *carl*, an archaic term for a man of the people.

Some of Olmsted's notes are downright derivative. When Olmsted missed a train connection in Odin, Illinois, he took the opportunity to watch the people waiting in the station. Trollope had also missed a train during his American visit, and over the course of a lengthy layover, he had recorded memorable impressions of his fellow travelers. Other writings are merely cranky. A stay at the Burnet House in Cincinnati prompted him to list the establishment's myriad shortcomings, followed by: "What else is necessary to justify the assertion that the palatial hotel is the dreariest of all American humbugs? . . ." But there are also sharp observations to be found among these jottings. During his travels, he was often struck by how the demands of commerce crowded out anything of lasting value—a venerable Olmstedian theme. "It seems useless to describe Chicago," he writes at one point. "What it was when I saw it, it will not be by the time this is read."

Ultimately, Olmsted was unable to shape his Carl journals into a book. Even he couldn't find the time.

Lee's army was on the move again. Once again, he was crossing onto Northern soil. This was a strategic move, an effort to capture Union territory, but also a pragmatic one. While camped in Virginia, his soldiers had eaten everything in sight—every cow, every chicken, every vegetable, every last morsel—and the barren farmland needed time to recover. Hungry Confederates were now massing in Maryland and Pennsylvania.

Lee issued Order No. 72: no theft of private property, but federal property was fair game. The general knew that victory would be twice as hard for an invading army that enraged civilians by pillaging their farms. Instead, Southern troops visited Northern farms to "purchase" food using Confederate scrip. Who was going to say no to men with guns?

One thing was for certain: A major battle was brewing, though no one was sure quite where it would take place. Olmsted ordered that stores of supplies be moved to a variety of locations, including Baltimore, Harrisburg, and Frederick. Whole sprawling armies were on the march, and everything was fluid, uncertain. The Confederates briefly occupied Frederick, forcing the USSC to hide its supplies there. The goods were federal property, after all, subject to seizure under Lee's order. Presently, it became clear that the two armies were converging near the town of Gettysburg, Pennsylvania. The USSC started sending wagons laden with supplies to the front.

The battle began on July 1, 1863, and lasted for three days. Opposing Lee was General George Meade, in the job less than a week. He'd relieved General Joseph Hooker, who, in turn, was Lincoln's replacement for Mac the Unready—McClellan. The USSC continued to send a steady stream of wagons onto the battlefield. Many wagons were captured by Confederates, who stole the supplies and imprisoned the drivers and doctors onboard. But plenty got through, often at crucial points in the conflict. At the very moment that General James Longstreet was attacking the Union's left flank, a pair of supply wagons marked "U.S. San. Com." pushed through under heavy fire. They were carrying brandy, beef stock, bandages, and chloroform. Several hundred gravely injured Union soldiers had been laid out in an orchard behind a barn. Upon the approach of the wagons, a beleaguered battlefield surgeon supposedly cried, "Thank God! Here comes the Sanitary Commission. Now we shall be able to do something."

Olmsted was in Philadelphia when news of Gettysburg began to trickle in with wounded soldiers. Apparently, the Union had come within a hair's breadth of defeat on several occasions. But its fortunes had swung when General George Pickett led his disastrous charge across three-quarters of a mile of open field, right into the teeth of Union fire.

On July 5, pelted by a heavy rain, Lee's defeated army filed along Hagerstown Road, headed back to Virginia. The Union army pursued, but it was a halfhearted effort. Olmsted sent a telegram to Bellows: "Private advices tend to confirm reports of capture of over fifteen thousand prisoners and one hundred guns. Lee retreating." One of the USSC commissioners posted the telegram on a bulletin board, commenting, "Olmsted is wary, shrewd, and never sanguine. This despatch was not sent without strong evidence to support it."

Olmsted proved correct in assigning victory to the North. But the USSC's real work had only just begun, as a mass of wounded remained on the battlefield. The Union death toll, 3,155 soldiers, was dwarfed by its injuries, 14,531 men; a smaller Confederate force had lost 4,708, with 12,693 wounded. Rails to the east of Gettysburg had been knocked out during the battle, but as soon as they were restored, the USSC began a massive relief effort.

Olmsted went on a buying mission in Philadelphia, purchasing tons of fresh eggs, butter, mutton, and milk. He also bought a vast quantity of ice. This he used to turn a boxcar into a makeshift refrigerated car. He filled a second railcar with tents and other supplies. On July 6, he was able to arrange for both cars to be attached to the very first train into Gettysburg.

He then traveled to Gettysburg to supervise a relief station. It was a larger version of the station the USSC had created on the Virginia peninsula and again featured iron kettles hanging over a fire pit, cooking soup and heating coffee day and night. Tents were set up to care for wounded soldiers until trains could evacuate them.

During the week following the battle, Olmsted arranged for an average of 40 tons a day of supplies to flow into Gettysburg, which included 300 yards of surgeon's silk, 3,500 fans, 6,100 pounds of fresh butter, 4,000 pairs of shoes, 1,200 pairs of crutches—such a variety of items both humdrum and precious to serve so many men in so much pain.

By July 18, the emergency had died down sufficiently that Olmsted was able to walk the fields of Gettysburg, as countless others would in the years to come. He was struck by the scale of the place; everything had happened across distances far greater than he had supposed. He also noted that the hills were gentle and rolling, so very out of kilter with the carnage that was everywhere still in evidence. "At some points," he wrote, "where the ground was taken and retaken, I found plenty of evidence of terrible fighting."

Olmsted came across spent shells and twisted bayonets, broken-down wagons and half-buried dead horses. Particularly touching, to Olmsted, was the random strew of Union and Confederate caps, often together on the ground, shot through with bullet holes.

CHAPTER 18

"The Country Cannot Spare You"

JULY 4, 1863, marked the turning point of the Civil War. On the very day Lee conceded defeat at Gettysburg, General John Pemberton surrendered at Vicksburg. Grant had figured out how to take the fortress city, though the canal plan had been abandoned.

VICTORY! WATERLOO ECLIPSED! screamed the headline in the *Philadelphia Inquirer*. When news of the defeats reached England, the overseas market for Confederate war bonds collapsed, and the rebel cause was further hobbled. The chance that the South could win was now infinitesimal; hopes shifted to the possibility that a battered Union army might be too weary to keep fighting. What remained was an agonized denouement, stretching over nearly two more years, as the war slouched toward Appomattox.

This was also a turning point for Olmsted. Gettysburg was the last major battle in which he played a role; his relationship with the USSC was souring fast. It's almost as if the prolonged conflict was exposing tensions within the USSC, and factionalism—the very evil Olmsted had railed against—was now cropping up between him and his colleagues. The USSC board began to snipe at Olmsted, raising issues that struck him as picayune. A directive was issued, for example, requiring Olmsted to get approval for all expenditures over $1,000. On another occasion, a fellow USSC commissioner demanded that Olmsted dismiss four employees for causes ranging from "oafishness" to "beastly drunkenness." Olmsted thought that the charges were trumped up; he took the call to fire the employees as a personal slight.

Olmsted met the pettiness with still greater pettiness. The New York metropolitan police force had donated fifty boxes of lemons earmarked for soldiers at Vicksburg. Olmsted complained that it was wasteful to transport lemons all that distance. *Why not send fifty boxes of lemons from a closer depot—from Tennessee, say, now under Union control? Why did the troops in Mississippi have to receive the New York lemons specifically?* It's a simple point, but Olmsted made it exhaustively and exhaustingly in a letter to the Reverend Henry Bellows. This was followed by a flurry of dispatches to Bellows, more long letters raising other small points. "I chafe and fume like a caged lion," Olmsted wrote. "You can chloroform me or beat me blue and silent."

For Olmsted, infighting with the board had echoes of Central Park's politics and his dealings with Andrew Green. Once again, bureaucrats and bean counters were mucking around, trying to bring down something that he had built. He began floating the idea that he might resign.

George Templeton Strong, a fellow USSC commissioner, crafted an entry in his diary that includes a kind of plus-column and minus-column assessment of Olmsted. "He is an extraordinary fellow," wrote Strong, "decidedly the most remarkable specimen of human nature with whom I have ever been brought into close relations. Talent and energy most rare; absolute purity and disinterestedness. Prominent defects, a monomania for system and organization . . . and appetite for power."

In another diary entry, Strong speculated that his colleague's extreme drive was causing the worst traits in his nature to win out: "Olmsted is in an unhappy, sick, sore mental state. Seems trying to pick a quarrel with the Executive Committee. Perhaps his most unsanitary habits of life make him morally morbid. He works like a dog all day and sits up nearly all night, doesn't go home to his family for five days together, works with steady, feverish intensity till four in the morning, sleeps on a sofa in his clothes, and breakfasts on strong coffee and pickles!!!"

Olmsted resented the challenges from his USSC colleagues. But something else was going on, too. By now, Northern victory was pretty much ensured, and Olmsted finally had the chance to contemplate life after wartime. It filled him with panic. Even if Olmsted didn't leave the

USSC, this wartime job would be ending soon enough anyway. He wouldn't be able to return to work at his beloved Central Park, either. Vaux had recently resigned, worn down by political battles of his own. He'd gone ahead and submitted Olmsted's resignation, too, a move to which Olmsted agreed. What could Olmsted do next to make a difference? What would he do to make a living? Minus the USSC job's salary (which had been settled at $2,500 per year) and $1,200 from Central Park, his income would be nil.

During this period, Olmsted got into a rare scrape with his father. Why, if his son was so worried about the future, the elder Olmsted demanded, was he limiting his options, battling his colleagues at the USSC, agreeing to quit Central Park in league with Vaux? Wasn't firming up existing prospects the wise course? Olmsted responded defensively, listing some of his accomplishments and throwing around terms like *principles of management* to remind his father that he was a man of the world. That he'd hurt his son's feelings clearly upset John Olmsted. Both father and son moved quickly to smooth things over. "However wanting in sagacity I may be, I am obstinate only in honest dutifulness," wrote Olmsted, signing the letter, "Your affectionate Son."

Still, Olmsted was restless, unsettled by ill-focused ambition. He started looking for new work. He considered landscape architecture. His recent visit to Chicago had convinced him that the city was sorely in need of a pleasure ground. But landscape architecture was also a nascent profession, albeit one that he and Vaux had pioneered. He wasn't sure whether there was enough demand for him to make a living at it.

Journalism seemed a surer bet. Olmsted even came up with a promising idea in collaboration with Edwin Godkin, a friend and fellow journalist. Like Olmsted, Godkin had traveled across the South writing about slavery as a correspondent for the *London Daily News*. Now, the pair hit upon what seemed like a potentially winning journalistic formula: a serious magazine of ideas, similar to the *Atlantic*, covering weighty issues, like federalism—but rather than a monthly, it would be a *weekly* magazine, something of an innovation at this point.

Olmsted and Godkin tossed around various names: *Comment*, *Reviser*, *Scrutiny*, perhaps the *Maintainer* or the *Holdfast*. They even drew up a business plan, *Prospectus for a Weekly Journal.* The pair was able to raise only $3,000 of the $40,000 they estimated was needed to start the magazine.

Olmsted approached Charles Dana, hoping he might invest in the venture. Dana—a onetime colleague at *Putnam's Magazine*, and long-time second in command to Horace Greeley at the *New York Tribune*—was a field observer for the Union army. His job was to visit generals at their camps and report back to Washington. A particularly delicate assignment involved spending time with Grant to address rampant rumors of the general's alcoholism. Dana concluded that Grant was an extremely capable commander and tactician, heavy drinking notwithstanding. Lincoln called Dana "the eyes of the government at the front." Olmsted pitched his weekly journal idea to Dana. Dana thought launching a new magazine in the middle of a war was terrible timing. He told Olmsted, "I don't believe it will succeed."

Early in August 1863, Olmsted received an envelope marked "Private." It contained a letter from Dana concerning something called the Mariposa Estate, a sprawling gold-mining property near Bear Valley, California. Until recently, the owner of the enterprise had been John Charles Frémont, the famous explorer. But he'd recently sold a majority stake in the mines to a group of eastern financial backers that included George Opdyke, mayor of New York City. They were looking for a manager. Qualified candidates were in short supply during wartime, and finding someone willing to live in the wilds of California only upped the challenge. This was reflected in the enticingly generous salary, $10,000 a year plus stock incentives. Dana had been offered the job but turned it down, recommending Olmsted instead. "You are less rooted than I am," Dana wrote. "It seems a chance you may like to accept."

Olmsted immediately set off to New York to meet with Mayor Opdyke and the other backers. The position was his, he was told, if he chose to accept it. As he weighed the Mariposa offer, he generated far more than his usual volume of letters to friends and family. These letters show Olmsted divided, wrestling with various issues: his obligations to the war effort, the turmoil of uprooting his family once again, and whether by taking the position he'd be selling out. In choosing jobs, Olmsted had always placed the ability to effect social reform above financial considerations; running a gold mine decidedly did not equal social reform. He also felt a vague misapprehension about the eastern moneymen. Yet for every argument Olmsted could summon, a part of him was already leaning westward.

The money was a draw, no question. Olmsted had borrowed $5,500 from his father in buying into *Putnam's*, and the publishing company's collapse had saddled him with an additional obligation of $8,000. He'd retired very little of this debt and still owed $12,000 by his own calculations. Olmsted worried about what would happen if he fell seriously ill, went blind, or broke his other leg. If—God forbid—he died, Mary and the children would be left in "absolute poverty."

Even more so than the money, Olmsted appears to have been thrilled by the opportunity to try something new. He had built up the USSC, set it on its course, and now all that was left were maintenance and aggravation. Mariposa was a fresh, blank canvas. He was caught up in the romance: California, the West, epic scenery, a gold mine.

Bellows tried to talk Olmsted out of leaving. Despite their recent scuffles, the reverend valued Olmsted as an administrator and viewed the younger man as a good friend, too. Bellows appealed to Olmsted's ambition, deeming him one of just "a half-dozen men in the whole North" with the potential to shape weighty affairs of state in the years ahead. And Bellows appealed to Olmsted's patriotism. "*The country can not spare you at such a juncture*," wrote the reverend, italicizing generously. "I think *you* must *feel this* in *your bones*."

Olmsted's mind was made up. On September 1, 1863, he resigned from the Sanitary Commission.

The USSC continued on to the end of the Civil War, operating under two more general secretaries that followed Olmsted. Its record of battlefield relief is stunning. Working with 286 local aid societies, the USSC solicited an estimated $15 million (in 1860s dollars) worth of supplies and another $5 million in cash that was used to buy medicine and other items.

Right after Antietam, Olmsted had launched a hospital directory to better connect wounded soldiers with their loved ones. The USSC set up a department for discharged veterans, helping them fill out forms, obtain pensions, and otherwise navigate the bureaucratic maze in Washington. A series of pamphlets, produced by the USSC and circulated to army field surgeons, offered some of the era's best medical guidance. The USSC's Bureau of Vital Statistics, initiated by Olmsted, conducted 1,482 camp inspections. The data gathered has been of immense value to the historians.

The USSC also gets credit for goading the Medical Bureau into action, by pushing for the 1862 reform bill. The same army that began the Civil War with 26 surgeons finished with 11,000! The same army that started the war with a handful of field hospitals ended it with 204, featuring 137,000 beds. When General Meade described the "inestimable blessings and benefits conferred by that noble association upon the sick and suffering soldiers," he was referring, of course, to the USSC.

There's even a crucial connection between the USSC and the American Red Cross. After the Civil War, Bellows sought to keep the spirit of the USSC alive. He founded an organization called the American Association for the Relief of the Misery of Battlefields. The AARMB's primary purpose was to get the United States to comply with the Geneva Convention. This treaty (signed on August 22, 1864) conferred neutrality on medical workers on the battlefield, along with the injured soldiers in their care. It was signed by countries such as Belgium, France, and Prussia, but not the United States. The AARMB's board featured substantially the same cast as the USSC's board, including George Templeton Strong, Oliver Wolcott Gibbs, and Olmsted. The outfit also had its own flag, a white Greek cross on a red background, reminiscent of the Sanitary Commission flag.

Clara Barton, the legendary Civil War battlefield nurse, who had operated independently of both the Medical Bureau and the USSC, also took up the cause of getting America to ratify the Geneva treaty. Through tireless effort, Barton convinced President Garfield to sign. But he was assassinated before he could make good on the promise. At this point, Barton turned to Bellows, asking him to write a letter supporting her efforts.

Bellows did so only a few weeks before his own death in January 1882. President Chester Arthur signed the Geneva treaty on March 1, 1882. This gave official recognition to an organization Barton had founded the previous year, the American Red Cross.

The Red Cross began life as a battlefield relief outfit with substantially the same mandate as the original USSC. Over time, it would evolve into an organization that also provided aid during peacetime disasters such as earthquakes and hurricanes. As one historian put it, the USSC played "mid-wife to the Red Cross."

But all this was years in the future. Right now, Olmsted was headed to California.

V
"There Seems to Be No Limit"
CALIFORNIA, 1863–1865

CHAPTER 19

Gold Dust

ON SEPTEMBER 14, 1863, Olmsted departed New York bound for the Mariposa Estate, a sprawling concern in the heart of California gold country. This stretch of land was legendary, described by Horace Greeley, who had visited during a recent cross-country journey, as "perhaps the finest mining property in the world." It also had a colorful back story, full of intrigue and double-dealing, some of which was known to Olmsted and some of which would soon be revealed.

John Frémont, the famous western explorer, had purchased the Mariposa Estate for $3,000 in 1847, when the land was still under Mexican control. The 44,387 acres were a floating grant, a Mexican real estate anomaly whereby the size of a property was fixed, but the precise location was not. This made it possible to shift a claim, akin to moving a blanket on a beach.

In his youth, Frémont had been an imposing figure. People who met him were often struck that every facet of his being—his hard-angled face, distant gaze, and compact muscular build—seemed designed only for action, never contemplation. Once, as an Indian prepared to fire an arrow at Kit Carson, Frémont rode to his friend's aid, rearing up on a horse and stomping the Indian to death.

When gold was discovered in the Sierra Nevada, Frémont simply floated his land grant to cover some of the most coveted territory. Prospectors who had already staked claims on the land were apoplectic. Once California gained statehood in 1850, they finally had a means to pursue their grievances. The ensuing legal wrangle went all the way to the Supreme Court, where Frémont won in 1859.

Mariposa gold made him a very wealthy man. But he fell just as quickly into debt, thanks to his legal fees, the cost of maintaining the mines, and the financial toll of his heady political ambitions. (Frémont was the brand-new Republican Party's very first presidential candidate in 1856. Olmsted voted for him, but Frémont lost the election to Democrat James Buchanan.) "Why, when I came to California I was worth nothing," he once joked, "and now I owe two millions of dollars."

In 1863, Frémont managed to erase some of this debt by selling most of his property to the group of investors that included Mayor Opdyke. It was a different time, one when a big-city mayor could launch a business while in office. The investors organized the Mariposa Company, headquartered at 34 Wall Street, and drew up a prospectus, filled with projections from mining consultants. One consultant calculated that the Mariposa Estate would yield one hundred tons of raw ore daily for the next 388 years. Another stated, "There seems to be no limit to the extent to which mining and milling operations can be carried out." The Mariposa Company quickly sold $10 million worth of stock to a gold-fevered public. Frémont was named a trustee of the new entity, and he retained an equity stake. If the company proved successful, he'd be able to pay off still more of his debts. Frémont dreamed of one day reclaiming full control of his mining business.

As manager, Olmsted was to be paid his $10,000 salary in gold, worth at least 20 percent more than the same salary paid in greenbacks, then racked by wartime inflation. During his first five years of service, he was also to receive $10,000 in stock annually, potentially worth many thousands more.

Just to get to his new job was no easy task. Olmsted elected to take the Panama route, one of several options for getting to the West Coast in those days. The Panama route, established in 1855, required traveling by steamer down the Atlantic Coast, then crossing the narrowest point in Central America, the Isthmus of Panama, via a forty-eight-mile interoceanic train ride. On the Pacific Coast, travelers boarded a new steamer and sailed up the coastline. The trip covered 5,500 miles and took roughly three weeks. Cheaper choices, sailing around Cape Horn, the very tip of South America, or going overland by wagon, were more time-consuming, requiring three months, minimum. There was also a Nicaragua route, both cheaper and potentially quicker than the Panama route, but featuring a harrowing land passage. In the years before the transcontinental railroad (1869) and the opening of the Panama Canal (1914), traveling from coast to coast was an ordeal.

Olmsted traveled without his family, planning to get settled on the Mariposa Estate before bringing them out in the spring of 1864. For the first leg of the journey, Olmsted sailed on the *Champion*, a rickety side-wheeler, operated by Cornelius Vanderbilt. Vanderbilt had a reputation for stinting on safety. "The steamer on the Atlantic side was small, ill-supplied, dirty and crowded," Olmsted noted.

Before arriving in Panama, as was the practice, Olmsted started taking several grains of quinine each day, prophylactically, so as to ward off malaria. The "Chagres shakes"—named after a river that ran alongside the rail line in Panama—was a particularly virulent strain. In 1852, Ulysses Grant had lost 250 men while marching across Panama. As an old man, he'd remember the horrors of Panama more vividly than those of the Civil War.

At Aspinwall (now Colón), a Panamanian port, Olmsted made the switch from ship to rail. The train's seats were made of cane, and it was open-air—venetian blinds were the only thing separating passengers from the elements. The forty-eight-mile trip took roughly four hours, following the Chagres through deep gorges and requiring refueling stops every few miles at wood stations along the route. Olmsted was stunned by the natural drama unfolding outside his open window. Pelicans, looking prehistoric, floated in lazy circles, with the Andes towering in the distance. The punishing noonday sun was broken by a sudden shower, then sunlight again, stretching from the heavens in luminous shafts. Nearer the ground, directly across the Chagres, the foliage was so lush that the sun could scarcely get through, providing just a dappling of light amid deep shadows.

The variety of plants and trees seemed almost infinite, Olmsted noted, and they grew so close together, their branches interlaced, that you didn't know where one began and another ended, and through everything twined thick tropical vines. There were fat yellow breadfruits, ripening coconuts, thick clusters of bananas. As Olmsted recounted in a letter to his wife that evening, the tropical luxuriance "makes all our model scenery— so far as it depends on beauty of foliage very tame & quakerish."

Mary would be making this same passage soon enough. "Remember to point out the mountains to the children & tell them they are the Andes," he urged. Like his own father, Olmsted wanted to make sure his children appreciated the scenery.

On the west coast of Panama, Olmsted boarded a new boat, the *Constitution*, operated by the Pacific Mail Steamship Company. The vessel was superior in every way to Vanderbilt's *Champion*—newer, cleaner, safer. In fact, the *Constitution* was the largest and best-appointed boat on which Olmsted had ever traveled. "It's Fifth Avenue with the park, after Greenwich Street with the battery," he wrote to Mary.

Chugging up the Pacific coastline toward San Francisco, Olmsted could not shake his memory of the scenery he had witnessed on the train ride. He puzzled over the landscape's meaning, morally speaking. Did it denote bounteousness, creativity, freedom, lack of restraint? He also began to wonder if it would be possible to reproduce some of this tropical superabundance in the Ramble, his ever-evolving wild garden in Central Park.

Olmsted no longer had a formal role with the park, having shed first his architect-in-chief duties and then the consulting position he shared with Vaux. But he still thought of the park as his own—his creation, his masterpiece—and always would. In fact, it would please him mightily the following year when park brass introduced a flock of sheep onto the parade ground. The move effectively prevented troops from conducting drills during the Civil War in Central Park—a place of peace, in his reckoning, above the fray. Forever after, the parade ground would be known as Sheep Meadow.

Onboard the *Constitution*, Olmsted dashed off a letter to Ignaz Pilat, the park's gardener. Would it be possible, Olmsted inquired, to plant some species such as purple barberry and honey locust, apt analogies to the tropical species he'd seen, but capable of growing in New York City's climate? He also suggested covering trees such as sycamores in clematis

vines. Such plantings, he wrote, "would under favorable natural circumstances, I believe, produce an effect having at least an interesting association with or, so to speak, flavor of tropical scenery and I should hope
some little feeling of the emotion it is fitted to produce."

Upon receiving the letter, Pilat would dutifully try out some of Olmsted's ideas, planting a few select new species thickly in the Ramble and
training vines to snake through some of the existing trees. It wasn't a disaster—Olmsted's wild garden was a pretty forgiving space—but somehow the
intended tropical effect failed to translate in the middle of Manhattan.

On October 11, 1863, a month after leaving New York, Olmsted arrived
in San Francisco. As he disembarked from the steamship onto the
crowded wharf, a horse kicked him in his lame leg. The kick didn't result
in serious injury, but it struck Olmsted as an omen. Before him, there still
lay a grueling two-hundred-mile journey to the town of Bear Valley,
headquarters of the Mariposa Estate.

Olmsted had time only for a cursory impression of San Francisco. It
wasn't a good one. Something about the way the town was laid out—a
simple grid work against a hillside—well, he couldn't put his finger on it,
but it unnerved him. He boarded a new steamer, which carried him by
river into the California interior and to Stockton.

In Stockton, the last town of any size before Bear Valley, Olmsted
rented a coach and two horses. Then he set out across the stifling San
Joaquin Valley toward the foothills of the Sierra Nevada range. California
was in the midst of its worst drought in the nineteenth century. The contrast to the rain forests of Panama was stark; Olmsted described this portion of his journey as a trip through "a dead flat, dead brown prairie,
with scattering remnants of trees. . . . The shade of one tree never con-
nects with another, so far as I have seen."

In the distance, the Sierra Nevada were like a painted backdrop. The
coach clattered onward, mile upon dusty mile, but the mountains remained frozen, never drawing closer. The only thing breaking the general
monotony, Olmsted noted, were the graves. Everywhere he looked, the
dry plains were dotted with makeshift graves, a disturbing number of
them belonging to children.

And then Olmsted's coach began to climb. At first the ascent was so subtle as to be nearly imperceptible. Olmsted had reached the Sierra Nevada foothills. Then, suddenly, his coach was climbing at a steep grade, through a mountain pass and into a densely wooded plateau. Here, the trip paused to give the horses a rest. After that, the coach climbed still higher into the mountains, through another pass, and down to his destination, Bear Valley.

Olmsted checked into Oso House, the town's lone inn. Olmsted ate his dinner sitting on a stool, as the inn didn't have a single chair. Then he retired to a room, only slightly larger than a closet and with walls made out of canvas. These provided little barrier to sound, of which there was plenty—men drinking and fighting and gambling well into the night. It would do—for now—but Olmsted knew he'd need to find different accommodations when his family arrived.

Besides Oso House, Bear Valley consisted of about twenty establishments lining a single unpaved street, perpetually aswirl with thick red dust. There were three saloons, including the notorious Bon Ton, a billiard hall, two laundries, an Odd Fellows lodge, and a bathhouse. There was also a butcher shop and the Frémont general store. Bear Valley's population— hard-luck eastern transplants stuck working as miners after their own gold dreams collapsed, Mexican immigrants, members of local Indian tribes, along with a smattering of wayward Europeans—was estimated at 1,000, but who really knew? For men with families, there were several extremely modest rooming houses run by the mining company. Single men, accounting for the bulk of the residents, were content to sleep in tents or booths—if they could raise the funds to purchase a few planks. Booths were little wooden structures with room enough to curl up and sleep.

Bear Valley had no churches and no schools. But it had the one establishment vital to a mining town—a Wells Fargo Express office. Bullion from the mines was regularly delivered to this office, from which it was transported by heavily armed coach along the arduous route to San Francisco. There, it was weighed, assayed, and credited to the mining company's account.

On waking the next morning, Olmsted immediately began a tour of the Mariposa Estate. The property consisted of seven separate mines. Despite his damaged leg, Olmsted shimmied down a mine shaft at one point. He loosed a piece of quartz with a pickax and, with the aid of a candle, spied glittering specks of gold embedded in the rock. Olmsted continued on, familiarizing himself with the vast property he would now be supervising.

Mariposa was a high-tech operation by nineteenth-century standards. Mechanized hoists were used to pull big chunks of quartz out of the mines. The quartz was loaded onto cars and sent along a rail—more like a roller coaster—that dipped and twisted through the mountains, carrying raw ore from the mines to the mills for processing.

Each mill had a number of stamps, big metal weights that struck the quartz repeatedly, upwards of fifty times a minute, until it was crushed to powder. Once the quartz had been pulverized, water was added, creating a thick slurry. The mixture was then run slowly across an amalgamation table, which featured a layer of mercury.

Gold is one of the heaviest elements on earth. As the slurry slid across the amalgamation table, even the tiniest specks of gold drifted to the bottom of the mix and dropped into the bed of mercury.

Gold and mercury's chemical relationship is nonexistent. Bits of gold simply collected in the mercury until the mercury was utterly laden. Then it was "clean-up time." The so-called amalgam was scooped into buckets and carried to a retort room. There, it was heated in iron kettles until all the mercury had vaporized, leaving behind gold. Gold captured in this fashion is called doré. Olmsted noticed that the doré looked like a filthy sponge cake.

Even at first glance, Olmsted could also see that a great deal was wrong with the operation. Sure, *Mariposa* and *bonanza* were synonymous in the popular imagination. In the months before the eastern investors purchased the property, the estate was turning a profit of $50,000 per month—unheard of. Yet the mines Olmsted visited were in great disrepair, and many of the mills were at a standstill. He immediately wrote a letter to his bosses back in New York: "These facts, all new and entirely unexpected to me, coming to my knowledge mostly in one day . . . gave rise at first to a feeling of very great disappointment."

The better Olmsted got to know the Mariposa Estate, the worse it looked. The drought was so severe that several streams indicated on maps had ceased to exist. The estate's most crucial source, the Mariposa River, was just one foot deep. With water so scarce, gold mining was difficult. Water was needed to power the mills that crushed the quartz. Water was necessary to create the gold-bearing sludge that washed across the amalgamation tables.

Besides the vagaries of nature, Olmsted began to hear whisperings about human schemes. Supposedly, Frémont had ordered the previous manager to work the property hard, upping the gold yield. Nothing about this was illegal per se. The estate had been for sale; stellar results were needed to entice a buyer. Frémont's real sin was ignoring a cardinal rule of gold mining: *Even in the midst of the gaudiest pay streak, you had better be thinking about the future.* All streaks eventually end. Frémont had pushed his mining machinery to the limit, deferring routine maintenance to the next owner. He hadn't bothered with exploration that might have located fresh veins of gold. Now, with the onset of a terrible drought, mining was drying up, quite literally.

Late into the night, Olmsted pored over his predecessor's financial ledgers. Only one thing was really clear. Recently, the mines had been turning a fat profit. Now they were losing $80,000 a month. "Things are worse here than I dare say to anybody but you," he wrote his wife, in a letter that he marked "X Private," as in *extremely private.*

Olmsted started making plans to revive the property to its recent glory. So-called deadwork—placing underground timber supports—had been neglected and needed to be done before a tunnel collapsed. Olmsted intended to drop a series of test shafts, looking for promising new spots to mine. He wanted to string a telegraph line to Bear Valley, opening communication with the outside world, making the mining property less remote. Most important, Olmsted proposed digging a long canal to convey water onto the estate from the Merced River, a deeper, more reliable source. "I can make nothing of it without water," he noted.

Before Olmsted could even get started, however, his plans hit a snag. Years earlier, Frémont had borrowed $7,847 at a usuriously high interest rate. Compounding monthly, the tab had by November 1863 reached $308,000, and what's more, the loan's contract specified that the amount must be repaid in gold.

A reorganized Mariposa company, freshly infused with capital from the sale of stock to the public, yet with Frémont still a legal trustee—what a perfect opportunity to collect this ancient debt. In fact, a San Francisco banker had been canny enough to purchase the debt from its original holder. Now, the banker signaled that he intended to pursue collection voraciously. Back East, Opdyke and the rest of the Mariposa board instantly recognized the severity of the situation. (The company would settle within months, agreeing to the following terms: $300,000, in gold, payable in three annual installments, no more compounding interest.)

Meanwhile, Olmsted received a dispatch from the Mariposa board. Due to this new and unforeseen Frémont debt, the company's financial position had worsened. Olmsted was forced to reevaluate his plans for refurbishing and upgrading the mines—this, when he'd barely gotten started. Some of his most ambitious ideas, such as the telegraph line and the canal, were now unaffordable. Going forward, capital improvements to the estate would have to be realized through increased gold production—as if that was even possible, paradoxically, without capital improvements.

What had he gotten himself into, Olmsted started to wonder? Looking at his surroundings through the prism of all this recent frustration, Olmsted was struck anew by what a barren land this was. The foliage—thorny chaparral and clumps of dwarf chestnut—seemed to him stunted and alien. Even the topography was needlessly severe. *California*, he was certain, was made up of two Latin words, *calor* (heat) and *fornax* (furnace).

On a Sunday night, Olmsted heard a commotion in the street in front of Oso House. Looking out, he saw that a dogfight was in progress, and the two animals were tearing at each other, kicking up dust. A crowd of miners had gathered, and they were whooping and cheering and laying down bets. "Evening services" was how Olmsted termed the event in a letter to Mary, adding, "I rather think that if I had known what the place was I should not have asked you to come here. You must be prepared for a hard life. . . . But it's too late to retreat. . . . A region possessing less of fertility—less of living nature—you scarce ever saw."

When he could sleep, always a problem for Olmsted, he began to have a recurring dream where he found himself in the English countryside.

The dream's locale was very specific: outside the town of Leamington Spa in the county of Warwickshire, a favorite spot from his travels.

Around this time, he also sent out a number of letters, exploring different ideas, trying to make something happen. He invited a doctor he'd known during his USSC service to set up a new practice in Bear Valley. He sent $75 to his friend Edwin Godkin, the New York editor, requesting that Godkin start subscriptions to a list of roughly thirty magazines—*Harper's, Punch, Mining and Smelting,* and the *Leisure Hour* among them—and arrange for them to be sent to the estate. Olmsted planned a reading room for the miners.

Olmsted also contacted David Parker and Company, an innovative Shaker-run company in New Hampshire that produced one of America's first automated appliances, a steam-powered washing machine. Perhaps cleaning the miners' filthy clothes would prove a route to increased productivity. "I think something of the sort is more wanted here than a church," Olmsted wrote to a friend, describing his plan.

But the doctor didn't come. War was still on, and his services were sorely needed. For want of water, the washing-machine idea was quickly abandoned. The magazines began to arrive, but there's no record of the miners' response to the *Leisure Hour* or any of the other titles. In his own way, Olmsted was hoping to reform this godforsaken place. But it was mere fancy; even Olmsted knew this at some level. Disappointment—that was reality of his new life out West—and it just kept coming.

Next, a letter arrived from Vaux. The letter was five weeks old; that's how long it could take for mail to travel from New York to Bear Valley. But Vaux's anger was still fresh: "My special object in writing is to speak of a matter about which, in view of your proposed long absence, something needs to be said. The public has been led to believe from the commencement of the Central Park work to the present time that you are pre-eminently the author of the executed design, and such we all know is the general impression throughout the country today."

Back in September, on the day Olmsted had left New York, a couple of newspapers had run articles about his new job running a gold mine in California. One article assigned the bulk of credit for Central Park to Olmsted, while the other neglected to even mention Vaux, slights duly noted by his erstwhile partner. Perhaps, Vaux suggested, Olmsted was receiving outsize credit because he had undertaken certain administrative duties that kept him in the public eye. Or maybe the credit flowed from the title of "architect in chief." Why had Olmsted been so comfortable accepting that title, Vaux demanded? And why hadn't Olmsted done more to correct misimpressions about their roles? He reminded Olmsted that they both shared credit for the park.

Olmsted's response—characteristically logorrheic—opened with a note of hurt. He'd received Vaux's letter right before Thanksgiving. "Your letter of the 19th October comes in to make its chilly, lonely dolefulness more perfect," he wrote. From here, Olmsted crafted a couple of surprising parries, meant to pull the rug out from under Vaux. Absolutely, Olmsted conceded, they should share credit for the park's *design*. But by being so fixated on the design issue, Olmsted pointed out, Vaux was guilty of an unwitting slight of his own. Clearly, Vaux placed no value on Olmsted's administrative achievements or policing innovations, treating these as though they were lesser endeavors. These were also crucial to the park's success, he pointed out. But perhaps Vaux was too much the artist, too hung up on his "superior education in certain directions," as Olmsted termed it.

As for "architect in chief"—the title Vaux so clearly coveted—well, that was just empty words. Rearing up, Olmsted asserted that no mere title could capture the breadth of his skills. He could move fluidly between art and administration, between the high-flown world of ideas and the practical world of men. That, *all of that*, is what he had brought to their work together, and how dare Vaux challenge him? He concluded, "By fact of natural gift . . . I have been worth most to the park."

There was an unexpected hauteur to Olmsted's letter. Also more than a hint of defensiveness. Broad skilled though he may have been, he had so far succeeded in bringing neither administration nor artistry to the Mariposa mines.

It had been a terrible autumn, and the clincher came when Olmsted received word that a fire had burned a couple of barns on the Staten Island farm. The fire destroyed some furniture he was storing, realia from his trips through the South, and an old letter he owned that had been written by George Washington. On New Year's Day, 1864, Olmsted composed a letter to his father. The recent barn fire, he wrote, "helps to strengthen an unpleasant sense of being cut off from my past life. . . . I confess I am sadly homesick. It is very hard to make up my mind to adopt this as my home or to begin life over again in making friends here."

Yet there was hope, hope being one by-product of Olmsted's boundless energy. When things were at their darkest, by ceaselessly casting about, he was often able to find that first tiny marker—a vague idea, a general direction, something, anything—pointing the way to redemption.

During a mine inspection, at the edge of the Mariposa property, Olmsted had spotted an amazing sight in the distance. This, he knew, was Yosemite. He hadn't had a chance to visit yet. Besides Indians, who until recently had lived in the valley for millennia, only a few hundred people had ever entered the place. But Olmsted had seen photographs. He'd read about this natural wonder in popular accounts published back East in magazines like the *Atlantic*. The most striking feature that Olmsted could make out was a huge bare cliff of palest granite. El Capitan. "Think of it as 13 times as high as Trinity spire," he wrote to Mary. It was a reference to Trinity Church, at 284 feet the tallest building then in New York City.

Way in the distance, Olmsted had spied something that promised an alternative to all this dust and disappointment.

CHAPTER 20

Yosemite

THE MARIPOSA OPERATION continued to stagger along. One month the yield would bump up only to fall right back the next—all very confounding.

Olmsted was starting to realize the cruel calculus of gold mining. Yes, there was gold in these mountains. Yes, Mariposa had once been profitable, had the potential to be so once more. But something had to change. He needed to luck into a serious pay streak. Or maybe Mother Nature would cooperate with a deluge, swelling the rivers, putting those defunct streams back on the map.

Instead, he contended with a steady flow of Frémont creditors. Former mine managers, equipment suppliers, and dry goods merchants showed up one after another, hands outstretched. "He (Fremont) seems to have worn out the patience, after draining the purses, of all his friends in California," Olmsted wrote to his father. "Whether he is more knave or fool is the only question. I am over-run with visits from his creditors who all hope to get something from the new owners of the estate."

The prospects looked bleaker each day. But 125 miles to the north, the mines in the Grass Valley section of California were on a production rampage, thanks to a quirk of geography. These mines were lower in the Sierra foothills and had more reliable water sources. Recently, the Grass Valley operations had grown highly profitable. The owners, wisely, were using some of their proceeds to buy new equipment and to invest in technology such as more efficient stamps and new amalgamation processes.

Spend money, make money; it was a virtuous circle, and Grass Valley was putting Mariposa to shame.

Olmsted dispatched his chief engineer to Grass Valley to learn the most current gold-mining methods. But there wasn't anything that could be readily applied to the Mariposa Estate. Unable to increase production, stymied on capital improvements, Olmsted used the only lever he had to keep the struggling concern going.

On March 1, 1864, after first hiding every weapon he could locate, Olmsted cut the miners' salaries. Pay on the Mariposa Estate, by his reckoning, was five times higher than in New York. It was higher than other California mining outfits, too, another sign of the previous management's carelessness. Olmsted cut the miners' wages from $3.50 to $3.15 per day. The miners immediately went on strike. This is what Olmsted *did*, whispered the men; this is *why* he had been brought out West. He held firm, content to lose many of the workers, particularly the bitter, failed prospectors who filled the ranks. "They hate regularity, order and discipline," he complained, "and they influence the whole body of our hands. They have never done with their recollections of the days when the working miners governed matters as they wished, with revolvers in their belts as they worked."

As a small concession, Olmsted lowered the cost of the company-run boardinghouses. This is where married men lived, the most stable element in his labor force. He wanted to encourage these particular workers to stay. Otherwise, Olmsted played rough. He placed ads seeking new hires in San Francisco papers. He brought in Chinese immigrants, willing to work for as little as $1.75 a day. With a flood of replacement workers, the strike broke quickly, and more than half of his original workforce simply walked away.

While Olmsted was busy putting down a mine strike, he became the beneficiary of a proposal put forth by a complete stranger. Olmsted wasn't even aware of the honor, but he would learn about it shortly.

Israel Raymond sent a letter about Yosemite to John Conness, a U.S. senator from California. Raymond was one of the earliest advocates for preserving the valley. His concern was partially borne out of his job as an executive with a steamship company. Conveying tourists to California to visit Yosemite could be a boon to his business. But steps were required to curb other commercial interests, ones that might not be so partial to the scenery. Already people were timbering near Yosemite, and miners couldn't be far behind.

Raymond urged that some kind of intervention was needed on behalf of this natural marvel. With his letter, he included a set of stereographic prints by Carleton Watkins, a photographer who had captured some of the first images of the valley. Raymond also provided a list of names, Olmsted's among them, of people who would be well qualified to serve on a Yosemite commission. There is zero evidence that Olmsted and Raymond had even met at this point. Rather, it appears that Raymond—aware that the distinguished gentleman behind Central Park was now in his midst—simply placed Olmsted's name on a list of viable candidates.

In a young America, a pioneering spirit prevailed, nowhere more than in California. All things were possible. Manage the staff of a wartime medical outfit, get tapped to supervise a gold mine. Supervise a gold mine, get included on a list of the wilderness advocates best qualified to preserve Yosemite. (With the environmental movement still decades away, the irony here—that Olmsted's gold mine was a terribly *un*green business—didn't even register.)

Senator Conness was moved by Raymond's plea. He forwarded the letter to California's General Land Office, requesting that it be used as the framework for crafting a bill. The legislative process was rolling and would move remarkably fast.

A welcome distraction from mine business was the arrival of Olmsted's family in California. Their original departure from the East Coast had encountered a series of delays. Then they'd spent a month journeying on the Panama route. When the family disembarked near midnight on March 11, after a full day sitting in the San Francisco Harbor waiting for the fog to clear, Olmsted was relieved that they'd made it at last.

Mary and the four children were accompanied by Harriet Errington, an English-born teacher who had run a school for girls on Staten

Island. Growing up, Mary had been her pupil. Miss Errington had been hired as a governess for the Olmsted children in schoolless Bear Valley.

Olmsted bid good riddance to Oso House and moved his family and the governess into a suite of rooms above the Mariposa Company general store. The children instantly took to the freedom and exoticism of a western mining town. Miss Errington tailored her teachings to the setting, taking the children outdoors for their lessons. She rode on horseback, pointing out plants and fossils embedded in stone, while the three older children tailed behind on donkeys named Fanny, Kitty, and Beppo. The kids got to pan for gold and found it thrilling. To everyone's delight, two-year-old Marion said her first full sentence: "I know what stage say—stage say God damn!" Apparently, the little girl had noted the colorful language used by coach drivers.

It was a happy reunion between Olmsted and his family. He'd been away for much of his marriage. He'd missed long stretches of the children's lives as they grew up. Olmsted felt the most at ease he had in months, perhaps years. An entry from eleven-year-old John Charles's diary captures the flavor of Olmsted family life on the frontier: "I was very busy sewing my overall so that I could climb the pine trees to get the nuts out of the cones to eat. We have an owl that is two months old. Mother and father rode out and they saw a brown fox limping along. The therm 96 [degrees]."

There was even a rapprochement with Vaux. As a kind of peace offering, Vaux sent a blueprint of a proposed Bear Valley home for the Olmsted family. It was called "Marion House"—a tribute to the youngest daughters in the Olmsted and Vaux families, both named Marion.

Whenever Vaux designed rural houses, especially during his partnership with Andrew Jackson Downing, one of his principal tenets was asymmetry. Taking a free-form approach, following nature's dictates, was key in Vaux's view to creating a proper respite for his clients, a place where they could escape overordered city life. For the Mariposa Estate, Vaux sensed, the design challenge was precisely the opposite. Chaos reigned in this place; order was the requirement if a family home was to be a sanctuary. Thus, Vaux designed Marion House to be utterly symmetrical.

(The house would never be built for lack of funds, and, sadly, the plan has been lost.)

In the summer of 1864, California was still in the throes of a terrible drought. Water had grown so scarce by late July that the Mariposa gold mills were working way below capacity. Precious little was getting done; Olmsted found himself supervising an operation that had grown skeletal.

To escape the oppressive heat, he decided to take his family on an extended wilderness camping expedition, with Yosemite as their ultimate destination. He planned to return alone to the estate periodically to check on the gold mines. In autumn, when production could be expected to bump up, he'd resume full-time duties.

The Olmsted family set out with another couple as their companions, the Ashburners. (William Ashburner was a mining consultant whom Olmsted had met through his Mariposa job.) The party also included Miss Errington, a housekeeper, and a guide—eleven people in total—requiring a caravan of ten saddle horses, eight mules, and two carriages. Traveling over treacherous mountain passes, two full days were needed to cover the forty miles to their first destination, Galen Clark's ranch. Clark was a garrulous, wild-bearded woodsman who spun out leisurely and vividly detailed adventure tales for his visitors. His log cabin and surrounding property served as a kind of way station for travelers bound for Yosemite.

A mere fifteen years earlier, Yosemite had been known only to Indians. That changed with the Gold Rush, as settlers flooded the California frontier. Hunting deer and other game, sometimes to the point of depletion, brought the settlers and Indians quickly into conflict. Partly out of retaliation, partly from sheer hunger, the local Ahwahneechee had taken to butchering and eating the settlers' horses. On March 25, 1851, an armed battalion of frontiersmen set out after a band of Ahwahneechee, pursuing them into a remote valley. The Indians promptly got away. But that was the first recorded "visit" to Yosemite.

By 1864, Yosemite still remained incredibly isolated; to go there was a true adventure. By one account, only about six hundred non-Native people had entered the valley. That meant Olmsted's eleven-person party represented 2 percent of the total traffic to this point. Clark seemed to have met every last one of these travelers, leading Olmsted to dub him "the doorkeeper of Yosemite." Each of these visitors, in turn, seems to have produced an account of their journey in one form or another.

Carleton Watkins entered the valley with twelve mules to lug his photographic equipment, including his "Mammoth camera" and another for taking stereographic pictures. He developed the photos on-site in a darkened tent. Watkins's work became the major draw at a New York gallery, generating great acclaim and much curiosity.

Fitz Hugh Ludlow had contributed to the *Atlantic* a widely read article, "Seven Weeks in the Great Yo-Semite." Albert Bierstadt had spent the summer of 1863, right before Olmsted arrived in California, making sketches in Yosemite. The sketches were studies for two paintings that caused a sensation, *Domes of Yosemite* and *Valley of Yosemite.*

Olmsted's party set up a base camp on the banks of a mountain stream that ran through Clark's spread. The men and boys slept under the stars wrapped in blankets. The women slept in tents. Not long after the party's arrival, Indians began to gather on the land directly across the stream from them. There were only a few at first, but even that was cause for concern. They kept arriving by the hour, and soon their ranks had swelled to more than fifty.

As it turned out, they were Miwok. Where the Ahwahneechee were legendary warriors, the Miwok were relatively peaceful. They had gathered for an annual tribal ritual. The Indians busied themselves catching trout in the stream. They sold some of their haul to the Olmsted party. Fish was far superior to bear. A couple of nights earlier, a hunter who had felled a grizzly had passed through the camp. He'd shared some of the meat. Olmsted decided that "poor, coarse beef" was the most charitable description of grizzly.

Olmsted's children established contact, through funny faces and laughter, with the Indian children on the other side of the stream. They begged to cross, and Olmsted let them go. Of course, the Olmsteds spoke no Miwok. The Miwok knew just a few words of broken Spanish, picked up from earlier California settlers. Lack of a common language proved no barrier whatsoever, and the children played together happily.

The trip was off to a great start, already qualified as a memorable adventure. Yosemite still lay ahead. But first, there was a side journey to the Mariposa Grove, a stand of giant sequoias. There were six hundred trees, the oldest dating to roughly 500 BC, making them contemporaries of Pythagoras and Confucius.

Giant sequoias are the largest living things on the planet if one takes into account both their height and their girth. Olmsted was awed by the Grizzly Giant, a sequoia that tops two hundred feet and is more than ninety feet in circumference. He deemed it "probably the noblest tree in the world." He and the others slept under this giant canopy. He noted that the campfire's flickering light didn't reach much beyond the foot of any given tree; from there, the black trunks seemed to stretch all the way to the stars. In the morning, he took measurements of some of the trunks—and then it was on to Yosemite.

The party split in two, with Olmsted, Mary, some of the children, and the guide setting off in advance. The plan was to establish a camp on the valley floor, and then the guide would return for the others. Olmsted paused at Inspiration Point to take in what would become the classic Yosemite vista, a wooded valley bracketed by El Capitan on one side, Half Dome on the other. Olmsted scribbled some notes: "Previous expectations—photographs, sketches—reports of several visitors . . . Yet taken by surprise."

Descending into the valley on horseback was challenging. It took most of a morning. Olmsted and his advance party arrived in time for a picnic lunch on the banks of the Merced. Afterward, searching for a suitable campsite, Olmsted selected a spot with a view of Yosemite Falls, the highest waterfall in North America. It's incredibly dramatic, featuring a river that flows over a cliff, crashes onto a shelf of rock, regrouping into rivulets that flow over another cliff, only to repeat this again—water plunging down three separate tiers, plummeting nearly a half mile.

Olmsted put great effort into positioning the tents just so. He wanted to make sure that Yosemite Falls was perfectly framed. Tie back the flaps, and a tent dweller's view was a triangle, precisely bisected by a line of crashing water in the distance. The effect was akin to Vaux's ever-artful archways framing Central Park scapes as if they were living paintings.

The guide went back for the other half of the party. In the days ahead, they explored the valley, sometimes on horseback, sometimes on foot. Mary was an equestrian quick study, regaining the skill from a youth spent riding. Miss Errington, an especially fearful rider, was given a docile horse.

Olmsted was struck by the extent of the greenery. The ground was thickly carpeted with ferns and wild flowers, such a contrast to dusty Bear Valley. The Merced, he found, reminded him of nothing so much as the Hockanum, a river that flowed near his boyhood home in Connecticut. There was something remarkably gentle about the valley. But one need only look up, he found, and that gentleness was overwhelmed by grandeur. All around, sheer cliff faces jutted straight up from the valley floor, perpendicular for thousands of feet. He had the perception, common to Yosemite visitors, of being remarkably enclosed. And he was intrigued by how even subtle shifts—a morning haze, a cloud's shadow creeping over a rock outcropping—changed the mood of his surroundings.

Olmsted spent more than two weeks in Yosemite. Though he grew familiar with the individual landmarks, he saw this landscape as a total composition. "The union of the deepest sublimity of nature with the deepest beauty of nature," he wrote, "not in one feature or another . . . but all around and wherever the visitor goes, constitutes the Yo Semite the greatest glory of nature."

In Bear Valley, Olmsted had experienced a recurring dream about the English countryside. A mere thirty miles away, he had found wilderness that took his breath away.

In the first week of September 1864, the camping party returned to Bear Valley. On arrival, Olmsted received some pleasant and unexpected news: He had been named to a committee to preserve Yosemite, a place he had only just visited for the first time.

Earlier in the summer, Senator Conness's bill had passed both houses of Congress. Because the nation was still in the midst of the Civil War, the measure generated little discussion and less interest. President Lincoln had signed the bill into law on June 30, 1864. The bill deeded Yosemite Valley and also the nearby Mariposa Grove to the State of California,

meant to ensure that this land didn't fall into the hands of private developers. The national park system didn't even exist yet. Preserving a piece
of land for its scenic value alone was a novel idea. The best way to go
about it, therefore, appeared to be a federal law dictating an action to be
taken by a state.

As for choosing the committee, California governor Frederick Low
simply copied the names suggested in the original letter from Raymond,
the steamship executive. Among the eight members were Raymond; Ashburner, the mining consultant; and Galen Clark, Yosemite's doorkeeper.
Since Olmsted's name headed the list, he became the de facto chairman
of the commission. All members were to serve without pay.

As his first act, Olmsted commissioned a survey of the boundaries of
Yosemite. He paid for it himself. As a man with a "game" leg, as he called
it, he recognized that Yosemite was a challenging destination, difficult
even for intrepid adventurers. So he proposed that more convenient
campgrounds should be established for tenderfoots. He also envisioned a
kind of carriage circuit, connecting Yosemite, the Mariposa Grove, Galen
Clark's ranch, and the gold-mining estate, the last civilized settlement,
such as it was. This would make it possible for people to access these
wilderness wonders more easily. In a letter to one of the surveyors, he advised, "There should be no very long hills of a grade so high that six good
horses could not be kept upon a slow trot, taking up an ordinary stage
coach load."

In the year since Olmsted had left the East, his life had taken on a curious seesaw rhythm. He'd been down and then up: He'd been desperately
lonely, and then the arrival of his family had ushered in one of his happiest times. He'd been up and then down: Olmsted made a great deal of
money, but he'd never seen it slip away so fast.

Recently, he had sold a block of his Mariposa Company stock for a
good profit. Yet he was devoting a considerable portion of his earnings to
repaying the debts he owed, giving priority to what was due his father. He
was alarmed by how quickly he was burning through what was left. There
were unexpected expenses, like employing a governess to teach the children in the absence of a school. Factor in the need for basic items—a

piece of cloth, a chair to sit in—and the cost of frontier life became downright exorbitant.

Through that first year, the one constant had been the drought. But that changed in November 1864, and in spectacular fashion. The heavens opened, and dusty Bear Valley was hit with a deluge. It washed out coach roads, swelled streams, and drowned cattle. It also returned the mills to capacity, and then some. For the month, the Mariposa Estate yielded $83,000 in gold, nearly three times the July yield of $30,000.

Unfortunately, the production surge was partly due to a backlog of ore. Big chunks of raw quartz had been piling up at the stamp mills, awaiting the water necessary for processing. The next month, production fell again.

Down, then up. Up, then down. Olmsted just wished he knew where things were going.

CHAPTER 21

Unsettled in the West

GEORGE OPDYKE AND Thurlow Weed were the worst of enemies. Opdyke, now the former mayor of New York City, remained a principal of the Mariposa Company. Weed was the powerful editor of the *Albany Evening Journal*, who had lately taken to filling the pages of his paper with scandalous allegations about Opdyke.

Among Weed's claims: During his term as mayor, Opdyke had used his political clout to land a lucrative contract to supply blankets to the Union army. He'd proceeded to furnish the troops with ones that were threadbare and shoddy. Weed's paper also asserted that Opdyke had placed himself on a committee to investigate the case of a munitions plant destroyed during the New York City draft riots. The committee recommended that the city pay the plant's owners hefty damages, nearly $200,000. But Opdyke failed to disclose that he had a financial stake in the munitions plant.

Then there was the matter of a legendary California gold-mining property. When Opdyke and his colleagues had joined with Frémont to form the Mariposa Company, Weed maintained that they'd seized on the explorer's financial desperation to cut him unfavorable terms.

Opdyke sued Weed for libel. Weed, in turn, opted for a straightforward legal defense: He and his lawyers planned to prove that all the things the *Albany Evening Journal* had printed were patently true. The sensational trial played out in a New York City courtroom, packed with members of the press. Each day's testimony brought a stream of notable public figures and a fresh torrent of sordid accusations.

The highlight of the trial came on December 21, 1864, when John Frémont himself was called as a witness. Many Americans still viewed Frémont as "the Great Pathfinder," a heroic figure instrumental in taming the frontier and settling California prior to statehood. But time had not been kind to Frémont. Years of financial anxiety had taken their toll on his famous man-of-action bearing. As he took the stand, onlookers noted that he looked haggard and gray.

Weed's lawyer grilled Frémont about the sale of the Mariposa Estate. At a crucial point, the lawyer asked the onetime explorer, "Was any unfair advantage taken of you by any of these gentlemen in any of the negotiations?"

Fremont paused for way too long.

"No, I-I-I think not," he finally replied.

The stammer was telling. Frémont had just revealed that he viewed himself as the victim of a swindle. That made Opdyke and his colleagues swindlers, supporting Weed's newspaper accounts.

But Frémont-as-business-naïf was only half the story. During a lengthy questioning, Weed's lawyer teased various damning admissions out of Frémont. As it turns out, he had also swindled the swindlers. Frémont had engaged in all sorts of shenanigans, such as failing to disclose some big debts that later came back to bite the new company. These details—many of them already suspected by Olmsted since his arrival in Bear Valley—also came to light during the trial.

Opdyke had gone to court hoping to clear his name. It backfired. Instead, Weed succeeded in proving that it ain't libel if it's true.

During Frémont's testimony, however, another thing became abundantly clear to the assembled newspaper scribes. The Mariposa outfit was a den of thieves. A group of disreputable men had joined forces, cheating each other at every opportunity, but reserving their worst for the public to whom they sold shares in a gold company with modest production and a mountain of debt.

The jig was up. During the days immediately following the trial, Opdyke, Frémont, and the rest of the Mariposa chiselers raced to unload their shares. The company's stock, which had recently traded as high as $45, fell below $10.

Olmsted wasn't immediately aware of any of this. News from the East often took weeks to reach Bear Valley. In fact, the first Olmsted heard of the Opdyke-Weed libel trial and its disastrous fallout was on January 6, 1865, when three men showed up at the estate. The first was a representative of the Bank of California, which had just stopped honoring all Mariposa Company financial transactions due to insufficient funds. The second was a representative of Dodge Brothers, a wholesale supplier to the estate's general stores that was owed a great deal of money. The pair was accompanied by a sheriff, who planned to seize the property. It would be sold to pay back the various creditors.

Olmsted sat down with the three men and pieced together the story. He was flabbergasted. But he persuaded them to hold off on any action until he could get in contact with the Mariposa board. Of course, a telegraph on the estate would have facilitated long-distance communication. But plans for one had been scrapped due to financial problems. Instead, Olmsted resolved to go to San Francisco. Once there, he hoped to establish a dialogue with the board via telegraph and maybe learn what options were even possible.

Before departing, Olmsted gathered up $4,000 in gold bullion and some mining equipment. He wrote a bill of sale, transferring this property to himself. Olmsted's handshake deal with the Mariposa board—he had failed to get a written contract—called for him to receive his entire salary at the *end* of each year's work. He was owed $10,000. He figured the gold bullion and equipment would about cover what he was due and that this might be his only chance to get paid. (Luckily, Olmsted had sold much of his stock a month before the Opdyke-Weed trial.)

It took Olmsted three days to travel to San Francisco, a hard journey that ordinarily required two days. Ironically, the same rainstorm that had caused a temporary bump in the Mariposa Estate's gold yield had damaged the coach roads. At the Bank of California's offices, he used the company's telegraph to send an anxious dispatch. He waited. No answer.

Olmsted checked into a hotel. Over the next few days, he visited the bank offices repeatedly, hoping for some word from back East. None. "I have made no progress & heard nothing from New York," he wrote Mary from San Francisco. " . . . A lingering death of Mariposa—uncertainty and hope deferred, seems the most disagreeable prospect for us—for me."

But there was news from Bear Valley. And it was ominous. Because the miners had stopped getting paid, they'd stop working. They were panicked, hungry, and threatening to loot the general stores. Olmsted sent yet another telegram to New York, still more urgent than the last. Finally, he received a reply: "Should a few guarantee present indebtedness can we rely implicitly on early profits of Estate for reimbursement."

Olmsted couldn't believe it. Even by telegraphic standards, this was an enigmatic response. It reminded him of the bewildering counsel provided by Jack Bunsby in *Dombey and Son*, Dickens's novel concerning a shipping company.

By now, Olmsted knew he was working for a bunch of crooks. Even so, the extent of their brazenness seems to have taken him by surprise. The Mariposa Company still owned real working mines full of expensive equipment and capable of producing gold, overhyped expectations notwithstanding. He figured the board would offer something—a directive, a strategy, a warning. But all they had provided was this "Bunsbyish impertinence," as he termed the telegram.

Olmsted asked the bank to give him one hundred days to sort things out. As a first step, he composed an executive order and mailed it to one of the managers back at the Mariposa Estate. He requested that it be read aloud in front of each mine and then posted. The decree has been lost, but the gist of his message to the miners was as follows: Get back to work, as the mines are the source from which everything else flows. Olmsted arranged for a sheriff to distribute the miners' pay directly from the gold that was produced. Gold would also be used to pay off the debt to the general stores, so they might agree to reopen. The miners would have employment and something to buy with their salaries; the general stores would have a market for their goods.

It was a total improvisation on Olmsted's part, a kind of Wild West bankruptcy workout. Many of the miners, seeing the logic in Olmsted's order, returned to their jobs. Olmsted opted to remain in San Francisco, sending out telegraphs, hoping for some kind of resolution.

Waiting was excruciating. For much of the time, Olmsted sat by himself in a hotel room. Looking out the window, at one point, he counted six hundred people walking along Montgomery Street. He noted with alarm that nearly all the passersby were vigorous, fast moving, displaying a marked sense of purpose. Olmsted counted only two people—two!—who were unequivocally over forty. He was forty-two now. The West was a young man's world, and he wasn't sure that he had what it took.

Periodically, he met with angry creditors and tried to keep them appeased. Or he'd drop by the bank office checking for dispatches that never came.

One advantage of this exile in San Francisco, at least, was that it was possible to stay current on the progress of the Civil War. Here, it was so much easier than in remote Bear Valley. When he heard about the fall of Richmond, the Confederate capital, he knew the conflict was nearing an end. It was only a matter of time.

On April 9, 1865, Olmsted went alone to a morning service at San Francisco's First Unitarian Church. As the congregation launched into "The Battle Hymn of the Republic," Olmsted pitched suddenly into a mood of near-unfathomable darkness. It was as if all the events of recent months washed over him. He was devastated. Why, he wondered, had he traded duty with a wartime medical outfit for the sucker promise of a gold mine? Now, Union victory was drawing near, and he was away in a distant outpost. What was he doing in San Francisco? Where was he headed?

All these feelings, coursing about, found focus in an upwelling of longing for John: "But, today, singing *Glory! Hallelujah!* with a great congregation and looking at the great flag of victory held over us, though of all with whom I ever had conscious sympathy or hope and prayer for this day I stood alone—and my heart cried back stronger than ever to my poor, sad, unhopeful brother, who alone of all the world, ever really knew me and trusted me for exactly what I was."

That very same day, on the other side of the continent, General Lee was defeated in the battle of Appomattox Court House. It was the final major battle of the Civil War. Less than one week later Lincoln was assassinated. He was pronounced dead on April 15, 1865, at 7:22 a.m.

Olmsted was on his way to the bank office when the news reached San Francisco. All around him, the ordinarily bustling streets fell silent; people were in shock, moving as if in a dream. "I have never seen such an intense and pervading public feeling," Olmsted wrote to his father. In a letter to a friend, he added: "I can't help feeling that the best part of me is pining here in a sort of solitary confinement, & a man is never so lonely as in a crowd of strangers—even though a sympathetic crowd."

Olmsted joined a group of 15,000 San Franciscans in a solemn march from Washington Square to a pavilion on Stockton Street, where the Reverend Horatio Stebbins delivered a eulogy. It was all so sudden. When Lincoln died, a formal treaty ending the war had not even been signed yet. But the South was done, utterly vanquished. "At any rate the nation lives and is immortal and Slavery is dead," Olmsted wrote.

Olmsted sent a letter to Mary in Bear Valley, instructing her to drape their home in black cloth in Lincoln's memory. "I would do so simply to impress the event in the minds of the children," he wrote, adding that "the awful calamity of the country . . . almost disables me from thinking of anything else."

Soon the one hundred days that Olmsted had requested from the bank was up. There was still no word from New York, so Olmsted had to make a decision himself. The mining firm remained thousands of dollars in debt. He worked out a deal with Dodge Brothers, the general-store supplier. Dodge Brothers agreed to run the mines, using the proceeds to pay themselves back along with the many other creditors. As part of the arrangement, Olmsted stepped down as manager.

Late in the spring of 1865, Olmsted rejoined his family in Bear Valley. Money was quickly running out. Despite everything he'd been through, he clung to a perverse hope that something might change with the Mariposa Company. Maybe there would be a fresh twist and he'd be rehired at his old salary. Too much had happened, too soon, and it was hard to process.

Barring that, Olmsted would need to stir up new work. He planned to use the Bear Valley as a base, such as it was, and periodically make the long, dusty commute to San Francisco to try to stir up opportunities.

That was his plan—*plan* being a very loose term at this point. He began casting about. As a sailor-turned-farmer-turned-park maker, lately a gold-mine supervisor, there were so many things he had done, more still that he might do. He found himself pulled this way and that by all the possibilities—a tyranny of choices.

Journalism was an option. Godkin had finally lined up funding for the publication that he and Olmsted had tried to launch at the height of the Civil War. Rather than any of the names Olmsted had suggested, it was to be called the *Nation*. Godkin wrote Olmsted suggesting that he write a series of West Coast dispatches for the new publication similar to his earlier Southern dispatches: "Why won't you prepare to do for the *Nation* about the Pacific Coast what you did for the *Times* about the Seaboard States?" Olmsted declined. With a startup publication, whether his work would actually appear in print was a speculation, and low pay was an outright guarantee.

Maybe he'd try the oil industry instead. Oil had recently been discovered in California. There was a ready market: It could be burned for heat or used to lubricate heavy machinery. During the past year, he'd traveled to several spots in the state to visit wells. Of all things, he had been elected in abstentia as president of an oil company. The tiny upstart offered no salary, only a block of valueless stock. Olmsted had said no thanks to that offer. The more he thought about oil, the less sense it made. Oil appeared even more speculative than mining for gold, if that was possible.

Olmsted even checked out the wine business in Sonoma. Because California wine making was still very much in its infancy, Olmsted was actually able to land a consulting assignment. Olmsted visited the Buena Vista Vinicultural Society run by Agoston Haraszthy. Since emigrating from Hungary, Haraszthy had worked as a steamboat captain on the Mississippi and served as the first town marshal of San Diego. In 1861, he traveled to Europe, returning with 100,000 grapevine cuttings. He introduced them in his Sonoma vineyard to see what grew. Olmsted spent two days on his property before producing a report that concluded, "The business is one promising extraordinary profits."

As a wine consultant, Olmsted's advice was dubious. During his visit, the first evidence of phylloxera, also known as root louse, must have been visible. Within a year, the infestation would decimate Haraszthy's vineyard, prompting him to abandon Sonoma for Nicaragua. There, he tried to start a sugar plantation before disappearing under mysterious circumstances. Haraszthy's horse was found tied near the banks of an alligator-infested river, but he was never heard from again. He was presumed eaten.

Haraszthy is often called the "Father of California Viniculture." If Olmsted was wrong about the state of his vineyards, he was right at least about the prospects for California wine.

Unsettled in the West, desperate for money, Olmsted rattled this way and that. Tellingly, he reserved his greatest energy for seeking out landscape architecture jobs. Yet despite his enduring passion for the outdoors and his success with Central Park, he was less certain than ever that there was enough demand to make a living as a landscape architect.

The first project he embarked upon was actually one that he'd been handed while still supervising the Mariposa Estate. It was also his first solo commission, landed without Vaux. Now that his gold-mine obligations appeared finished, Olmsted turned his attention to the job.

The Mountain View Cemetery was to occupy 200 acres in the hills above Oakland. In preparing a design sans Vaux, Olmsted worked with a hired draftsman. As with Central Park, he showed an unusual sensitivity to the unique requirements of the site. He came up with a variety of thoughtful cemetery-design touches. Many of the people who would be buried in the cemetery were Chinese immigrants. So Olmsted's plan included a "receiving tomb" to hold bodies temporarily until they could be returned to China, as was then the practice. There was also a preponderance of single men in California's highly transient population, as Olmsted had noted. So his plan included an unusual number of single plots.

The land set aside for the cemetery was a bowl consisting of a flat, dusty floor surrounded by steep barren hillsides. When it came to plantings, this was quite a challenge. A stately canopy of elms was simply not going to be possible. Here again, Olmsted proved extremely imaginative, suggesting a tree—the cypress—that he believed would thrive on the grounds while striking the perfect note of reverence:

Being an evergreen, and seeming more than any other tree to point toward heaven, it has always been regarded as typical of immortality. For this and other reasons, it was considered by the Persians and Hebrews of old, as it is by the Turks and Oriental Christians of the present day, more appropriate than any other tree for planting about graves. Thucydides mentions that the ashes of the Greeks who died for their country were preserved in Cypress; and Horace speaks of the custom among the Romans of dressing the bodies of the dead with Cypress before placing them in the tomb. It is the gopher-wood of Scripture, of which, according to the tradition of the Hebrews, the Ark was made; and it constituted the "exalted grove" of Mount Sion, spoken of in Ecclesiastes. Here, then, is a tree which seems peculiarly fitted by its associations, as well as its natural character, for your purposes.

Olmsted's plan greatly pleased his client; he received a much-needed $1,000. He also chased several other landscape architecture projects, but with far less success.

Earlier, during his lonely stay in San Francisco, Olmsted had haunted the Bank of California office, awaiting telegrams that never came. It was a display of doggedness that greatly impressed the bank's president, Darius Mills. While Mills was appalled by the Mariposa Company and its team of Wall Street chiselers, he developed a great respect for Olmsted and asked him to draw up a plan for his large country estate. Back in Bear Valley, Olmsted received word that he'd failed to win the commission. But the name Olmsted suggested for the estate stuck: Millbrae. (Over time, a city grew up on the land, still known today as Millbrae, California.)

Another possible landscape job came from Henry Coon, mayor of San Francisco. He met with Olmsted, and the pair walked over a desolate, wind-whipped section of land. Apparently, there was some desire to create a park here. But the city commissioners and other interested parties were intent on a reprise of Central Park in San Francisco. Olmsted argued for a park more appropriate to the city's climate and topography. Mayor Coon asked Olmsted to draft a proposal. Meanwhile, the trustees of the soon-to-be-opened College of California contacted Olmsted. He was asked to submit a preliminary design for the campus grounds and also the surrounding community. Both of these projects struck Olmsted as highly speculative; neither seemed likely to progress quickly.

While Olmsted cast about, Vaux was busy back in New York. He entered into a heated battle with Richard Morris Hunt. Hunt, the first American to attend Paris's École des Beaux-Arts, was an architect with a flair for the grand. His star was lately on the rise, and he had proposed that a series of monumental gates be placed at various entry points into Central Park. This was very out of keeping with Olmsted and Vaux's human-scale, rustic treatment. Vaux succeeded in derailing Hunt's proposal. To achieve this required Vaux to reopen communication with the Central Park board of commissioners. This was his first real contact with them since he and Olmsted had resigned a couple years earlier.

There were also encouraging signals about a possible Brooklyn park. Plans had been on hold for years. But with the end of the Civil War, there was a sudden burst of progress. The park's commissioners decided to reconsider a design they had accepted some years back, generally agreed to be a thoroughly lackluster effort. They approached Vaux, asking him to submit a competing proposal.

During the spring and summer of 1865, while Vaux pursued the commission, he wrote Olmsted repeatedly, trying to enlist his participation. Olmsted dutifully responded. Given the vagaries of the mail— it could take a month for a letter to travel between the coasts—there was a crazy-quilt quality to their correspondence. Sometimes Vaux reiterated a point, not realizing that Olmsted had already addressed it in a letter then in transit. Other times, Olmsted tried to anticipate an argument that Vaux might make, only to receive a letter that went off in a totally different direction.

Despite this fractured time sequence, the major themes of their exchange remained intact. Vaux felt certain that he was closing in on a commission—a major park commission. Olmsted felt compelled to hold back. There was nothing firm yet; it was a tentative prospect at best. Vaux's letters only added to his dizzying array of possibilities. "I trust you are getting on pretty well," Vaux wrote. "We may have some fun together yet. I wish you could have seen your destiny in our art. God meant you should. I really believe, at times, although he may have something different for you to do yet he cannot have anything nobler in store for you." He signed the letter, "With love, Yours, C. V." Back in the autumn of 1863, when they'd gotten into a scrape, Vaux had used the far chillier "Yours faithfully." With the reference to "your destiny in our art," Vaux reopened those earlier arguments about art versus business, the world of ideas versus the world of men.

Olmsted wrote back, "I love beautiful landscapes and rural recreations and people in rural recreations—better than anybody else I know. But I don't feel strong on the art side. I don't feel myself an artist, I feel rather as if it was sacrilegious in me to post myself in the portals of Art." He protested again that there was more to him, so much more, than could be summed up in simple art. He had such diverse abilities; he'd occupied so many roles in life. Why, the job he'd lately done—and many of the options he was considering—were far afield from art, capital *A*, Art.

"Nobody cares two straws for the mines in St. Francisco," Vaux asserted. "As yet you are the representative man of the C. P. [Central Park] and not much else to New Yorkers, and very likely the majority of those who think of the matter at all suppose you still to be at work there." In this, Vaux showed a wily side and a deep understanding of his friend's psychology.

Olmsted suggested that park work was unattractive because it would necessarily subject him to meddlers such as Andrew Green. "A scheme that can be upset by a Green is sure to be upset, for men of his caliber are to be found everywhere," answered Vaux.

Why, Olmsted demanded, didn't Vaux simply plan to do the Brooklyn park by himself? Vaux's response: "Your objection to the plan is I believe at heart because it involves the idea of common fraternal effort. It is too republican an idea for you, you must have a thick line drawn round your sixpen' worth of individuality. . . . Well! Well!"

Eventually, Vaux grew weary of Olmsted's heel dragging. As the correspondence carried on, he couldn't resist a few zingers. He called Olmsted a "stubborn cemetery maker in California." In another, Vaux dubbed him "Frederick the Great, Prince of Park Police." Even these jibes were carefully crafted—sly, remarkably candid, designed to get what he wanted. He saw Olmsted clearly. Moreover, he knew how Olmsted preferred not to see himself. Vaux let fly: "If I go on and do Brooklyn alone, well or ill, you suffer because the public naturally will say, if Olmsted really was the prime mover in the C. P., why is he not ready to go forward in the path that he started in."

Right in the middle of this epistolary slugfest, another letter arrived from a man of whom Olmsted had never heard: William B. Scott. Olmsted received it in late July 1865. Apparently, the Mariposa Company had reorganized; Scott was the new president. It was the first message Olmsted had received from New York in nearly six months. And it was far simpler and clearer than that earlier Bunsbyish telegram. Under the new management, Scott explained, Olmsted's services were no longer needed. Just like that, any lingering hopes Olmsted had about renewing his work as a gold-mine supervisor were extinguished.

Scott's tenure as president would last just one month. He was replaced, then his replacement replaced, and so it would go. The Mariposa Estate would stagger on for decades to come. No end of people were beguiled by the promise of riches. There was always someone willing to try where others had failed, and soon a company would be formed and investors found, but never much gold, and so the Mariposa mines kept on through endless iterations right up to the eve of World War II. "Its business history," as historian Allan Nevins once wrote, "is a thorny and profitless maze."

As for Frémont, he'd go down as one of the nineteenth century's greatest riches-to-rags story. Within a few years, he'd be forced to look to the kindness of his few remaining friends for his next meal and a place to lay his head at night. Once worth $10 million, he died nearly penniless.

The seesaw rhythm of Olmsted's life—and indeed of his times—continued. Hot on the heels of Scott's letter came news from Vaux. He had landed a commission to submit a preliminary design for the Brooklyn park. Not only that, but the Central Park board had requested that he and Olmsted return as landscape architects. These were two real jobs

offering real money—the kind of opportunity that might prompt someone to uproot his family again and move back across the continent.

Olmsted replied at once, agreeing to return to New York. In a subsequent letter, Olmsted would rather imperiously ask Vaux to find him a
horse and locate suitable housing for his family. There could be no doubt
as to the terms of this partnership: It would be Olmsted and Vaux, never
Vaux and Olmsted. Vaux didn't mind. There was art to be done, and he
knew that he needed Olmsted.

Before leaving California, Olmsted had one last act, one that would re-
verberate through the centuries ahead. It involved his role as chairman of
the commission on Yosemite and the Mariposa Grove. In a local paper, he
had seen a mention that Schuyler Colfax was planning to visit Yosemite.
Colfax was the Speaker of the U.S. House of Representatives. Back in
1860, when an overland mail route across the United States was completed,
Colfax had planned to commemorate the event with a cross-country trip,
ending with a visit to Yosemite. But his plan, like so many other plans,
had been interrupted by the Civil War.

At last, Colfax had embarked on his journey. He planned to arrive in
the Sierra Nevada in early August. Several journalists were accompanying
Colfax, among them reporters for the *New York Tribune* and *Chicago
Tribune*, as well as Samuel Bowles. Bowles was the much-respected editor of the *Springfield (Mass.) Republican* and an advocate of brevity when
bloated passages were the rule. Olmsted greatly admired Bowles and considered the *Republican* one of the best papers in America.

Olmsted arranged to meet up with the Colfax party to accompany
them on the Yosemite leg of their journey. In preparation, Olmsted wrote
an 8,000-word treatise about Yosemite.

On August 8, 1865, Colfax and his entourage of journalists entered the
valley. Olmsted had managed to round up several of his fellow commissioners such as William Ashburner and Galen Clark. The party had swelled
to nineteen people, likely the largest group to visit Yosemite since that first
battalion pursued the Ahwahneechee. The Colfax party hiked and swam,
hunted and fished. At night, they sang rollicking versions of Civil War anthems such as "John Brown's Body" and "Marching Through Georgia."

On August 9, Olmsted gathered everyone together for an impromptu reading of his treatise. The work sounded many of Olmsted's long-held concerns. There was Olmsted as reformer, urging that Yosemite must be made available to everyone in a democratic society: "Yosemite should be held, guarded and managed for the free use of the whole body of the people forever."

There was also Olmsted the futurist, though that was then a term that lay ahead in, well, the future. It's apt nevertheless; Olmsted often demonstrated a surprising capacity to see where the world was headed. Back in 1858, Olmsted had cautioned the Central Park commissioners that any viable park design must take into account the built-up Manhattan of 1878 and beyond. Now he applied the same idea to Yosemite, telling his small audience that—believe it or not—masses of people would one day descend on the place. "Before many years," he declared, "if proper facilities are offered, these hundreds will become thousands and in a century the whole number of visitors will be counted in the millions. An injury to the scenery so slight that it may be unheeded by any visitor now, will be one of deplorable magnitude when its effect upon each visitor's enjoyment is multiplied by these millions."

Yosemite needed to be protected for posterity. Olmsted was addressing the gathering as a kind of proto-environmentalist. The masses would visit Yosemite—and they should—but this land must be preserved for their benefit, something that no private interest could be counted on to do. It was the rightful role of government. And it was a role, he said, that should be expanded to other wild spaces as well: "The establishment by the government of great public grounds for the free enjoyment of the people under certain circumstances, is thus justified and enforced as a political duty."

His address concluded with a request that California set aside $37,000. These monies would be used to manage Yosemite and also to build the carriage circuit and campgrounds for tenderfoots that he envisioned. Following the trip, Olmsted tried to submit his treatise to the legislature. While Conness's bill had deeded the land to the state, there was no provision for any funding. Olmsted's request, and the entire fifty-two-page report that accompanied it, was promptly put aside. Fortunately, however, Olmsted had already read this treatise to the Colfax party, many of whom were journalists. Several of them wound up writing books about the cross-country excursion, expending much ink on Yosemite. Even Congressman Colfax—a journalist by training, later to become the first journalist to serve as vice president, under Grant—produced a tome. Bowles wrote a travel classic, *Across the Continent: A Summer's Journey to the Rocky Mountains, the Mormons, and the Pacific States.*

Earlier written accounts of Yosemite had dutifully related the valley's wonders. Paintings and photos had captured its beauty. But the Colfax party's various books differed in that they also included calls for conservation, echoing Olmsted. Not only should Yosemite be passively appreciated by visitors, but the valley also required active protection by an enlightened government. Bowles even listed some other sites deserving the same consideration, such as Niagara Falls and parts of Maine.

Famously, the idea for a *national* park system was born in 1870 around a campfire in Yellowstone. But that campfire gathering was picking up on a notion that had been building for some time: There was steamship executive Raymond's original letter to Senator Conness, followed by Olmsted's address to the Colfax party, followed by a collection of books that sent the idea of wilderness preservation ricocheting through American culture.

Things came full circle in 1906, when after years of mismanagement by the State of California—and following the tireless efforts of Galen Clark and John Muir—Yosemite became a national park. With his August 1865 address, Olmsted played a key early role in the conservation of America's wild spaces.

Olmsted's work in California was done. He and his family returned to New York by way of Nicaragua—the cheap route.

VI
"Where Talents and the
Needs of the World Cross"

SHAPING THE NATION,
1865–1877

CHAPTER 22

New Prospects

ON NOVEMBER 21, 1865, Olmsted and his family began their approach into New York Harbor aboard the steamer *Ericson*. Passage from California had taken exactly forty days. But then came a hitch. A fierce storm prevented the *Ericson* from docking. The family passed an anxious night drifting in the water, riding the storm out.

Next day, when they finally arrived in New York, they were met by a small group of people. Vaux was waiting on the pier along with a couple of employees from his architectural firm. Godkin, editor of the *Nation*, was also there. Olmsted and his family moved into a boardinghouse at 167 East 14th Street—a temporary arrangement. Meanwhile, most of their California possessions had been shipped separately and were making a slow circuit around Cape Horn.

Olmsted and Vaux got directly to work on the Brooklyn park. They were charged with creating a new design for a project that predated their involvement and had been bouncing around for about five years. Back in 1860, a newly formed Brooklyn park commission had obtained a 300-acre tract of undeveloped land, the future site of what was then known as Mount Prospect Park. Brooklyn was a separate community from New York. It was, in fact, the third-largest city in the nation after New York and Philadelphia. Brooklyn's civic leaders were intent on building a grand park, a suitable equivalent to Central Park in their rival community just across the East River. What they sorely lacked was an attractive site. The property slated for the park was broken by an existing thoroughfare, carving it into two pieces. One parcel featured Mount Prospect—in actuality, more of a steep hill than a mountain, but a difficult piece of topography to integrate into a park plan nonetheless. At the top of the hill sat a reservoir, holding Brooklyn's drinking water.

The original design commission fell to none other than Colonel Egbert Viele, Olmsted's old nemesis. Viele had drawn up a profoundly uninspired plan. He had simply done his best to work with Mount Prospect. To connect the two sections of parkland, he had proposed a couple of ungainly looking overpasses. In an accompanying written report, Viele attempted to obscure his design choices behind bloated sentiments about the beauty of nature, such as this description of a tree: "Whether bursting the fast of winter, it opens its buds in spring-time, or yielding to the chilling blasts it scatters its autumn leaves." The park commissioners were thoroughly underwhelmed. Viele's plan was tabled. Then, with the onset of the Civil War, progress on the park came to a halt. It wasn't until it became clear that the conflict was nearing an end that the subject was revisited.

In January 1865, James Stranahan, president of the Brooklyn park commission, invited Vaux to stroll over the proposed parklands. Vaux immediately saw that the two mismatched pieces of land—one flat, one a steep hill—broken by an existing road, pretty much guaranteed an awkward park design. He urged that Mount Prospect should be removed from the park scheme. Instead, he suggested that the commissioners should purchase some undeveloped land that bordered the second parcel. That would create a single contiguous stretch of land.

The commissioners followed Vaux's suggestion. They also asked him to draw up a new park design. At that point Vaux started pursuing Olmsted about returning east from California. Now, the two partners were together again. They launched an instant business, Olmsted, Vaux & Company, using Vaux's existing offices at 110 Broadway. During Olmsted's West Coast sojourn, Vaux had been working as an architect, mostly designing houses. Vaux would maintain this architectural practice as a separate business. The new Olmsted, Vaux & Company would be devoted to landscape architecture. In a delicious twist, the reunited team was once again stepping in where the arrogant Viele had failed. And again, they had a grand canvass on which to work.

Prospect Park, as it was now known—the *Mount* had been dropped from its name—was 526 acres (60 percent of the size of Central Park) and roughly the shape of an arrowhead. Olmsted and Vaux saw opportunities to learn from their earlier experience. Skating mania, for example, had drawn throngs of people to Central Park, filling the Lake beyond its capacity. This time, they proposed to build an artificial lake more than twice the size of the one in Central Park. And they suggested that it include a concert island. Olmsted's experiments with across-the-water acoustics led him to plan a permanent aquatic concert venue.

During the autumn of 1866, Olmsted and Vaux devoted their days to crisscrossing the parkland, getting to know its features. They noted that the highest point was 168 feet above sea level—no Mount Prospect. Still, given how low-rise Brooklyn was in this era, the view was breathtaking. From this point, it was possible to see New York, its harbor, the bluffs of the New Jersey Palisades, and, way in the distance, the city of Newark. Some days, it was even possible to catch a whiff of salt breeze blowing in from the ocean. They dubbed this spot the Look-Out and planned to create a formal viewing area here.

Fresh from the West Coast, Olmsted proposed that Prospect Park should include a ravine and waterfall, both wholly man-made features. These would provide a small-scale echo of Yosemite's grandeur. He and Vaux also paced out a vast meadow. It was labeled "The Green," "The Green," "The Green"—three times due to its extent—on the blueprint in progress.

Because Prospect Park was an unbroken piece of land, uncut by even a single transverse road, traffic circulation was going to be less of a challenge than in Central Park. Once again, Olmsted and Vaux opted for a tripart separation of ways, featuring paths for carriages, horseback riders, and pedestrians. This time, they also proposed that dedicated multilane roads should extend from Prospect Park to other smaller parks then being contemplated for Brooklyn. Perhaps it would even be possible to lay down one of these roads from Prospect Park to the East River. From there, people could take a ferry across to Manhattan. Then they could connect with Central Park via another dedicated multi-laned road. Olmsted and Vaux envisioned a network of these special roads connecting the various green spaces within the metropolitan area—an idea both grand and forward-looking.

By December 1865, Olmsted and Vaux were scrambling to complete their proposal. They spent their days on the parklands and then worked deep into the night at Vaux's home in Manhattan. Vaux drafted a polished, submission-ready version of the plan. Olmsted enumerated their ideas in an accompanying written report for the commissioners. Where Viele's earlier report had read like a purple nature poem, Olmsted played up the social-reform attributes of his and Vaux's design. This would be a place of refuge for all classes of people in Brooklyn. It would provide fresh air and open space to the city's residents. "Here is a suggestion of freedom and repose," he wrote, "which must in itself be refreshing and tranquilizing to the visitor coming from the confinement and bustle of crowded streets."

Olmsted and Vaux finished their plan in January 1866. Vaux hosted a party at his home where they celebrated with claret and orange-juice punch. And then they . . . waited. The partners had been commissioned only to create a *design* for Prospect Park. Whether their design was accepted and what firm would actually construct the park—those questions rested with the commissioners. Construction couldn't begin during the cold winter months, in any case.

While awaiting word from the commissioners, Olmsted turned to the speculative projects he'd drummed up while in California. These had become part of Olmsted, Vaux & Company's book of business, though Olmsted appears to have worked on them without input from his partner. He also worked on them relying solely on maps and memory. Olmsted was happy to be back East, and he wasn't about to make the lengthy trip out to California to revisit the sites.

The city supervisors in San Francisco had expressed a desire for a West Coast version of Central Park, only larger and grander. But this had struck Olmsted as a wrongheaded approach. First, there was the matter of the city's climate. Certain trees and plants just weren't going to be possible; he thought it best to go with greenery suited to an arid, Mediterranean-style climate. For inspiration, he drew on more memories—really old memories, in this case—of his trip to Italy a decade earlier, on which he'd been accompanied by the three young women. At that time, as he put it, he had "no more thought of being a landscape architect than of being a Cardinal."

There was also the wind to consider. The land he'd walked over with Mayor Coon, as Olmsted recalled, was whipped by cold winds coming in off the ocean. So he dreamed up a radical solution. He suggested several separate smaller parks, set up in parcels of land well removed from the Pacific. To connect the parks, he envisioned a promenade sunken twenty feet below ground level. In his proposal, he described this promenade as being like a dried-up creek bed along which people could travel from park to park. Steep embankments would provide a break against the relentless winds.

For the College of California, meanwhile, he had been commissioned to lay out a large property that would include a university, a park, and a new residential community. In his plan, Olmsted suggested that the residences should extend right onto the campus lands. Rather than living in dorms, the students could live in clusters of houses. In Olmsted's view, this would erase artificial distinctions between campus life and the life of the larger community. It was akin to what he'd experienced as a farmer who nonetheless hung out at Yale.

On receiving his recommendations, the College of California trustees were not convinced. His plan was promptly tabled and then lost. Several years later, he would receive a check for $2,832 for his work. (By this time, the university had been rechristened "Berkeley," as had the surrounding community.)

Olmsted's San Francisco park proposal was similarly ill met. "I like the plan myself," Mayor Coon wrote to Olmsted, "but find at present great opposition to it." He sent along payment for $500, and that was that.

While awaiting a verdict on Prospect Park, Olmsted also focused his attention in an entirely other direction—journalism. When Olmsted had sailed into New York Harbor aboard the *Ericson*, Vaux was waiting to meet him, but so was Godkin, editor of the *Nation*. This was no coincidence. There were rival claims on Olmsted—Vaux in the landscape architecture corner and Godkin in the name of journalism. Godkin, less than a year into his tenure as editor of the *Nation*, already found himself deeply embattled. He hoped that Olmsted could come to his aid.

During the *Nation's* brief life, there had already been many twists and turns, and no shortage of intrigue. Back in 1863, recall, Olmsted and Godkin had contemplated a weekly publication devoted to serious issues. This notion, simple as it was, actually addressed an unfilled market niche given that there were serious monthlies (the *Atlantic*) and dailies (the *New York Times*), but few weeklies. Fervent as always, Olmsted came up with forty-five possible names, including *Tide*, *Reviser*, *Scrutiny*, and the *Key*. There was a war on, however, and the timing was wrong for starting a new publication. So Olmsted headed out to the Mariposa mines. Godkin was forced to take a job offered to him by the Reverend Henry Bellows, as editor of a house organ, the *Sanitary Commission Bulletin*.

Launching a new publication became a better proposition when it was clear that the Civil War was about to end. In 1865, a group of abolitionists started the *Nation*. It was meant to succeed papers such as the *Liberator*, soon to be obsolete once slavery ended. But new publications would be needed to cover "freedman's issues." The abolitionists raised $100,000 in start-up capital, even set up an office for the *Nation* in New York, sharing space with the American Freedmen's Aid Union. They tapped Godkin to edit the new publication.

Godkin was a fitting choice. A stout English expat with a thick beard and reddish brown hair, he was avowedly committed to the rights of freed slaves. But he also had a broader agenda. On taking the job, he felt that he received assurances that he would have complete editorial control. He'd even written to Olmsted in California, calling the new publication "substantially the same as that which we had projected."

For the *Nation's* first issues, Godkin devoted ample ink to freedmen's rights but covered a variety of other subjects as well. As a consequence, the financial backers soon split into two rival factions. Half agreed with Godkin. This group was led by James McKim, a prominent Quaker social reformer. McKim, in fact, was the person who had come up with the name, the *Nation*. He envisioned a general-interest publication, addressing the welter of complex issues facing a reunited *nation*. But half felt that the *Nation* should be exclusively devoted to issues related to former slaves. This faction was led by George Stearns, a wealthy Bostonian who had helped finance John Brown's raid on Harper's Ferry.

In January 1866, Olmsted entered this fray, signing on as an associate editor. Godkin was delighted. It gave him an ally in the fight for editorial independence. Godkin wrote to a friend, "Olmsted's coming in relieves my mind a good deal, particularly in ridding me of the hateful burden of over-caution."

The impact of bringing in Olmsted was instantaneous. If Godkin hoped to throw "over-caution" to the wind and to increase the *Nation*'s eclecticism, he could not have teamed up with someone more catholic in his interests than Olmsted. Articles in the *Nation* during the 1860s were unsigned. Through records and correspondence, it's clear that Olmsted wrote very few pieces. Rather, he dreamed up story ideas and shaped existing copy to reflect his interests and concerns. He'd learned well during his stint at the ill-fated *Putnam's*. Now, he'd assumed the same role occupied at that magazine by the talented editors Curtis and Dana. Olmsted tapped various friends and acquaintances to write for the *Nation*, including Bellows, Charles Eliot Norton, and James Russell Lowell.

Olmsted's active tenure as associate editor of the *Nation* is confined to the first six months of 1866. Yet the variety of Olmstedian themes and ideas visited in the stories that ran during this brief period is quite simply astounding. As an editor, he managed vastly greater range than was possible for a mere harried scribe. An article in the March 1 issue, for example, takes a skeptical look at a new stamp-mill technology being touted by an eastern inventor. Fresh from the Mariposa mines, this was certainly familiar territory for Olmsted. A piece in the March 15 issue covers the brutal conditions faced by sailors, a concern dating back to Olmsted's days on the *Ronaldson* with Captain Fox. Although Olmsted wasn't the author of either of these articles, his editorial fingerprints are all over them.

The *Nation* dispatched a correspondent to travel through the former slave states, providing weekly dispatches for a column called "The South

As It Is." This was kind of a post–Civil War retracing of Olmsted's earlier travels as "Yeoman." But in this case, the correspondent was J. R. Dennett, a recent Harvard graduate. He received $150 a month for his dispatches. There were also a number of articles on various agricultural topics, harking back to Olmsted's years as a farmer. There was an article on the migration from farm to city, a transition Olmsted had made. There was also a piece about proper nutrition for soldiers, an echo of his time with the USSC.

Olmsted's presence is clearly felt in the selection of books the *Nation* reviewed during this brief period. There was a review of *Short Sermons to News Boys* by Charley Brace. In his role as Children's Aid Society founder, Brace had become focused on outreach to newsies, boys who lived on the street under particularly harsh conditions and hawked papers to get by. There was also a review of Samuel Bowles's *Across the Continent,* a book that includes an account of the author's visit to Yosemite where he met up with Olmsted. There was even a review of a memoir, *Life of Benjamin Silliman, M.D.* Professor Silliman taught the lone course that Olmsted enjoyed during his brief Yale stint, inspiring Olmsted to found the "Infantile Chemistry Association."

Sometimes the consonance between Olmsted's interests and a *Nation* article borders on the absurd. A piece in the March 22 issue is based on a Connecticut state survey of clergymen's salaries. The conclusion: Endemically low pay forces the clergy into side professions such as running schools, thereby diluting their focus on spiritual matters. There's no evidence that Olmsted wrote this piece. More likely, he learned about the survey and assigned a writer to cover it. As an editor, he probably shaped the copy to reflect his own very personal experience with this matter. Another piece titled "Hints for Tourists and Invalids on Italian Climates" features the following opening passage:

> The annual tide of travel from this country to Europe will very shortly set in, with the usual tendency after traversing the Continent during the intervening months, to rest in Italy during the winter. This will especially be true of such as are in feeble health, and are led to anticipate the most salutary effects from their sojourn upon the peninsula. As their

disappointment will be most serious, and ought as far as possible to be
prevented, we have thought some suggestions as to what to expect, what
to avoid, and what of benefit and enjoyment may be obtained in the
kingdom of Victor Emanuel [*sic*], would have a timely interest and value.

Of all things, this is an article about how misconceptions about
Mediterranean weather pose a danger to Americans suffering from
chronic ailments. Olmsted's own brother had just such an experience.
He'd arrived in Nice, desperately ill with tuberculosis, only to be told by
a doctor that the climate might not be so beneficial to his health.

Of course, Olmsted had also grown over the years to be a staunch abolitionist. As part of the *Nation*'s editorial mélange, there continued to be
frequent articles on issues related to the freed slaves. But the subject wasn't
covered sufficiently to satisfy an increasingly agitated George Stearns.
By the summer of 1866, Stearns—John Brown's erstwhile benefactor—
had had enough. It was clear that the *Nation* was anything but a journal
devoted to freedman's rights. He withdrew his considerable stake in the
venture; the others in his faction followed suit.

The *Nation* was reorganized as a new company. Godkin held one-half
of the stock, McKim held a third, and Olmsted took the remaining one-
sixth. As for the name of the new venture: E. L. Godkin and Company.
"I wanted Olmsted's name," Godkin wrote to a friend, "but he was afraid
it would injure his other business." In any case, Olmsted would be a relatively absentee shareholder and within a few years' time would transfer
his interest (worth only a pittance) to the other partners. But he'd already
made his mark on the publication. During a critical few months in the
spring of 1866, Olmsted had boldly chosen a direction—broad inquiry
over narrow focus—and had helped set the *Nation* on its course.

As for that "other business" mentioned by Godkin, it scored a major victory to offset the pair of California setbacks. Olmsted and Vaux's design
won the overwhelming approval of the Prospect Park commission. On
May 29, 1866, the partners were officially appointed as landscape architects, and their fee was fixed at $8,000 per year. Earlier in the spring,
Olmsted had moved to a new home on Amos Street in the Clifton sec-

tion of Staten Island. He was now able to commute each day by ferry to his new job. John Olmsted, aged seventy-four, paid a visit. Olmsted proudly conducted his father over the grounds of his latest project.

From the outset, Stranahan and the other commissioners were extremely supportive. With his strong features and aquiline nose, Stranahan had a face like a Roman statesman. But the illusion was quickly broken by his manner and garb: Stranahan perpetually carried a black silk top hat in his hand, as opposed to wearing it on his head. He usually had an overcoat draped over his arm. He was a man in a hurry. After making a fortune as a railroad contractor, he'd devoted himself entirely to becoming Brooklyn's number-one booster. To secure maritime commerce for his city, he'd taken the lead in developing the Atlantic Docks in Red Hook. A few years hence, he'd be a prime mover behind the Brooklyn Bridge, and many years later he'd urge the combination of Brooklyn, Manhattan, and the other boroughs into a single city.

Olmsted found Stranahan to be the opposite of Andrew Green. Stranahan didn't interfere, and he didn't pinch pennies. To work with so little oversight was an unexpected and gratifying experience. Early in the project, Olmsted wrote to his friend Norton, "It grows upon me and my enthusiasm and liking for the work is increasing to an inconvenient degree, so that it elbows all other interests out of my mind."

As with Central Park, the creation of Prospect Park demanded a knack for illusion. The landscape had to be totally engineered yet made to look utterly natural. This presented ample technological challenges from a nineteenth-century standpoint. It also required a substantial workforce. By the summer of 1866, 300 men were at work on the park, and in the years ahead that number would swell to nearly 2,000. Whereas some of the tasks required brute force—digging holes and hauling stone—some demanded expertise and precision. To execute their design, Olmsted and Vaux oversaw a team of talented engineers and gardeners and architects.

A major technical challenge was filling the artificial lake. Initially, the plan was to rely exclusively on a network of drainage pipes. These pipes would conduct rain runoff from the parkland into the lake. But Olmsted wasn't certain that rain alone would be sufficient to feed this vast 57-acre sheet of water. So a sixty-foot well was dug, and a state-of-the-art Worthington duplex pump powered by a 50-horsepower engine was installed to draw water. Capacity: 1 million gallons a day. The pumped water, in turn, could be directed through a series of natural-looking streams that merged, entered a ravine, and flowed over a waterfall before emptying into the lake—an ingenious solution. A set of sluices was built to drain water in the event that the lake got too full.

Olmsted's tree-planting scheme also demanded a creative solution. The land slated for Prospect Park had a fine assortment of old-growth trees; problem was, they weren't in the right places. Fortunately, John Culyer, a park engineer, invented a tree-moving machine.

Such a device would have come in handy at Central Park, especially during the construction of the Mall. At the time, Olmsted tried to bring in mature elms uprooted from the grounds of Sing Sing prison. But the transplanted trees all died very quickly. The only solution was to plant saplings. As a consequence, during Central Park's earliest years, the Mall was flanked by scrawny juvenile elms rather than overhung with an intricate canopy. Once again, it had required time for the Greensward vision to be realized.

Culyer's machine attached tightly to a tree trunk, then yanked the tree directly out of the ground, in the process pulling up an ample plug of dirt that kept the roots encased. It was like pulling a weed, but on a large, mechanized scale. Olmsted ordered hundreds of trees moved to comply with the blueprint that he and Vaux had prepared. When he encountered an especially striking specimen tree, he had it moved to a spot where it could really stand out and be viewed full-on in all its glory.

Shortly after work began, the commissioners announced an official opening day for the public. Thousands of people showed up. The routes of future pedestrian paths were marked by a series of red flags, and future waterways were marked with blue flags. But there really wasn't much to see yet. It was more akin to a construction site. Like Central Park, Prospect Park's magic would reveal itself slowly.

One of the first areas to be completed was an oval plaza that served as the main entryway into the park. The plaza featured a basin fountain and a statue of Lincoln. The nine-foot-tall bronze rendering (the work of

Vaux's friend Henry Kirke Browne) was the first statue of Lincoln to go up anywhere in the United States.

That Prospect Park was the site for this very first statue is somehow fitting. After all, the park was a grand civic work commenced immediately after the Civil War's end. Lincoln was the man who saved the Union. It's hard not to see the park in the context of a reunited America, though nothing about the park's general design overtly addresses this theme. (Olmsted and Vaux were far too subtle for that.) But remember: Vaux had rejected two mismatched pieces of land in favor of a single unbroken stretch. Olmsted had recently devoted his attention to turning the *Nation* into a publication devoted to the broad interests of a postwar America.

As Prospect Park took shape, it would be notable for its *unity* (that's the word often used) of design. Among the various elements—water, woods, and meadow—there was an undeniable harmony. Who knows? Maybe, like other artists, Olmsted and Vaux were simply caught up in the flow of events, of history, and this subconsciously informed their work.

Vaux created some of his finest structures in Prospect Park. In keeping with his motto, "Nature first, second, and third—architecture after a while," he designed a series of rough-hewn stone archways that nestled into the sides of hills. To up the rustic feel still further, the archways' masonry was generously draped in creepers and vines. Walking through one of Vaux's masterful Prospect Park arches, one literally walks directly through a hill. The Endale Arch, constructed of alternating bands of New Jersey brownstone and yellow Berea sandstone, is particularly striking.

But the tour de force of Olmsted and Vaux's design was the Long Meadow, the feature thrice marked "The Green" on the original plan. When completed, it just rolled and rolled, luring visitors around come-hither corners, whereupon a new expanse would open up ending in another enticing turn—the whole thing stretching out over nearly a mile.

As a brilliant touch, Olmsted and Vaux designed the pedestrian paths that crisscrossed this long green so as to be depressed below ground level. Perhaps this was inspired by the promenades of the failed San Francisco park plan, though these paths were sunk a matter of inches rather than twenty feet. This time, the intent was to provide someone looking out across the meadow with a view unbroken by paths. If any people happened to be walking on the paths, they appeared to a viewer to be gliding, because their feet were not visible. It was quite an effect, especially given the formal attire of the nineteenth century. One might look out across the Long Meadow, only to see a woman in a long skirt carrying a parasol, mysteriously floating along.

Olmsted and Vaux had expected their generously proportioned skating pond to be Prospect Park's main attraction. But that distinction fell to the Long Meadow instead. Rather than skating mania, the park soon became the site of croquet mania.

Croquet had been invented in England less than a decade earlier. When the game stormed U.S. shores, no better venue presented itself than the ample green of the brand-new Prospect Park. Like skating, it was another outdoor activity that could be pursued by both men and women. Against a backdrop of strict Victorian morals, it provided another suitably chaste opportunity for the sexes to mingle. A croquet concession was set up in Prospect Park, where it was possible to rent equipment for 28¢ an hour. Some days, the Long Meadow was filled with people playing croquet. "He must be an exceptional compound of coarse clay and coarser habit who cannot in pleasant days of Summer find pleasure in this place," waxed a reporter for the *Brooklyn Eagle*. "There are hundreds of maidens and their suitors busy at croquet on the lawn."

It would require seven years and $5 million, on top of the $4 million spent acquiring the land, before Prospect Park could be officially declared finished. But even early on, one thing became abundantly clear: Olmsted and Vaux had done it again. In this, their sophomore effort, they had created another masterpiece.

But for Olmsted, the experience was marred. While a refreshing sense of ease surrounded the creation of Prospect Park—Stranahan wasn't meddlesome, Vaux wasn't combative, the design just seemed to coalesce—turmoil found its way into other parts of his life just the same. As was so often the case for Olmsted, professional triumph was intertwined with personal tragedy.

On November 24, 1866, Mary gave birth to a baby boy who lived for only six hours. Olmsted and his wife never even gave the baby a name. Mary was crushed. For months afterward, she lived like an invalid, remaining in bed for long stretches, visiting friends in the country in search of peace, just some peace. She was thirty-six now, and getting pregnant again was going to be terribly difficult. Mary was tough, but she was reaching her limit.

More than ever, Olmsted's relationship with his wife seemed forged in sorrow. The couple had gotten married after John's death had left Mary a widow. Three of the four children the couple was raising were Olmsted's brother's natural offspring. The eldest, John Charles, was fourteen now and the namesake of John Hull Olmsted. Meanwhile, Owen, age nine, bore a striking physical resemblance to his natural father. Even his temperament and mannerisms were eerily similar. With each passing year, Owen seemed more like the carefree young man who used to shoot a smirk at Kingsbury while Fred and Charley Brace argued. For Olmsted, his two adopted sons were a constant reminder of love tied closely—so achingly close—with loss.

To deal with the death of the newborn, Olmsted fell back on his now familiar way of managing grief. He lost himself in work. Of that, there was plenty. While Olmsted and Vaux referred to Prospect Park simply as "The Park" in their correspondence, their primary focus at this time, the partners had many other jobs as well. Most notably, Olmsted and Vaux had revived their association with Central Park in an official capacity as consulting landscape architects.

For all intents and purposes, the park was complete. But maintenance was perpetual and demanding. Bridges needed to be fixed, paths refurbished, dead trees taken down and new ones planted in their place. There was also the issue of clarifying certain sections of Central Park and developing these sections for the benefit of visitors. During this time, Olmsted and Vaux focused in particular on developing the children's district at the southern end of Central Park. It was a poignant choice, given that Olmsted had lost two babies, the first during the park's initial construction. Olmsted suggested that the children's section would benefit from a shelter where mothers and tots could congregate. So Vaux designed one of his most inspired rustic wooden structures, a large octagonal pavilion (one hundred feet in diameter) featuring a roof that was wildly atwist with interlaced branches.

This same children's district would later become home to the Dairy. This Gothic-style stone building (designed by Vaux in 1869) is one of the most beautiful edifices ever conceived for the benefit of cattle. It was meant as a place where a child could get a glass of milk "warm from the cow." This was no mere novelty. Pasteurizing milk wasn't a practice yet; New York City was full of unscrupulous purveyors who sold tainted milk or even cut it with various additives to stretch out their supply. Due to these practices, children frequently became sick or died. The Dairy was intended as a kind of certified milk station, a place where a child could get a free drink in the safe confines of Central Park.

If Olmsted wished to lose himself in work, there were plenty of other tasks demanding his attention. In early 1867, he was named recording secretary of the Southern Famine Relief Commission (SFRC). The outfit was based in New York, and its board included J. P. Morgan and Theodore Roosevelt, a wealthy reformer and father of the future president. During the nearly two years since the Civil War ended, the South had been stricken by a terrible famine. The disaster resulted from the collision of a number of unfortunate variables: Many Southern farmers turned soldiers were now dead or dispersed, farmland had been damaged during the war, there had long been an overreliance on cotton over food crops, the system of slave labor had ended, and sealing the deal—just a grim coincidence, courtesy of Mother Nature—much of the region was starved for rain.

The SFRC was remarkably similar to Olmsted's USSC. During the Civil War, the USSC had coordinated the activity of local women's groups, making sure everything from shoes to preserved peaches was routed to the Union soldiers who most needed the items. Now, the SFRC coordinated efforts among various famine-relief organizations such as church groups and various benevolent societies. Thousands of Northerners wished to help, both out of simple human decency and also as a way of extending an olive branch to Southerners.

Olmsted helped gather information about which regions of the South were most afflicted. He also prepared handbills and circulars requesting aid. Due to his wealth of journalism connections, he was very successful

at getting these pleas printed in newspapers. There's a particularly striking exchange between Olmsted and Edward Bright, a fellow SFRC executive, in regard to a circular titled *Famine at Home*. Bright contributed a
passage in which he suggested that aid would help restore the South to
"the wealth in which she once luxuriated." Olmsted disagreed with this
conceit. He'd traveled to the antebellum South and found it anything
but opulent: "Judging from my own experience, therefore, I think the
appeal would be forcible perhaps if the idea of abounding wealth among
the people were not emphasized." Olmsted prevailed; the phrase in question did not appear in the printed version of the circular.

By November 1867, the crisis had ended, and the SFRC disbanded.
Olmsted wrote the organization's final report, which recorded that
169,316 bushels of corn had been sent to the South, enough to feed a
half-million people for six months. The SFRC had also distributed clothing, potatoes, beans, flour, and money for medicine. He concluded the
report with this: "It remains to be seen whether the war, which has cost
us so much, has, after all, brought us nearer in our public or our private
life to the divine requirement: 'Do unto others as ye would that they
should do unto you.'"

Olmsted's service with the SFRC is notable because the outfit saved
untold numbers of lives during its brief ten-month existence. It is also notable because it marks the last time that Olmsted would participate in a
substantial way in an endeavor outside the field of landscape architecture.

"Where your talents and the needs of the world cross, there lies your vocation," said Aristotle. Olmsted's *talents* were many and various. He'd
been a sailor, farmer, journalist, and abolitionist—and that's just a partial
list. As for what the world *needed*, it was parks, more parks. Olmsted and
Vaux now found themselves inundated with requests from various cities
around the United States. It was quite a turnabout, given that only a few
years earlier Olmsted had wondered whether there was sufficient demand
for landscape architecture to make a living.

Much had changed. By now, Olmsted and Vaux had created show-
piece parks—Central Park and Prospect Park—in two of the nation's
three largest cities. The post–Civil War economy was on an upswing, and

other cities were eager to build parks of their own. Olmsted, Vaux & Company was contracted to provide designs for Philadelphia; Newark, New Jersey; and Fall River, Massachusetts. In Bridgeport, Connecticut, the firm designed Seaside Park using land donated by one of the town's leading citizens, P. T. Barnum. And the demand wasn't confined to park making. Olmsted, Vaux & Company was also called upon to do other landscape architecture work such as creating a campus plan for the new Maine College of Agriculture and the Mechanic Arts. The firm also designed the grounds of a summer cottage in Long Branch, New Jersey, later owned by Ulysses Grant.

Olmsted grew so busy that he couldn't have pursued one of his assorted sidelines had he wanted to. He was forced to give up the idea—subject of the lively exchange with Vaux—that he was more an administrator than an artist, that his greatest talents lay in supervising gold mines and battlefield relief outfits. Even journalism—long a shadow career of sorts—fell by the wayside. He would rarely write articles, and when he did, they would usually be about landscape architecture. A big book on the drift of civilization, which he'd been tinkering with for years—that would be abandoned. Olmsted was done working as an editor, too. At the age of forty-five, Olmsted had finally found his vocation, or, rather, it had found him.

Going forward, as a landscape architect exclusively, he would draw on the varied interests and experiences of his earlier life to craft a series of inspired designs that would literally change the face of America. As always, his professional heights would exist in a queer close blend with devastating personal events.

CHAPTER 23

City Planning

Buffalo and Chicago

TWO MORE CITIES came calling, Chicago and Buffalo. In 1868, representatives of proposed projects in both communities approached Olmsted, Vaux & Company. The fact that two separate groups contacted the firm at virtually the same time says a lot about Buffalo and Chicago. Both were booming and both had emerged as preeminent American cities, and with their runaway growth came a need for green space. Naturally, it made sense to turn to the nation's foremost landscape architecture firm.

In the course of a few decades, Buffalo had transformed—as one contemporary observer put it—into a "commercial Constantinople," a place that handled countless tons of grain, iron, coal, and timber as it was transported from the West back East. Chicago was quite simply the fastest-growing city in America. Its population had shot from around 100,000 in 1860 to nearly 300,000 by 1868. It now ranked as the nation's fifth-largest city and was fast gaining on St. Louis. Such urban density demanded some kind of relief.

In mid-August 1868, Olmsted set out by train from New York, planning stops in Buffalo and Chicago. In Buffalo, he took a Sunday horseback ride into the countryside just beyond the city limits, scouting for possible park locations. Olmsted was accompanied by William Dorsheimer, a prominent lawyer and leader in the drive to build a park for Buffalo. Olmsted and Dorsheimer were on slightly familiar terms, both having served on the USSC during the Civil War.

Then it was on to Chicago. Olmsted traipsed out to view a stretch of prairie nine miles west of town. The site was called Riverside. The plan was to develop the property into a parklike suburb, meant to be a haven from bustling Chicago.

On the return train trip to New York, Olmsted made another stopover in Buffalo. He was met with quite a surprise. As he wrote to his wife, "What was my horror on arriving here to find that a public meeting had been called for this evening. Mr. Fillmore to preside, special invitations to over 200 leading citizens sent out, to hear an address on the matter of a public park from the distinguished Architect of the N.Y.C.P. [New York Central Park] Fred Law Olmsted Esq. There was no help for it."

Mr. Fillmore was Millard Fillmore, the former president now settled in his hometown of Buffalo. He was a longtime park booster. During his administration, recall, President Fillmore had hired Andrew Jackson Downing to landscape the Mall in Washington, D.C. Downing had enlisted the aid of his young assistant, Vaux. But Downing's death had brought the project to an abrupt end.

The meeting in Buffalo was held at the home of Sherman Jewett, a man who had earned a fortune manufacturing stoves. No transcript exists, nor has so much as a quotation survived from Olmsted's comments to the assembled two hundred leading citizens. But apparently, he held forth spontaneously for roughly an hour, laying out a whole-cloth vision for parkland in Buffalo.

Olmsted was a talented speaker, a fact that's often overlooked. Of course, his written park proposals are full of winning ideas and persuasive arguments. But landing—and *hanging on to*—a design commission required a great deal of communication. That's one of the reasons that Vaux, a gifted artist but stumble-tongued speaker, was so eager to team up with Olmsted.

Olmsted could be an eloquent and convincing salesman, as evidenced by this account from a participant in one of his many park pitches during this era: "Mr. Olmsted has a mastery of language commensurate with the magnitude of his plans. Nothing short of upsetting the entire status quo is worthy of being considered in his gigantic schemes; and then his fluent dissertations overwhelm the astonished listener, and drown the natural objections to such revolutionary changes and extravagant 'improvements.'"

Olmsted emerged from the Buffalo meeting feeling confident. He sent another letter to Mary that concluded on a note of optimism: "I think it will go." Back in New York, he quickly drew up proposals for both Buffalo and Riverside. He worked without Vaux, who was on a lengthy inspiration-gathering trip to Europe, visiting assorted architectural treasures. Olmsted managed to wow both clients with the proposals. Both hired Olmsted, Vaux & Company.

Riverside got under way first. As a suburban development, at a time when very few true suburbs existed in the United States, this was a novel undertaking. Cities were densely built and teeming, but as a general rule, right beyond their limits, the land almost instantly took on a rural character. Country living provided the antidote, with clean air and open space, but there was little infrastructure and services were nonexistent. *Want running water? Run and fetch some from the well.*

Riverside was meant to combine the best of both modes of living. The setting was scenic, 1,560 acres along the banks of the Des Plaines River. Critically, the land was also near a stretch of track recently laid by the Chicago, Burlington, and Quincy Railroad. The plan was to build a station, the first stop on the line, making commuting to Chicago easy.

Building a model suburb in Riverside was not Olmsted's idea. Rather, the idea originated with the Riverside Improvement Company. The RIC was a consortium of eastern investors that had recently purchased the property. Its president was Emery Childs, a manic and jowly business promoter. Upon first meeting with Childs and his crew, Olmsted was reminded of another consortium of eastern investors, Mayor Opdyke and his Mariposa cronies. He had sent a letter to Vaux in Europe, describing the Riverside enterprise as a "big speculation." But it seemed like the RIC was in earnest—and in a hurry as well. In a letter to Mary, he marveled, "They want to go to work at once & employ 2000 men."

This was a private effort in contrast to the public works in which Olmsted and Vaux had been involved, such as Central Park and Prospect Park. No legislative approval was needed; there just wasn't the same level of bureaucracy as in a public-sector job. By autumn of 1868, work was under way.

Childs had hired Olmsted assuming he'd approach suburb design with the keen artistry on display in his firm's park making. From the outset, Olmsted was adamant that the highest priority for Riverside was something crushingly mundane: serviceable roads. He was wearing his farmer's hat. Olmsted had done his share of country living; he'd ridden over enough rutted, ill-graded, miry rural roads to know that such matter had the potential to sink this suburban experiment, no matter how comely the grounds. Roads, Olmsted stressed, must "be the first consideration" in planning a suburb, and he added, "Let them cost what they will."

For Riverside's roads, the solution Olmsted suggested was macadamization, a process where a foundation of large stones is overlaid with layers of successively smaller stones progressing to gravel. The layers are tamped down with heavy rollers. When Scottish engineer John Loudon McAdam dreamed up the idea in the early 1800s, it was the biggest innovation in road construction since Roman times. Even in 1868, it was still a pretty newfangled approach. Per McAdam's model, the surfaces of Riverside's roads were to be cambered, that is, given a convex shape that allowed rain to run off. State-of-the-art paved gutters would be installed to carry water by underground pipes into the Des Plaines River.

Yet Olmsted didn't skimp on beauty. Laying out Riverside's streets on unsullied farmland provided a rare opportunity to get away from the dreaded grid plan. Olmsted designed the streets to travel in sweeping, generous curves. This was meant to impart an unhurried vibe to the future residents of Riverside. The intention was to place their domestic life in stark relief to nearby Chicago, where the street scheme was angular and the mood frenzied. The "absence of sharp corners" in Riverside's streets, as Olmsted put it, was meant to "imply leisure, contemplativeness, and happy tranquility."

Olmsted also named many of Riverside's streets. There are Michaux and Nuttall roads, for example, named after a couple of Olmsted's dendrology heroes. François André Michaux came to the United States from France in the early 1800s and produced an exhaustive three-volume study of America's trees. Englishman Thomas Nuttall picked up where Michaux left off, traveling extensively in the States before writing his landmark *North American Sylva: Trees Not Described by F. A. Michaux.* Carlyle Road was named in honor of the author of *Sartor Resartus,* the novel that provoked so much philosophical pondering by Olmsted in his youth. As one might expect, the voraciously read Olmsted opted for a variety of other literary references. There are Akenside and Shenstone roads named after English poets. Of course, there's a Downing Road.

Probably the most significant concept Olmsted brought to Riverside was that of communal spaces. Roughly 40 percent of the 1,560 acres was set aside as greens and commons. This decision, too, has its roots in an earlier Olmsted experience. While traveling in the South, he'd observed the cultural vacuum that resulted from people living great distances apart. Ample shared spaces were meant to ensure that Riverside's residents connected socially, traded information, discussed the issues of the day. Riverside was meant to be a community; Olmsted wanted to promote civic discourse.

He even went so far as to propose that a dedicated road be built to Chicago. That would serve horse and carriage traffic. The railroad was quick, to be sure, but he wanted people to have another, more leisurely, way to travel home to Riverside.

As payment for the design, Olmsted accepted lots of land. This was against his better judgment, but the terms were just so enticing. According to Childs, the land that the RIC transferred to Olmsted, Vaux & Company for the design alone would be worth $15,000 once those lots were sold to residents. Supervising construction would net the firm additional lots, potentially worth more than $100,000. If just a fraction of this amount were realized, it would be quite a payday.

Still more earning potential would derive from the fact that Vaux was a trained architect with considerable experience designing houses. Riverside was 1,560 blank acres demanding homes, not to mention all the houses and other structures needed along the boulevard to Chicago. "There will probably be a large demand upon us for cheap little cottages growing out of it, wood chalets," Olmsted wrote his partner, referring to that long road, "—also for spring houses, arbors, seats, drinking fountains & c." Riverside had the potential to be a genuine bonanza.

In tandem with Riverside, Olmsted set to work in Buffalo. This was an Olmsted, Vaux & Company job, but once again, Olmsted very much took the lead. His plan—first enumerated during those impromptu remarks before the two hundred citizens—was nothing if not revolutionary.

He designed a set of three separate parks, each with a distinct purpose. One park was called the Parade and was intended, as the name implies, to be the scene of large gatherings and vigorous activities such as sports. It occupied 56 acres. A second larger greensward was meant for passive pursuits such as strolling and sitting in quiet contemplation. Because this was the only fitting use for a true park, to Olmsted's mind, he designated this 350-acre parcel as, simply, the Park. (Later, it was rechristened as Delaware Park.) The Park featured a natural-looking lake—totally man-made—with a meandering shoreline and plantings of weeping willows and other trees that looked more soft than stately, touches meant to lend a subtle, dreamlike quality to this creation. The third park was called the Front. For this one, Olmsted chose a 32-acre piece of land with a commanding view, a bluff overlooking the spot where Lake Erie starts to narrow as it feeds into the Niagara River. The Front also had a distinct purpose. Olmsted considered the Front to be a place with "a character of magnificence admirably adapted to be associated with stately ceremonies, the entertainment of public guests, and other occasions of civic display."

The land Olmsted selected for the three separate parks showed a genuine grasp of Buffalo's landscape. Besides his Sunday horseback tour with Dorsheimer, Olmsted had also visited the city on USSC business during the Civil War. He was well aware that Buffalo didn't adhere to a simple street grid like New York and so many other American cities. Rather, Buffalo's street plan had a distinctly French accent. This was due to a blueprint for the city's future growth, drawn up by Joseph Ellicott back in 1804. At the time, Buffalo had a mere two dozen residents. But its founders had a sense of manifest destiny. They hired Ellicott, who had worked with French-born Pierre-Charles L'Enfant during the early stages of planning Washington, D.C. In an echo of Paris, L'Enfant had suggested a radial plan for Washington, with the U.S. Capitol in the center and streets radiating out like the spokes on a wheel. Buffalo, at its inception, was designed by Ellicott with streets radiating out from a hub, Niagara Square.

Because the city was founded on the shores of Lake Erie, however, expansion in all directions wasn't possible. So Ellicott designed Buffalo as a partial radial—a wedge shape. Think of Niagara Square as home plate on a baseball field. And picture Buffalo growing outward, continually outward, but within the confines of the foul lines. In placing his three parks, Olmsted was careful to stay true to Ellicott's original blueprint. Per the baseball-field analogy, think of the parks as being placed in left field (the Front), center field (the Park), and right field (the Parade).

Olmsted also sited the parks at a considerable distance from the city center. They were arrayed along the town's edge, not yet built up as of 1868. That made it possible for the city to obtain the selected parcels of land at low prices. Olmsted knew full well that as Buffalo grew, it would eventually surround these parks; land on the city's outskirts would over time become priceless green space well within the city limits. In the years since 1858, when work on Central Park commenced, he'd watched this same process happen as development crept northward around the park's periphery.

Olmsted brought another dazzling innovation to the Buffalo project. He suggested a series of broad roads to connect the three separate parks. This was an idea that he and Vaux had been kicking around for some time. During one of his visits to Paris—the one he took in 1859 ostensibly to gather ideas for Central Park—he'd seen a variety of things that he simply tucked away in his mind for future reference. He was especially inspired by such grand thoroughfares as the Avenue de l'Imperatice and the Champs-Elysées, which he described at the time as "the most magnificent urban or interior town promenade in the world."

For some earlier designs, Olmsted had attempted to adapt Paris-style byways to his own idiosyncratic purposes. There's the long road to Chicago in the Riverside plan. His rejected San Francisco proposal had suggested a sunken promenade connecting several parcels of land. The original plan for Prospect Park had called for a series of roads that would tie together various green spaces in the metropolitan area, maybe even connecting with Central Park. To describe this novel concept, Olmsted and Vaux had even coined a term: *parkway*. Two would be built in Brooklyn, Eastern Parkway and Ocean Parkway. These were grand roads, no question, but Eastern Parkway would simply serve as an approach to Prospect Park, and Ocean Parkway would travel to Coney Island. They didn't tie any parks together.

Maybe it had something to do with Buffalo's original French-ified scheme, but Dorsheimer and the other civic boosters immediately grasped Olmsted's intent. From the outset, he was given carte blanche to develop the parkways concept to the fullest. Per Olmsted and Vaux's vision, the Buffalo parkways were ample, two hundred feet wide, and provided a quad-part separation of ways with dedicated pedestrian and bridle paths along with carriage and service roads. Elms were planted along the edges to create an overhanging canopy, and the medians were planted with flowers and shrubs. These were linear parks in effect. The idea was that a person could travel the entire six miles from the Front to the Parade without ever leaving green space. Everything was tied together.

Buffalo was now the site of something brand-new—the world's first park system. The system was even designed to help pay for itself with its own built-in revenue source. This, too, was an Olmsted idea. Whereas the parks and parkways were public land, the surrounding grounds were available for private development. As the parkways were laid out, the lots fronting on them became especially desirable addresses. In the years ahead, wealthy Buffalonians such as John Larkin, a soap baron, and George Birge, a wallpaper tycoon, would build grand houses along these roads. Assessments on their property would help defray the cost of the park system and served to maintain it going forward.

Of course, a plan as ambitious as the Buffalo park system couldn't be completed overnight. While Olmsted conceived of the design on his own, he was joined by his partner to see it through. Vaux collaborated with Olmsted and helped refine the plan. Per his standard role, Vaux also contributed structures to the parks such as bridges. In the Parade, he designed a long two-story refectory that was one of his most elaborate buildings. The Parade was close to a neighborhood that was home to many recent German immigrants; Vaux's refectory was meant to serve as a place for festive gatherings. (In 1904 the building was torn down.)

When Olmsted, Vaux & Company first opened for business, the following advertisement for the firm ran in the *Nation*: "LANDSCAPE ARCHITECTS. The undersigned have associated under the above title for the business of furnishing advice on all the matters of location and Designs and Superintendence for Buildings and Grounds and other Architectural and Engineering Works including the Laying-out of Towns, Villages, Parks, Cemeteries, and Gardens."

That's quite a scope of services. At the time the ad ran, Olmsted and Vaux had only a handful of jobs in their portfolio. With Buffalo, these ambitions were realized. This project was so much more than mere park making. It was about planning for the growth of a city and making sure that ample green space was set aside for the future. It also served a democratic purpose, ensuring that parkland was available to all the diverse citizens of Buffalo. As the city grew, it would have a set of three beautifully designed spaces, meaning that people in a number of different neighborhoods were in close proximity to a park. Olmsted would proudly describe Buffalo as "the best planned city, as to its streets, public places and grounds, in the United States if not the world."

Olmsted, Vaux & Company was like a ball of wax. As time went on, as the firm continually took on new work, none of the earlier projects ever seemed to be put to rest. That's the nature of landscape architecture. While working on Buffalo and Riverside, it wasn't as if Brooklyn's Prospect Park, for example, was entirely finished. Why, the partners still had duties regarding their very first project, Central Park, now more than a decade old. To manage all this, Olmsted, Vaux & Company was a very flexible outfit. It took on surveyors and draftsmen on an as-needed basis.

The two partners made a point of visiting project sites frequently in the early stages. Then once matters were well under way, they would turn the jobs over to others. Whenever possible, they tried to install people who would be sympathetic to their interests. The Buffalo park system was typical. To oversee construction, they recommended George Radford, an English-born engineer who was friends with Vaux. Radford was later replaced by William McMillan, another Olmsted and Vaux loyalist who had earlier worked on Prospect Park.

The client was responsible for the salaries of the superintendents, horticulturalists, and other professional staff necessary to execute the plans. These people worked in close consultation with Olmsted and Vaux, keeping them updated through regular correspondence. They were executing the firm's designs, after all. To do so required them to oversee large teams of local laborers, also paid by the client. That very first job, Central Park, provided the model: These were grand-style collaborations, requiring the work of vast numbers of people.

When a problem or a major alteration to a plan arose, it sometimes became necessary for Olmsted or Vaux to personally visit a site even when a project was well under way. Meanwhile, new work was forever coming into the firm; the ball of wax just kept growing.

Riverside led to another project in Chicago. The city hired Olmsted and Vaux to design a park system like what was underway in Buffalo. They proposed two large parks: one occupying an expanse of land right on the shores of Lake Michigan and the second roughly a mile inland. Picture this park system as looking sort of like a barbell with the two parks as weights and a thin strip of land—akin to a barbell's metal bar—connecting them. At nearly 1,000 acres in total, the two parks and the mile-long connecting strip would represent Olmsted and Vaux's largest work to date.

The partners approached this big job with fittingly big ideas. The piece of land that fronted Lake Michigan was low-lying, soupy marshland. Their plan was to thoroughly dredge it and to create an intricate network of waterways. Visitors would get around by boating or swimming. This would be a park that people traversed by water—a new idea, utterly without precedent.

For inspiration, the partners drew partly on Olmsted's 1863 trip across Panama on route to California and the Mariposa mines. They dubbed a section of this lakefront park the Lagoon Plaisance—*lagoon* being evocative of a languid, meandering waterway, and *plaisance* a French word that roughly translates to "pleasantness." Yes, this park on chilly Lake Michigan was meant to have a distinctly tropical ambience. Olmsted planned to drape the shoreline thickly with native plantings. "You certainly cannot set the madrepore or the mangrove to work on the banks of Lake Michigan," he wrote, "you cannot naturalize bamboo or papyrus, aspiring palm or waving parasites, but you *can* set firm barrier to the violence of wind and waves, and make shores as intricate, as arborescent and as densely overhung with foliage as any. . . . [I]f you cannot reproduce the tropical forest in all its mysterious depths of shade and visionary reflections of light, you can secure a combination of the fresh and healthy nature of the North with the restful, dreamy nature of the South."

As for the strip of land that connected the shoreline park with the inland park, Olmsted and Vaux dubbed it the Midway Plaisance. The plan was to cut a mile-long canal running its length. That way, it would be possible to travel by boat right to the entryway of the inland park. In winter, it would be possible to skate along the canal, a scene right out of Amsterdam.

Compared to the rest of their design, the inland park was pretty conventional—a mix of woodland and meadow. But oh, the approach to this place! Getting there would be all the fun.

The Buffalo park system led to another project in that city. Olmsted and Vaux were commissioned to landscape the ample grounds (200 acres) surrounding the Buffalo State Asylum for the Insane. Architect Henry Hobson Richardson, then at the beginning of his distinguished career, was in the process of designing the asylum itself.

Richardson was a rotund man with a vast appetite for food, drink, and convivial conversation. He was only the second American to attend the École des Beaux-Arts in Paris. (The first was Richard Morris Hunt, who drew the ire of Vaux after proposing a series of monumental entryways into Central Park.) Richardson's time in Paris gave him a thorough survey of French architecture. But he was far too ebullient to be constrained by rigid stylistic concerns.

On returning to the United States, he took the Romanesque style that he'd seen in ancient French castles and cathedrals and pushed it and prodded it until it simply exploded. The result was an untamed architectural vocabulary all his own, replete with towers and turrets and rough-hewn stone walls that look like something out of a medieval hallucination. This style has come to be known as Richardson Romanesque.

Richardson and Olmsted lived near one another in the Clifton section of Staten Island. While in Buffalo, the two men began to grow close personally and laid the groundwork for future professional collaborations. Olmsted was in his late forties during this period; Richardson was in his early thirties. They even took a trip, accompanied by Vaux and Dorsheimer, to nearby Niagara Falls. This great scenic attraction was at risk of being overwhelmed by a combination of circus-style amusements and industrial development. The four men met in Dorsheimer's room at an inn called Cataract House and had a lively discussion about how Niagara Falls might be preserved.

Olmsted and Richardson were soul mates of sorts, though decidedly mismatched in other ways. Olmsted was slightly built with a refined manner; Richardson was big and demonstrative. Olmsted was a wildly original thinker, yet there was an intense discipline, a precision even, to his creativity. Richardson followed a creative process as messy as his napkin after one of his epic meals. No work was ever finished, as he put it, until it was "in stone beyond recovery."

Because the Buffalo asylum was one of his first major commissions, Richardson was brimming with ideas, many of them probably better suited to structures with other purposes. The result: a twin-towered castle fantasia that's like no mental institution built before or since. Unfortunately, Olmsted and Vaux's landscaping plan for the surrounding grounds was lost before it could be executed. Olmsted later drew up a vastly simplified version of the initial scheme.

But there is one touch from Olmsted and Vaux's original plan that survived. They suggested rotating Richardson's building so that it was on a diagonal to the line of the street. Initially, the directors of the Buffalo asylum were puzzled. It seemed such an awkward placement for this monumental structure. But then they realized that Olmsted and Vaux

wanted the building to face to the southeast so that as much soothing
sunlight as possible would pour through the residents' windows. When
Richardson's mental institution was built, it would be positioned exactly
as Olmsted and Vaux had specified.

An asylum in Buffalo, a park system in Chicago—the ball of wax kept
growing. But that's not to mention the various failures. There were plenty
of those. The late 1860s and early 1870s were an incredibly productive
time for Olmsted and Vaux, yet for everything they accomplished, their
efforts came to naught in a shocking number of cases.

Their proposals for parks in Albany, New York, and Providence,
Rhode Island, were rejected. Plans for a park in Newark, New Jersey, were
stalled indefinitely. Plans for the campus of the Maine College of Agriculture and the Mechanic Arts were abandoned. Landscaping surrounding a memorial chapel at Yale was never carried out. Olmsted and Vaux
spent a huge amount of time drawing up a plan for a suburban development in Tarrytown Heights, New York. That, too, came to nothing. Typically, Olmsted, Vaux & Company would collect a modest fee for its
efforts. Given that much of the pair's work was on the front end—visiting a site repeatedly in the early going, preparing a detailed plan, writing
a proposal—the failures took nearly as much time as the projects that
moved forward.

The heavy workload took its toll on Olmsted. He wrote to Samuel
Bowles, "I feel myself so nearly desperate that I have to school myself
against the danger of some wildly foolish undertaking—such as putting
all I can get together in a farm, cutting the world and devoting myself to
asceticism." Bowles, the editor of the *Springfield (Mass.) Republican*, and
Olmsted had first met during the Colfax party's visit to Yosemite. The
two men had stayed in touch and developed a friendship. "But I say to
myself ten times a day that I positively must find some way of living in
the country and escaping this drive." Olmsted added, "I cannot live another year under it."

Olmsted had tried farming and had had his fill of it. But the deeper
root of his dissatisfaction appears to lie in changed domestic circumstances. There was a new baby in the household. Olmsted was feeling

added financial responsibility and was also troubled that the crushing workload was taking him away from his family.

Henry Perkins Olmsted was less than a year old. Olmsted and Mary referred to him simply as "Boy," as if saying "Henry" was tempting fate. The nickname was like a desperate prayer. The couple had lost two sons in infancy, and they grappled with terrible anxiety that the unthinkable might happen yet again.

Bowles urged Olmsted to move up to Massachusetts, maybe near Springfield, and slow down. He also counseled him to split with Vaux. After all, Bowles pointed out, Olmsted did the bulk of the work in the partnership. He could set himself up as an independent consultant instead. But Olmsted was forty-nine years old and worried whether he could make enough money on his own to support a family of seven. Furthermore, he responded, "Even if there were no ties of sentiment & obligation I have not courage enough left to dispense with V's cooperation."

Nevertheless, Olmsted continued to grouse about his hectic life. "I am looking in earnest for some less irritating & exasperating method of getting a living than I have lately followed," he wrote to Kingsbury.

Unbeknownst to Olmsted, on the very day he posted the letter—October 8, 1871—the Great Fire broke out in Chicago. That's the conflagration that occurred, according to myth, when Mrs. O'Leary's cow kicked over a lantern. The truth was that the fire raged for two days, killed several hundred people, and destroyed $200 million worth of prime property in America's fastest-growing city. In an unfortunate coincidence, the entire United States slipped into an economic depression not long after the Great Fire. The effect of the depression was especially pronounced in Chicago, and Olmsted and Vaux's work in the city was sorely affected.

Among the business casualties was the Riverside Improvement Company, which went bankrupt. Thus ended a maddening chapter for Olmsted and Vaux. They had battled Emery Childs at every turn. The partners had been forced to sue the RIC twice for nonpayment before simply resigning from the project. The home-design bounty never materialized; before ties were cut with the RIC, Vaux designed but a single house in Riverside that was actually built. As for the grand boulevard to connect Riverside and Chicago, only a tiny stretch was ever completed. (A vestigial sliver of this roadway still exists today in the Lawndale section of Chicago.)

Olmsted and Vaux had taken on the project dazzled by the possibility of earning in excess of $100,000. But as payment, only a handful of lots were ever transferred to them. And Childs wildly overestimated their value. Once Chicago was hit by a severe economic downturn, they proved to be worth still less. When Olmsted and Vaux finally managed to unload their lots, they collected a fee believed to be just $2,000, representing their total payment for Riverside.

Childs confirmed the partners' worst fears. He turned out to be a swindler very much in the Mariposa mold. But at least he was a swindler with taste. By the time the RIC went bankrupt, 1,176 of the 1,560 acres were finished, and, crucially, the work had been done in accordance with the original plan. Construction of the roads, sewers, and other features was faithfully carried out by the firm of William Le Baron Jenney, the architect that Olmsted had met during the siege of Vicksburg. Once Chicago recovered economically, people began moving to Riverside in droves. In the future, the suburb would feature houses by such notable architects as Louis Sullivan and Frank Lloyd Wright. Riverside, with its curving streets and abundant common space, would become the template for a model suburban community. Any modern suburb—if it's well thought out—likely owes a debt to Olmsted and Vaux's 1868 plan.

The Great Fire had a more direct effect on their plans for a park system in Chicago. Various deeds and property records pertaining to the project and in the possession of assorted local attorneys and real estate agents burned up. Although the documents could be replaced, momentum was irretrievably lost. In the aftermath of a terrible disaster, the idea of building a new park system in Chicago was just no longer a priority. Four square miles of downtown had been destroyed and were in need of rebuilding; nearly 100,000 residents had been left homeless.

Even so, work on the inland park—the more modest composition of woodland and meadow—proceeded, albeit slowly. Horace W. S. Cleveland, a landscape architect who had worked on Prospect Park, supervised the construction of what came to be known as Washington Park. But what about the shoreline park? What about those lagoons, the lush plantings, people gliding along in boats on languid July evenings, skating down the frozen Midway mile in January? Following the Great Fire, such an extravagant place seemed like something out of a dream, a dream with a huge price tag attached. For the next two decades, Chicago would pretty much forget about the shoreline park. But one person would remember. During all the long years ahead, Olmsted would hold on to the dream and serve as its keeper.

CHAPTER 24

Battling Boss Tweed, Splitting with Vaux

THERE WERE FAILURES. There was the Great Fire. But for Olmsted and Vaux, the greatest fear of all was that a park already done would be undone. Nowhere was this anxiety more pronounced than with Central Park. As a great civic work in the middle of a vast and unruly metropolis, there was never a shortage of people eager to mess with Olmsted and Vaux's original design or to propose new features for the park, new purposes for the land.

Generally, these were fended off. But the pair had never before encountered a menace the equal of Tammany Hall, the preposterously corrupt political machine that managed to seize power in New York City by trading jobs and favors for bribes and votes. During the early 1870s, it achieved ascendancy under the leadership of William Marcy Tweed—the notorious Boss Tweed—a demagogue of rare and diabolical talent. Tweed had worked his way up from volunteer fireman to Democratic Party boss and had amassed a fortune rumored at $200 million.

Tweed's most trusted henchman and the brains of the Tammany machine was Peter Sweeny. Whereas Tweed was the aw-shucks populist, Sweeny was the cunning, remain-in-the-shadows operator. He had a variety of nicknames, none flattering, including Sly Sweeny and Spider Sweeny. A stout, ugly man with a big black walrus mustache, he was once described as having eyes that shined "like little dollars in the night."

Boss Tweed installed Spider Sweeny in a plum job as president of the newly created Department of Public Parks. Just like that, Sweeny became ruler of a large fiefdom that included all of the city's parks and public squares. For some reason, the job even gave him control over street improvements in Upper Manhattan. But Central Park was the jewel; as an ample space that employed a large number of people, the park represented an irresistible opportunity for a patronage-based political machine.

Sweeny immediately went on a hiring binge, pushing the head count—which had hovered around several hundred during the late 1860s—to several thousand. This vast crew was wholly unqualified for park work; many of the hirees were old or infirm and had simply been handed a job as a political payoff. Under Sweeny's direction, they set to work on such tasks as cutting low-hanging branches, until the first thirty or so feet of many of the park's trees looked like poles. This was done, according to the minutes of a Tweed Ring park-board meeting, to increase the "circulation of air" in the park. An army of Tammany hires was loosed upon the Ramble, where they busied themselves trying to remove lichen from boulders. Others were given the task of banishing all traces of rusticity from Vaux's structures; they were instructed to pumice those archways until they fairly shined.

Sweeny retained Olmsted and Vaux as consulting architects, but that was only for show. They were not consulted. Also for show, Andrew Green was kept on as a member of the board. Actually, Green was deeply loyal to Central Park in his own parsimonious way. Now, Olmsted would have welcomed some form of intervention from his old nemesis. But Green was utterly impotent. He'd show up for a park-board meeting and would be the only one present. The new commissioners were in the habit of lying to Green; they'd hold their own private meetings at undisclosed times.

Sweeny and his Tweed toadies had ambitious plans for the park. At the southern end, they planned a trotting course for horses. They also began work on a zoo on the grounds of the hourglass-shaped North Meadow, at that time the park's most fetching open space. The Dairy—the place where mothers brought children for untainted milk—was converted into a restaurant. There was also talk of erecting in Central Park a fittingly lavish monument to Boss Tweed. For Olmsted, never a fan of statues, this was anathema.

Olmsted and Vaux protested loudly against the whole situation—the damage already done their park and that which was planned for the future. Not only was their masterpiece in jeopardy, but the partners worried that if Sweeny had his way, Central Park might cease to be a professional calling card. It could hurt their future business. Potential clients might conclude: *Why spend heavily on such a project? Just look at Central Park! Look at what an eyesore a park can become in the space of a few short years.* Once again, the press-savvy Olmsted tried to engage public opinion, just as he had when Dillon and Belmont tried to overhaul the original Greensward plan. He wrote a series of articles attacking the Tweed Ring's plans. But that only got the partners fired as consulting architects.

Things looked bleak. Olmsted despaired of saving Central Park. "It is disheartening to have the best work of my life made nothing of by Hilton & Sweeny," Olmsted wrote to his old friend Kingsbury. (Henry Hilton was another member of the Tweed park board.)

But then the *New York Times*, the paper for which Olmsted had worked in its earliest incarnation, came to the rescue. It devoted some of the finest reporting of its history to exposing the Tweed Ring. In the autumn of 1871, the Tweed Ring collapsed. Boss Tweed was arrested and would be in and out of prison for the few years of life that remained to him. Sweeny fled to Canada, then France. Eventually, he snuck back into the United States, where he lived incognito in and around New York City.

Following the fall of the Tweed Ring, a new Central Park board was assembled. Among its members was Frederic Church, the Hudson River School painter who was also a close friend of Vaux's and a distant relative of Olmsted's. For Olmsted, the inclusion on the board of an artist—especially one as notable and civic-minded as Church—represented a genuine commitment to change. "Church's name was first suggested by Vaux, and we both did what we could to secure his appointment," wrote Olmsted to Brace, adding, "The appointment of Church signifies more—That offices (for the present) are not for sale to those who want them, but are to seek and draw in the best men."

Olmsted and Vaux were restored to their posts as consulting landscape architects. A provision was adopted whereby no structure could be placed in the park until they had first viewed plans for it and discussed the matter with the board. Green was asked to serve on the new board as treasurer, but he declined. Instead, he accepted a job as New York's comptroller; he would apply his talents to cleaning up the entire citywide fiscal mess wrought by the Tweed Ring.

Shortly into the new board's tenure, its president took a five-month leave of absence. Henry Stebbins set off on a business trip to Europe. On May 29, 1872, Olmsted was chosen to act as temporary president and treasurer. Although the Tweed Ring's grip on Central Park was relatively short, only lasting about a year, they managed to make quite a mess. "The Park has suffered great injury," Olmsted lamented. Sweeny had run up $1.5 million in debts and had entered into another $500,000 worth of bogus contracts. Olmsted set to work razing the zoo structures that had been built on the North Meadow. (The familiar zoo that exists at the southern end of the park is a different, non-Tweed, creation.) He planted thousands of shrubs to replace ones that had been grubbed out by careless workers.

When Stebbins came back from Europe, Olmsted returned to his position as consulting landscape architect. But the fact that Olmsted was named president, albeit temporarily, says something about the profile he had managed to achieve. The nineteenth century didn't have celebrities in the same frenzied fashion as later eras, but Olmsted had become what might properly be termed a notable public person. All manner of entreaties came his way. He was offered, and turned down, the presidency of Iowa's agricultural college. He was also offered, and turned down, the presidencies of a variety of companies, among them a maker of earth closets (an alternative to the privy) and an outfit devoted to photo sculpture (making statues based on pictures snapped from a variety of angles).

Olmsted also received numerous letters from strangers. Naturally, many wrote requesting information about landscape architecture. *How do I break into this new field?* Or simply: *How do I tastefully landscape the grounds surrounding my home?* But others wrote with off-kilter requests—for example, seeking tips on how to stop drinking.

Among the most notable of Olmsted's correspondents was William Hammond Hall. Hall was a bold young engineer who had landed a big job, designing a park in San Francisco. When it came to park making, Hall had zero training and zero credentials, something Olmsted could surely appreciate. Ironically, Hall was also dead-set on doing the exact thing that Olmsted had refused to do in San Francisco. Olmsted had felt that the city's climate and topography required a unique treatment. But his plan, sunken promenades and all, had been roundly rejected. Hall had won the commission by promising that he could somehow manage to re-create Central Park in windswept San Francisco.

As a first step, Hall started teaching himself all about landscape architecture. He obtained Olmsted and Vaux's reports on Central Park and Prospect Park and read them religiously. Once he summoned the nerve, Hall wrote directly to Olmsted. "Please excuse the liberty I take in addressing you without being even an acquaintance," Hall began. He then requested that Olmsted send him a list of books that might aid him in his work. Hall closed by writing that he had "visited and carefully studied and noted the principal parks and grounds about London, Paris, and the United States; particularly have I roamed through your Central Park . . . and the Brooklyn [park] . . . to say nothing of those beautiful spots on the Hudson with which that gentleman of great taste, Mr. Downing, and yourself too I am told, had so much to do."

That Hall had actually visited all these spots was a stretch, at best. And Olmsted hadn't designed any "beautiful spots" along the Hudson. But the reverent tone was duly noted. And the reference to Downing was a touch guaranteed to win Olmsted's favor. Olmsted wrote back with a long list of titles that Hall might consult. Among them, Olmsted suggested works by John Claudius Loudon, Humphry Repton, and Uvedale Price, an author that he had read as a boy in the Hartford library. Olmsted ended his letter with a word of caution: "I have given the matter of pleasure grounds for San Francisco some consideration and fully realize the difficulties of your undertaking. . . . But the conditions are so peculiar and the difficulties so great that I regard the problem as unique and that it must be solved if at all by wholly new means and methods. It requires invention, not adaptation."

The indefatigable Hall approached the task in exactly this spirit. The land chosen for Golden Gate Park was a rectangle roughly three miles

long and a half mile wide, the exact shape and nearly the same size as
Central Park. At its western edge a large portion of land was entirely given
over to barren dunes. Stiff winds blew sand over the rest of the land, making parklike plantings virtually impossible. Hall believed the solution lay
in a technique he'd read about known as plant succession. He decided to
start with yellow broom, a hardy shrub that might grow in the dunes.
This shrub could act as an anchor, making it possible to grow larger
plants and eventually trees. But the yellow broom wouldn't take.

Then a fortunate accident occurred. Hall and some colleagues were
riding over the dunes on horseback, studying them. They fed their horses
barley. Some scattered barley seeds sprouted in the sand. Hall had found
his anchor. With some tweaking, he figured out that a sequence of barley, lupine, and then maritime pine would still the shifting sands. It then
became possible to landscape Golden Gate Park after the fashion of Central Park or Prospect Park. In doing so, Hall consulted the various titles
that Olmsted had recommended.

Throughout the early 1870s, during the initial construction of
Golden Gate Park, Hall carried on a vigorous correspondence with Olmsted. He asked Olmsted to recommend a gardener; Olmsted suggested
Frederick Poppey, a man who had worked on Prospect Park. To create
various rustic structures, Hall hired Anton Gerster, the Hungarian crafts-
man who had worked with Vaux on Central Park.

People often mistakenly credit Golden Gate Park to Olmsted and
Vaux. The design is all Hall. It's more accurate to view Olmsted as a kind
of mentor, offering encouragement, suggesting pertinent books, steering
talented employees Hall's way. Olmsted is the man behind the man who
created Golden Gate Park.

On June 21, 1872, Olmsted was nominated in absentia as vice president
of the United States by a small group of prominent citizens. This was a
political *splinter* group in the sheerest sense. Incumbent Ulysses Grant
was the presumptive nominee for the Republican Party. A dissident faction of Liberal Republicans was instead backing Horace Greeley as its
candidate. A group of twenty-two men who favored neither Grant nor
Greeley met at New York's Fifth Avenue Hotel.

Among those present was James McKim, one of the financial backers of the *Nation*, and Robert Minturn, a New York philanthropist instrumental in the original call for Central Park. They proposed a ticket featuring Olmsted as VP, and as president William Groesbeck, a former U.S. representative from Ohio who had served as a counsel to Andrew Johnson during his 1868 impeachment trial. The party dubbed itself the National American Democratic Republicans, a name that "seems to have nearly a word for each member," as Greeley's own *New York Tribune* sneered.

Olmsted immediately quashed his own nomination. He took out a card in the *New York Post* that read, "My name was used without my knowledge in the resolutions of the gentlemen who met on Friday at the Fifth Avenue Hotel . . . but, while thanking them sincerely for their very good opinion, I must express my regret they should have thought it expedient to take up as a representative of their requirements one who is so completely separated from the political field, and so much absorbed in professional and official duties as I am."

Secretly, Olmsted was pleased by the VP nod. In a private note to McKim, he wrote, "I am surprised & gratified that it is so well received." This was yet another episode that served to underscore what an estimable public figure Olmsted had grown to be.

Olmsted's high profile intensified the long-simmering tensions with Vaux. On the one hand, Vaux had coaxed Olmsted back from California by insisting that he required Olmsted's unique palette of skills. At the same time, Vaux resented Olmsted's prominence. Vaux was particularly thin-skinned about even the barest insinuation that Central Park wasn't an equal collaboration. For his part, Olmsted was forever correcting journalist friends who referred to him in articles as Central Park's "creator" or its "prime mover." Then again, more recent collaborations between the two were unequal. Olmsted truly had acted as the driving force behind the jobs in Buffalo and Riverside.

On October 18, 1872, Olmsted and Vaux dissolved their partnership. The pair's relationship had always been heavy on squabbles. Even impersonal discussions—on design philosophy, say—were quick to devolve into personal arguments. Olmsted would later say, "Mr. Vaux's ways are not my ways and I could not fit mine to his," adding, " . . . [I]t was a relief to me to part company with him." Underneath it all, however, Olmsted and Vaux shared a deep bond of loyalty and friendship. They even respected one another as artists, although they couldn't be in the same room together for long. What's more, Olmsted would always gratefully remember that it was Vaux who first approached him about collaborating on Central Park. Without Vaux, Olmsted once said, "I should have been a farmer."

Of course, none of this flavor appears in the bland official statement issued by Olmsted and Vaux, stating that their break was for "reasons of mutual convenience." They agreed to jointly handle any lingering business involving earlier projects such as Prospect Park. Going forward, the two would still collaborate when it suited them, notably on New York City's Riverside and Morningside parks. But Olmsted, Vaux & Company was no more. A partnership that stretched back fourteen years—with a few sidelines by Olmsted along the way—was at an end.

The timing was right for Vaux. For his separate architectural practice, he had recently landed a pair of huge and prestigious commissions to design the buildings for New York's Museum of Natural History and Metropolitan Museum of Art. Rather than working as a *landscape* architect, designing bridges and refectories in parks that were increasingly Olmsted creations, he saw the potential to establish himself as one of the nation's leading architects. Olmsted's immediate prospects were less promising.

The very first job Olmsted took on sans Vaux was McLean Asylum. This was a modest job, especially when compared to his erstwhile partner's Museum of Natural History, slated to be the largest building in America. But Olmsted—as a reformer and out of a special empathy, too—was always drawn to mental-institution commissions. He approached this latest job, like all his work, with a winning combination of earnestness and intensity.

The McLean Asylum had opened in 1818 in Charlestown (now Somerville), a town right outside Boston. By 1872, Charlestown had grown into an industrial center, and McLean's bucolic grounds had been completely transformed. The air hung thick with smoke and foul odors, wafting from such nearby businesses as a slaughterhouse, tannery, and a bleach-and-dye works. Four separate railway lines skirted the property. This was no longer a restful place for a person suffering from mental illness.

McLean's trustees hired Olmsted to identify a piece of land suitable for building a new hospital. He visited several sites before settling on a 114-acre property in Belmont, Massachusetts. In a letter to the trustees, Olmsted described this property as having a "decided advantage in the great numbers of well-grown trees and in local picturesque interest." A natural spring flowed though the property, ensuring a supply of fresh water for the patients.

Olmsted also suggested a building scheme for the new hospital. He proposed that the patients be housed in a small collection of cottages. This would create a setting that was more domestic in feel, less institutional. It would also make it possible to separate patients by degree of affliction. Unruly and agitated patients could be grouped together, while the "worried well" (as people with less severe mental illness were known) could have separate accommodations.

Olmsted's proposal was a departure from the Kirkbride plan, the standard for mental institutions in the mid-1800s. This design scheme, named for Philadelphia psychiatrist Thomas Kirkbride, was all about maximizing control. Patients were housed in vast wings that could be locked down quickly in the event of some kind of disturbance. But such an arrangement had considerable disadvantages: Fires could advance quickly through the wings, diseases traveled easily among the crowded patients, and the lack of fresh air, the result of poor ventilation, was not exactly conducive to improved mental health. Olmsted's proposed cottage plan addressed all these issues by spreading out the patient population. Once again, he was very explicit that the cottages be positioned so as to receive ample sunlight.

McLean's trustees accepted Olmsted's recommendation on a site for the new hospital. They purchased the Belmont property. But it would be many years before there were sufficient funds to build a new facility. When the new McLean was finally built, it would depart in many significant ways from Olmsted's cottage plan.

Two months after the split with Vaux, Olmsted received a letter from his half-brother Albert, casually informing him that his father had slipped on the ice and broken his hip. Olmsted caught the next train to Hartford.

John Olmsted was surprised and pleased to see his son. Olmsted sat at his bedside, and they had a pleasant talk until his father drifted off. The next morning Olmsted returned to New York. The following day, Albert sent a telegraph with the news that John Olmsted had taken a turn for the worse. Olmsted rushed back to Hartford. He arrived to find his father sleeping. He also noticed that his father looked terribly much older than the day before. When he awoke and saw his son, he smiled and said, "Who's this? Fred? So you've come back!"

John Olmsted was feverish and in great pain. He appeared to be failing fast. At the nurse's urging, he was given Dr. McMann's Elixir, an opium-laced sedative. He slept fitfully for a while. Olmsted wet his father's lips. The old man awoke briefly at one point and gasped, "Air—give me all the air you can." Olmsted's stepmother, his half-sister Bertha, and his half-brother Albert gathered around the bedside in vigil. John Olmsted died at one o'clock on the morning of January 25, 1873. He was eighty-one.

Olmsted was deeply moved when he happened upon the little business diary that his father had maintained his entire adult life. The final neat pencil notation, spelling out some mundane matter, was only a few days old. Olmsted was also touched when he opened a drawer, only to find it packed with newspaper clippings going back twenty years, all about his parks and books and sundry endeavors. "He was a very good man and a kinder father never lived," Olmsted wrote to Kingsbury. "It is strange how much of the world I feel has gone from me with him. The value of any success in the future is gone for me."

CHAPTER 25

Blindness and Vision

AT THE TIME of his father's death, Olmsted was about halfway moved into a brownstone in Manhattan. Besides providing a home for his own large family, the dwelling was meant to serve a couple of other purposes as well. Now that he'd split with Vaux, Olmsted needed a professional office, and Staten Island was just too far off the beaten path. The new quarters were also meant to provide a place to care for his father and step-mother in their old age. Olmsted had bought the place figuring some of the rooms could be set aside for them as a kind of apartment. Sadly, his father wouldn't be joining him.

The brownstone was located at 209 West 46th Street, right off Long-acre Square (now known as Times Square). It was four stories plus a base-ment. Olmsted converted the first-floor dining room into an office. As with the Vaux partnership, the new company would be a lean outfit, this time operating out of Olmsted's home. He'd hire mostly part-timers to meet shifting workloads, and many of his charges would remain in the field. Two large north-facing windows in the dining room converted into an office provided abundant light. Olmsted placed a drafting table in front of them. (For professional-quality drafting, he'd turn to assistants, as always. He was a big-idea person; his own drafting skills were limited.) On a mantelpiece in the office, he placed some photos, including ones of Ruskin and Vaux. A large map of New York City hung in a hallway that connected the office and a bathroom. Otherwise, Olmsted's home office was pretty spare of ornament. Another small ground-floor room was turned into a reception area for clients.

Having Olmsted's office on the first floor necessitated placing the dining room on the second. The kitchen was in the basement. Thanks to a dumbwaiter, it was possible to communicate between the kitchen and dining room. There was also a second-floor parlor; its walls were lined with Carleton Watkins's photos of Yosemite, scene of some of the family's happiest times together. Mary placed a piano in the parlor and enjoyed playing and singing. The top two floors were bedrooms for the family.

Everywhere, all over the house, there were books. The office had reference works such as Augustus Mongredien's *Trees and Shrubs for English Plantations*, G. M. Kern's *Practical Landscape Gardening*, and *Gardening for Ladies* by Jane Loudon. Elsewhere, books simply overflowed their cases; stacks grew on every available surface, and tottering piles were arrayed on the floor. According to a rough inventory, he owned about 2,000 books. The titles reflected his eclectic interests and concerns: *Principals of Political Economy* by John Stuart Mill and Darwin's *Origin of Species*, collections of poems by Browning and Burns, Macaulay's *History of England*, Hawthorne's *Marble Faun*, Defoe's *Robinson Crusoe*, and *Short Sermons to News Boys* by Brace. There was also a work on insomnia, *Sleep and Its Derangements*, by William Hammond.

The brownstone had a backyard, short and sixteen feet wide. It had been many years since Olmsted had lived in a home surrounded by so little land. But he made the best of it, using his well-honed perspective tricks to plant the tiny yard so as to give the illusion of space—as much as was possible.

In a new home now, Olmsted slipped back into his accustomed domestic relationships, ones that bore a marked similarity to those of his late father. As a widower with two small boys, John Olmsted had been in a hurry to wed Mary Ann Bull back in 1827. The couple had fallen into a relationship that was largely practical, hardly passionate. Over time, Olmsted and Mary had also achieved a kind of mutuality, an essential element of love, to be sure. But there seemed to be something muted about their feelings for one another, a lack of spark. Theirs was a love born of obligation—the death of Olmsted's brother—and deepened through successive sorrows.

Years earlier, Olmsted had confided to Brace that he feared he might have to settle in marriage and be left "believing that the 'highest element of love' is not of earth." That's precisely what had come to pass. In another confession, Olmsted once told Vaux that Central Park had been his grand passion and that while working on it, "a great deal of disappointed love and unsatisfied romance and down trodden pride fastened itself to that passion." *Disappointed love* and *unsatisfied romance* are curious choices of phrase, more so when one considers that Olmsted wed Mary while work on Central Park was under way.

As for his relationship with his children, Olmsted was capable of great affection, as his own father had been. Both often showed a genuine sweetness toward their children that wasn't so common among fathers in nineteenth-century America. But both men also maintained some distance from their offspring. Work required Olmsted often to be absent from home; his father had sent him away to school for long stretches of his childhood. But here's where the two differed: Olmsted could at times be remarkably underindulgent—something for which his father could never be accused. His father was a comfortable Hartford burgher; Olmsted was a hard-driven and pioneering artist. Olmsted had high expectations when it came to parenting as well, and when these expectations weren't met, the results could be chilling.

Olmsted was fifty-one now; Mary was forty-three. Between his brother's three children, whom he had adopted, and two natural offspring, he had five children. His father also had five who lived to maturity.

John Charles, age twenty, was the oldest in the Olmsted brood. He'd grown into a deadly serious and painfully shy person. Because he was the firstborn, perhaps, he had an intense, overdeveloped sense of duty. As a boy, Olmsted had called him "Charley," but the nickname proved entirely too lighthearted. By 1873, when the family moved into the brownstone, Charley had come to be known as John and was studying at Yale's Sheffield Scientific School. John had a talent for rendering. He was thinking about becoming a painter or an architect, perhaps even following his father into landscape architecture. John had also recently grown a beard, though not for the usual reasons. He'd slammed into a stone wall while sledding with the Brace children. His chin was left so scarred that he wore a beard the rest of his life.

Among the various children, Charlotte, age eighteen, provoked the most concern for Olmsted and his wife. She was a bright young woman, who was studying at a boarding school in Massachusetts. Her dream was to run a kindergarten. She was tiny, like her mother, but given to violent mood swings. Charlotte's nickname was Chatty, though that seems like a euphemism for far darker personality traits. Olmsted once described how Charlotte "on the least provocation turns down almost to the bottom, pale, thin, blue, and hysterical."

Owen, age fifteen, continued to look unsettlingly more like his father—Olmsted's dead brother, Mary's dead husband—with each passing year. He also shared John's casual, winning disposition as well as his fragile physical makeup. Owen was attending boarding school in Plymouth, Massachusetts, along with the Vaux boys. At one point, Olmsted wrote the headmaster, trying to ensure that Owen was receiving a rigorous outdoor training to go along with book learning. Perhaps exposure to the rougher side of life would fortify his delicate constitution. The letter is a litany—a form in which Olmsted excelled—detailing all the skills that Owen might properly be taught:

> To saddle & bridle a horse—to harness him. . . . To ride, drive, pack, clean, feed, bleed & physic a horse. . . . To make a fire, & cook under difficulties. To swim, with & without support; to aid others in swimming, to rescue drowning persons. . . . To make and understand common signals & signs of seamen & woodsmen. To measure distances by the eye—by pacing—by trigonometry without instruments. . . . To ford a river. To kill animals without cruelty; to preserve meat. To preserve life & health under difficulties when ordinary provisions are lacking—from cold, from heat, hunger & thirst—fatigue, debility, nervous prostration, excessive excitements. To make slight repairs in & run a steam engine safely. To take care of a watch; to preserve clothing from moths. . . .

That's not even the half of it. On and on goes the letter, though it appears that Owen mostly learned the standard reading and math at his boarding school. At home, he showed a talent for tinkering. Owen cobbled together some telegraph equipment and strung lines between the brownstone and the homes of four friends, one more than ten blocks away.

Marion, age eleven, was Olmsted's first child with Mary to survive infancy. She was energetic, a tomboy who enjoyed outdoor activities like hiking. There was also something incredibly stolid and dependable about Marion. "Just the nicest girl—little old maid—possible; patient; happy, indefatigable" is how Olmsted once described her.

And then there was Henry, the baby of the family, now two. At age seven, in a truly bizarre turn, he'd be rechristened as Frederick Law Olmsted Jr. By that point, Olmsted and Mary figured that he had a real chance of surviving, of carrying that name—and all that went with it—into adulthood. For now, Henry, née Boy, future FLO Jr., delighted in traveling from floor to floor in the dumbwaiter.

Throughout the mid-1870s, the Olmsteds would have a lively household on West 46th Street, and many people would come to visit. The Braces were regular guests, as was architect H. H. Richardson, critic Clarence Cook, the Putnams, and the Perkins cousins. Poet and *Post* editor William Cullen Bryant was a frequent visitor at a time when he was preparing a translation of the *Odyssey*. He read from the original Greek text in a stentorian voice, making quite an impression on the youngest Olmsteds.

But 1873, the first year spent in the new brownstone, proved most of all to be a difficult time. Within days of John Olmsted's funeral, Mary Ann Olmsted, Fred's stepmother, began questioning the terms of the will. She had always left financial matters entirely in her husband's hands, and when he died, she was stunned by how little money was left. She had assumed he had sizable real estate holdings, or maybe a large portfolio of investments. But chronic overindulgence of his children had left John Olmsted's estate quite diminished.

In the will, Fred was designated as a trustee along with his half-brother Albert, who was a banker in Hartford. The pair was left with the unenviable task of convincing Mary Ann that, given financial exigencies, she'd need to cut back. Fred suggested she sell one of the two horses and downsize from a double to a one-person carriage.

Instead, Mary Ann chose to contest the will and hired a lawyer. The lawyer went on the attack, trying to have Fred and Albert removed as trustees. Albert sent Fred regular updates from Hartford of the probate proceedings, in one describing Mary Ann as "the enemy/mother" and in another warning, "I write that you may be prepared for an attack from any quarter." Meanwhile, Mary Ann sent a series of letters to Fred, containing everything from grave accusations—in one, she claimed he was cheating her out of her rightful share—to small jibes, such as a demand that he return to Hartford at once to pick up some old copies of the *Nation* stored in the house. Invariably, she signed these letters: "I remain your affectionate, Mother."

Things grew progressively more ugly. Settlement of the estate, something that should have taken weeks, dragged on for months. Mary Ann even went so far as to claim that Olmsted and his half-brother had bribed the probate judge. At this point, Olmsted sent a letter to Central Park. Even in the best of times, Olmsted's longtime consulting role with the park was fraught with tension, and given his current family blowup, he felt that he needed to be "relieved of responsibilities which under present circumstances I can not satisfactorily meet." Back came a telegram insisting that he stay on.

But then, just when the legal wrangle was beginning to look unending, the matter settled. John Olmsted's will was upheld. Per its terms, Mary Ann was to receive the Hartford house and a modest allowance. There was a portfolio of stocks and bonds sufficient to provide each of his children roughly $1,500 a year. This was nothing to scoff at, but it meant that Olmsted couldn't really pursue his occasionally voiced desire to slow down. The will proceedings also had another result: The acrimony left Fred's relationship with his stepmother in ruins. They would never manage to patch things up. And she would also not be coming to live at 209 West 46th Street.

Olmsted fell into genuine despair. His father's death had brought pain and consequences beyond anything he could have imagined. He wondered whether he really could go it alone without Vaux. Now, more than ever, it was necessary to strike out and find fresh clients.

Instead, Olmsted went blind. A doctor examined him and concluded that nothing was physically wrong. He was simply overcome with anxiety and needed to rest his eyes. Olmsted appears to have been suffering from something like hysterical blindness. The whole episode has echoes of the sumac poisoning that spread to his eyes as a teenager, preventing him from going to college.

During the late autumn of 1873, Olmsted was confined to a darkened bedroom, doctor's orders, unable to work, unable even to read, just alone with his thoughts. Letters from potential clients piled up. P. T. Barnum wrote inquiring whether Olmsted might be interested in landscaping the grounds surrounding his mansion in Bridgeport, Connecticut. The Board of Education in Elmira, New York, sent a worrying note: "I hope you have not forgotten our school grounds."

Even after Olmsted regained his eyesight, his mood remained black. In December 1873, he sent a rambling letter to Brace. Olmsted attempted to summon the spirit that had first bound the two in friendship—argument, endless argument—but his tone was so bleak that this came off as pessimism rather than provocation. Olmsted even took a few tired swipes at religion. "Do you suppose that it is a much smaller misfortune for a Chinese child to lose its Pagan mother than for an English child to lose its Christian mother?" he asked. "Do you suppose there is a whit more tenderness toward her child in an English mother than in a Digger Indian mother?"

But religion was a matter he'd settled long ago. Olmsted had made his peace with the rigid Congregationalist faith of his upbringing and the years spent with cruel country parsons. Over time, Olmsted had become what might best be called an agnostic. He frequently described himself in such terms, though he didn't use the word *agnostic*. No matter: In this letter to Brace, it seems clear, Olmsted's real anger was directed not so much at religion as at his puritanical stepmother. He also made an oblique reference to his recent medical condition: "Suppose a man who sees things so far differently than the mass of ordinary healthy men is thereby classified as of defective vision, as of diseased brain. Thus I have not a doubt that I was born with a defect of the eye, with a defect of the brain."

As the year ended, Olmsted pulled himself together, as he somehow always seemed to do. In previous months, during the ugly inheritance battle, he'd carried on a sporadic correspondence with Justin Morrill, senator from Vermont. Morrill was chairman of the Senate Committee on Public Buildings and Grounds. In the new year, matters took on increased urgency. Congress had just obtained some land that expanded the grounds surrounding the Capitol in Washington, D.C. Senator Morrill asked Olmsted to prepare a preliminary design.

Olmsted traveled to Washington twice in January 1874. He was shocked anew by the shabbiness of the Capitol. When he lived here during the Civil War, the building's dome was under construction, girded with scaffolding. The dome was finally finished, but the surrounding grounds were a disgrace: 58 acres of incoherence, unplanned, unloved, dotted here and there with scraggly trees and marred by large patches of wind-whipped dirt. "In short, the capital of the Union manifests nothing so much as disunity," he wrote Senator Morrill.

To Olmsted, this chaos spelled a great opportunity. Transforming the misbegotten grounds was exactly the kind of high-profile project he'd been seeking. It had the potential to be so far beyond whatever eccentric demands P. T. Barnum had for his private estate, a commission Olmsted now chose not to pursue. The job also represented a new type of challenge for Olmsted. Ordinarily, the emphasis of his landscape designs was the landscape: compositions of foliage, water effects. To succeed here, he perceived, the landscape needed to be secondary to the Capitol itself. Olmsted's task was to create a design that would enhance people's view of that great marble pile, symbol of democracy. This was noble work, to Olmsted's mind, a chance "to form and train the tastes of the Nation."

In March 1874, Congress appropriated $200,000 for work on the grounds. Olmsted was officially hired at a salary of $2,000 a year. He'd remain in New York but travel frequently to Washington. As usual, there would be an army of people on-site to execute his plan.

One of the first orders of business was clearing the existing scraggly trees. He left a few, such as an elm planted by George Washington, at least according to legend. But the bulk weren't worth saving. Better to start over with trees such as sweet gum, mulberry, and magnolia, species he chose for their ability to survive Washington's harsh summers. Starting from scratch allowed Olmsted to pursue a tour-de-force planting scheme. Olmsted envisioned discrete stands of tightly bunched trees. The open space between them would provide sight lines. By carefully arranging the stands of trees, it would be possible to treat someone walking over the grounds to the very best views of the Capitol from the best-chosen angles. The building was always the star here; in planting trees, Olmsted wanted always to adhere to this guiding principle. Foliage was just a frame.

Clearly, the Capitol grounds were nothing like a park. Thousands of people visited each day, including tourists, those on official business, and members of Congress and staff. Generally, they could be expected to move quickly over the grounds en route to the Capitol. This posed a thorny circulation challenge. As it stood, twenty-one different streets touched the Capitol grounds. Carriage drives and footpaths entered at forty-six different places. Olmsted puzzled over this mightily before devising a system that fed visitors, regardless of the point where they entered the grounds, into just a handful of main thoroughfares. These thoroughfares were laid out in gentle curves, Olmsted's signature.

His most ambitious idea involved the Capitol building itself. This was not something that Senator Morrill and his committee had requested. But as Olmsted saw it, if he was going to create a landscape to accentuate a building, well, that building had better be flawless. It wasn't. The Capitol featured two wings that were recent additions. Work had begun on them in the 1850s, a time when Congress had outgrown its quarters, thanks to all the senators and representatives from newly admitted states such as California and Texas. The new wings doubled the length of the building, a circumstance that necessitated that new dome. It was 288 feet tall where the original had been 140 feet tall.

To Olmsted, these changes were aesthetically unnerving: the Capitol was now an overlong building with an overhigh dome, the whole structure looking like it might topple over at any moment. As a metaphor for American democracy, it was frightening to contemplate.

Olmsted proposed a massive marble terrace that would surround the building on three sides, grounding it visually on Capitol Hill. As he put it, "The building will appear as standing on a much firmer base, and thus gain greatly in the supreme qualities of stability, endurance, and repose."

The terrace would also serve a second, equally important, purpose. It would restore the Capitol's original aspect. L'Enfant's eighteenth-century plan had called for the building to face west. But the Capitol was built facing east, owing to the idea that Washington was bound to grow in that direction. As it turned out, the White House, the Treasury and Commerce buildings, and the Mall all wound up to the west. The terrace would serve to reorient the Capitol. "The larger part of the city," Olmsted argued, "the Executive Mansion and the other government buildings will no longer appear to tail off to the rear of the Capitol, but what has been considered its rear will be recognized as its more dignified and stately front."

Though Olmsted's Capitol plan involved a mere 58 acres, there was a momentousness about it. It would take many years to complete and would require drastic measures such as importing tons of bat guano from Peru to enrich Capitol Hill's nitrogen-starved soil.

His design was also meticulous, packed with thoughtful little surprises. Olmsted hired architect Thomas Wisedell, who had done some wonderful sandstone carvings in Prospect Park, to design benches and trellises and lampposts. Olmsted himself designed a small structure, discretely tucked into the side of Capitol Hill and meant to serve as a way station for weary people coming off the Mall. He sweated every last detail of this so-called Summerhouse. He commissioned Tiffany and Company to custom build a carillon, a set of bells, that was ingeniously triggered by the flow of water. When a thirsty tourist stopped in the Summerhouse for a drink from its water fountain, the carillon would play a few tinkling notes.

Of course, getting all these features built required epic determination on Olmsted's part. He'd found various Central Park boards difficult enough, but now the client was Congress. "I heard that it was a house for some man's monkey," sneered Senator James Beck of Kentucky in an attempt to strike monies earmarked for the Summerhouse. The exorbitant marble terraces proved a particular sticking point. Year upon year, Congress refused to grant the funding necessary to begin construction. At one point, Olmsted hand-delivered pamphlets to members of Congress, explaining the rationale for the terraces. He even went so far as to put up scaffolding to provide an idea of what they would look like.

The project would drag on many years into the future. Along the way, Olmsted would even manage one last round with Egbert Ludovicus Viele—Congressman Viele. Olmsted had bested Viele on Central Park and again on Prospect Park, but he'd never been able to quite shake his vainglorious onetime boss. Viele had a knack for coming back. Years after being fired by the Central Park board, he had mounted a lawsuit for wrongful termination against the City of New York. He actually won and was awarded $8,625. Viele put his own spin on the verdict, treating it as validation that he was actually the park's rightful author. Ever after, he claimed that Olmsted and Vaux stole his design. As a congressman masquerading as Central Park's creator, Viele was a vocal critic of Olmsted's design for the Capitol grounds. Fortunately, Viele managed only a single two-year term and was voted out of Congress before he could do much damage.

In the end, the terraces got built. The whole thing got built. Amazingly, the grounds surrounding the Capitol today are remarkably true to Olmsted's original plan. Even the lovely Summerhouse remains, though sadly the carillon never worked properly and was removed long ago.

In the autumn of 1874, during the early stages of the work in Washington, Olmsted received another large commission. The city of Montreal wanted a public park. Oddly, this was his first proper park job since the break with Vaux. As with the Capitol grounds, Olmsted would bring a sense of vision to this project that was intense, bordering on incandescent. Sadly, this time he'd be in some measure thwarted by forces far beyond his control.

Olmsted made his first official visit to the site in November 1874. The future park's overriding feature was a hump of trap rock, one mile long by a half mile wide, and 764 feet high. Montreal, then a city of 120,000, had grown up at the base of—indeed, derives its name from—this "mountain." In his first communiqué to the park commissioners, Olmsted proposed to draw out "the genius of the place." The phrase dates to Roman times (*genius loci*). "Consult the genius of the place in all," Alexander Pope famously exhorted in his poem *Epistle IV to Richard Boyle*. The ever-literary Olmsted planned to follow Pope's counsel and find the natural essence of this particular landscape.

To accomplish this, Olmsted devised one of the most outré designs of his career. He proposed to plant different types of trees at different points along the mountain slope, creating distinct regions of vegetation. This is exactly how trees grow in nature up the sides of a majestic, snowcapped peak. By imposing the same growth pattern on this 764-foot demipeak, Olmsted hoped to craft an illusion capable, as he told the commissioners, of "making your mountain more mountain-like."

At the base, Olmsted proposed to plant the kind of trees one might see in a valley, such as butternut and cherry. Further up, he suggested deciduous trees native to lower elevations, such as hemlock and moose maples. At the highest point, he envisioned scrubby pines and thorny bushes, planted in spare little clumps so as to leave large outcroppings of rock clearly visible. A key feature was a carriage road to the top, periodically curving whether it needed to or not, giving the impression of a demanding climb.

As always, Olmsted's design was not confined to mere artistry but was also meant to confer societal benefits. Perhaps because this park site was particularly dramatic, Olmsted had a vivid, almost mystical, sense of what his landscape could accomplish. In his first report to the commissioners, he described how beleaguered city dwellers would benefit from the "power of their scenery to counteract conditions which tend to nervous depression or irritability." At another point he suggested that his park would be a "prophylactic and therapeutic agent of vital value."

And it would be accessible to all. Because the park would in reality be the most modest of mountains, imposing only in appearance, it would invite use by people who weren't exactly physically rugged. His plan called for a children's playground in an area that was supposed to *feel* like a high mountain meadow. He designed a walking path with a grade so gentle that it would be possible to meander all the way to the top of the mountain without encountering a single set of stairs. The path could even be used by what Olmsted termed "the feebler sorts of folks"—the elderly, handicapped, even people in wheelchairs. These visitors, too, would be able to conquer Mount Royal's awesome summit. Olmsted knew a thing or two about feeble folk. His father had recently died following a fall in which he broke his hip. Olmsted still walked with a limp, thanks to the carriage accident that had shattered his thigh many years back.

Olmsted was joined on the Montreal project by his eldest stepson. John Charles, newly graduated from Yale, signed on as an assistant in the autumn of 1875. He was charged with various clerical duties. Because he had a talent for drawing, he learned quickly from the other draftsmen whom Olmsted hired on a part-time basis. Soon John would develop into a skilled draftsman in his own right.

In the autumn of 1875, Olmsted got a bite from a prospective client that had the potential to be huge. Charles Dalton was commissioner of the newly formed Boston parks commission. He was also a onetime USSC executive and a McLean Asylum trustee—again those incestuous interrelationships.

As a fast-growing city of roughly 300,000, vital cultural center, and civic rival of New York, Boston was a natural for a new park project. But like Chicago, the city's aspirations had been slowed by a great fire, in 1872. Now, Dalton invited Olmsted to travel to Boston and visit some sites. There was discussion of a possible park system. But everything was still at a preliminary stage. When work might begin and how many parks would be needed, such details were unclear—as was the most crucial issue of all, whether Olmsted would be tapped for the job.

Meanwhile, construction began on Mount Royal that winter. This was an unusual season to break ground on a park. But Canada had fallen into a terrible economic depression. The commissioners were anxious to launch a public project that would employ people. Unfortunately, the work was commenced hastily, without consulting Olmsted and without much fidelity to his plan. The carriage road failed to follow the route he'd meticulously mapped out, gracefully winding past specific rock outcroppings and other interesting natural features that he'd identified on the site.

Olmsted was furious. He fired off a letter to the commissioners, describing the road that had been built as something that "any boy who had been a year with a surveying party might have laid out & any intelligent farmer might have constructed." Twisting the knife, he added that the "opportunity of making such an attractive way up the mountain as I had designed, has been lost forever."

Problems mounted as the work progressed. It turned out that the commissioners had requested Olmsted's plan before they knew whether they could purchase certain parcels of land at the base of the mountain. As that became clearer, they asked him repeatedly to redo parts of his plan to reflect ever-fluctuating boundaries. Then the commissioners sprang on Olmsted that a reservoir was planned in the middle of his mountain meadow. There was also talk of building a smallpox hospital on the park's grounds.

When Olmsted encountered resistance, his energy, ordinarily focused and constructive, could curdle into something maniacal. He bombarded the commissioners with angry letters. He adopted the same wounded tone that had characterized the end of his tenure at the USSC, or the worst of his dealings with Andrew Green on Central Park. Underneath the rain of verbiage hummed a constant, pained insinuation: *You aren't merely deviating from a plan. You're hurting me!*

Finally, in the autumn of 1877, Olmsted arranged to travel to Montreal and take his case directly to the public. This had worked in Buffalo. He'd dazzled a large audience, setting the stage for a park-making coup. Maybe, he figured, he could sell the good citizens of Montreal on the merits of his plan and, in so doing, rescue some of its best elements.

Olmsted was scheduled to speak in a hall with a capacity of eight hundred. At the appointed hour, only about ten people had shown up. Another thirty or so trickled in during his speech. He described the exercise as a "farcical failure" in a letter to John.

Like the Capitol grounds, work on Mount Royal would stretch out over many years. But here, many of Olmsted's ideas were not adopted. His intricate tree scheme was mostly ignored. The gentle-grade walking path, suitable for the feeble folk, was never laid out. Sometimes the world understood. Sometimes the world was blind to Olmsted's vision.

VII

"I Have All My Life Been Considering Distant Effects"

SUMMITS AND SORROWS, 1877–1903

CHAPTER 26

A Troubled Wander Year

OLMSTED WAS PLEASED that his stepson had joined the practice. Now there was the possibility of passing his firm along, keeping it a family business when the time came, not to mention a chance to ensure a future for landscape architecture, the profession he had pioneered in America. But John Olmsted had a lot to learn. If he was going to be more than a draftsman, if he was going to design landscapes, he needed to broaden his horizons.

Time and again, when Olmsted was a younger man, he had taken breakneck tours abroad careening from park to park, soaking up knowledge and ideas. In a pre-Google era, when images weren't widely available and were often of poor quality, it was highly necessary to go see things in person. In fact, visual artists such as painters and sculptors were in the habit of taking dedicated sojourns, typically through Europe, to view the great masterpieces. Such a trip was sometimes called a "wander year," though the time allotted might be less than twelve months.

In 1877, it was decided that John should have a wander year. He'd devote some months to visiting England and France, places from which Olmsted had drawn ample inspiration. "I could not keep down my own excitement in sympathy with him," Olmsted confided to Mary after seeing off their eldest.

John departed with six pages of written instructions from his stepfather, to be "read over and committed substantively to memory while at sea, re-read in London and again in Paris." The instructions included a list of parks John should visit as well as assorted estates, castles, and cathedrals. Olmsted also provided the names of various people he knew in London and Paris; John might benefit by making their introduction. The instructions, on all points, included an incredible level of detail and demand: "Everywhere examine closely and accurately all small architectural objects adapted to park-work—pavilions, lodges, entrances, chalets, refreshment stalls, bridges, conservatories, plant-stands, fountains, drinking fountains, lamps, flagstaffs, seats, railings, parapets, copings, etc. If you find anything novel and good, especially in plan and arrangement; take sketches & notes & be prepared on return to make full drawings." Olmsted was anxious that John make the most of this opportunity. "Steep your mind as much as possible in the scenery," he urged, "so as to fix strong, permanent impressions." That's how Olmsted had always worked, and he expected nothing less from his stepson, his employee.

Upon arrival, John wrote to his stepfather nearly every day, providing full accounts of his doings. Olmsted seemed pleased with the initial dispatches. "They show that you were well prepared to profit by the journey; better than I had supposed," Olmsted wrote back. " . . . Your notes are just what I want; full & nothing redundant. I look with great interest for what are to follow."

Meanwhile, Olmsted's longtime position as landscape architect to Central Park was experiencing one of its periodic flash points. Boss Tweed was safely behind bars in the Ludlow Street Jail now, and Spider Sweeny was hiding out somewhere in France. But Tammany had reconstituted as a political force that was still plenty corrupt, just not as visibly, publicly so. As always, Central Park was viewed as a patronage gold mine. The park's board had lately been reduced to just four members, three of whom were Tammany loyalists. Once again, they had designs on the park such as building a horse-racing course.

The machine took shots at Olmsted, whenever and however it could. For example, the *New York Evening Express*, little more than a Tammany house organ, carried an article that attacked Olmsted from an absurd revisionist perspective. The piece claimed that the Tweed Ring's approach to Central Park had upheld the public trust, while Olmsted was actually part of a "Greensward Ring" that for years had cynically exploited the citizens of New York. Here's a typical passage: "The Greensward Ring, whose babble in the papers and Society Circles, about aesthetics and architecture, vistas and landscapes, the quiver of a leaf and the proper blendings of light and shade bamboozled the citizens of that day. These were the Miss Nancies of Central Park art, the foes of nature, and the aids to money-making."

Olmsted was directed to contribute $112 to a Tammany reelection fund. He refused. At another point, the board refused to pay his salary for several months, claiming that he had too many professional obligations besides Central Park. Olmsted would have conceded as much himself. (Tellingly, the commissioners didn't claim he was abdicating his duties, only that he was frequently occupied with nonpark matters.) Olmsted was forced to sue to collect the money that had been withheld.

No doubt, all this contributed to another run of poor health for Olmsted. During the summer of 1877, New York was hit with a heat wave, and he had developed a mysterious illness characterized by fever and chills. As the fall drew on, his relations with the Central Park board grew increasingly strained, and Olmsted grew peevish.

He barraged John with letters on an almost daily basis. John was methodically working his way through the six pages of instructions. But now Olmsted demanded to know whether he was actually appreciating the things he saw. Perhaps his stepson was "too much in haste to get with the mood of enjoyment." What about all the various contacts Olmsted had provided? Had John connected with Mr. Brale, the barrister who was an accomplished amateur geologist? Why, he might prove an invaluable contact. What about Leopold Eidlitz, the noted New York architect? Eidlitz was visiting London at this very time; had John managed to look him up? And why hadn't John spent more time at the British Museum? Why was his lodging arrangement so unsatisfactory? The place did not even serve breakfast. Olmsted worked his way up to a seventeen-page letter that included the following:

> When I have reminded you that (so far as your letters indicate) you have
> failed of enjoying more of the great things you have seen, I do not in the
> least mean that you have not enjoyed them as a child enjoys a show or as

a school girl enjoying jewelry & nice dresses, much less that you have not *enjoyed* the freedom and stir and novelty of traveling in foreign lands, nor that you have not *enjoyed* the observations you have recorded, but that *you have* not had that enjoyment of them which an artist's imagination could have given him. There is no sign that they have taken possession of you and enlarged your artistic capacity. I want you to recognize that if they have not it is because you have not studied them or contemplated them from the right point of view. You are not a man of genius in art, a man of less artistic impulse I never knew. You have no care to produce anything—to carry to perfect realization any conception. Consequently, as you have insisted on making yourself an artist, you must spend great labor, years of study with little satisfaction of any worthy contribution—of all this I thoroughly warned you.

The letter was simply cruel. When John wrote back, he avoided the harsh glare of his stepfather's assessment, confining himself instead to setting straight a few small points: "I have been to the reading room of the British Museum, but they close at 4, as there are no lights allowed in the building, so I have not time to read much."

John's strategy was to remain dutiful, almost to the point of masochism. He continued to write letters home, cataloging the parks and art he saw, going now to great self-conscious lengths to express how these things *moved* him. This succeeded in appeasing Olmsted somewhat. "It is evident that there was little occasion for the long letter which I wrote," he indicated to John. And that was the end of the matter: no apology, no reassessment of John's abilities, at least not at this point.

Olmsted was feeling worse. In December 1877, a doctor advised him to take some time off to recuperate. Olmsted lit upon an idea: He would join John overseas. Together, they would visit some of Europe's finest green spaces, and Olmsted could direct his stepson's appreciation of these masterworks. He requested and was granted a leave of absence by the Central Park board. He laid out an ambitious itinerary that included Amsterdam, Munich, Vienna, Pisa, Turin, Florence, and Dijon, just to name a few stops. Given his stepfather's current mood, the idea of traveling across Europe together filled John with dread. This time John wrote directly to his mother: "His mention of a long string of cities he intends visiting fairly makes my head swim."

Then the other shoe fell in Olmsted's Tammany fracas. The Central Park board announced that it was eliminating his position. The board slyly timed the decision to fall right as Olmsted was preparing to leave. He asked the commissioners to table the matter until after he returned, but they refused.

Olmsted sailed on January 8, 1878. While he was away, his friends and colleagues rallied to his defense. Virtually every New York daily including the *Times, Herald,* and *World* published editorials calling for Olmsted's reinstatement. Godkin, Olmsted's onetime *Nation* collaborator, voiced his outrage in a piece that appeared in the *New York Tribune.* A petition decrying Olmsted's dismissal was signed by 158 prominent citizens, among them banker Morris Jesup, editor Whitelaw Reid, painter Albert Bierstadt, and Willard Parker, the doctor who had both instructed John and treated Olmsted after his carriage accident. The petition included the following passage: "It is not unnatural that we, as taxpayers, should ascribe the successful management of the Park for the last twenty years largely to Mr. Olmsted's connection with it during the greater part of this period."

Notably absent from all this activity was Vaux. The outpouring of support for Olmsted opened an old wound. Vaux was particularly irked by Godkin's piece, which treated Olmsted as Central Park's sole creator, while failing to even mention his name. Vaux wrote a furious rebuttal to the *Tribune,* asserting that Godkin's "greedy misrepresentations" had ignored his role. He also contacted Mary directly, requesting that the record be set straight. Since Olmsted and John were both overseas, she asked Owen to pen a brief statement for publication. The statement asserted that Olmsted and Vaux deserved equal credit for Central Park. But Mary was rankled by what she termed Vaux's "chivying English disposition."

Olmsted did his best to ignore the hubbub. For this trip, he made a point of not even picking up a New York paper. He was determined to enjoy the wander year, this one intended for John's edification as well. Early on, he succeeded. They visited Regent's Park in London, and on the Continent, they particularly enjoyed the Englischer Garden in Munich.

Olmsted filled his pocket notebook with copious scribblings on all he observed—trees, gateways, shelters, fountains—and John recorded his parallel impressions.

But as time went on, Olmsted found that he was unable to shut out the worry. Mount Royal had gone badly, and now his consulting role with Central Park had ended. He was anxious about the lost income. Olmsted had other work such as the ongoing Washington, D.C., project and service on an advisory board regarding the New York State capitol at Albany. But he was concerned about the future of his business. John found his father increasingly quiet and brooding. Olmsted even started to pare back the ambitious itinerary, striking Berlin, Vienna, and several other places. "He is continually fearing that he will never be able to work again at all," John wrote to his brother Owen. "In fact there is no anxiety that he could imagine that he is not thinking about all the time." John added: " . . . Half the time he pays no attention to my remarks about things we are passing."

Olmsted maintained the Italian leg of the trip. Maybe the warm weather would do him good. In Venice, according to John, his stepfather passed an entire gondola ride in silence but appeared soothed by the rocking motion. Then it was on to France. In Paris, John described the previous night's stay at the Hotel de Lille et d'Albion as "one of the worst nights he has had, more depressed thoughts & less sleep, so that today he is despondent." John added: "A good hearty 1 o'clock breakfast made him feel better but he does not know what to do. He has bought a novel by Miss Thackeray [Anne Thackeray Ritchie] but finds it hard to keep his mind to it."

Olmsted returned to New York in April after nearly four months abroad. He was stunned by his situation: His work on Central Park was truly over. It was twenty years since he and Vaux had submitted the Greensward plan. Going forward, he'd have no official say in the fate of the park, although he would still weigh in with his pen. He'd even write a pamphlet called *The Spoils of the Park*, a double entendre, one edge dripping with bitterness. A couple years hence, he'd also be treated to the absurd spectacle of Egbert Viele finagling his way onto the board for a brief spell, while he was left to watch helplessly from the sidelines. Still, he'd remain forever protective of his creation. "It all makes me sick and keeps me sick," he would later say, describing this lifelong vigil.

On returning to New York, Olmsted also received another piece of discouraging news. The Boston commission was going forward with plans for a park. It was just one park; there wasn't sufficient funding at this point for a whole system, which was what he had earlier discussed. What's more, the chosen site for this lone park was a swamp in Boston's Back Bay section, a place where city residents dumped their sewage. One contemporary account described it as "being without a single attractive feature. A body of water so foul that even clams and eels cannot live in it."

This was one nasty spot for a park. Uglier still, from Olmsted's standpoint, was the fact that the commissioners had not chosen him for the job. Rather, they had decided to hold a design competition. Adding to the slight, Olmsted received a letter in which commission head Charles Dalton inquired whether he would act as a judge in the contest. He shot back an angry reply, flatly refusing.

The competition received twenty-three entries. First prize went to Hermann Grundel, a florist. Ignoring the realities of the site, Grundel simply designed a pretty ornamental garden—somehow to be superimposed onto the swamp. The *American Architect and Building News* declared Grundel's design "childish."

For Olmsted, there had been plenty of unhappy endings of late. It would have been hard for him to believe that a fresh beginning was to be found in all this mess.

CHAPTER 27

Stringing Emeralds

OLMSTED'S ANGRY LETTER to Charles Dalton had an unexpected result. "They must have you and they would have you," architect H. H. Richardson wrote to Olmsted in May 1878. Olmsted's friend and one-time Staten Island neighbor had moved to Boston after receiving a prestigious and lucrative commission, designing Trinity Church. He knew Dalton and some of the other park commissioners. He knew, too, that they had quickly grown disenchanted with Grundel's design. The commissioners paid the florist the $500 prize he was due and sent him packing. True to Richardson's word, an offer soon came Olmsted's way. The commissioners wanted him to prepare a preliminary design for the Back Bay park.

For the summer of 1878, Olmsted and his family left New York and moved in with the Godkins on Kirkland Street in Cambridge. This temporary arrangement made it possible for Olmsted to visit the site daily, familiarizing himself with the project's dimensions and demands.

The future Back Bay park was a thin strip of land, roughly 100 acres, containing a swampy stretch of water that connected with the Charles River. In the 1800s, this section of the Charles River was a tidal estuary. As a consequence, the swampy stretch often backed up during high tide, overflowing its banks. During low tide, the water receded, leaving behind a fetid plain strewn with the waste of the city's residents. "Offensive exudations arise from the mud," Olmsted noted, "when exposed by the falling tide to the summer's sun, which are perceptible at a great distance."

As unappealing as these grounds had become, Olmsted immediately recognized what they had been. This was a salt marsh—a particularly vile specimen to be sure—but a salt marsh nonetheless. Salt marshes were a staple landscape when America was young, though they were fast disappearing as the country became more urban. Growing up, while ambling around Connecticut, Olmsted had seen plenty of salt marshes. He had always found them achingly beautiful. Now they reminded him of his departed father and of home in Hartford, where ties had been so cruelly cut by the estate battle.

Salt marshes were also untamed places, suggestive of nature's abundance, very much in keeping with his artistic vision. He was never one for manicured gardens. The presence of saltwater made ornamental flowers, per the discarded design, a ridiculous notion anyhow. Olmsted knew that he would need to select plants that could grow in this specialized environment. Olmsted also recognized that this design job was largely a sanitation job, something with which he had ample experience.

Olmsted worked closely with John. Olmsted's drafting skills were limited, so he drew rough sketches—this was how he typically worked. Once he'd settled on a design, his stepson gave it a more polished treatment. On October 24, 1878, Olmsted presented a preliminary plan to the commissioners. They instantly accepted it.

But Olmsted wasn't sure. He requested a meeting with Boston's city engineer. He wanted to make certain that the plan was feasible from a technical standpoint. The city engineer brought along the superintendent of sewers, and the men huddled for four hours. Once he was convinced, Olmsted was ready to move forward. The commissioners formalized the arrangement, hiring him for the job. In a better mood now, Olmsted saw his stepson in a better light. He gave John, now twenty-six, a financial stake in the business.

As a first step, Olmsted had the swampy stretch dredged and reshaped so that the water traveled in a sinuous line—more natural than nature. In cooperation with the city engineer, intercepting sewers were built to catch refuse before it flowed into the waterway and gates were installed to regulate the flow with the Charles River. Olmsted wanted to maintain a constant water level that never varied more than a foot. After all, he didn't want the grounds to flood afresh at every high tide.

As for plantings, Olmsted called for a huge variety: sedges, salt grass, salt cedar, sea-buckthorn, and beach plum. He even suggested Oregon holly grape, a species brought back East by Lewis and Clark. Olmsted was a master at arranging plants in artful compositions but an undistinguished talent at actually growing them. For this project, he simply suggested a long list of salt-tolerant species. The idea was to see what would take. Just as Ignaz Pilat oversaw the plantings in Central Park, trained nurserymen did the actual planting here.

Not even lowly eels had been able to survive in the foul creek. But Olmsted was certain that abundant plantings coupled with cleaner water would provide a habitat. Birds like swans could be introduced, and he also hoped that wild fowl would be drawn here of their own accord. "The collection of water-birds should not be confined," he wrote in a report to the commission, " . . . to a few sorts of swans, ducks, and geese, but include as many varieties of these as practicable, and also pelicans, cormorants, cranes, and other waders, and fishers."

Olmsted's creation can fairly be called America's first wetlands restoration. What it was not was a park, at least by any ordinary definition. The commissioners were intent on calling the place Back Bay Park. But Olmsted was a stickler in such matters. Olmsted owned a dictionary published in 1706, which he often consulted when looking for suitably oldfangled names. He provided commissioner Dalton with a list of possibilities such as "Sedgeglade" and "The Sea Glades." But then he hit upon it: the Back Bay Fens. *Fens* is an archaic word for a marsh or boggy piece of land.

Olmsted's plan called for pathways in the basin above his salt marsh so that people could amble past the landscape without trampling the plantings—or falling into the water. To cap his creation, Olmsted invited Richardson to design a bridge. That placed Richardson in the Vaux role, amplifying a landscape with architectural flourishes. In temperament, the effusive, bearlike Richardson was nothing like Olmsted's slight onetime partner. And the bridge he designed was nothing like one of Vaux's subtle, nature-first creations.

But it worked. Richardson's Boylston Street Bridge—mammoth, hewn out of blocks of Cape Ann granite—succeeded in pulling the design together. It provided a needed focal point, visible from all over the Back Bay Fens. It doubled as an observation deck; a person standing on top of the bridge could gaze out across this piece of landscape memory smack in the bustling heart of Boston.

In 1879, while work on the Back Bay Fens progressed, Olmsted began on another project in Boston. Once again, Olmsted moved his family away from New York for the summer, this time taking a rented house in Brookline. The project involved designing the grounds for an arboretum. Like so many Olmsted jobs, this latest grew out of an idea that had been bouncing around for years. Back in 1873, he had visited Boston to attend a rhododendron show held on the Common. At the time, he was still employed by Central Park, and he was on official business, scouting for flowers. While at the show, he met Charles Sprague Sargent, and the two became fast friends. Sargent was a man very much in the Olmsted mold. Like Olmsted, Sargent didn't exactly cotton to formal education. In fact, he'd finished eighty-eight out of a class of ninety at Harvard. Yet so intense was his passion for trees, that he had recently been named director of Harvard's fledgling arboretum.

Sargent had a dream of turning the arboretum into a public park. Although Olmsted admired Sargent's resolve, he didn't think this was a very good idea. An arboretum is essentially a collection of trees, where different species are grouped together, often following a scientific order. This would be so limiting, Olmsted felt, when it came to a park design.

But Sargent kept pursuing his idea for years. By 1879, the ever-strapped Boston park commission had finally come up with the money. Sargent asked Olmsted to collaborate, and Olmsted reluctantly agreed. The plan was to create a public park, with the city responsible for such things as policing and routine maintenance. At the same time, a proper arboretum required the expertise of trained botanists at a place like Harvard.

Sargent was a cantankerous man, more at ease with trees than people. Thus, it fell to the worldly Olmsted to work out a unique arrangement where Harvard sold the land to the City of Boston, which, in turn, leased it back to Harvard for 999 years. Olmsted brokered this unique public-university partnership and found the negotiations exhausting.

That was the easy part. Olmsted also had to design the grounds of the arboretum. Here was the challenge: Hundreds of trees had to be planted in a precise order dictated by the Bentham and Hooker system, a Victorian Era scientific classification. Lindens need follow tulip trees need follow magnolias in rigid sequence. A suitable roadway had to be fashioned—winsome and winding—yet ensuring that visitors viewed the trees in the proper order. The idea was that this would be a drive-through park, where people traveled by carriage, looking at the trees.

All through the summer of '79, Olmsted produced study after tortured study. In his initial plans, the carriage road was so twisted as to make a pretzel look like a straight line. But he loved a good challenge. Although he'd initially been dismissive, he grew very passionate about Sargent's public arboretum. Eventually, he figured out an elegant road to carry people past the trees in the exact order spelled out by the Bentham and Hooker system.

Today, visitors walk over the grounds of Boston's Arnold Arboretum following the same path Olmsted originally designed for carriages. The trees are arranged in the exact same order. Some of the original trees are still alive, including a silver maple and a cherry.

Olmsted's focus was shifting from New York to Boston. He received yet another project from Dalton and the commission, for a park treatment along a section of the city's Muddy River. This was another unlovely stretch of fetid water, per its name, and once again Olmsted had to contend with both aesthetic and sanitary engineering challenges. He also teamed up with Richardson on a couple of private estate commissions in communities near Boston. In Easton, Massachusetts, Richardson designed the Ames Gate Lodge for railroad scion Frederick Ames, while Olmsted laid out the surrounding grounds. The pair also collaborated on the Ephraim Gurney House in Beverly, Massachusetts.

Meanwhile, Olmsted had ongoing jobs such as the Capitol grounds in D.C. And he was becoming increasingly involved in a project that was more like a personal mission. He was fighting to preserve Niagara Falls, an outgrowth of that meeting at Cataract House back in 1869. The falls were fast becoming a wretched tourist trap, the stunning natural scenery slipping into ruin.

But in New York City, Olmsted's work had pretty much evaporated. In the winter of 1881, Olmsted spent a weekend with Richardson at his home in Brookline. On awaking Sunday morning, Olmsted looked out the window and saw a team of men clearing the streets of snow. "This is a civilized community," he announced. "I'm going to live here."

The idea of returning to New England where he'd grown up was appealing. Olmsted entered into yet another rental situation, this time moving to a house on Walnut Street in Brookline. He rented out the brownstone in New York City. But just as the family was getting settled, Olmsted received disturbing news about Owen. Apparently, his stepson had fallen gravely ill.

Owen, now twenty-four, had headed out West after graduation from the Columbia University School of Mining. As a sickly person, he'd pursued a nineteenth-century medical regimen that prescribed counteracting one's constitution through rugged outdoor activity. His natural father, John, had tried this, too. But Owen took it to the extreme. He'd spent two years learning cattle ranching from Clarence King, a man who had years back helped Olmsted survey Yosemite. Afterward, Owen had run a ranch of his own on the Powder River in Montana. Olmsted put up some of the money to help him buy cattle. He'd seen Owen, too, within the past year, and his stepson had appeared healthy, thriving even. But now a telegram arrived saying that Owen was "very low."

Stepson John Charles was dispatched west to attend to Owen. He met up with him at Spearfish, South Dakota, where Owen had gone to convalesce in a fleabag hotel. The backwater town was one hundred miles east of his ranch, but it boasted a doctor—in name, at least. John sent telegram after telegram back to the family in Brookline. On one day, Owen would appear to be rallying. But on the next day, John would report that Owen seemed to have taken a dire turn. "We are again under the tension of a great domestic anxiety," wrote Olmsted to Norton.

Finally, John packed Owen onto a train and brought him back East. Olmsted and Mary met up with the train in Albany. By this point, Owen was comatose. He never regained consciousness. On a clean white piece of card stock, in a hand much clearer than his usual rapid-fire scrawl, Olmsted wrote: "Albany, 21st Nov. 1881. Owen died here tranquilly at noon today."

Owen had looked eerily like Olmsted's brother John. He shared the same easy temperament. And now he had died from the same malady, tuberculosis. Olmsted, curiously, insisted on claiming that Owen succumbed to diabetes. It's quite possible that he suffered from this disease, too. There's a link between the two illnesses. But Olmsted was in denial, unable to accept the fact that tuberculosis had actually killed Owen.

Condolences flooded in to Olmsted and Mary. But there's an air of puzzlement in many of the letters. "The whole thing seems to me incredible," reads one from a man named John Platt. "How could he have been so ill as he must have been? . . . I can not understand. It is all very sad, but what extraordinary pluck and resolution the boy must have had."

Vaux's note to Olmsted was particularly dissonant. "John certainly felt that you were suffering less than might be anticipated from such a shock—but the actual suffering is not always the criteria." *Actual suffering not always the criteria?* Apparently, Olmsted didn't appear to be in as much pain as one might expect under the circumstances. In a letter to Brace, Olmsted described the effect of Owen's death on him as "tranquilizing." There's that word again. Olmsted had suffered so many tragedies. With this latest one, he appears to have simply gone numb.

Still, he managed to feel something. Shortly after Owen's death, Olmsted lost control of his horse, was thrown, and fractured his sternum.

Olmsted longed for something, anything—in work, in life—that didn't feel ephemeral. Meanwhile, the Boston commission finally managed to line up ample funding. Olmsted had been working on a park-by-park basis. Now the commission asked him to create an entire park system, like what he'd done earlier in Buffalo. Olmsted was charged with designing new parks and also cobbling together the odds and ends he'd designed so far—a wetland preserve, an arboretum—into a single integrated system. The whole thing would be connected with ribbons of green space, or waterways in some cases, as well as his signature parkways. In

February 1883, Olmsted was officially named "landscape architect advisory." He signed a three-year contract at a salary of $2,000 per annum.

Several years of guaranteed work were just the inducement Olmsted needed. He was ready to cut his last ties with New York. Olmsted began looking for a permanent home in Brookline. Richardson wanted Olmsted to move next door—as in, take up residence on his lawn. He offered to design him a house there, and in a letter to Olmsted he included a rough sketch, labeled: "Your house—a beautiful thing in shingles." Richardson was in earnest, but Olmsted viewed this as just a lark.

Still, Olmsted was set on moving to the "civilized community" of Brookline. In an era when his Riverside, Illinois, suburb was a novelty, Brookline was one of the few established suburbs in America. The place appealed to Olmsted for a reason that would become a venerable American cliché in the years ahead: Here, it was possible to have a big yard yet still be close to the city. No less a talent than Downing had landscaped the grounds surrounding several Brookline homes. Olmsted had lived in the country, the city, and now he was ready for the suburbs.

Olmsted was especially taken with an old farmhouse at 99 Warren Street owned by Sarah and Susannah Clark, a pair of elderly spinster sisters. Olmsted made them an offer, but at first they refused. Then he hit upon a compromise. If they would sell him the house, stepson John would build them a cottage on the edge of the property. The sisters would have a place to live for the rest of their lives, and they'd have the proceeds of the sale. The Clark sisters agreed to sell Olmsted the house for $13,200.

Being the nation's premiere landscape architect had made Olmsted famous. It hadn't made him rich. Olmsted's new house was large, comfortable, but well short of a mansion. Still, he gave it a grand name: Fairsted. Fairsted was his family's ancestral village in the county of Essex, England. Olmsted had visited the place during his 1850 walking tour.

Olmsted converted the large north parlor of the new house into an office. Mary had never been enamored of Olmsted's blending of domesticity and work. So at Fairsted, he built a "sleeping porch" above his office. He slept there by himself surrounded by books. Piled high on his nightstand were old favorites such as Carlyle, Gilpin, Ruskin, and Zimmermann's *Solitude*. If he awoke in the middle of the night, gripped by an idea, he could shuffle downstairs to his office without disturbing Mary.

As in the New York brownstone, this office was modestly appointed. There were bookshelves lined with titles on landscaping and reports from various parks. Hanging on the walls were a few framed reproductions of favorite plans such as Central Park, the Capitol grounds, and Mount Royal. The part-time draftsmen worked in little cedar-lined cubicles.

This was nothing like Richardson's flamboyant home office on nearby Cottage Street. Richardson's office featured a huge fireplace elaborately filigreed with ironwork imported from Venice. Everywhere, there were elegant sofas and window seats. To create beauty, Richardson felt, one needed to be surrounded by beauty.

Olmsted couldn't have agreed more. But he had a different approach. He had once been a farmer, had signed his Southern dispatches "Yeoman." Though he'd become a premier artist, he had never really been comfortable with the trappings of the artist's life. His home office was utilitarian, a place for work. But fittingly, for a man so enamored of nature, Olmsted contrived it so that one need only walk out the front door. Here beauty held sway.

Olmsted turned Fairsted's 2-acre yard into a glorious personal park. It featured specimen trees such as a large elm that had drawn Olmsted to the property in the first place. Charles Sargent, who lived across the street, gave Olmsted a cucumber magnolia tree as a present. Olmsted also planted an area that was untamed and overgrown, his own private Central Park Ramble. He lined Fairsted's walls with trellises and let the wisteria creep and crawl until it was hard to see where his garden ended and his house began.

Olmsted was sixty-one years old when he moved to Fairsted. He'd gone completely bald on top, making his forehead appear prominent, domelike. This was what the Victorians referred to as a "noble brow." On the sides, he let his hair grow into a long gray mane. He'd just added a shaggy beard. People had been telling him that he looked like Benjamin Butler, the Massachusetts governor. Olmsted didn't approve of Butler's politics. The beard, he claimed, was to distinguish himself from Butler, who sported only a mustache. Sometimes, Olmsted's light-blue eyes still filled with their old spark. He'd seen more than his share of misfortune, but with age he was learning to take joy where he could find it.

Three of his children lived with him. Shy and dutiful John had just turned thirty. He'd remain at Fairsted until he got married in late middle age. Marion, Olmsted's "little old maid," was twenty-two. Frederick Law Olmsted Jr. was thirteen now and attending Miss Rideout's School in Brookline. He had a mischievous streak, like his father. Charlotte had married a doctor and was living nearby in Cohasset. Richardson—fond of saying, "I'll plan anything a man wants from a cathedral to a chicken coop"—designed a modest house for the couple. Charlotte had two children, making Olmsted a grandfather.

Living in Brookline, Olmsted enjoyed a vibrant social life. Besides Richardson and Sargent, both minutes away, his good friends Godkin and Charles Eliot Norton were nearby in Cambridge. Norton was a prominent critic and professor of art history at Harvard. Olmsted joined the St. Botolph Club, which numbered among its members William Dean Howells as well as publishers Henry Houghton and George Mifflin. Olmsted was surrounded by people who were accomplished, challenging, and socially conscious. "I enjoy this suburban country beyond expression," he wrote to Brace.

Shortly after moving to Fairsted, Olmsted took on his first apprentice, Charles Eliot. The decision was inspired by Richardson. Richardson, who had attended Paris's École des Beaux-Arts, was one of the few formally trained architects in the United States, a distinction he shared with Vaux. He viewed it as an obligation to teach his skills to others, and a series of apprentices passed through his Brookline workshop. As the pioneer of landscape architecture in America, Olmsted realized that he needed to do more than simply bequeath his firm to his sons at some future point. He also needed to draw others to the field.

Olmsted was thrilled by Eliot's qualifications—also his pedigree. Eliot, son of the president of Harvard, had just graduated from the university's horticulture program. He was also the second cousin of Olmsted's friend Charles Eliot Norton. Soon, young Eliot was joined by a second apprentice, Henry Codman. Codman was a recent graduate of the Massachusetts Institute of Technology and the nephew of Charles Sargent. There's an incestuousness at work here, like so much in Olmsted's professional life. But it was certainly a heartening sign that young people such as these were attracted to landscape architecture.

There was plenty to keep the apprentices busy. Olmsted had recently landed a major commission for Belle Isle, an island park in Detroit. There was a land subdivision in Providence, Rhode Island, and he had just started designing the campus of the Lawrenceville School in New Jersey. Still other jobs involved further collaboration with Richardson, such as more private estates as well as some Massachusetts train stations. Olmsted made John a formal partner in the business. The firm was rechristened F. L. & J. C. Olmsted. Olmsted instructed John to "throw more upon Eliot and let him throw more on Codman."

But the Boston park system remained Olmsted's primary obligation. "Nothing else compares to the Boston work," he stated. During this period in his career, his goal was "doing the best for Boston all the time." In 1884, he began work on a new park for the city. During his 1875 visit with commissioner Dalton, Olmsted had singled out this piece of land as particularly attractive and parklike. At the time, it was considered the potential site for a future West Roxbury park. Now it was a go. The place was dubbed Franklin Park. Benjamin Franklin had left a bequest to the City of Boston that was scheduled to mature soon. The plan was to tap some of the money for park-construction costs. This didn't happen, but the name remained.

For his design, Olmsted conceptualized Franklin Park's roughly 500 acres as two distinct parcels destined for very different treatments. The larger piece was a hilly section dotted with hemlocks and other attractive old-growth trees. Experience had taught Olmsted that on those rare occasions when one is blessed with a truly fetching piece of land, the task is simple: Just leave things alone.

For the other parcel, he pursued a serious overhaul to convert it into a recreational space. Times had changed in the nearly quarter century since Olmsted and Vaux had designed Central Park. America was becoming more active, and people were increasingly enjoying outdoor sports. For Franklin Park, Olmsted designed a raised terrace, nearly three hundred feet long, with a wall of boulders that were Roxbury pudding-stone. This elevated plateau was meant so spectators could overlook the fields where people engaged in baseball, tennis, and other games. Olmsted also designed a long fieldstone building to serve as a locker room and a shelter. He called it Playstead. Olmsted was a landscape architect; designing a building was the province of architects. But Olmsted was nothing if not versatile. (Unfortunately, his terrace and shelter have fallen into ruin today.)

Franklin Park is the biggest park in the Boston system. Ultimately, Olmsted would provide a park treatment for a large glacial kettle hole (Jamaica Pond) and add several smaller parks to go along with the Back Bay Fens, Arnold Arboretum, and Franklin Park. He'd use a variety of means to stitch the whole thing together. Olmsted even made some adjustments to Commonwealth Avenue, integrating this existing grand thoroughfare into his system. Commonwealth Avenue, in turn, connected with two established smaller parks, the colonial-era Boston Common and the Public Garden from 1837.

Taken together, this was a bountiful green space, 1,100 acres arrayed over nearly seven miles from downtown Boston. It was far and away the most ambitious park system of Olmsted's career. Olmsted referred to the system as the "Jeweled Girdle." He had a knack for nomenclature, but this was not a winner. An unknown someone came up with the name that stuck: the Emerald Necklace.

CHAPTER 28

Saving Niagara, Designing Stanford

AT THE STROKE of midnight on July 15, 1885, a ceremony was held where Niagara Falls was officially "opened," free of charge, to the public. Thousands of people were on hand to view this American icon. Many of those present were first-time visitors who lived within mere miles of the falls. But they had never before seen them because the place had grown into such a racket, such a horrid hassle. "From this hour, Niagara is free," announced William Dorsheimer during the ceremonies. Dorsheimer, Olmsted's onetime patron on the Buffalo parks, was chairman of the newly formed Niagara commission. This was a major victory for Olmsted, too, as his involvement in the cause stretched back over many years.

During the nineteenth century, Niagara Falls had become the number-one tourist destination in America. In the process, it had become a grotesque parody of the natural wonder famously glimpsed by Father Hennepin in 1678. On arriving at the falls, visitors were immediately mobbed by barkers and sharps intent on diverting them to various entertainments. There were amusement parks, sideshows, and fireworks. Acrobats such as the Great Blondin regularly crossed the gorge beneath the falls on tightropes. If that wasn't enough, the Niagara River was fairly choked with industry; pulp mills and flumes and piers lined the banks. And everywhere there were billboards for products like "Parker's Hair Balsam." Getting an unobstructed view of the falls was a challenge, and people paid for the privilege. The best spots were on private property, and sightseers were assessed hefty fees. "To drive around and visit all the places worth seeing costs a single person at least ten dollars," lamented one contemporary account. "If you are on foot, at every few yards a hackman shouts to you for your patronage, or a low shop-girl affectionately invites you into a store."

Olmsted had first glimpsed the falls at age six during a family trip. Ever since the 1869 meeting at Cataract House, Olmsted had been working to focus attention on the sorry state of this once-grand piece of scenery. He had been part of a New York State survey team that had explored the feasibility of tearing down the mills, removing the carny-style amusements. He had also spearheaded a petition drive demanding that Niagara be restored to a more natural state. In this effort, Charles Eliot Norton had joined him. Like Olmsted, Norton had a deep well of contacts. The pair managed to gather hundreds of signatures, including those of Emerson, Longfellow, and Whittier as well as Morrison Waite, chief justice of the U.S. Supreme Court, and seven of eight associate justices. Because the falls are also visible from the Canadian side of the Niagara River (and because Canada was then a dominion of Great Britain), Olmsted and Norton also obtained the signatures of such English notables as Ruskin, Lord Houghton, and Sir James Stephen. "Carlyle signs," crowed Norton, when the literary hero of Olmsted's youth added his name to the petition.

The survey report, penned by Olmsted and accompanied by the petition, prompted New York State legislators to draw up a bill calling for the preservation of Niagara Falls. But it failed to pass due to the vehement opposition of Governor Alonzo Cornell. He was against spending taxpayer money, especially given that nothing was wrong with the natural wonder itself. What would be the point, he demanded, of removing the mills and amusement parks? "I don't see that it will make any difference—the water will run over the falls all the same," said Cornell.

Olmsted kept up the pressure. He perceived that this was a cause best furthered via the press, a forum where he had always enjoyed an advantage. This would be another of his nineteenth-century public relations battles. But he would wage it by proxy. By this time, Olmsted had grown extremely busy with the Boston system and other jobs. So Olmsted and Norton arranged to have Henry Norman, a recent Harvard graduate, write a series of articles that appeared in the New York and Boston papers as well as the *Nation*. Olmsted directed Norman, instructing him how to frame the Niagara Falls problem for public consumption. Olmsted and Norton also tapped Jonathan Harrison, a clergyman, to write more articles and even go on a speaking tour.

Meanwhile, hostile Cornell left office and was replaced by Buffalo native Grover Cleveland, an advocate of preserving the falls. "Governor Cleveland *strongly* in favor of Niagara," wrote Richardson to Olmsted in 1883. He had gathered this scuttlebutt while having dinner with Cleveland and Dorsheimer, for whom he had designed a mansion along one of Olmsted and Vaux's Buffalo parkways. Within months, the state finally passed legislation to preserve Niagara Falls. Following that, an even more critical bill was passed, setting aside the money necessary to purchase the land from private interests. "I congratulate you, prime mover," Norton wrote to Olmsted. "I hail you as the Saviour of Niagara!"

In 1885, a five-person commission was appointed, and Dorsheimer was named chairman. As a first act, he presided over that midnight "Niagara is free" festivity. Then it was on to the complicated business of purchasing forty parcels of land held by twenty-five different owners. It would be necessary to tear down roughly 150 different structures. Once the structures were down, someone would need to give the grounds surrounding Niagara Falls a proper landscape treatment.

Olmsted was the obvious choice. But Niagara was like an echo chamber of his past associations. One of the five commissioners was actually Andrew Green, his old Central Park tormentor. Green declared that the choice of Olmsted was "particularly offensive" to him. Whom did Green favor instead? Maybe Green was simply trying to stick it to Olmsted. His suggestion—Vaux!

Actually, Vaux was a logical choice. Vaux was one of the parties present for that seminal 1869 visit that set the "Preserve Niagara" movement in motion. Vaux was also close friends with Frederic Church, the civic-minded artist who had done the definitive Niagara Falls painting in 1857. Church and Olmsted were distant relatives. Echoes and more echoes.

Ultimately, the Niagara commission voted four to one to hire Olmsted for the project. Green was the lone dissenter. As a compromise, Olmsted simply agreed to team with Vaux. His old partner needed the work.

The bumbling, agitated manner; the constant fiddling with his spectacles—these had always conveyed that Vaux was a pure, uncompromising artist. It also communicated that he was difficult. As for the Metropolitan Museum and Museum of Natural History, the twin commissions that had promised to elevate him to the highest echelon of American architects—he'd been cut loose from both. In each case, structures designed by Vaux were actually built. But as the buildings expanded, he lost control of the commissions. Over time, his original work on both the Met and the Museum of Natural History would be almost entirely obscured by later work by other architects.

The years since Olmsted, Vaux & Company had ended had been cruel to Vaux. He was sublimely talented, yet his own business had dried up. Charley Brace had helped by hiring him to build a series of residences for the Children's Aid Society. It was modest work. Vaux was sixty-one now and filled with worry—about the future, about slipping into poverty, about his uncertain legacy. A diary entry by painter Jervis McEntee concluded sadly that for his old friend Vaux, "life seems a struggle."

Olmsted and Vaux began working out their plan for Niagara Falls in 1886. (They would submit their formal report early the following year.) The site was such a contrast to Yosemite, Olmsted's first effort at preservation. Yosemite was isolated and forbidding and even by the 1880s received only a handful of visitors. But Niagara Falls was the ultimate tourist destination, a simple fact that could be neither ignored nor undone.

Olmsted and Vaux perceived that the challenge, from a landscape architecture standpoint, lay in framing the falls, but also making them accessible to the masses. The Niagara railroad depot was the stepping-off point for thousands of travelers who arrived weary, hungry, and confused. Olmsted and Vaux suggested adding a large building where tourists could check their possessions, purchase food, and use lavatories. Information signs—something that had been sorely lacking in the otherwise cluttered environs—should be strategically posted to guide people to the various sites. They also proposed simple "furniture" such as benches facing especially fetching vistas. For safety's sake, Vaux designed railings to be placed in front of various precipices. The railings were utterly unobtrusive—just posts with three crossbars—and in a strange way, they were the apotheosis of his nature-first ethos. Awed by the falls, visitors wouldn't even notice the railings.

Olmsted was especially fond of the islands in the Niagara River above the falls. He felt the spectacle of the falls overshadowed the more subtle charms of these places. "I have followed the Appalachian chain almost from end to end," noted Olmsted, "and traveled on horseback, 'in search of the picturesque' over four thousand miles of the most promising parts of the continent without finding elsewhere the same quality of forest beauty which was once abundant about the falls."

Olmsted and Vaux's plan sought to restore wildness to places such as Goat Island and the Three Sisters Islands. But per the mandate, these also had to be accessible. They suggested a system of carriage paths and footpaths that would guide visitors through the scenery. The carriage paths were one-third the width ordinarily used in a park. (At around this time, in a separate effort, Canada also began restoring its side of the falls.)

Vaux traveled to Fairsted at one point to work on the Niagara plan. "He helped me and I helped him and at some points each of us crowded the other out a little" is how Olmsted described their collaboration. In other words, they fell back into their old pattern. Vaux wrote Olmsted a long worried letter wondering when they were going to get paid. Olmsted offered to lend Vaux four or five hundred dollars. Olmsted had other work, and money was coming in, making him "well windward of expenses," as he put it. Going forward, he would pretty well turn the job over to Vaux, who would supervise construction of the railings, benches, and other touches. It would give Olmsted's old partner a needed source of income.

On April 27, 1886, around the time work on Niagara Falls was getting started, H. H. Richardson died. He was forty-seven. The cause of death was Bright's disease, a kidney disorder now known as glomerulonephritis. Only a few weeks earlier, Olmsted had seen Richardson. His friend, always of ample girth, had ballooned to a massive weight, a symptom of the illness. At the beginning of the visit, Richardson seemed downcast. But then he grew suddenly animated on the topic of an architectural commission. As Olmsted described it, "He went on discussing for the better part of an hour, growing to sit up erect, his voice becoming clear, his utterance empathetic, his eyes flashing, smiling, laughing like a boy, really hilarious."

The funeral was held at Trinity Church with many of his fellow architects in attendance. Mourners passed around a story that Richardson had been blessed with a peaceful death. This was comforting: Richardson had created such great beauty during his brief lifetime that it seemed only fitting that he achieve some measure of grace as he exited this world. But it was far from the truth.

Richardson died as he'd lived, messily. He left behind a wife and six children. Though he was one of America's most successful and prolific architects, he also left behind a mountain of debt, a final display of what Olmsted called Richardson's "characteristic unconquerable recklessness." He didn't just slip peacefully away, either. Richardson spent the last day of his life in excruciating pain.

Richardson's death was a hard blow for Olmsted. He lost a dear friend and a professional collaborator; he had anticipated that their best works together lay in the future. But he'd experienced so much loss of late. Sorrowful events had come one after another, packed tight. Shortly after having her third child, Charlotte—always unstable—had fallen into the grip of serious mental illness. She was sent to an asylum, where she would spend the rest of her life.

Olmsted had seen many old friends pass away. The Reverend Henry Bellows, from Civil War days on the USSC, had recently died, as had George Geddes, the man who gave Olmsted his start in scientific farming. On learning that Friedrich Kapp, one of the Texas Germans, had died, he had written to Brace that "changes in our time have been so great that while I feel myself in the full fruit of the life of today, I feel that the life of our early days was almost another life." He added, "Instead of being shocked by the death of old friends, I wonder they could have lived till so lately—most of all that I am still living."

So much change. So much loss. It made Olmsted feel the need to take stock. His self-assessment was unsparing: "I have done a good deal of good work in my way too but it is customarily & every where arrested, wrenched, mangled and misused. It is not easy to get above intense disappointment & mortification." He was more generous toward Brace: "You decidedly have lived the best and most worthily successful life of all whom I have known. The C.A. [Children's Aid] is the most satisfying of all the benevolent works of our time."

Brace passed Olmsted's letter along for Kingsbury to read. It was like the old days of the "uncommon set," where everyone knew everyone else's business. Only now the set's ranks had thinned to three: brother John was long departed, and Charley Trask had drifted to the point that the others weren't even certain of what city he lived in.

Kingsbury wrote Brace back commenting on Olmsted's letter: "It's a pity he should attach so little influence to the much he has accomplished and so much to the little he has not succeeded in doing to his mind. No man even comes close to his ideals who has any." Kingsbury had always seen Olmsted with particular clarity. He knew that his old friend wasn't about to rest easy.

Soon an intriguing opportunity came Olmsted's way, courtesy of Leland Stanford. Stanford had built the western portion of the transcontinental railroad; he'd driven the famous golden spike during the ceremony when the two sections were connected. During the 1860s, he'd served as California's governor. Stanford was iron-willed and ursine and wore a perpetual scowl. As one of the age's foremost rail barons, he'd amassed a fortune and also an ample list of enemies, such as journalist Ambrose Bierce, who insisted on writing his name: "£eland $tanford."

Stanford had recently lost his only child, Leland Stanford Jr. While the family was traveling in Europe, the fifteen-year-old boy had died in Florence of typhoid fever. Stanford and his wife, Jane, were devastated. The couple consulted mediums and conducted séances, hoping to contact the boy's spirit. But even in grief, there was a limit to Stanford's tolerance for the ethereal realms. He soon hit on the idea of founding a university in his dead son's honor. And not just any university: This would be on the grandest scale conceivable, akin to an opera aria that keeps rising and swelling because there's no other place for such great sorrow to go.

Stanford traveled east to discuss his big plans with educators at universities such as Harvard, Yale, and Cornell. Stanford was especially taken with General Francis Walker, president of the Massachusetts Institute of Technology. MIT was still a young institution (just a couple decades old), and it had recently almost gone under. Walker had stepped in to turn the school around; he was Stanford's kind of can-do man. As it happened, Walker was acquainted with Henry Codman, a recent MIT graduate who also happened to be one of Olmsted's young apprentices.

It was Codman who forged the connection between Olmsted and Stanford. He also urged Olmsted to ask Stanford for $10,000 for a preliminary plan, an unheard-of amount. Olmsted was resistant; demanding a huge fee was a technique he sometimes used to drive away clients he didn't wish to engage. To his surprise, Stanford readily agreed to the $10,000. Clearly, this was quite a project. "There is not any word half big enough for his ideas of what it is to be," marveled Olmsted, wryly adding that the only fitting term was "Universitatory."

In August 1886, Olmsted set off for California accompanied by Codman. He also brought along his youngest child, Frederick Jr., whom he called Rick. Olmsted figured such a trip would benefit the sixteen-year-old. The three traveled by train to Portland, Oregon, then south to San Francisco by stagecoach. From there, they took a trip to the Mariposa Grove of Big Trees. Olmsted visited Galen Clark, seventy-two now but still voluble and still acting as "doorkeeper of Yosemite." Olmsted also paid his first visit to Golden Gate Park. He'd traded letters with its designer, William Hammond Hall, and offered him much useful advice, but had never actually seen the park.

The California trip was mostly devoted to studying a 7,000-acre tract of land set aside for Leland Stanford Jr. University. It was in Palo Alto, the senior Stanford's sprawling estate. MIT's Walker came out as well. Olmsted expected to go far beyond simply designing the campus grounds. As the U.S. pioneer of landscape architecture, he'd worked relentlessly to expand the scope of his field. Projects like the Buffalo park system and Boston's Emerald Necklace were exercises in urban planning as much as landscape design. Olmsted had ample experience with campus jobs besides. At the time, he was working on a plan for the Lawrenceville School in New Jersey, and he had done discrete design tasks on existing campuses, including Amherst and Yale. He also had some failed college commissions in his past: Early in his career he devoted a huge amount of time and thought to a never-executed plan for the Maine College of Agriculture and the Mechanic Arts. But that only meant that he was brimming with unrealized ideas.

Olmsted spent more than a month in close consultation with Stanford, Walker, and Codman. In far-ranging discussions, Olmsted began to hone his concept for the campus grounds, but he also had ideas for the architecture of the buildings—and even about how thoughtful design could promote a better educational experience.

No shrinking violet himself, Olmsted also got his first experience with the immovable object that was Leland Stanford. The Palo Alto estate included a stretch of hills, an ideal spot, thought Olmsted, for placing the university. The hills' rolling topography would allow him to create a unique naturalistic campus design. But Stanford was adamant: The school belonged on the broad plain at the base of the hills. He pointed out that his son had enjoyed riding his horse across this plain. "The site is settled at last—not as I had hoped," wrote Olmsted to his stepson John.

In September 1886, Olmsted set off for home. Once there, he'd draw up a formal plan for the university. At Salt Lake City, Rick and Codman continued east, while Olmsted split off for a deeply personal errand. Olmsted and Stanford were temperamentally unalike, but they had a shared bond in loss. Olmsted headed north to Montana, where he visited the ranch once run by Owen, his deceased stepson. He'd never seen this place before. But he had helped finance the venture, and he still held a considerable stake. With sadness, he noted the ranch was in poor shape. It was proving to be a pitiful investment, and not exactly a fitting tribute to Owen's life and work.

Back in Brookline, Olmsted got to work on the university plan. Olmsted agreed with Stanford that it ought to be organized around quadrangles, starting with a single main quad. As the university grew, it would be possible to add more quads, equivalent to lining up dominoes end to end. Olmsted also pushed for arcades on all the buildings. Such arcades provide shelter from both sun and rain. They would suggest an orderly path for students to follow. Arcades would also give the buildings, regardless of height, a consistent feature.

The quads and arcades were meant to create unity, architecturally, but they also served a subtler social-engineering goal. Olmsted was intent on providing ample common space, where students in diverse fields of study—literature, mathematics, philosophy—could meet and mingle their ideas. This was a hallowed Olmsted notion; he'd even coined a term for it: *communitiveness.* Mixing disciplines was the key to his professional success and the crux of his plan for Leland Stanford Jr. University. To bump up this concept further, Olmsted suggested that the students live in cottages. Intermingled with the student housing would be cottages available to people who weren't attending the university, forming a still larger sense of community. This was an idea revived from Olmsted's long-ago, shelved-then-lost plan for the university that became Berkeley.

As for planting, Olmsted urged Stanford to go with a scheme suited to an arid climate. Thanks to his recent tour of schools such as Harvard, Stanford had other ideas. "I find Governor Stanford bent on giving his University New England scenery, New England trees and turf, to be obtained only by lavish use of water," complained Olmsted.

He suggested that the campus grounds be paved in brick as much as possible. In his report, he pointed to the example of Rome, a place with a Mediterranean climate similar to Palo Alto, adding that the grounds of St. Peter's Basilica features "not a tree, nor a bush, nor a particle of turf." The paved campus grounds, however, should be periodically broken by little oases, discreet areas planted with palms and other flora suitable to an arid climate.

Olmsted submitted his report. Stanford seemed pleased. Meanwhile, General Walker lined up an architecture firm to design the campus's buildings: Shepley, Rutan & Coolidge. Stanford simply rubber-stamped this choice. Shepley, Rutan & Coolidge was a brand-new outfit formed after Richardson's death by three of his young associates. The university would be the firm's first major commission. Olmsted was thrilled. Working with these architects would be almost like a posthumous collaboration with his old friend Richardson.

In the spring of 1887, Charles Coolidge traveled to California with a master plan of the university. Stanford took one look and immediately started demanding changes. This was not unexpected; he was the client, after all. The challenge was the time constraint he suddenly introduced. He wanted to lay the cornerstone in two weeks, on a date corresponding with his deceased son's birthday. Young Coolidge made the mistake of arguing with Stanford. He said Stanford's changes would disrupt the plan—and to give this view weight, he summoned Olmsted's name. It was to no avail. "Gov. replied a Landscape Arch't and an Arch't might be disappointed but he was going to have the buildings the way he wanted them," wrote Coolidge to Olmsted, adding: "The Gov. means business."

Stanford insisted that Coolidge race to redo the design. One of the new features Stanford demanded was a huge memorial arch to serve as a formal entry into the main quad. This disrupted the intimate human scale of the quad in Olmsted's view. At the same time, if there was ever an architect with a grasp of the monumental, it had been Richardson. Under time pressure, Coolidge and his colleagues simply cribbed one of their deceased boss's designs, from an arch in Buffalo. They did the same thing with a number of other buildings designed for the campus.

Coolidge traveled up to San Francisco, where he hired a band and purchased a silver spade. On the prescribed date, Stanford dug up a clod of dirt and laid the cornerstone. Work was officially under way.

But Stanford kept making changes. Initially, he'd agreed to Olmsted's cottages—or at least appeared to. Instead, he decided he wanted a tall dormitory modeled after a building he'd seen during a vacation in Switzerland. He okayed Olmsted's plan for an arboretum featuring native California trees. Then he abruptly pulled the plug. Not only was he capricious, but he was nearly impossible to reach. He was constantly traveling. The governor placed his wife's brother, Ariel Lathrop, in charge of the project and asked that all inquiries now be directed to this man. Lathrop promptly fired the superintendent that Olmsted had installed in Palo Alto as the firm's on-site representative. To Olmsted, this was a serious breach. What's more, he felt reduced. Where before he'd had Stanford's ear, now he was forced to deal with this Lathrop. Olmsted protested directly to Stanford, writing, "We are now compelled to make a formal remonstrance." Stanford didn't even bother to reply.

Feeling stymied, Olmsted would taper off his involvement in the project over time. When the university opened, he wasn't even invited to the ceremony. Nonetheless, he wrote Stanford a letter of congratulations. Back came a terse note that included: "We are gradually improving the grounds in accordance with your plans."

This was partly true. Stanford's main quad, one of the great pieces of university architecture, still retains such Olmsted touches as the arcades and the oasis plantings. But the idea of a connected row of quads was abandoned. Stanford made all manner of other changes, many of them sensible but also at odds with Olmsted's original plan. After the governor died, his wife was equally demanding, but even more fickle in her architectural whims. Stanford University is best viewed as a collaboration—with a very headstrong client.

CHAPTER 29

Big House in the Big Woods

THIRTY YEARS HAD PASSED since Olmsted began work on Central Park. For the past twenty, he'd built a career as a landscape architect. Olmsted was sixty-six now, well past the age when his father and most other people retired. His shaggy mane and beard were starting to speckle gray to white. It made his eyes appear that much bluer, but they weren't filled with peace. Although he had received great acclaim, he worried about the lasting impact of every last work he'd ever done. He need only look at his most recent project, Stanford University. Or he could go back to his very first, Central Park, or most anything in between. All served as painful reminders that there was always someone eager to meddle with his designs. Olmsted wanted to leave a legacy. He wanted to elevate the profession of landscape architecture. He wanted to leave a thriving business to John and Rick. But he'd witnessed so much tragedy that he had a keen sense—beyond morbid—of his own impending demise.

During the years left to him, Olmsted would greedily seize on commissions, building a large book of far-flung projects that would send him careening across the United States in late-night railcars. This was the most successful stretch for his firm. But two particular commissions would stand out as being sufficiently lofty to provide what he craved. On these, he would expend massive energy and endure terrible anxiety. He'd race against time. He'd endeavor to outrun his fast-declining health. In the end, he would struggle against his own mind, would battle against the failure of memory itself, the very seat of his creative power. Those are losing fights, always. But with fate on the threshold, Olmsted would deliver a pair of spectacular triumphs.

In August 1888, Olmsted traveled to North Carolina to meet with George Washington Vanderbilt. As grandson of the Commodore himself, George had inherited a fortune worth $13 million. But he was also the first Vanderbilt heir not to take an active interest in building a business empire. He was twenty-five, and Olmsted described him as a "delicate, refined, and bookish man."

For the past several years, Vanderbilt had been traveling to Asheville with his mother, who suffered from malaria. Because of its mountain setting and clean air, smallish Asheville (population 10,000) had earned a national reputation by the late nineteenth century as a spot for rest cures. He came to know the surrounding area by taking horseback rides. During one, he'd discovered a particularly comely spot, a hill looking down on the French Broad River and in the distance, Mount Pisgah, one of the highest peaks in the Blue Ridge range. Vanderbilt decided he wanted to build a country estate here and started buying up parcels of land, anonymously, through an agent. If anyone learned that a Vanderbilt was in the market, property values would soar. Because Asheville was a renowned resort, rail service already existed from Vanderbilt's home in New York. It was a twenty-four-hour trip.

Vanderbilt wanted to be associated only with the best for this princely undertaking. For a landscape architect, Olmsted was the obvious choice. While living on Staten Island forty years earlier, Olmsted had done his very first landscaping job on the farm of William Vanderbilt, George's father. The Vanderbilts were well acquainted with Olmsted. In the past two years, he had begun projects with two of George's four siblings, designing the grounds of their private estates in Lenox, Massachusetts, and Lake Champlain in Vermont. The other two would soon commission Olmsted to work on estates in Madison, New Jersey, and Newport, Rhode Island.

For an architect, Vanderbilt turned to Richard Morris Hunt. French trained with a talent for elegant, formal designs, Hunt was one of the few Americans who could execute a house that would be at home in the vast spread Vanderbilt contemplated, one that would be suitably imposing and grandiose. Hunt was sixty-one and at the height of his career. He was somewhat of a court architect to New York high society, designing Fifth Avenue mansions and Newport redoubts. As described earlier, Vaux had clashed with Hunt years back over a proposal to place a series of monumental entryways into Central Park. Vaux won that one. But Hunt got the last laugh (metaphorically, as he rarely even smiled), by seizing the job to design the façade of the Metropolitan Museum after Vaux fumbled the commission. Hunt had also designed the Vanderbilt family mausoleum on Staten Island. Olmsted had collaborated with him on that project. Each man was old enough to be George Vanderbilt's grandfather. On matters of art and taste, the young scion would defer to both to an unusual degree. Vanderbilt's wealth was on par with Governor Stanford's, but his temperament couldn't be more different.

During their initial consultation, Vanderbilt sought Olmsted's advice on how best to utilize his land. He'd already purchased 2,000 acres and planned to buy tens of thousands more. The hilltop Vanderbilt had chosen for his house was striking. The distant views of the mountains were awesome. But Olmsted was shocked by the pitiful condition of the surrounding acreage. Generations of tenants had abused the land, cutting down the trees to build homes and fences. Entire stretches of forestland had been burned away to create pasturage for hogs. It was reminiscent of nothing so much as the barren rectangle once slated for Central Park.

"What do you imagine you will do with all this land?" asked Olmsted, according to an account of the meeting that he wrote to Kingsbury.

"Make a park of it, I suppose," answered Vanderbilt.

But Olmsted counseled him that a vast private park would be expensive to build and challenging to maintain. Better to set aside just a small portion for gardens and perhaps a small deer park. The rest could be restored to forest. Olmsted was more familiar with the varied U.S. landscape than just about anyone. During recent travels, he had grown conscious of a myth: America the primeval, land of limitless forest. From train-car windows and stagecoaches, he'd noted what big timber was doing, clear-cutting huge stretches of land. The proto-environmentalist in Olmsted, the same side that led him to become involved in Yosemite and Niagara Falls, drew him to this issue.

In Europe, where land was viewed as finite, forest management was a centuries-old practice. But Olmsted was one of only a tiny group of Americans who were thinking about the subject, and he was intimately familiar with the other players. A few months earlier, his Brookline neighbor Charles Sargent had launched a new magazine, *Garden and Forest*, which focused on this very subject. This was also a topic of concern for Horace Cleveland. Cleveland, who worked with Olmsted on Prospect Park and Chicago's Washington Park, had built up about the only American landscape architectural practice to rival FLO's. He'd recently written a pamphlet, *The Cultivation and Management of Our Native Forests for Development as Timber or Ornamental Wood*.

Olmsted even had some specific knowledge of the area surrounding Asheville. During the third leg of his Southern travels, the journey through the backcountry, Olmsted had spent an entire month meandering through the forests of North Carolina. "There is no experience of my life to which I could return with more satisfaction," he told Vanderbilt. He knew what had once been here; he saw now what had been lost. And Olmsted was intent on re-creating what he had enjoyed so mightily on a visit back in 1854.

Olmsted could be a convincing salesman. "Such land in Europe would be made a forest," he continued, "partly, if it belonged to a gentleman of large means, as a preserve for game, mainly with a view to crops of timber. That would be a suitable and dignified business for a man like you to engage in. It would, in the long run, be probably a fair investment of capital and it would be of great value to the country to have a thoroughly well organized and systematically conducted attempt at forestry made on a large scale."

Vanderbilt mulled this for a few months. As follow-up, Olmsted sent him a copy of Cleveland's pamphlet. Vanderbilt liked the idea of harvesting timber on his property; that would provide a source of income. And he was intrigued by the notion of a showcase for managed forestry. Eventually, he agreed to Olmsted's experiment.

At the beginning of 1889, Vanderbilt and Hunt set off on a trip together to England and France. They gathered ideas and inspiration during visits to assorted châteaus, such as Waddesdon Manor in Buckingham, an estate done over in French Renaissance style, then popular in England and increasingly in America as well. Stateside, Olmsted began to work out his plan for the Asheville grounds. He was to receive $3,000 per year for his services.

From the outset, Olmsted recognized the Vanderbilt job as peculiar but full of potential. On the grounds immediately surrounding whatever manse Hunt designed, it would surely be necessary to lay out geometric, ornamental, manicured gardens, something anathema to Olmsted. But on the outlying acreage, he'd have free rein, the opportunity to plant an entire forest. The job was a private estate, a type of commission that, while lucrative, had often left Olmsted feeling compromised. But Olmsted's public projects were also full of compromise, thanks to combative and money-starved city commissions.

This job could be ideal: A rich man's estate promised him more latitude as a reformer than some of his people's parks. Vanderbilt would be receiving many powerful and influential visitors; Olmsted's work here could serve to disseminate his ideas about forest management. "This is to be a private work of very rare public interest in many ways," Olmsted wrote. " . . . I feel a good deal of ardor about it, and it is increased by the obviously exacting yet frank, trustful, confiding and cordially friendly disposition toward all of us which Mr. Vanderbilt manifests."

For Vanderbilt, Hunt designed a house—or, rather, a palace—that when complete would be the largest private residence in the history of the United States. Everything about it was huge, right down to its 4-acre footprint. He designed it before he had ever visited the Asheville site. Olmsted, who once described Hunt as "earnest, tempestuous and used to having his own way," wasn't about to let this pile simply be plunked down on the hilltop. Olmsted positioned the house, orienting it to take in the best views. And Olmsted also insisted that Hunt add a significant feature, a long terrace extending off one side of the house.

Walking the grounds, Olmsted had noticed that a ferocious wind sometimes blew in from the mountains. Hunt might know big, bold, and beautiful, but Olmsted had a grasp of the practical. The walls of the terrace would act as a windbreak. Moreover, when visitors ventured outside of *Hunt's* house, the terrace would prevent them from being wind-whipped while strolling in *Olmsted's* landscape.

On the hillside, beneath the terrace, Olmsted designed a series of gardens. Everything was on such a vast scale: He had 40 acres to work with. To address the uneasy stylistic collaboration with Hunt, Olmsted's design started out formal near the house site and became consecutively wilder on the way down the hillside. At the base of the hill, the final, most untamed, garden was to give way to forest, a logical and satisfying progression. Olmsted had a pair of observation towers built that reached the height of two aspects (the terrace and the windows in the music room) of Hunt's design. By climbing the towers, Vanderbilt was able to get a preview of how Olmsted's landscape would look from the house, before it was even built.

But to Olmsted the forest was the thing. He immediately began planting thousands of white pines on Vanderbilt's ever-expanding, though shabby, acreage. Given the demand for untold numbers of trees, shrubs, and flowers, Olmsted quickly realized that a nursery was needed. Growing plant stock on the estate would allow for greater control, as well as being cheaper, than shipping in more mature plants. To oversee the nursery, Olmsted hired Chauncey Beadle, a Canadian-born botanist who had studied at Ontario Agricultural College and Cornell. Beadle's vast horticultural knowledge filled Olmsted with awe. In his mind's eye, Olmsted could vividly picture that youthful horseback journey through dense Carolina woods. Grudgingly, he could lay out an ornamental garden design. As always, an expert such as Beadle was needed to do the actual care and coaxing of plants, to execute Olmsted's vision.

As a kind of corollary to the forest, Olmsted also started planning an arboretum. For Olmsted, who likened arboretums to "tree museums," this would be the Louvre to the Arnold Arboretum's Uffizi. In the moderate Carolina climate, it was possible to grow so many more varieties of trees than in Boston. Where the Arnold Arboretum featured single specimens, Olmsted planned to grow entire stands of different species. That would make it possible to study how tree species grow in proximity, to learn whether some species crowd out others, all in the service of Olmsted's novel experiment in forest management.

During the project's early stages, one last task that Olmsted took on was christening the estate. Bringing a landscape to life was helped immeasurably by dreaming up the perfect name. It was a favorite challenge for Olmsted. The name should "fall tripingly [*sic*] off the tongue" he wrote to Vanderbilt, before offering a series of suggestions. Perhaps the estate could take its name from a local Indian tribe, often a winning formula. Or what about the nearby French Broad River? Olmsted offered up "Broadwood." Riffing off Olmsted, Vanderbilt hit upon the name: Biltmore. It combines *Bildt*, the region in Holland from which his family hailed (and his name's last syllable), with *more*, an old English term for rolling hills.

By 1890, Olmsted was making several lengthy visits to the estate per year, often traveling there in the Riva, a private rail car provided by Vanderbilt. With commissions, Olmsted's typical MO was to pay a visit or two to a site, then hand off the ongoing work to a local superintendent. But a project as big as Biltmore required more extensive personal consultation.

Upon arrival, Olmsted typically fell ill and was laid up for several days with assorted maladies such as sciatica, lumbago, and facial neuralgia. He stayed at Brick House, guest quarters on the grounds, while the mansion was under construction. When feeling up to it, he played whist in the evenings.

The Biltmore Estate was Olmsted's first southern landscape architecture project, and in some ways he felt like he'd come full circle. Where he'd once chronicled the antebellum South's moral turpitude for the *New-York Daily Times*, now he was creating something—with his planned model forest—of abiding social value in the same region. What's more, the Biltmore Estate was like a beachhead from which Olmsted could venture elsewhere in the South, stirring up other potential work. Olmsted was committed to giving the Biltmore his best, but he had such a surfeit of energy that he couldn't possibly give it his all.

Olmsted met with officials in Montgomery, Alabama, to discuss landscaping the grounds surrounding the state capitol. The job went to someone who quoted a smaller fee. In 1890, Olmsted also traveled to Atlanta to discuss a planned suburb akin to Riverside, Illinois. That commission he won, and he set to designing the neighborhood known as Druid Hills.

Besides making southern inroads, Olmsted also sought to expand westward. An ambitious park system of his design was well under way in Rochester, New York. He also began working on a set of parks in Milwaukee. He was even laying out a subdivision on the outskirts of Denver, called Perry Park, though he would withdraw from the job after several visits. Olmsted hired more employees to meet the increasing workload. In 1890, he made Harry Codman a partner and changed the firm name to F. L. Olmsted and Company. "My office is much better equipped and has more momentum than ever before," he crowed in a rare moment of optimism.

Then sad news. Olmsted learned that Brace was dead. Olmsted had been aware of Charley's recent trip to Europe for health reasons but had no notion of the direness of his condition. Brace had been suffering from Bright's disease, the same malady that killed Richardson. With his strength rapidly waning, he had traveled through Germany, along the way seeing some places fondly remembered from his long-ago walking tour with Fred and John. Brace died in Switzerland in a cottage near Lake Silvaplana. He was sixty-four. With Charley's passing, Olmsted's oldest and dearest friend was gone. Olmsted received the news while at the Biltmore Estate. "His death was a shock to me," Olmsted wrote to Kingsbury, his last remaining link to the uncommon set, " . . . and the shock has been growing greater since."

Shortly after learning about Brace, Olmsted took ill with a bad case of the flu. He was certain that he caught it from Hunt. Olmsted was treated by a doctor whom he described as a "Confederate physician." The man "dosed me excessively with calomel, quinine, whisky, and opium," reported Olmsted.

Woozy, half out of his mind, Olmsted wrote a letter in pencil on a piece of wrapping paper to Elizabeth Baldwin Whitney. She was married now—had been for some years—and was none other than the celebrated Miss B., object of his youthful infatuation. Apparently, Brace's death had thrown Olmsted into a tailspin of nostalgia. The letter hasn't survived. But in relating the episode to Kingsbury, an embarrassed Olmsted described the contents as "in vino veritas." One thing is for certain: Mrs.

Whitney, who hadn't communicated with Olmsted in decades, found a measure of impertinence in the rambling wrapping-paper missive. She wrote back a formal letter, politely inquiring about Olmsted's life and accomplishments in the years since they had known one another.

Olmsted was relieved to have a second chance. He composed a reply that was sober, quite literally. By way of apology, he made quick mention of his previous "queer note" before launching into a lengthy letter, heavy on details about his career and professional achievements. "I know that in the minds of a large body of men of influence," he wrote, "I have raised my calling from the rank of a trade, even a handicraft, to that of a liberal profession—an Art, an Art of Design. I have been resolute in insisting that I am not to be dealt with as an agent of my clients but as a councillor—*a trustee in honor*." Olmsted added: "I am thinking that of all the young men that you knew I was the last to have been expected to lead such a life as I have." In a surprising turn, he gave the former Miss B. credit for setting him on the course that led him to become a landscape architect: "And you gave me the needed respect for my own constitutional state and an inclination to poetical refinements in the cultivation of them that afterwards determined my profession."

The handwritten letter is fourteen pages long. It makes but the briefest passing reference to Mary. The mention occurs when Olmsted describes his 1860 carriage accident, relating how his wife saved the baby as she was thrown clear and how little John Theodore died soon afterward.

At a time when Olmsted felt compelled to gaze at his distant past, he also couldn't help but look forward to the future. The future was stepson John, to be sure, but Olmsted saw it even more clearly in his natural son and namesake, Frederick Law Olmsted Jr. Rick had been born to Olmsted and Mary late in life. As a consequence, while Olmsted was in his sixties now, Rick was only just headed off to college to begin his freshman year, and would be attending Harvard. This was an event guaranteed to stir emotions in a parent—doubly so, given that Rick's departure came within weeks of Brace's death.

Olmsted wrote Rick a series of letters, inquiring about his studies and his social life. In one letter, he instructed Rick to draw up a memorandum, "stating on honor" the times at which he went to bed each night.

He also furnished Rick with an account of the firm's current success: "I have, with an amount of forethought, providence, and sacrifice and hardship of which you can hardly have an idea, been making a public reputation and celebrity of a certain kind, which at last has a large money value. We have, as a consequence, more business than we can manage. The business increases faster than we can enlarge our organization and adjust our methods to meet it. And it is plain that this depends as yet almost entirely on me."

And then, a few paragraphs later, Olmsted delivered the kicker: "I want you to be prepared to be the leader of the van." He added: "I have all my life been considering distant effects and always sacrificing immediate success and applause to that of the future. In laying out Central Park we determined to think of no results to be realized in less than forty years. Now in nearly all our work I am thinking of the credit that will indirectly come to you. How will it as a mature work of the Olmsted school affect Rick? I ask, and then, with reference to your education, How is Rick to be best prepared to take advantage of what in reputation I have been earning? Reputation coming as the result of what I shall have done, but not coming in my time."

This was a lot for the young man to process. In response, Rick wrote a letter almost entirely devoted to a football game between Harvard and Yale. Football was a new sport, not generally embraced by those in his father's generation. In his description, Rick concentrated on the incidentals—the spirited crowd that he estimated at around 18,000, the fact that Harvard won, the postgame celebratory bonfire. "It would be no use for me to try to tell you about the game itself as you could not understand it," wrote Rick.

C H A P T E R   30

A White City Dreamscape

WHILE OLMSTED BEGAN WORK on the Biltmore Estate, and as he clattered southward and westward collecting new jobs, the city of Chicago was battling to land a World's Fair. This was a time when World's Fairs were transformative cultural events. Cities that hosted one could claim serious bragging rights, not to mention reap considerable economic benefits. But unlike the modern Olympics, say, these fairs weren't held on any regular schedule. There was no agreed-upon World's Fair designation among the international community. Fairs were more like parties: some good, some dreadful, all dependent on the host's magnetism and the list of guests who showed up.

Starting with London in 1851, there had been about a dozen events sufficiently large and well organized to merit the title "World's Fair," along with countless pretenders. Philadelphia had hosted a bona fide fair in 1876, and most recently, in 1889, Paris had held its Exposition Universelle.

The Paris Expo was widely considered a smashing success. Unfortunately, U.S. participation in Paris met with a mixed verdict. Visitors and judges alike were wowed by American exhibits related to agriculture and industry, and the country collected numerous medals. But America made a very poor showing in areas such as the decorative and fine arts. To deliver such artistic mediocrity in Paris—moreover, to be an aesthetic featherweight at a fair distinguished by the debut of the majestic Eiffel Tower—well, it all served to reinforce those good old American cultural insecurities. Afterward, there was a groundswell movement to host a U.S. fair that would set matters right.

To put on a proper fair, however, a host country needed to commemorate a suitable anniversary. The '76 Philadelphia fair coincided with the centennial of American independence, and Paris fell on the centennial of the storming of the Bastille. Boosters lit on 1892, the four hundredth anniversary of Columbus's voyage. That was a momentous historical date, no question. What's more, the date could work as a subtle jab at France and the rest of Europe, since the case could be made that 1492 marks the beginning of a power shift from the Old World to the New.

Once a date was settled, Chicago entered into a bruising competition, pitted against such rival candidates as New York, St. Louis, and Cincinnati. The battle first played out in the press. Chicago papers called Cincinnati a "toothless, witless old dotard" and referred to St. Louis as "our impotent neighbor." A New York City paper suggested that if Chicago won, there was danger the event would be a "cattle show." During these preliminary skirmishes, Olmsted's only involvement was making an emphatic public pronouncement: If New York hosted the fair, he sincerely hoped Central Park wouldn't be the site. He and Vaux's creation, lined with exhibition halls, tourists stomping about—it was beyond his worst nightmare.

As it turned out, the matter would be decided by Congress, not cities, anyhow. It made sense, given that so many communities were vying for the honor. To be host would require congressional approval this time around. The battle soon moved to Washington, with Chicago and other rivals hiring lobbyists to plead their cases. The spring of 1890 found Congress debating this highly divisive issue. New York came on strong. Even tiny Cumberland Gap managed to get a single vote during a House roll call. In the end, Chicago took the prize.

Congress set the fair's date for the summer of 1893. Although 1892 would be the anniversary of Columbus's landing, it didn't leave enough time to plan such a massive undertaking. The event could still be called the World's Columbian Exposition even if it happened the following year. Why quibble over the details?

Winning the fair was confirmation that Chicago had fully recovered from the Great Fire. Back then, Joseph Medill's *Tribune* had famously declared: "Chicago Shall Rise Again!" It had, coming back even stronger than before. Chicago was an economic center and transport hub, famed for its stockyards and featuring some of the nation's tallest buildings. As of 1890, Chicago's population had just crossed the 1 million mark. It moved ahead of Philadelphia to become America's second-largest city.

But there was one problem. It's nicely summed up by a nineteenth-century visitor to Chicago: "In all the world, there is perhaps no site better suited for a prosperous city, no site less adapted for a beautiful one." Chicago was modern, thriving, and—to some observers—homely. Even three months after congressional approval, the forty-five men who sat on the fair's board of directors remained paralyzed. They had yet to settle on a place in their city that was right for hosting such an event, an event seen as a crucial world-stage test of Chicago and America.

James Ellsworth was president of a Chicago-based coal-mining firm and a member of the fair's board. While on a business trip to Maine, without first consulting any of his fellow forty-four directors, Ellsworth dropped by Brookline to meet with Olmsted. He asked Olmsted to help select a fitting site in Chicago and to landscape the fairgrounds. Olmsted said no. He was far too busy. Furthermore, the grounds of a fair would be temporary, making this a highly unappealing proposition. Ellsworth begged Olmsted to reconsider, adding that he would drop by again on his return trip from Maine. Ellsworth was insistent, even going so far as to play on Olmsted's sense of patriotic duty. The fair would exist only temporarily, that was true enough, conceded Ellsworth. But during the fair's brief life, thousands of people could be expected to visit. The grounds would help form a lasting impression of Chicago, not to mention America.

On his return trip, Ellsworth stopped again in Brookline. Apparently, while Ellsworth had been in Maine, Olmsted had been thinking the matter over. Olmsted was far more receptive this time around and agreed to take the job. Back in Chicago, Ellsworth secured permission from the rest of the board to hire Olmsted. On August 6, 1890, a telegraph arrived at Fairsted: "When can you be here?"

Three days later, Olmsted was in Chicago. He brought along Codman, figuring his partner would be an invaluable resource. Codman had devoted much of 1889 to a wander year in Europe, visiting various parks to gather ideas for his work with Olmsted. He'd spent three months in Paris on the grounds of the fair. Young Codman, age twenty-six, could provide an edge on this particular project. He and Olmsted visited seven different potential sites in Chicago. At each successive one, they grew more convinced of the city's manifold scenic disadvantages. Chicago was so unrelievedly flat. There was a paucity of natural scenery, to Olmsted's eyes. But there was one feature that he thought suitably grand. Chicago sits on the shores of Lake Michigan. As discussed earlier, Olmsted and Vaux had designed a park system for Chicago back in the early 1870s. Their design had played off the lake. But then the Great Fire had raged through the city, disrupting everything.

Although the city had rebuilt, taller than before, progress on their park system had been slow. The inland part, known as Washington Park, had actually been completed, though it had taken many years. But the waterfront portion, known as Jackson Park, was in an arrested state. A little work had been done, such as building some piers, but it was only about 10 percent finished. As for the Midway Plaisance, the mile-long connector between the two parks, it was nothing but a vacant strip of grass.

Returning now after so many years, Olmsted felt certain that this was the spot. Never mind that Jackson Park was a wasteland, a mix of sand hills and swamps with a few unloved trees thrown in. Never mind, either, that Jackson Park was about seven miles from downtown Chicago. A striking setting was needed for the fair. To Olmsted, all other problems were mere details, easily surmounted. Moreover, rail lines traveled directly past the uncompleted park, making it possible to convey large crowds to the place.

Still, it was a hard sell. Jackson Park was in such a pitiful state that it was difficult for anyone else to grasp Olmsted's logic. He had to write two separate reports, but he managed to convince the directors. "We have carried our first point, that of tying the Fair to the Lake," wrote Olmsted to John.

F. L. Olmsted and Company was given the official title of consulting landscape architects to the World's Columbian Expo. Olmsted and the directors agreed to terms: $22,500. It was a hefty fee to accompany a huge job. Olmsted told John that it would be necessary to reapportion their workloads. Codman would need to devote 100 percent of his time to the fair; Olmsted planned to put in 50 percent, and John would need to allot 20 percent. Olmsted also intended to devote at least half his time to the Biltmore Estate. That left 0 percent for Rochester, Atlanta, and all his other current and future jobs. But Olmsted wasn't one to let a little thing like math get in the way of his big plans.

Olmsted began to work out a landscaping scheme for the fair grounds. Essentially, he revived his nearly twenty-year-old plan for a waterfront park, featuring a series of winding lagoons and waterways. To create these, it would be necessary to cut channels through roughly a square mile of soggy land. But earth removed when the channels were cut could be hauled to other spots, tamped down and shaped, thereby creating solid land. Lake Michigan would form a sensational backdrop and would literally flow, via the waterways, right onto the fairgrounds.

From the outset, Olmsted and Codman worked closely with Daniel Burnham and John Root. Burnham, age forty-four, was director of the fair. Root, age forty, was his longtime partner in an architectural firm that had designed some of Chicago's most notable buildings. In his younger days, Burnham had failed the entrance exams to both Harvard and Yale before setting off for Nevada mining territory, hoping to strike it rich. In other words, he was Olmsted's kind of guy. The two developed an instant rapport. Over time, like Olmsted, Burnham had discovered where his real talents lay and had learned to focus them. He was a brilliant businessman, and his organizational skills were unrivaled. Root, by contrast, was the artist: inspired, spontaneous, erratic. They made a dynamic team, and one observer likened their partnership to "some big strong tree with lightning playing around it."

Olmsted and Codman opened a Chicago field office in the Rookery, a building where the firm Burnham and Root had its headquarters as well. One day late in the autumn of 1890, the four men were together, discussing their scheme for the fair. Root laid out a huge piece of heavy brown paper, forty feet square. Then he began to sketch on it furiously, capturing their ideas. He drew the waterways to Olmsted's specs, and he indicated where various buildings would sit. Root also sketched out a Court of Honor, a formal space with exhibition halls arranged around a basin and presided over by a large statue. Root gripped his pencil so low and tight and sketched so rapidly that it "looked as if he were drawing with the tips of his fingers," according to historian Donald Miller. When he finished, he had produced the fair's master plan.

Burnham and Root agreed not to design any buildings. Every ounce of Burnham's organizational skill was needed; it was agreed that partner Root wouldn't design any, either, as it would show favoritism. Instead, Burnham opted to assemble an all-star team of architects. In close consultation with Olmsted, Burnham began approaching various candidates. Hunt, Olmsted's Biltmore collaborator, was a natural choice. So was Charles McKim of the New York firm McKim, Mead, and White. McKim was the son of James McKim, leader of the friendly *Nation* faction, the one that had supported Olmsted's catholic approach during the publication's earliest days. Early in his career, the younger McKim had worked for H. H. Richardson. Other possibles included Boston's Robert Peabody as well as Chicago's own Louis Sullivan and William Le Baron Jenney. Jenney had worked with Olmsted on Riverside. Vaux wasn't even considered. Four decades earlier, at a time when American architects were in short supply, he'd been a groundbreaker. It was a testament to how far he had fallen.

On January 10, 1891, the architects from out of town met in Chicago and traveled to look at the Jackson Park site. Landscape architect Olmsted was present, too. The temperature was frigid, the sky overcast, and Lake Michigan roiled and pitched. Far from providing a striking backdrop, the lake merely looked ominous. The architects were soon overcome with pessimism.

Peabody walked out onto a pier. He turned to Burnham. "Do you mean to say that you really expect to open a fair here by '93?"

"Yes," answered Burnham, "we intend to."

"It can't be done," said Peabody.

"That point is settled," rejoined Burnham.

That evening, the skeptical architects convened at the University Club. Olmsted was present once again. Lyman Gage, president of the fair's board, sat at the head of the main table, Olmsted and Hunt in places of honor on either side of him. The architects were no doubt happy just to be somewhere warm. Burnham plied his guests with vintage Madeira, fine cigars, and green-turtle consommé. When the moment was right, he delivered a rousing speech: "Gentlemen, 1893 will be the third great date in our country's history. On the two others, 1776 and 1861, all true Americans served, and so now I ask you to serve again!" Burnham's patriotic appeal reached the architects, just as Ellsworth's earlier one had reached Olmsted. They committed to the project.

Olmsted no longer required such goading. By now, he had a clear idea of what was possible on the soupy piece of land slated for the fair, and his vision grew more intense with each passing day. One of his principal features, captured in Root's lightning sketch, was a wooded island. Creating it would involve taking an existing lonely hillock and bulking it up with dirt dredged in the course of making the lagoons. Despite being man-made, it would serve as the primary naturalistic feature at the fair. The event was sure to be crowded and hectic. Olmsted conceived his wooded island as "a place of relief from all the splendor and glory and noise and human multitudinousness of the great surrounding Babylon."

Because water was such a key element in his landscape, Olmsted also came up with the idea of offering boats for hire. Most people could be expected to traverse the fair on foot, but this would provide an elegant alternative. Olmsted was downright obsessive about these boats. Not just any type would do. They needed to be small craft, geared to intimate groups of passengers. He was also dead-set on using the new breed of electric launches rather than boats powered by steam. These would glide over the water, almost silently. Olmsted even had strong notions about the boats' appearance. They should feature brightly colored awnings, modeled on the sampans that he remembered from his voyage to China, half a century before.

On February 24, 1891, another architects' meeting was held in the library on the top floor of the Rookery. This time everyone was present: the out-of-towners and the local architects such as Sullivan and Jenney. They gathered to present their designs for the major buildings such as the exhibition halls.

Olmsted watched as each architect walked to the front of the room and unfurled his blueprint. Weeks before, the architects had agreed to work in the same style, giving them a kind of common visual vocabulary. They had lit upon classical architecture, a fitting choice. Many of the architects were either French trained or devotees of the beaux arts, a neo-classical style then in vogue. From a practical standpoint, the choice guaranteed a unity of design. Even so, the buildings showed dazzling variety. "You're dreaming, gentlemen, dreaming," said Expo president Lyman Gage. "I only hope that half the vision may be realized."

The buildings were huge, big as the architects' egos. Yet the plan was to make these structures out of simple skeletons of wood and chicken wire, overlaid with staff. Staff is a kind of glorified papier-mâché. It's durable, thanks to its hemp content, yet highly malleable. It can be shaped to mimic a marble column or a terra-cotta frieze. Almost all the major buildings were to be painted white. When the fair ended, almost the whole set of them was meant to come down. There was one last consistent feature, and it pleased Olmsted mightily. Each building featured two entrances, one by land, the other by water to accommodate his boats.

As the weather grew warmer, Olmsted began working on a planting scheme. He intended to line the banks of his waterways thickly with foliage. But to survive Chicago's climate, Olmsted knew he'd need to go with indigenous plants, throwing in a few exotics. Under his direction, foraging parties were dispatched to lakes and rivers throughout Illinois and Wisconsin to gather cattails and rushes and willows. The plants arrived at the grounds by the trainload. Olmsted also planted honeysuckle and other fragrant plants so that fairgoers would have something to smell as well as see. He was contemplating a full sensory experience.

Rick, preparing to be "leader of the van," came out from Harvard after his freshman year to spend a summer working on the grounds. He'd spend the next summer here, too, finding it a great experience.

As the fair drew closer, Olmsted engaged in assorted battles, as per usual. Everyone wanted a piece of the Wooded Island. It represented 16 pristine acres in the center of what was certain to be a very crowded fairgrounds. Participating countries wanted to place their pavilions on the island. Companies thought it an ideal spot for promotions. Burpee Seed suggested a display garden of marigolds and petunias. Olmsted's response to this request is unknown but can probably be summed up as *Perish the thought!*

Even Theodore Roosevelt had designs on Olmsted's island. He wanted to build a model hunting camp to demonstrate the woodsmanship of his Boone and Crockett Club. Olmsted gave a flat no to the future president. Still, the clamor eventually grew so intense that Olmsted had to relent. He agreed to share his island with the Japanese government, which proposed to build something called the Ho-O-Den, a replica of a temple near Kyoto. The temple would be modest, low-rise, and integrated into the scenery.

Olmsted also got into scrapes over the boats. No one seemed to grasp his small-quiet craft fixation, not even his staunch ally Burnham. Olmsted was troubled when he learned that Burnham had entertained an offer from a steamship company that promised to cheaply convey large numbers of fairgoers. "I suspect that even Codman is inclined to think that I make too much of a hobby of this boat question," he wrote Burnham in a memo, "and give an amount of worry, if not thought, to it that would be better expended on other more critical matters, and I fear that you may think me a crank upon it."

In a follow-up memo to Burnham, Olmsted laid out his objections. Yes, a big, honking steamboat could convey the masses. True, small boats could carry only a handful of people at a time. But watching small, colorful boats glide over the lagoons would create a memorable experience for *everyone*. What's more, he proposed that if small boats proved a big attraction, if more people started lining up for them, it would make sense to hike the fares. Counterintuitive though it was, Olmsted's premise was curiously democratic since it promised to extend the greatest benefit—enjoying the ambience of a small collection of boats—to the largest number of people. He reminded Burnham that his aim—the aim of all the great artists working on the fair—was to create something of beauty: "You know that if boats are to be introduced on these waters, it would be perfect nonsense to have them of a kind that would antagonize this poetic object." Burnham was convinced and agreed to give Olmsted his boats.

The major points were now settled. In the spring of 1892, with Codman holding down the Chicago project, Olmsted set off on an ambitious business trip that took him from the Biltmore to Knoxville, Louisville, and Rochester, among other places, and on to Brookline. He was nearly seventy. He covered nearly 3,000 miles.

He returned in terrible health, racked by conditions old and new. He was suffering from insomnia and neuralgia, and there was a constant ringing in his ears. He'd also had a recent bout of what he thought was arsenic poisoning. He believed that the culprit was the new "Turkey red" wallpaper in his Brookline home. For Olmsted, about the only good health development was that his damaged left leg, an ancient injury, was feeling better. During one of his constant trips, the train on which he'd been traveling got into a minor accident, and this, bizarrely, appeared to be the cause of the improvement. He was walking with greater ease now, feeling less pain. It wasn't exactly a medical diagnosis, but Olmsted thought perhaps the crash had succeeded in stretching out some of his tendons. Otherwise, he felt wretched.

Olmsted decided to make a trip to England and France. He could visit various sites and gather ideas, while regaining his health in the process. At least, that was the plan. On April 2, 1892, Olmsted sailed to Liverpool accompanied by Rick, Marion, and Philip Codman, Henry's younger brother. He stayed briefly with relatives of his wife in Chislehurst, on the outskirts of London. Then he traveled to Paris with the two young men. Marion remained behind in Chislehurst.

In Paris, Olmsted walked over the grounds of the recent Exposition Universelle. He soaked up every last detail, as was his wont. The ornamental gardens left him unimpressed, and he wrote a letter to John back in Brookline, containing a strong reminder that such "petty effects and frippery" must be avoided in Chicago. But the fact that the Paris buildings made ample use of color intrigued him. In fact, it left him downright worried. He wondered whether the Chicago buildings were too severe, too bound up in "grandiloquent pomp," too . . . white.

He grew more aware that he was the fair's color man. He'd selected the site, and on a clear day Lake Michigan would offer a sea of blue. Any other colors would flow from him as well. At the same time, Olmsted had a well-honed aesthetic that didn't conscience gaudy palates. He valued subtlety. Green, in the form of impossibly lush greenery—that was the way, he was certain, to offset the unremitting whiteness of the architecture.

Almost as an afterthought, Olmsted went up in the Eiffel Tower. Then he left Paris for the Loire Valley, where he visited some châteaus, gathering ideas for the Biltmore Estate.

Then it was back to England, where his health took a bad turn. He had a flare-up of facial neuralgia. Insomnia, his old foe, returned with a vengeance. He tossed in bed deep into the night, worrying about the Expo and the Biltmore and other jobs and his legacy and the future and . . . as the sun rose, he would snatch a few hours sleep, if he was lucky. That was his pattern.

Henry Rayner, a friend of Mary's London relatives, dropped by the house in Chislehurst. He simply wanted to meet the great Olmsted, celebrated American landscape architect. By sheerest coincidence, he also happened to be a doctor who specialized in nervous disorders. Dr. Rayner was astounded by Olmsted's haggard appearance. He asked if Olmsted would submit to a physical. The examination found no "organic trouble," Olmsted reported, but the doctor also concluded that "it is a peculiarity of my case that over-exertion does not produce the sensation of fatigue." Dr. Rayner suggested that Olmsted stay at his home in Hampstead Heath, where he could personally oversee his care.

Shortly after arriving, Olmsted received disturbing news about Vaux. Vaux had recently managed to get reappointed to the Central Park board, a promising development professionally. During a meeting, a fellow member asked Vaux the scientific name for the flower rose of Sharon. Vaux wasn't sure. The man pursued him, demanding to know why he lacked this knowledge. Increasingly agitated, Vaux sputtered and fumed and toyed with his glasses.

Of course, Vaux was an architect of bridges and buildings, not a designer of foliage compositions. For that matter, Olmsted most likely didn't know the scientific name of rose of Sharon, either. Still, Vaux was deeply humiliated, and he sensed that his standing with the board had been badly damaged. After receiving news of Vaux's latest setback, Olmsted didn't sleep for forty-eight hours.

Dr. Rayner did his best to shield Olmsted from other excitements. He fed Olmsted a steady diet of sedatives. After many weeks in Hampstead Heath, Olmsted began to feel terribly constrained. "You know that I am practically in prison here," he wrote to Codman. Yet he gradually started to show improvement and was finally released from Dr. Rayner's care.

As was his habit, following a period of inactivity, Olmsted exploded into action. He spent a couple days traveling along the Thames from London to Hurley, trying out two different electric launches along the way. During this trip, he also took the opportunity to closely observe the foliage that grew along the riverbank. He was struck anew by the bounteousness that nature could achieve, even in temperate England. He was overwhelmed by the sheer variety, the mystery—willows jutting out over the water at unexpected angles, vines snaking this way and that. He knew that at the fair he would need to capture that elusive, lush, almost tropical quality that he was forever chasing in places like Central Park's Ramble. "A most capital school is found on the Thames banks for the study of what we want at Chicago in the lagoon banks," Olmsted wrote in a letter addressed jointly to his partners, John and Codman.

In September 1892, Olmsted sailed back to the United States. The ship encountered severe weather, and the return voyage can only be described as a rough passage. For Olmsted, it always was.

October found Olmsted back in Chicago. Less than a year remained before the fair was scheduled to open. He was surprised to see how much had been accomplished during the time he'd been away. Many of the buildings were well under way, rising up from the ground, as if they were living, growing things. Great progress had been made even on the Manufactures and Liberal Arts Building. Designed by architect George Post, it was slated to be the largest building in history with an exhibit space covering 44 acres.

But Olmsted was also disturbed by how much still remained to be done. He was especially critical of his own firm's efforts. Waterways had been dredged; the fairgrounds themselves had been created with compacted muck and thousands of tons of manure carted in from the Union stockyards. Still, he wondered, how could all the remaining planting and filling and grading possibly get done in time? "I am tired and have a growing dread of worry and anxiety," he wrote to John.

Olmsted headed down to the Biltmore Estate but was back in Brookline in time for Christmas. Reports trickled in indicating that Chicago was grappling with a particularly ferocious winter. And then in early January, a telegram arrived at Fairsted. Codman was dead. He had succumbed to complications following a routine appendectomy. He was twenty-eight years old.

There was a sad symmetry to Codman's death, as Burnham had also lost his business partner during the course of the project. Root had died of pneumonia. The night Root died, someone claimed to have overheard Burnham muttering, "I have worked, I have schemed and dreamed to make us the greatest architects in the world—I have made him see it and kept him at it—and now he dies—Damn! Damn! Damn!"

Olmsted could well have said the same, substituting *landscape architect* for *architect*. Actually, what Olmsted said about Codman's death was: "I am as one standing on a wreck and can hardly see when we shall get afloat again." He rushed back to Chicago. At his firm's field office at the Rookery, he sat down at Codman's desk and began riffling through the various letters and memorandums. But it was hard to make sense of anything. Better to assess matters out on the grounds—the frigid grounds. The temperature on February 4, 1893, was minus 8°F, Olmsted noted, and the ground was frozen three feet deep. Olmsted directed men to use dynamite to loosen earth that needed to be moved. Then he oversaw teams as they pressed and molded this godforsaken dirt to build up the fairgrounds and build out the lagoon banks until they appeared suitably varied and mysterious.

So much was left to do. Olmsted felt overwhelmed, and his health was suffering once again. He had a new ailment, an ulcerated tooth. And he faced an old demon, insomnia. Olmsted was staying at the Wellington Hotel. He wrote to John back in Brookline, begging him to send a new pair of Pulitzer's-brand earplugs to replace a pair that he had simply worn out. He couldn't possibly quiet the noise inside his head, but at least he could silence the clangs and clatters and other street sounds coming from without.

Olmsted intended to throw everything into a final sprint in Chicago, but he wondered whether it would kill him. Most certainly, he'd have nothing left for the ever-expanding practice. He wrote a hopeless letter to John that included: "It looks as if the time has come when it is necessary to count me out."

He needed sleep. He needed help. If he added a new partner, perhaps that person could pick up some of the slack on all the other projects—all over America—that were weighing on him. Olmsted decided to bring Charles Eliot, his onetime apprentice, into the partnership. Eliot had been pursuing his own landscape architecture practice in Boston. In March 1893, the firm became Olmsted, Olmsted & Eliot.

By now, Burnham had 12,000 men on the grounds, working around the clock. This was possible due to a recent invention, electric lights. A large crew set to painting the massive structures white. This was done with the aid of another innovation, the world's first spray-painting apparatus.

As spring drew on, the ice gave way to hard rain. Olmsted continued to work outdoors, exposed to the elements, directing the last of the plantings. Often, he even took his meals outside, alongside the other workers. "The dirt of the provisional mess table, the noise & scurry and the puddles and rain do not leave a dilapidated old man much comfort," he wrote to John.

The ulcerated tooth bothered him more than ever. In another letter, he confided: "I am living on toast & tea."

But he kept going. Olmsted was frustrated because he had to wait for buildings to be completed before he could plant around their bases. Elsewhere on the grounds, he directed the last of the plantings, supplementing what had taken root in the two previous seasons of work. Everywhere he pushed to turn up the volume—thicker, lusher, greener—per his recent trip along the Thames.

When it became clear that the fair was truly going to happen, that gala event was held at New York's Madison Square Concert Hall, forerunner of the current Gardens. Several hundred guests were present, including a generous sampling of the fairgrounds' creators: architects and painters and sculptors. The press was there along with a smattering of politicians. Two of Olmsted's old friends, Edwin Godkin and Charles Eliot Norton, had traveled down from Boston for the event.

Following a two-hour dinner, there was a show of stereoscopic images, projected onto a large screen. It was an incredible display: Hunt's Administration Building, featuring a dome larger than the U.S. Capitol's, followed by Daniel Chester French's *Statue of the Republic*—massive, gilded, *Lady Liberty*-like, given pride of place at the head of the Court of Honor. Olmsted's Wooded Island met with high approbation. The stereoscopic show closed with an image of Daniel Burnham, director of the fair.

Hunt, hobbled by gout, slowly took the stage and presented Burnham with a silver loving cup. Burnham filled it with wine, took a big swig, and then sent it circulating through the crowd. Burnham then launched into that memorable speech, quoted earlier, reflecting glory away from himself and onto Olmsted, describing Olmsted as an artist who "paints with lakes and wooded slopes," thanking him for "what his brain has wrought and his pen has taught for half a century," and calling him "our constant mentor" and "the planner of the Exposition" and a "genius."

Meanwhile, the loving cup continued to make the rounds. It was engraved with the names of the event's 272 attendees. Among those names was Olmsted's, of course. But there was one small matter. Olmsted wasn't actually there. He had taken the opportunity to slip down to Asheville to work on the Biltmore Estate.

Press accounts made the natural mistake of assuming Olmsted was present for his own glittering tribute. In the aftermath of the event, both Harvard and Yale announced they planned to confer honorary degrees on him. What a turnabout: high recognition from two preeminent universities for a man who had attended one of them for all of three months. In an odd twist, both ceremonies were set for the same date. Olmsted accepted the honors but wrote letters explaining that he'd have to receive both in abstentia. He was just too busy. "I doubt if a man ever came to such honor before as to have L.L.D. [doctor of laws] from both Yale and Harvard the same day," remarked an astonished Kingsbury, "and I suspect that nobody ever cared so little about it."

Olmsted had his priorities. He was back in Chicago on May 1, 1893, for the opening ceremonies of the World's Columbian Exposition. That day, an estimated 500,000 people were packed along the Court of Honor to hear President Grover Cleveland deliver an address. Shortly after noon, the president touched a gilded telegraph key, which sent a signal traveling through the fairgrounds. In perfect sync, banners unfurled from the buildings, jets of water rose from Frederick MacMonnies's *Columbia Fountain*, a shroud fell revealing the *Statue of the Republic*, two hundred doves were released, and a band struck up "America." Olmsted ignored the hullabaloo. He was busy making one last tour of the grounds, making sure everything was just so.

But he didn't stick around for long. At last, he felt comfortable turning the project entirely over to a superintendent, per his usual practice. Of course, it wasn't as if work ended now just because the fair had opened. What's more, there was *re*work to be done. Every day, visitors trampled the landscape, and people uprooted plants to take home as souvenirs. Mercifully, these concerns would now fall on someone else.

Olmsted knew he had made a mockery of his 50 percent rule during that mad-dash period leading up to the fair. He felt the press of the Biltmore and all his other business. Soon he hit the rails once more, making his most ambitious business trip yet, one that would carry him through sixteen states.

Unfortunately, the fair got off to a slow start, due to poor weather. Attendance was far below expectations. As Olmsted traveled, he interviewed fellow rail passengers about the fair, a throwback to his long-ago days as a reporter for the *New-York Daily Times*. Even from a distance of hundreds of miles, Olmsted still couldn't entirely disengage from events in Chicago. He concluded that many people planned to visit the fair, but they were waiting for better weather. Some people were holding off because they expected the event to be at its height closer to its autumn closing date. "Everywhere there is growing interest in the Exposition," Olmsted reported to Burnham. "Everywhere I have found indications that people are planning to go to it." In his letter, Olmsted also suggested some ways to liven up the fair. Maybe there could be wandering banjo players, for example. Burnham had given in to Olmsted on his boats. But banjo players—no way!

As part of Olmsted's travels, he visited Atlanta, which was planning its own Cotton States Exposition as an answer to Chicago's Columbian Expo. In the year ahead, he would make several more visits to the city. During one, the *Atlanta Constitution* would treat his mere presence as front-page news. "Mr. Olmstead Talks," reads the headline, followed by: "He says the grounds can be made very beautiful. His visit for consultation only." Note that the paper misspelled Olmsted's name. As often happened, he lost out on the commission to someone who agreed to do it for less.

Meanwhile, the Columbian Expo turned out to be an outsize success. Paid attendance just kept growing through the summer and early autumn, eventually passing the 20-million mark. The big sensation, the feature that managed to upstage even the Eiffel Tower, was the world's first Ferris wheel. It was placed on the Midway Plaisance, that narrow connecting strip from the original plan. Also relegated to this spot were Buffalo Bill's Wild West Show, Hagenback's circus, a replica Hawaiian volcano, and the World's Congress of Beauty, promising "40 Ladies from 40 Nations." Thanks to this memorable and colorful section of the Expo, the term *midway*, coined by Olmsted and Vaux, entered the language. It's used to refer to the more raucous part of a fair, featuring sideshows and other more blueish entertainments.

But more than the Ferris wheel, more than any single attraction, what visitors took away from the fair was a general feeling, an ambience. People were awed by the massive buildings set on the banks of winding lagoons, little brightly colored boats gliding languidly past. These elements were potentially discordant, yet they achieved a strange harmony. The fairgrounds were not of this world. They were laid out according to the logic of dreams. "Words fail," declared a kindergarten teacher, visiting from Kankakee, Illinois. "The magic splendor of that sight can never be excelled on earth."

At night, the sense of otherworldliness was greater still. The buildings were lined in electric lights, an innovation many visitors had never before seen. The *Chicago Tribune* referred to the "graceful outlines of the White City." And that was the name that stuck: the White City.

Even Olmsted's Wooded Island achieved its aim, providing an oasis of calm. Irascible architect Louis Sullivan declared it the very best feature of the fair, high praise since he had designed one of the buildings. Sullivan's young assistant spent many hours wandering around the island and was especially taken with the Japanese Ho-O-Don. The assistant's name: Frank Lloyd Wright.

It's estimated that somewhere in the neighborhood of 5 percent of the U.S. population attended the fair. And then: curtains. On October 31, 1893, the gates closed for all time. Within the space of a few years, almost all of the buildings would come down. A large number burned, quite possibly due to arson, during a violent Pullman workers' strike. Left behind was a landscape, Chicago's Jackson Park, designed by Olmsted and Vaux back in 1871.

Clever Olmsted; he'd figured out a way to make real a long-ago dream.

CHAPTER 31

"Before I Am the Least
Prepared for It"

DOWN IN NORTH CAROLINA, work was progressing. In fact, it had never missed a beat, thanks to Olmsted's slipping off to Asheville at every opportunity. Hunt, too. For the past two years, Hunt's mansion for Vanderbilt had kept growing, just as surely as the architect's supersize Administration Building in the White City. The Biltmore Estate was starting to take discernible shape, rising from the hilltop like a huge sand castle. When complete, it would be 175,000 square feet, featuring 250 rooms, 43 of them bathrooms.

Olmsted's plan for a model forest had also moved forward at startling speed. Vanderbilt had gone on a buying binge, and his North Carolina holdings had grown to a size that was simply mind-boggling. He now owned around 100,000 acres, and his holdings would ultimately grow to roughly 125,000 acres (equal to nearly 200 square miles). Some of this was hearty, old-growth woods, but much of it was scraggly and abused like the land Olmsted had seen during that first visit.

While Vanderbilt's property grew exponentially, Olmsted had come to realize that forest-management acumen far beyond his own was required. He had personally recommended that Vanderbilt hire a young man named Gifford Pinchot. Vanderbilt had agreed. Pinchot hailed from a wealthy New York family and was of French descent. He was one of the first Americans to attend the École Nationale Forestière in Nancy, France. While there, he had studied under the school's leading theorists. He had toured England, Germany, and Switzerland and returned to America versed in the latest European thinking on forestry.

Upon going to work for Vanderbilt, Pinchot immediately began putting these methods into practice. He had even made a contribution to North Carolina's exhibit at the Columbian Exposition, a forty-nine-page pamphlet detailing his revolutionary forest-management plan for the Biltmore. Pinchot's pamphlet was awarded an "honorable mention" during the Chicago festivities.

Olmsted was impressed by how much Pinchot was accomplishing at Biltmore. With the fair finally behind him, Olmsted seized the opportunity to renew his own focus on the estate. Still, lavishing exclusive attention on any one project felt alien, and he couldn't shut out the creeping suspicion that he was neglecting others. He'd been in a state of emergency for so long that it had become his normal state. "Am I needed at Kansas City? It is so long since I have been at Louisville that I shall be lost if I go alone," he wrote to John back in Brookline. "You must send me the names of the people whom I shall need to renew acquaintance with. At this moment I cannot recall one." In another letter, Olmsted worried that if he took a trip to visit various clients, it would kill him: "My health is extremely frail and I may be tipped out any day."

John assured Olmsted that matters were under control. His stepfather could cut back his travel. That's why Eliot had been brought into the partnership. With projects that were sufficiently advanced, that's what superintendents were for. Olmsted slowed down, but not surprisingly, he couldn't resist making certain trips. It was reminiscent of his youth, when he'd pinballed from infatuation to infatuation. There was so much yet to be done, and he was aware that the time left him was limited. Olmsted was especially likely to slip off to jobs near Asheville, such as the Atlanta suburb or the Louisville park system.

Biltmore, however, promised the greatest glory. "*This* is a place and G. W. V. [Vanderbilt] is a man that we must do our best for," Olmsted declared in a letter to his partners. " . . . It is far and away the most distinguished private place, not only for America, but of the world, forming *at this period*. It will be critical and reviewed and referred to for its precedents and for its experience, years ahead, centuries ahead."

Olmsted put great effort into designing an approach road for the estate. In effect, this was a driveway for Vanderbilt's house. But there are driveways and there are *driveways*: Like everything else in this project, outrageous scale was in order. He designed a three-mile approach that took its sweet time, curving and looping and winding up the hillside. He directed that the sides of the carriage road be thickly planted with native Blue Ridge flora such as rhododendron, mountain laurel, and white pine. The idea was to create a screen, albeit a visually arresting one. It was key that a visitor be deprived of all distant views, until he rounded a bend, and then the mansion "breaks suddenly and fully upon him," as Olmsted put it.

Olmsted's design contrived to keep the huge house a surprise. But he planned another, still greater, surprise. Once inside the house—from windows, off balconies—visitors would get their first glimpse of where they truly were. Their view had been entertainingly diverted during the long journey up the approach road. Now it would become clear. They were on a hilltop surrounded by a forest that stretched endlessly, endlessly, into the distance. "Hasn't Olmsted done wonders with the approach road," commented Hunt. "It alone will give him lasting fame." Apparently, the imperious Hunt had forgotten that Olmsted had secured lasting fame back in 1858. Lord knows Hunt had designed enough mansions overlooking Central Park.

Olmsted also worked on his ambitious plan for the Biltmore arboretum, a tree museum to dwarf all others. Here, he faced a setback. Vanderbilt wasn't particularly compelled by the idea. Then Charles Sargent withdrew his support. This was a critical blow. Sargent, Olmsted's Brookline neighbor and his collaborator on the Arnold Arboretum, had his doubts about such an undertaking on a private estate. An arboretum not associated with an institution such as a university, Sargent felt, would be of dubious scientific value.

Vanderbilt set December 25, 1895, as the deadline for completing the Biltmore. He planned to debut the estate on Christmas with a gala party for his many powerful and influential friends. Fortunately, this was not turning out to be a mad dash like Chicago. In fact, by the autumn of 1894, things were moving forward with unusual ease, at least by the standards of an undertaking this large and complex. True, Olmsted's arboretum was stalled.

But the other pieces of his plan—the forest, the approach road, the gardens—were taking spectacular shape.

At the same time, Olmsted was feeling worse than ever. He had driven himself so hard in recent years; his ever-precarious health was now slipping fast.

Rick had recently graduated Harvard, magna cum laude. He'd majored in zoology (landscape architecture didn't yet exist as an academic discipline). Olmsted summoned his son to Asheville and installed him as an apprentice on the project. He figured Rick could get some needed training. Then Olmsted returned to Brookline for a period to attend to other firm business. But the moment he arrived home, his thoughts immediately turned to Rick and the Biltmore. Olmsted sent his son a long letter. "Write in a personal way to me personally giving me some account of what you are doing and thinking," Olmsted demanded. "I want to know a great deal more about you than I do. How is your health—physically, mentally, morally? Do not be backward in telling me." He continued: "Are you getting any practice shooting, fishing or hunting? . . . Have you shot a wild turkey? Are you going to any balls, or dances? Are you punctual and regular in your social—'society'—duties?"

Most of all, Olmsted wanted to make sure Rick took every advantage of the rare opportunity before him. He would be working in close proximity with some truly renowned experts. "But whatever you can get from others, Beadle and Pinchot are your principle [sic] mines," Olmsted wrote. "You cannot work them too much." He was particularly concerned that Rick acquire the botanical expertise that he himself lacked. Olmsted possessed vast knowledge of plants in a folk-wisdom kind of way. At conceiving foliage compositions, he was unrivaled. But he lacked a scientific grounding in botany and was certain this could be a professional drawback. He'd seen as much with Vaux and the recent rose-of-Sharon episode. "You must, with the aid of such inheritance as I can give you, make good my failings," he continued. "That is one of the thoughts that dwell with me. Also, I recognize wherein John (& wherein Eliot) is imperfectly fitted, and I want you to be fitted to make good, years to come."

The letter carried on for twenty-one pages and countless exhortations: "Review! Review! And train *yourself.* . . . *If you don't get it now you never will.*" The italics are Olmsted's, and, once again, he left his son a lot to ponder. Rick wrote his father from Biltmore: "I am compelled to answer, with pain and regret, after the most serious and thorough thought, that I believe I would better enter upon another career."

This only succeeded in triggering a flurry of letters. Olmsted wasn't about to accept such an answer. He implored Rick not to follow the same course as him, bouncing from profession to profession. He pointed out that his own father had been "overmuch indulgent and easy going" toward him. That's why Olmsted was being tough. Didn't Rick see that there was a ready-made career just waiting for him? Olmsted declared himself "anxious to get you under training here before I die."

In the spring of 1895, Olmsted returned to Asheville. He was accompanied by Mary and Marion. This time, his visit was meant to serve a dual—though not entirely logical—purpose. Olmsted planned to oversee Rick's development and attend to some final details on the project. He also hoped to reap some of the recuperative benefits of that legendary Asheville spa climate. Vanderbilt put the Olmsted family up at Rivercliff, a guest cottage on the estate grounds.

The Olmsted who arrived was different from the Olmsted who had been there only months before. It was subtle, but his family could see it. Olmsted was growing forgetful, Rick noticed. For a while now, he'd been having trouble remembering names, but it had been chalked up to the fact that he juggled so many projects. More ominously, his blue eyes, always so alert, sometimes filled with a strange bewildered look.

When Olmsted directed the planting of some tulip trees in front of the Biltmore mansion, he got the scheme confused. Fortunately, Rick caught the mistake. Olmsted was pleased that Rick was paying attention but was also deeply embarrassed. He worried about what would happen if Vanderbilt became aware of his condition. Abruptly, Olmsted announced that he wanted to return to Brookline.

Vanderbilt talked him into staying on for a while longer. He had commissioned John Singer Sargent to do portraits of the two artists behind the Biltmore, Olmsted and Hunt.

Sargent's painting of Hunt captures the architect standing in the mansion's grand entry hall, staring fiercely ahead. It's a bold image but also a considerable illusion. Hunt was in terrible health himself. Apparently, Mrs. Hunt hovered throughout the sessions, begging Sargent, who was known for his realism, to be charitable in depicting her husband. Two months later, Hunt would be dead.

For Olmsted's portrait, Sargent selected a thickly planted spot on the side of the approach road, about a half mile from the mansion. Dogwoods and kalmia were in full blossom—a perfect setting for the great landscape architect. Alas, the sessions proved too demanding for the increasingly frail Olmsted. Before Sargent could finish, Olmsted headed home to Brookline.

To complete the portrait, Rick stood in for his father. He even donned the same clothing that Olmsted had worn during the first few sessions with Sargent. It had happened far too quickly. Rick felt wholly unready. But in some fashion, this sad, strange little episode represented a changing of the guard.

Back in Brookline, Olmsted plummeted. He was sometimes his old self but was just as often confused and agitated. To compound matters, Fairsted was a home office, headquarters of an increasingly successful practice. From moment to moment, one never knew which Olmsted would appear. During this period, he did his very last pieces of actual work (as opposed to the obsessive *thinking* about work that would characterize the time ahead). He inspected some recently completed touches in the Boston system and wrote something about the parks in Hartford, the town where he'd grown up. But one day, in the summer of 1895, he also composed three letters to Vanderbilt. The letters were nearly identical.

Clearly, Olmsted was suffering from Alzheimer's or some other kind of senile dementia, though no such diagnosis existed in those days. His family made preparations to remove him from Fairsted.

Mary secreted her husband away to the village of Sunset on Deer Isle, off the coast of Maine in Penobscot Bay. This was a spot that Mary and Marion had visited during recent summers. They were often joined there by John and Rick. Olmsted had rarely gone. He'd been too busy and had never liked the place, besides.

From Deer Isle, Olmsted mailed a steady stream of letters—sometimes several a day—to the office in Brookline. He demanded action on mat-

ters large and small, real and imaginary. A particular source of anxiety
for Olmsted was the Biltmore arboretum. In letter after letter, he asserted
that John simply did not get it, was incapable of grasping the importance
and complexity of this issue. "I can't think that you recognize how serious a matter the Biltmore crisis is," he wrote.

Of course, there was no crisis. There wasn't going to be an arboretum;
that had been pretty much settled. Still, Olmsted managed almost endless varieties of this same conceit (*you just don't get it*) in his correspondence with John. The repetitiveness was a symptom of his disease. But
there was something unnerving about what he kept cycling over. It was
shades of the harsh assessment ("you are not a man of genius") that Olmsted had leveled against his stepson many years before.

Faced with such an onslaught, ever-dutiful John tried to remain calm
and businesslike toward his stepfather. That was hard. "It would help us
very much if you would constantly bear in mind that your memory for
current events is no longer a working basis for your thoughts," he wrote.
"Until you do so, realize you will give us no end of trouble and worry." In
the same letter, he couldn't resist a jab, though it was ever so slight: "Your
failing memory will in time necessitate some slight readjustment of firm
matters but you need not give it further thought for some weeks to come."

In the village of Sunset, Olmsted was tossing and turning through almost every night. He paged blankly through yellowed periodicals he
found in the cottage. He grew fixated on the idea that John was planning
a coup designed to deny Rick his rightful place in the firm. There was a
terrible logic to this thought. John was his stepson. Frederick Law Olmsted Jr. was his natural son, his namesake, the vehicle of his legacy.

Even as his condition deteriorated, Olmsted had moments of lucidity.
That's the curse of such conditions: periodic insight into how far one has
declined and a sense of what lies ahead. As a consequence, Olmsted's
Deer Isle correspondence has a schizoid quality. Hectoring letters alter-
nate with contrite letters, where he acknowledges that he's unwell and
has been unkind. He wrote an especially poignant one to partner Eliot,
who had not escaped rough treatment. "In my flurry I have done some
things which I would not do now and for which I am sorry," he wrote by
way of apology. Then he added: "You cannot think how I have been

dreading that it would be thought *expedient* that I should be sent to an 'institution.' *Anything* but that. My father was a director of an Insane Retreat, and first and last, having been professionally employed and behind the scenes in several, my dread of such *places* is *intense.*"

The very next day, his mood had taken an entirely different turn. Mary wrote to John, complaining that Olmsted was "in a dreadful state—he makes me nervous he is so violent." Apparently, Olmsted never attacked Mary physically. But as his conditioned worsened, he would throw a box at a caretaker and would also beat a horse. "Do not tell anyone that your father's state is pitiful," Mary continued. "Let us keep it to ourselves as long as we can—else his name will be useless to the business."

Mary had faced her share of life's emergencies. She handled this latest with equanimity. Even the decision to bring her husband to Deer Isle was practical. The place was an island, after all. And Mary was a very small woman. Here, it was possible to let her increasingly troubled and belligerent husband move about freely, or at least be under the illusion that he had some control. But Mary assured John that he needn't worry about Olmsted's slipping back to the Brookline office: "We have adopted the policy of letting him do as he likes so long as he does not offer to go off the island."

Mostly, Olmsted passed his time inside his own fevered brain. While he sent a stream of letters to his partners, he sent a raging river to Rick. "I am lying awake nights in a perplexed state of mind about Biltmore affairs and your professional training, especially in matters of foliage. I am not sure that the object of your being at Biltmore is being accomplished." In another, Olmsted wrote, "Observe, inquire, read, discuss all such matters, all you can. Don't be content with off-hand statements and explanations. Read, compare, inquire, cross-examine. Keep at this sort of work in *every* department, until you have sucked every source of information dry. . . . Make the most of the *special* Biltmore opportunity."

Olmsted couldn't stop thinking about Rick, and he couldn't stop sending letters to him. "I write only in yielding to a constant impulse," begins one missive, "vain tho' I feel it to be, to be doing something for you." And from another letter: "I am thinking more of you, these bitter days, than of anybody and all else. . . . It is not childishness. It is the assurance that you are taking up what I am dropping."

Whenever Rick responded, Olmsted was ecstatic. "You cannot think how much your long letter of 5th October interests and gratifies me," Olmsted wrote. "I will confess to you that twice last night I lighted my bed lamp to read it over *again*. It has been the most satisfactory circumstance of my life here."

This particular letter to Rick is one of Olmsted's last and one of his most heartrending. On those occasions when the fog of his disease cleared, the old Olmsted was visible—penetrating, aware, humane. Olmsted related how during his boyhood, away at some poor country parsonage, he had been forced to memorize a passage from the book of Ecclesiastes. The passage related to life's fleetingness. As a young boy, he told Rick, it struck him as incredible that the years ahead might pass so quickly. But they had. Now, he found himself wonder struck once again to have reached life's end. "And now, before I know it, before I am in the least prepared for it, I am there," he wrote to Rick. Olmsted concluded the letter: "I love you and take joy in you with all my heart. Your father."

Olmsted continued to decline. Caring for him on Deer Isle finally proved too difficult, even for Mary. So she brought her husband back to Brookline, where a doctor examined him and made recommendations about the future course of his treatment. Incredibly, the doctor held out hope that a cure for Olmsted might still be possible—or at the very least, his condition might be mitigated. But he shouldn't be treated anywhere in the Northeast. Proximity to his Brookline office would be agitating. Despite its therapeutic climate, the South was out, too. It would only make him pine for the Biltmore Estate. Instead, the doctor suggested that Olmsted be taken to England, where the treatment of nervous disorders (as this was termed) was supposedly more advanced than in the United States.

Olmsted wrote Rick, begging to be sent photos of his beloved Biltmore. He feared, correctly, that he would never set foot in Asheville again.

The Biltmore was his swan song. The winding three-mile approach road is one of his finest designs. And his call to create a model forest was quite simply prophetic. Within a few years, America's first forestry school—an idea that Olmsted and Pinchot had dreamed up together— would be established on Vanderbilt's land. That's why the Biltmore Estate is sometimes called the "cradle of U.S. forestry." As for Pinchot, he would soon leave Vanderbilt's employ to head up the forestry division of the Department of Interior. When Teddy Roosevelt transferred the division to the Agriculture Department, it was renamed the U.S. Forest Service, and Pinchot became its first chief. Years in the future, following Vanderbilt's death, 83,398 acres of the estate would be sold to the government for safekeeping. That land would become the core of North Carolina's Pisgah National Forest, one of the largest woodland preserves east of the Mississippi.

On November 16, 1895, Olmsted departed Boston for Liverpool aboard the *Cephalonia*. Mary and Marion accompanied him. So did Rick, who planned to help get his father settled in England. Despite all the anxiety and ink expended on the Biltmore, there wasn't really much work left to be done there.

Rick rented a two-story house in Lympstone, a village in the county of Devon. Then he returned to the States. Mary arranged for Olmsted to be cared for by Dr. Rayner, the nervous-disorder specialist with whom Olmsted had stayed during his previous visit to England. His treatment wasn't any more effective this time around. "I am going down hill rapidly," Olmsted wrote to John back in Brookline.

Unknown to Olmsted, there was tragic news of Vaux. Mary was aware of it, but she elected to shelter her husband from the details for as long as possible. On November 19—while Olmsted had been onboard the *Cephalonia*—Vaux had drowned. Apparently, he'd been taking a sunset walk on Brooklyn's Gravesend Bay, when he'd slipped off a pier. When his body was found two days later, he was missing his hat, one shoe—and his spectacles.

Vaux was seventy-one, and his health, along with his architectural practice, had been failing for some time now. He was also deeply lonely: His wife had died a few years earlier in a carriage accident. Such details led to natural speculation that Vaux's death was a suicide. In fact, a man told the *Brooklyn Eagle* that he'd encountered Vaux on the pier and found his demeanor curious. The point is moot. Slip or jump, the water had pulled tiny Vaux down then deeper all the same, just as it had Andrew Jackson Downing, his beloved mentor, all those years earlier.

Mary could keep the news from Olmsted for only so long. She felt honor bound to inform him about Vaux's death. When she finally did, to her surprise, Olmsted appeared weirdly energized. It gave him something to do: Olmsted announced that he planned to write a fitting tribute to his old friend and partner. But in the next moment, the matter slipped from his mind.

About the only sustained pleasure that Olmsted managed was sitting by the side of a pond, watching ducks splash. His condition was so upsetting to sensitive Marion that Mary worried her daughter would "go off" like Charlotte. Mary rarely mentioned her other daughter, away in an institution. No one in the family did; it was easier that way.

One thing was becoming clear: This English experiment wasn't working. Earlier, Mary had purchased 46 acres of land on Deer Isle. Now, she wrote to John asking him to arrange for a house to be built there. She planned to move back to Maine and to care for Olmsted. Of course, she planned to have help this time, such as a live-in housekeeper and a nurse. "I am quite equal to looking after him three hours a day and that is all," Mary wrote in a letter to Brookline, addressed to her "dear boys"—John and Rick. She added: "I *really can not* sketch out a scheme of life—I feel too old." Mary was sixty-six, nearly a decade younger than her husband. She had always been tough. But this was taking its toll.

In a separate letter to John and Rick, Marion drew a plan for the house and the surrounding grounds. It includes a small body of water, marked *pond*, with a tiny sketch of a duck. Marion was showing an interest in the family line of work.

Before returning to America, there was a matter that Mary wanted to attend to—alone. She placed Marion on a ship and sent her back to the States. She parked Olmsted with a caretaker. Then Mary traveled to the Continent. In Geneva, she visited the house where her sons John and Owen had been born. She arranged to have a photo taken of the place. And she went to Nice, where she visited the grave of John Hull Olmsted, her first husband, Fred's brother. Mary was distressed to find the grave site in a neglected state. She arranged to have some repairs done. Then Mary returned to England, gathered up Olmsted, and sailed for America.

By early 1897, Mary and Olmsted were moved into the new house in Maine. It featured a little pond, just as Marion had prescribed. Mary dubbed the place Felsted. She sorely wanted to abide by her husband's wish to be cared for in a home setting. But Deer Isle didn't work the second time around, either. Olmsted's condition was just too far advanced. Sometimes he sat for hours watching the ducks, his blue eyes glazed and empty. Those were his good days. On bad days, his eyes filled up with uncomprehending rage.

In September 1898, the family made the painful decision to commit Olmsted to the McLean Asylum. This was the very institution for which he had designed the grounds years earlier. On becoming a patient, he reputedly said, "They didn't carry out my plan, confound them!"

By this point, John and Rick were business partners. The new firm was called Olmsted Brothers. John was forty-six and had been a landscape architect for years. Rick was twenty-eight and had no formal training. Then again, neither did his father, nor anybody else in this era. Luckily, Rick turned out to share his father's awesome ability for conceptualizing landscapes. Surely, parts of this talent were inherited. In the years ahead, he would create a whole other set of incredible spaces and places, scattered all over the United States. Of course, he would collaborate with John and others in the growing practice. But Frederick Law Olmsted Jr. was the driving force.

As for John, he had taken Rick into the partnership without any outward fuss. In his letter to Rick announcing the decision, he was coolly composed as always: "I said you could come in January 1st. I meant in name only because our fiscal year is February 1st."

What choice did John have anyway? He wasn't about to go against the wishes of his father, even if his father was in no condition to object. Furthermore, John recognized that Rick would be an asset. And John certainly knew the value of working with someone who was a visionary. He'd done so his entire adult life.

CHAPTER 32

Fade

LATE SUMMER OF 1903, a call was received at Fairsted from McLean. Olmsted was unconscious, his breathing terribly labored. He was not expected to live very much longer. Mary, John, and Rick raced to the institution in nearby Belmont, Massachusetts. They began a bedside vigil, but when Olmsted continued to hang on, John and Mary went home. Rick remained by his father's bedside. At two o'clock in the morning on August 28, 1903, Olmsted died. He was eighty-one.

Three days later a funeral service was held at Fairsted. It was a small affair, attended only by immediate family. Olmsted's body was cremated, and his ashes were placed in the family vault in Hartford's Old North Cemetery.

Olmsted's final years were isolated and apparently empty. Time was, he'd crafted landscapes, written books, blanketed the country in travel, generated more letters than seems humanly possible. But five long years at McLean had been passed by Olmsted in a kind of hush. During this time, a new century had dawned, with new promise and new problems. There were dazzling new inventions. The call that had summoned his family to McLean came via a telephone, an innovation just beginning to appear in American homes. Perhaps Olmsted was dimly aware of all this change, more likely not.

For those final years, Frederick Law Olmsted—a man capable of such epic drive, full of passion and moral fervor and creativity and unquenchable energy, so central to his times—had been slowly fading from this world.

EPILOGUE

Olmsted's Wild Garden

YET HE'S STILL with us. In the course of his career, Olmsted designed more than thirty major city parks, the U.S. Capitol grounds, and such planned communities as Riverside, Illinois, and Druid Hills in Atlanta. His work on campuses included Stanford, Amherst, and American University in Washington, D.C., and assorted other places such as the grounds of Moraine Farm in Beverly, Massachusetts.

He died uncertain whether any of his creations would survive into the future. His proposition—maintain valuable center-city land as green space—was tenuous and vulnerable to the developers of housing tracts and racetracks and shopping districts. But Olmsted's worst fears haven't been realized. Instead, his creations have become centerpieces, points of pride for scores of communities across the country. Far from receding, Olmsted's influence has only increased in the century since his death, growing and spreading like the Ramble, his beloved wild garden.

Olmsted Brothers turned out to be a smashing success, far beyond anything he could reasonably have expected. Just as Olmsted was the foremost landscape architect of the nineteenth century, the firm run by John and Rick became the preeminent practice for a new age. Much of its business involved circling back around to Olmsted's original creations to do maintenance or to add modern touches such as swimming pools. Olmsted Brothers did such work on their father's parks in Chicago, Louisville, and Rochester as well as Mountain View Cemetery. In 1908, the firm revised a plan for Bryn Mawr College that Olmsted had done some work on in the spring of 1895—one of his very last projects.

Over time, Olmsted Brothers also built up an impressive list of original works such as Memorial Park in Maplewood, New Jersey, the grounds of the University of Idaho, and the Seattle park system.

Frederick Law Olmsted Jr. fulfilled his uneasy destiny and truly became "leader of the van." He helped Harvard, his alma mater, to set up the first university course in landscape architecture ever offered in America. Following in his father's footsteps, he also became a pioneering environmentalist. When the bill to create the National Park Service was written in 1916, Rick contributed some of the key language and phrases. He helped establish national parks in the Everglades, the Great Smoky Mountains, and Acadia in Maine.

Rick also served alongside Daniel Burnham on the prestigious McMillan Commission, which reorganized various Washington, D.C., public spaces such as the Mall, the White House grounds, and Jefferson Memorial into a more coherent scheme. This experience pushed him into urban planning, far further than his father ever ventured. He drew up plans for the future growth of cities such as Detroit, Pittsburgh, and Boulder, Colorado. He also designed Forest Hills Gardens, a lovely and verdant 147-acre community smack in the middle of New York City (the community is not to be confused with nearby Forest Hills). This is Olmsted junior's masterpiece as surely as Central Park is his father's. Robert A. M. Stern, dean of the Yale school of architecture, recently described Forest Hills Gardens as "one of the finest planned communities ever."

Olmsted Brothers carried on—in one form or another—for many decades. Along the way, the firm employed such notables as Frank Lloyd Wright Jr. and Arthur Shurcliff, known among other things as the landscape architect of Colonial Williamsburg. Marion Olmsted, who never married and continued to live at Fairsted, was also involved in the family business. A talented photographer, she took pictures of sites and reputedly even did some drafting work. But this was a different era, so the contributions of an Olmsted sister to Olmsted *Brothers* success—unsigned and uncredited—are impossible to reconstruct.

The firm continued well beyond John's death in 1920, one year before Mary's death. It was still going strong when Marion died in 1948. It even outlasted Rick, who retired in 1949 and died in 1957.

After there were no brothers involved in the business, the name was changed to Olmsted Associates (never mind that no Olmsteds were involved, period). The name held considerable equity, enough to propel the firm to 1980—when the offices moved from Brookline to Fremont, New Hampshire—enough even to carry it all the way to 2000. In the final year of the millennium, the business finally shut down. By then, the impact on the American landscape of Frederick Law Olmsted and his successors was—quite simply—indelible.

Olmsted's influence also extends far beyond his own firm. From 1857 onward, there isn't a single U.S. landscape architect that doesn't owe a debt to Olmsted. During his lifetime, he provided counsel not only to William Hammond Hall of Golden Gate Park but also Horace Cleveland, who designed the Minneapolis and Omaha park systems. Olmsted also carried on an active correspondence with George Kessler, the prolific designer of Houston's Hermann Park; Deming Park in Terre Haute, Indiana; Overton Park in Memphis; and a variety of other places. Not one of these is an Olmsted park, yet his fingerprints—the naturalistic designs, emphasis on ease of use, bold feats of engineering when necessary—are all over them.

Olmsted's reach extends to the current era, to such modern landscape architects as Peter Walker. Considered one of the field's preeminent practitioners, Walker has designed a vast array of spaces, including Burnett Park in Fort Worth, Texas; the grounds of a new airport in Bangkok; and the campus surrounding Pixar's Emeryville, California, headquarters. In 2004, Walker's San Francisco firm won a competition to design a memorial on the site of New York City's World Trade Center. "With my work, I always keep in mind that the goal is creating something socially useful," Walker told me. "I think that comes mostly from Olmsted. That social vision is the thing that defines his greatness."

Olmsted also left behind a formidable literary legacy. During the 1850s, his dispatches from the South were among the first works to "signal" (in the words of his friend Edwin Godkin) that the *New York Times* was a serious paper devoted to vital issues. *The Cotton Kingdom*, the abridged version of Olmsted's Southern trilogy, first published in 1861, remains in print to this day. While in prison, Malcolm X read *The Cotton Kingdom* and later credited Olmsted with providing a startlingly unvarnished look at the institution of slavery. In an introduction to the 1953 edition, historian Arthur Schlesinger described *The Cotton Kingdom* as "the nearest thing posterity has to an exact transcription of a civilization which time has tinted with hues of romantic legend."

Olmsted was also involved in the startup of the *Nation* and helped steer that publication on to its course as a prominent left-leaning journal devoted to broad inquiry. Since then, the *Nation* has featured an incredibly varied group of contributors: George Orwell, Ralph Nader, Hannah Arendt, Langston Hughes, Hunter S. Thompson, and Naomi Klein.

And then there are all the names and terms that have entered the language—Olmsted loved to come up with these. Drive down any divided road, even one of terribly modest and uninspired design, and chances are it will be called a "parkway," a term coined by Olmsted and Vaux. Visit the wild section of a fair, filled with rides and carnival barkers, and chances are it will be called the "midway." That's a nod to the Midway Plaisance, a stretch of Olmsted and Vaux's original 1871 Chicago parks plan that wound up housing the Ferris wheel and other attractions during the 1893 World's Fair. Or you could visit Millbrae, California. In 1865, Bank of California president Darius Mills rejected Olmsted's design for his estate. But the name Olmsted suggested stuck, and today Millbrae is a community of 20,000 people just south of San Francisco International Airport. And then there's Fenway Park. The home of the Boston Red Sox takes its name from the nearby place that Olmsted called the Back Bay Fens.

Yes, Olmsted is still very much with us. You can read his work; let one of his choice phrases "fall trippingly from your tongue," as he once put it. Better yet, you can visit one of his green spaces. These transcendent creations provide a window into his spirit as surely as regarding the *Starry Night* will rouse Van Gogh.

Perhaps you have a favorite Olmsted spot. I know I do. I walk down the steps of Central Park's Bethesda Terrace, past the *Angel of the Waters* statue, and make my way to the edge of the Lake. Then I follow the shoreline to the Bow Bridge and walk across. I like to stand at the water's edge, soaking up this peerless composition: Vaux's beautiful bridge, both spanning the Lake and reflected in the Lake, and Olmsted's untamed Ramble all around.

But this is so far beyond a mere work of landscape architecture. Looking around, I'm always struck by the variety of people—every income group, every nationality, young and old, enjoying a dizzying number of different activities. Here it is, the twenty-first century, and one of Central Park's original purposes remains very much intact. In the truest sense, this place belongs to everyone. I think Olmsted would be proud.

NOTES

KEY

Unless otherwise indicated, correspondence is from the Frederick Law Olmsted Papers, Manuscript Division, Library of Congress, Washington, D.C.

Loeb Library: Used to cite letters from the John Charles Olmsted Papers, Francis Loeb Library, Graduate School of Design, Harvard University, Cambridge, Massachusetts.

NYPL: New York Public Library.

Papers: Used to cite the multivolume collection of Olmsted's writings, reports, and other documents edited by Charles Beveridge. On first reference, a full citation of the volume will be provided; for example, *The Papers of Frederick Law Olmsted*, vol. 1, *The Formative Years* (Baltimore: John Hopkins University Press, 1977). Subsequent citations of the same volume will use an abbreviated form, with the volume and page numbers separated by a colon, as in *Papers*, 1:30.

The following initials will be used for frequently cited figures:

FLO = Frederick Law Olmsted (subject)
FLO Jr. = Frederick Law Olmsted Jr. (son)
JO = John Olmsted (father)
JCO = John Charles Olmsted (stepson)
JHO = John Hull Olmsted (brother)
JM = Justin Martin (biographer)
MAO = Mary Ann Olmsted (stepmother)
MPO = Mary Perkins Olmsted (wife)

Introduction: Why Olmsted Matters

1   "**Each of you knows**": Daniel Burnham speech of March 25, 1893, Ryerson and Burnham Libraries, the Art Institute of Chicago.
2   "**I was born for**": FLO to JHO, March 27, 1856.
4   "**When Olmsted is blue**": George Templeton Strong, *Diary of the Civil War, 1860–1865* (New York: Macmillan, 1962), 243.

Chapter 1: So Very Young

7   **During this period, Hartford:** Lee Paquette, *Only More So: The History of East Hartford, 1783–1976* (East Hartford, CT: Raymond Library, 1976), 29.

8   **In 1632, this original:** Henry King Olmsted and George Kemp Ward, *Genealogy of the Olmsted Family in America* (New York: A. T. De La Mare Printing and Publishing, 1912), x.

8   **Voting records show:** Paquette, *Only More So*, 31.

8   **Fred's very first memory:** FLO, "Passages in the Life of an Unpractical Man," reprinted in FLO Jr. and Theodora Kimball, eds., *Forty Years of Landscape Architecture*, vol. 1 (New York: G. P. Putnam's Sons, 1922).

9   **suffering from postpartum depression:** For more on this topic, see Melvin Kalfus, *Frederick Law Olmsted: The Passion of a Public Artist* (New York: New York University Press, 1990), 96.

9   **she had attended:** MAO to JHO, April 14, 1846.

9   **"I chanced to stray":** Autobiographical fragment, undated, FLO Papers, Library of Congress.

9   **"No a/c kept":** JO diary, March 12, 1826, FLO Papers, Library of Congress.

10   **"celebrated beauty of the day":** *Life of Harriet Beecher Stowe: Compiled from Her Letters and Journals*, pt. 2 (Boston: Houghton Mifflin, 1890), 30.

11   **To learn grammar:** Books FLO used drawn from JO diary and Theodora Kimball's notes for *Forty Years of Landscape Architecture*, both in Library of Congress.

11   **"The way of man":** Noah Webster, *The American Spelling Book* (Hartford: Hudson, 1822), 43.

12   **"infinite love":** Autobiographical Fragment A, FLO Papers, Library of Congress.

12   **"Miss Naomi Rockwell buried":** JO diary, February 8, 1829.

13   **"I was strangely uneducated":** FLO to Elizabeth Baldwin Whitney, December 16, 1890.

13   **Fred headed out:** Details regarding FLO childhood rambles drawn mostly from Autobiographical Fragment A.

14   **"I was under no":** Ibid.

15   **explored his grandmother's book collection:** Ibid.

15   **"strong discipline":** *Hartford Courant*, January 19, 1830.

15   **"I was very active, imaginative":** Autobiographical fragment, reprinted in *The Papers of Frederick Law Olmsted*, vol. 1, *The Formative Years* (Baltimore: Johns Hopkins University Press, 1977), 110.

16   **Fred lived with three:** Details of life with Joab Brace drawn mostly from Autobiographical Fragment A.

17   **poison sumac:** Autobiographical Fragment B, FLO Papers, Library of Congress.

17   **Reverend George Clinton Van Vechten Eastman:** *Papers*, 1:110.

18   **"we begin to feel":** JO to FLO, Oct 7, 1838.

19   **"I hear Fred'k coming":** JO to JHO, 1840 [no month or day specified].

19   **"Dear brother," begins a letter:** FLO to JHO, June 9, 1840.

20   **Mrs. Howard's boardinghouse:** Laura Wood Roper, *FLO: A Biography of Frederick Law Olmsted* (Baltimore: Johns Hopkins University Press, 1973), 18.

20   **He hated the job:** Evidence that Olmsted hated working at Benkard and Hutton drawn from FLO to JHO, August 29, 1840, and FLO to Charles Brace, June 22, 1845.

Chapter 2: At Sea

21   **As captain of the *Huntress*:** Henry King Olmsted and George Kemp Ward, *Genealogy of the Olmsted Family in America* (New York: A. T. De La Mare Printing and Publishing, 1912), 36.

21 **In 1777, Olmsted was:** Joseph Olcott Goodwin, *East Hartford: Its History and Traditions* (Hartford: Case, Lockwood, and Brainard, 1879), 83–84.

22 **teamed up with Jim Goodwin:** *Papers*, 1:136.

23 **Fox impressed Fred:** FLO to JHO, April 8, 1843.

23 **"Now's the time":** Ibid.

24 **an almanac, a sea chest:** Laura Wood Roper, *FLO: A Biography of Frederick Law Olmsted* (Baltimore: Johns Hopkins University Press, 1973), 22.

24 **"drowndered":** FLO to JHO, April 10, 1843.

24 **nearly thirty other ships:** FLO's *Ronaldson* voyage diary covering April 24–August 9, 1843, FLO Papers, Library of Congress.

24 **To shed some weight:** FLO, "A Voice from the Sea," *American Whig Review*, December 1851.

25 **Fred was put to work:** Details about Olmsted's shipboard duties from FLO's *Ronaldson* voyage diary, Library of Congress.

25 **get to his sea chest:** FLO to parents, August 6, 1843.

25 **"Bah!":** Foul-food dialogue from FLO's *Ronaldson* voyage diary.

27 **"set the lee foretopmast":** Nautical lingo taken from various letters FLO wrote while onboard the *Ronaldson*.

27 **A sailor lost his purchase:** FLO to parents, August 6, 1843.

27 **Then Fred fell:** FLO to JHO, December 10, 1843.

27 **furl the sails:** FLO's *Ronaldson* voyage diary.

28 **captain's-table prerogative:** FLO to parents, September 5, 1843.

29 **Fox did not swear:** FLO to JHO, December 10, 1843.

29 **"Well, he's a most":** Ibid.

30 **"My opportunities of observation":** FLO to JO, September 24, 1843.

31 **"I've heard much more":** FLO to JHO, December 10, 1843.

31 **"But I was glad":** FLO to Maria Olmsted, November 30, 1843.

32 **"What are you taking":** Details of temple visit from "The Real China," an unpublished essay that Olmsted wrote in 1856, reprinted in *Papers*, 1:187.

32 **"turkeys & cranberry":** FLO to Maria Olmsted, November 30, 1843.

32 **"Fred's company much wanted":** JO diary, November 30, 1843.

32 **the fresher the tea:** Witold Rybczynski, *A Clearing in the Distance: Frederick Law Olmsted and America in the Nineteenth Century* (New York: Scribner, 1999), 53–54.

33 **flogged him repeatedly:** Details and dialogue from near-mutiny episode drawn from "A Voice from the Sea."

33 **On April 20, 1844:** Date taken from Theodora Kimball's notes for *Forty Years of Landscape Architecture*.

34 **looking yellow and skeletal:** MPO memo, FLO Papers, Library of Congress.

34 **"Well, how do you":** FLO to JHO, December 10, 1843.

Chapter 3: Uncommon Friends

35 **sat nearly an entire day:** FLO to Brace, July 30, 1846.

36 **Brace came from a family:** Description of Brace drawn from multiple sources, including *The Life of Charles Loring Brace*, ed. Emma Brace (New York: Charles Scribner's Sons, 1894).

37 **"Intense earnestness":** Ibid., 8.

37 **"uncommon set of common friends":** Letter from Brace to Frederick Kingsbury in 1846, quoted in ibid., 27.

37 "honorary member of the Class of '47": FLO Jr. and Theodora Kimball, eds., *Forty Years of Landscape Architecture*, vol. 1 (New York: G. P. Putnam's Sons, 1922), 5.

38 "Infantile Chemistry Association": FLO to Brace, July 30, 1846.

38 "I have a smattering education": FLO to Kingsbury, June 12, 1846, typed version in "Kingsbury Sketch," Library of Congress.

39 "'Twas a fine day": FLO to JHO, September 13, 1845.

39 "He has dreamed about": MAO to JO, August 8, 1844.

40 "I am desperately in love": FLO to Brace, February 5, 1845.

40 "rouse a sort of scatter-brained pride": FLO to Elizabeth Baldwin Whitney, December 16, 1890.

40 "Governor's daughter. Excellent princess": FLO to Brace, February 5, 1846.

40 "private opportunity": FLO to JHO, March 2, 1846.

41 "right smack & square": FLO to JHO, March 27, 1846.

42 "self-examination was carried": *Life of Harriet Beecher Stowe: Compiled from Her Letters and Journals*, pt. 2 (Boston: Houghton Mifflin, 1890), 35.

42 "I think there is nothing": MAO to JHO, March 1846 [no day specified in letter].

42 "how highly bless'd": MAO to JHO, April 3, 1846.

42 "Thank God for Miss Baldwin": FLO to Brace, March 27, 1846.

43 "God's fever attended me": FLO to JHO, April 7, 1846.

44 "any inclination for Agriculture": FLO to Brace, June 22, 1845.

44 just a few hundred feet: Geddes obituary, *New York Times*, October 9, 1883.

44 "Geddes Canal": Detail from Daniel Klein and John Majewski, *Promoters and Investors in Antebellum America: The Spread of Plank Road Fever* (Berkeley: University of California Transportation Center, 1991).

44 variety of different foodstuffs: Details about Fairmount farm such as acreage and what was grown there drawn from the *Cultivator*, July 1846.

44 "grind a bushel": FLO to JO, July 23, 1846.

44 inventor of the Geddes' Harrow: Details about Geddes's inventions from Klein and Majewski, *Promoters and Investors in Antebellum America*.

45 "I do think Carlyle": FLO to JO, August 12, 1846.

46 "Up, up! Whatsoever thy hand": Thomas Carlyle, *Sartor Resartus* (Boston: James Munroe, 1840), 200.

46 copied it into a letter to his brother: FLO to JHO, December 13, 1846.

46 "silver forks every day": FLO to JO, July 1, 1846.

Chapter 4: A Farmer and Finite

48 As he spelled out: FLO to JHO, September 1846 [no day specified in letter].

49 But the farm itself: Description of Sachem's Head farm taken largely from "Kingsbury Sketch," FLO Papers, Library of Congress.

49 "Real juicy": FLO to JHO, February 16, 1847.

50 "I don't believe": JHO to Kingsbury, March 27, 1847.

50 "fine capabilities": JHO to Kingsbury, May 1847 [no day specified in letter].

50 "I hope the present": JHO to Kingsbury, March 13, 1847.

50 "It is pretty much": Kingsbury to JHO, May 8, 1847.

50 very first published works: *Boston Cultivator*, March 13, 1847, as referenced in *Papers*, 1:290.

51 "F. L. Olmsted, Sachem's Head": *Horticulturist*, August 1847.

51 "There's a great *work*": FLO to Brace, July 26, 1847.

52 "so far look bountifully": Ibid.

52 "Well, the world needs": Kingsbury to JHO, May 8, 1847.

53 belonged to Dr. Samuel Akerly: Description of Tosomock Farm drawn from multiple sources including *Staten Island Historian* (January–March 1954) and "Kingsbury Sketch."

54 Olmsted considered "Entepfuhl": FLO to Kingsbury, November 17, 1848.

54 "Here I am now": Ibid.

54 a corruption of Tesschenmakr: *Staten Island Historian* (October–December 1953); FLO to William James, July 8, 1891.

54 "One thing, Fred": JHO to Kingsbury, March 1848 [no day specified in letter].

54 transforming the property: *Staten Island Historian* (January–March 1954).

55 Increasingly, Staten Island: Description of Staten Island drawn partly from Charles Leng and William Davis, *Staten Island and Its People: A History, 1609–1929* (New York: Lewis Historical Publishing, 1930).

56 "But the amount of talking": Letter from Brace to Kingsbury, September 30, 1848, quoted in *The Life of Charles Loring Brace*, ed. Emma Brace (New York: Charles Scribner's Sons, 1894), 61.

56 Olmsted began making improvements: "Kingsbury Sketch."

57 William Vanderbilt even requested: *Staten Island Historian* (April–June 1954).

57 learned that King Louis Philippe: Ibid.

57 "Here are two close": FLO to Kingsbury, December 13, 1848.

58 "just the thing for": FLO to Kingsbury, July 16, 1848.

58 "A marriageable young lady": JHO to Kingsbury, December 11, 1849.

59 "nothing but Hog-French": JHO to Kingsbury, October 30, 1848.

60 "We ask you, then": FLO, "Appeal to the Citizens of Staten Island," December 1849, reprinted in *Papers,* 1:331–334.

60 "For the matter of": FLO to Brace, June 22, 1845.

Chapter 5: Two Pilgrimages

61 "I have a just": FLO to JO, March 1, 1850.

62 costing them $12 apiece: FLO, *Walks and Talks of an American Farmer in England* (Amherst, MA: Library of American Landscape History, 2002), Charles McLaughlin's introduction, xxv.

63 had to see Birkenhead Park: Description of Olmsted's visit to the park, ibid., 90–96.

63 Olmsted's first brush: Description of first visit to English countryside, ibid., 98–99.

64 Crosskill's Patent Clod-Crusher Roller: Ibid., 192.

64 grounds of Chirk Castle: Description of Olmsted's visit to Chirk Castle, ibid., 224–225.

65 71¢ per day: FLO to JO, August 11, 1850.

65 "The fact is evident": FLO to Brace, November 12, 1850.

66 "The mere fact of": FLO to Brace, January 11, 1851.

67 His pronouncements, delivered: Characterization of Downing's aesthetics drawn from assorted issues of the *Horticulturist* and August 14, 2009, interview, JM with Francis Kowsky, author of *Country, Park, and City: The Architecture and Life of Calvert Vaux* (New York: Oxford University Press, 1998).

68 "A Note on the True": *Horticulturist*, December 1852.

69   "one farmer's leg": FLO, *Walks and Talks*, preface, 1859 edition, 9.

69   "Sit ye down now": Ibid., 212.

69   "What artist so noble": Ibid., 145.

70   "As it is": FLO to Brace, January 11, 1851.

70   "The sun shines": FLO to Brace, November 12, 1850.

70   "The conclusion is": FLO to Kingsbury, February 10, 1849.

71   "Sit erect when you": JO to JHO [undated].

71   "sentence of death": JHO to Kingsbury, August 11, 1851.

71   tuberculosis was an "incipient" form: FLO to Kingsbury, August 5, 1851.

71   "revulsion of feeling": JHO to Kingsbury, September 12, 1851.

72   "I am to be examined": JHO to Kingsbury, October 12, 1851.

72   "seems to me somebody": FLO to JO, November 21, 1851.

Chapter 6: "The South"

74   **During its first year:** Account of *Uncle Tom's Cabin* sales from "Tomitudes," *Putnam's Monthly Magazine*, January 1853.

74   **In Boston alone, three hundred:** Janet Badia and Jennifer Phegley, *Reading Women: Literary Figures and Cultural Icons from the Victorian Age to the Present* (Toronto: University of Toronto Press, 2005), 66.

75   **Olmsted remained a gradualist:** Characterization of Olmsted as a gradualist drawn from FLO, *Walks and Talks of an American Farmer in England* (Amherst, MA: Library of American Landscape History, 2002), 241, and FLO to JO, August 12, 1846.

76   **forebears had been slaveholders:** Support for Olmsted's forebears as slaveholders drawn from Lee Paquette, *Only More So: The History of East Hartford, 1783–1976* (East Hartford, CT: Raymond Library, 1976), 234.

76   **"red hot abolitionist":** FLO to Kingsbury, October 17, 1852.

77   **On the decline:** Elmer Holmes Davis, *History of the "New York Times," 1851–1921* (New York: New York Times, 1921), 7.

78   **"diverting the public mind":** *New York Sun* article quoted in Frank Luther Mott, *American Journalism: A History, 1690–1960*, vol. 2 (New York: Macmillan, 1962), 226.

78   **"We do not mean":** Prospectus, quoted in Davis, *History of the "New York Times,"* 21.

78   **Circulation had immediately shrunk:** Ibid., 26.

78   **"matter of fact matter":** FLO to Kingsbury, October 17, 1852.

79   **tailed a funeral procession:** Description of funeral procession from FLO, *A Journey Through the Seaboard Slave States* (New York: Mason Brothers, 1861), 24–26.

80   **"You can't imagine":** FLO to Brace, February 23, 1853.

80   **"The mean temperature":** "The South," no. 2, *New-York Daily Times*, February 19, 1853.

80   **In a letter to his father:** FLO to JO, January 10, 1853.

81   **"French friterzeed Dutch flabbergasted":** FLO, *A Journey in the Back Country* (New York: Mason Brothers, 1860), 135.

81   **"This is a hard life":** "The South," no. 2, *New-York Daily Times*, February 19, 1853.

82   **"I lubs 'ou mas'r":** FLO, *Seaboard Slave States*, 434.

82   **"Oh God! Who are we":** "The South," no. 10, *New-York Daily Times*, April 8, 1853.

83   **"They are forever complaining":** "The South," no. 7, *New-York Daily Times*, March 17, 1853.

84 "What! Slaves eager to work": FLO, *Seaboard Slave States*, 355.

85 "If I was free": Ibid., 679.

86 "I reckon a dollar": Ibid., 86.

87 "He tenaciously and patiently": Edmund Wilson, *Patriotic Gore: Studies in the Literature of the American Civil War* (New York: W. W. Norton, 1994), 221.

87 "What that? Hallo!": "The South," no. 44, *New-York Daily Times*, November 21, 1853.

Chapter 7: Tief Im Herzen Von Texas

89 "The *Times*, however": *Savannah Republican*, February 22, 1853.

89 it had returned to 25,000: Francis Brown, *Raymond of the "Times"* (New York: W. W. Norton, 1951), 106.

89 "The *Times* signaled itself": Rollo Ogden, *The Life and Letters of Edwin Lawrence Godkin* (New York: Macmillan, 1907), 113.

90 host of a Greenwich Village salon: Description of Anne Charlotte Lynch's salon drawn largely from Luther Harris, *Around Washington Square: An Illustrated History of Greenwich Village* (Baltimore: Johns Hopkins University Press, 2003), 96.

90 "knew all the distinguished people": FLO to JO, May 19, 1853.

90 "Here was another": FLO, "Gold Under Gilt," *Putnam's Monthly Magazine*, July 1853.

93 "Well, the moral": FLO to Brace, December 1, 1853.

94 "After a little practice": FLO, *A Journey Through Texas* (Lincoln: University of Nebraska Press, 2004), 76.

94 *Drovers* was the appellation: Witold Rybczynski, *A Clearing in the Distance: Frederick Law Olmsted and America in the Nineteenth Century* (New York: Scribner, 1999), 126.

94 "We should have": FLO, *A Journey Through Texas*, 71–72.

95 "She was made up": Ibid., 93.

96 He was surprised: Olmsted's first intimation of Germans in Texas was the copy of *San Antonio Zeitung* encountered in Bastrop, according to his own account in *A Journey Through Texas*, 133, and also Rudolph Biesele, *The History of the Germans in Texas, 1831–1861* (Austin: Press of Von Boeckmann-Jones, 1930), 225.

97 "I have never": FLO, *A Journey Through Texas*, 143.

98 Germans started pouring: Many details about Germans settling in Texas drawn from R. L. Biesele, "The Texas State Convention of Germans in 1854," *Southwestern Historical Quarterly* (April 1930).

98 community of 3,000: FLO, *A Journey Through Texas*, 180–181.

99 "We have no other": Ibid., 150.

100 fifty-seven papers: FLO, "Appeal for Funds for *The San Antonio Zeitung*," October 1854, reprinted in *The Papers of Frederick Law Olmsted*, vol. 2, *Slavery and the South* (Baltimore: Johns Hopkins University Press, 1981), 316.

100 one of five such settlements: Names of the five communities can be found at "Latin Settlements of Texas," *The Handbook of Texas Online*, http://www .tshaonline.org.

100 belted out "student songs": FLO, *A Journey Through Texas*, 198.

101 "But how much of": Ibid., 199.

101 John sent a letter: JHO to MPO, March 12, 1854.

Chapter 8: A Red-Hot Abolitionist

103 **Lately, Douai had become:** Many details of Douai's rift with fellow Germans drawn from Laura Wood Roper, "Frederick Law Olmsted and the Western Texas Free-Soil Movement," *American Historical Review* (October 1950).

104 **"A Few Dollars Wanted":** FLO, "A Few Dollars Wanted to Help the Cause of Future Freedom in Texas," October 1854, reprinted in *Papers*, 2:319–320.

104 **raise more than $200:** Ibid., 320n.

104 **Other Texas papers took aim:** FLO, *A Journey Through Texas* (Lincoln: University of Nebraska Press, 2004), 437.

104 **In a grim irony:** Roper, "Frederick Law Olmsted and the Western Texas Free-Soil Movement."

105 **launching the kindergarten movement:** *Papers*, 2:60–61.

106 **"I can't well write a word":** FLO to Edward Everett Hale, August 23, 1855, letter reprinted in ibid., 362.

106 **Abbott traveled back East:** Many of the details about James Abbott raising money for weapons drawn from W. H. Isley, "The Sharps Rifle Episode in Kansas History," *American Historical Association* (April 1907).

107 **raise more than $300:** FLO to Abbott, October 4, 1855, Kansas State Historical Society collection, accessed online.

107 **He consulted a veteran:** FLO to F. G. Adams, December 24, 1883.

107 **Olmsted sent him a series of letters:** See FLO to Abbott, September 17, October 4, 7, 24, 1855, Kansas State Historical Society collection, accessed online.

107 ***h* for howitzer:** FLO to Abbott, October 4, 1855, Kansas State Historical Society collection, accessed online.

107 **"prompt and energetic friend":** Kansas State Historical Society, "Selections from the Hyatt Manuscripts," *Transactions* 1–2 (1875–1880): 221.

107 **Olmsted's howitzer was mounted:** Account of howitzer's tangled history from Isley, "Sharps Rifle Episode in Kansas History."

Chapter 9: The Literary Republic

108 **"writing as much":** JHO to Bertha Olmsted, January 28, 1855.

109 **Joshua Dix:** Descriptions of Dix and Edwards drawn from a variety of sources, including Arnold Tew, "*Putnam's Magazine*: Its Men and Their Literary and Social Policies," PhD diss., Case Western Reserve University, 1970.

109 **distant relative:** Support for Putnam's being related to Olmsted drawn from *A Memoir of George Palmer Putnam* (New York: G. P. Putnam's Sons, 1903), 339.

110 **apartment at 335 Broadway:** *Papers*, 2:355.

111 **650 magazines in the United States:** John Tebbel and Mary Ellen Zuckerman, *The Magazine in America, 1741–1990* (New York: Oxford University Press, 1991), 8, 25.

111 ***Harper's* simply raided English magazines:** Frank Luther Mott, *American Journalism: A History, 1690–1960*, vol. 2 (New York: Macmillan, 1962), 384.

112 **"If we can get the writers":** FLO to JO, May 28, 1855.

112 ***Putnam's* physical offices:** Secret-office detail drawn from Laura Wood Roper, "'Mr. Law' and *Putnam's Monthly Magazine*: A Note on a Phase in the Career of Frederick Law Olmsted," *American Literature* (March 1954).

113   **"call from a queer fellow"**: FLO to JO, April 13, 1855.

113   **Denison Olmsted**: Detail about acting as consultant to the dictionary from the preface of the revised 1848 edition of *Webster's*, vi.

113   ***mould* to *mold***: Account of Olmsted copyediting changes drawn from *The Writings of Herman Melville: The Piazza Tales, and Other Prose Pieces, 1839–1860* (Evanston, IL: Northwestern University Press, 1987), 561nn.

113   **"hideous Websterian manner"**: George Curtis to Joshua Dix, September 1855, quoted in Tew, *"Putnam's Magazine,"* 94.

113   **"Oliver Basselin"**: The three poems by Longfellow appeared in the May, July, and August issues of *Putnam's*.

113   **"than the *Knickerbocker*"**: *Hartford Courant*, May 22, 1855.

113   **"much the best Mag."**: Curtis to Dix letter, September 7, 1855, quoted in Roper, "'Mr. Law' and *Putnam's*."

114   **"a sort of literary republic"**: FLO to JO, December 9, 1855.

115   **"This ponderosity becomes"**: FLO to JO, November 9, 1855.

115   **"This remarkable book"**: *New York Post*, April 8, 1856.

115   **"the most valuable"**: *Boston Daily Advertiser*, February 18, 1857.

116   **exclusive serial of the Dickens novel**: Miriam Naomi Kotzin, "Putnam's Monthly and Its Place in American Literature," PhD diss., New York University, 1969.

117   **"surprised if Bartholomew"**: FLO to Mary Olmsted, June 7, 1856.

117   **"But then it troubles me"**: FLO to Bertha Olmsted, June 18, 1856, reprinted in *Papers*, 2:380.

117   **Preston Brooks**: Account of Brooks-Sumner incident drawn largely from Allan Nevins, *Ordeal of the Union: A House Dividing, 1852–1857* (New York: Macmillan, 1940), 444–445.

118   **"The position of an American"**: FLO, "How Ruffianism in Washington and Kansas Is Regarded in Europe," *New-York Daily Times*, July 10, 1856.

118   **party that Thackeray threw**: Laura Wood Roper, "Frederick Law Olmsted in the 'Literary Republic,'" *Mississippi Valley Historical Review* (December 1952).

119   **promote his own book**: Ibid.

119   **"fallen off alarmingly"**: JHO to FLO, July 10, 1856.

119   **"Write me in a fever"**: FLO to Dix, August 29, 1856.

120   **"my best book"**: FLO to Mariana Griswold van Rensselaer, June 17, 1893.

121   **"special proneness to violence"**: Thomas Gladstone, *The Englishman in Kansas; or, Squatter Life and Border Warfare* (New York: Miller, 1857), FLO's introduction, viii.

121   **"I much fear"**: FLO to Edward Everett Hale, January 10, 1857, reprinted in *Papers*, 2:398.

121   **purchased by another publisher for $3,400**: Roper, "'Mr. Law' and *Putnam's*."

122   **bankruptcy by William Emerson**: *Papers*, 2:334.

122   **"We failed today!"**: Curtis to FLO, August 15, 1857, reprinted in Tew, *"Putnam's Magazine,"* 117.

Chapter 10: "Is New York Really Not Rich Enough?"

124   **James Alexander Hamilton**: *The Papers of Frederick Law Olmsted*, vol. 3, *Creating Central Park* (Baltimore: Johns Hopkins University Press, 1983), 93.

125   **"What else can I do"**: FLO to JHO, September 11, 1857.

125   **"P.S. After a very"**: Ibid.

126   **memories of Niblo's Garden:** For account of Niblo's, Contoit's, and other early
      New York green spaces, see FLO Jr. and Theodora Kimball, eds., *Forty Years of
      Landscape Architecture,* vol. 2 (New York: G. P. Putnam's Sons, 1922), 21.

127   **Manhattan Island had seventeen parks:** Roy Rosenzweig and Elizabeth Black-
      mar, *The Park and the People* (Ithaca: Cornell University Press, 1992), 19.

127   **"What are called parks in New-York":** *Horticulturist,* October 1850.

127   **"Is New York really not rich":** *Horticulturist,* June 1851.

127   **"very small space":** *New York Post,* June 17, 1851.

127   **"There are no lungs":** *New York Herald,* July 15, 1850.

127   **In 1850, both candidates:** Catherine Fredman, Central Park tour guide, to JM,
      July 14, 2009.

128   **Neither was willing to sell:** Rosenzweig and Blackmar, *The Park and the People,*
      21.

128   **"Give us a park":** *New York Commercial Advertiser,* July 29, 1853.

128   **British troops had once:** David Karabell, Central Park tour guide, to JM, July 1,
      2009.

128   **properties developed along:** Fredman to JM, July 14, 2009.

129   **A pair of bone-boiling plants:** Rosenzweig and Blackmar, *The Park and the Peo-
      ple,* 70.

129   **Seneca Village had 264 residents:** Leslie Alexander, *African or American? Black
      Identity and Political Activism in New York City* (Urbana: University of Illinois
      Press, 2008), 157.

129   **$5,169,369.90:** Figure comes from Clarence Cook, *A Description of the New York
      Central Park* (New York: Benjamin Blom, 1972), 22.

129   **Andrew Williams:** Rosenzweig and Blackmar, *The Park and the People,* 70.

130   **Downing was a skillful swimmer:** Account of Downing's drowning drawn in part
      from interview, August 14, 2009, JM with Francis Kowsky, author of *Country,
      Park, and City: The Architecture and Life of Calvert Vaux* (New York: Oxford Uni-
      versity Press, 1998).

130   **"There is no Downing":** *New York Herald,* September 9, 1857.

131   **"black and unctuous slime":** FLO, "Passages in the Life of an Unpractical Man,"
      reprinted in *Papers,* 3:89–90.

132   **"Everything is black & blacker":** FLO to Samuel Cabot, October 22, 1857,
      reprinted in *Papers,* 2:452.

133   **Many of the desperate job seekers:** Account of menacing workers taken from
      "Influence," an unpublished manuscript fragment by Olmsted and also from *Pa-
      pers,* 3:15.

133   **as little as 3¢ an hour:** Detail from FLO to CP board of commissioners, January
      22, 1861.

133   **"into a capital discipline":** FLO to JO, January 14, 1858.

134   **"Dear dear Fred":** JHO to FLO, November 13, 1857.

134   **"In his death":** JO to FLO, November 28, 1857.

134   **"Don't let Mary suffer":** JHO to FLO, November 13, 1857.

Chapter 11: Right Man, Right Place

135   **Vaux was an architect:** Portrait of Vaux and early work with Downing drawn from
      multiple sources including Francis Kowsky, *Country, Park, and City: The Archi-
      tecture and Life of Calvert Vaux* (New York: Oxford University Press, 1998).

137 **Vaux was a tiny man:** Description of Vaux's appearance and demeanor drawn from interview, JM with Kowsky, August 14, 2009.

137 **"Being thoroughly disgusted":** Vaux, quoted in the *Metropolitan Museum of Art Bulletin* (Winter 2008).

139 **"It would have been difficult":** FLO, "Public Parks and the Enlargement of Towns," reprinted in *Civilizing American Cities: Writings on City Landscapes*, ed. S. B. Sutton (New York: Da Capo Press, 1997), 52.

139 **"go ahead with the Children's Aid":** FLO to Brace, December 1, 1853.

140 **"The Park is intended":** FLO, "Description of the Central Park," reprinted in *Papers*, 3:213.

140 **A large improvised table:** Interview, JM with Kowsky, August 14, 2009.

140 **For their design:** Details regarding Olmsted and Vaux's design taken from the so-called Greensward plan, reprinted in *Papers*, vol. 3.

140 **"who in the best sense":** Greensward plan, reprinted in *Papers*, 3:126.

141 **Jervis McEntee—the notable painter:** Detail that McEntee did paintings for the Greensward submission checked on December 9, 2010, with Kowsky, author of *Country, Park, and City*.

142 **"Only twenty years ago":** Greensward plan, reprinted in *Papers*, 3:120.

143 **By late in the afternoon of March 31, 1858:** Sara Cedar Miller, *Central Park: An American Masterpiece* (New York: Abrams, 2003), 87.

143 **like the world's continents:** *Papers*, 3:112.

143 **plan dubbed "The Eagle":** *New York Post*, April 15, 1858.

144 **"Commonplace and tasteless":** Clarence Cook, *A Description of the New York Central Park* (New York: Benjamin Blom, 1972), 24.

144 **a mysterious submission:** Miller, *Central Park*, 234.

144 **"If, as is not improbable":** Greensward plan, reprinted in *Papers*, 3:132.

145 **"jewels of the Park":** Dillon and Belmont card, *New York Post*, June 10, 1858.

146 **"It is one great purpose":** FLO to CP board of commissioners, May 31, 1858, reprinted in *Papers*, 3:196.

146 **"The contrast will be sudden":** Dillon and Belmont card, *New York Post*, June 10, 1858.

146 **"It is not only":** *New York Courier and Enquirer*, May 31, 1858.

Chapter 12: A Park Is Born

149 **blast caused the very first fatality:** Roy Rosenzweig and Elizabeth Blackmar, *The Park and the People* (Ithaca: Cornell University Press, 1992), 166.

149 **"undignified tricks of disguise":** FLO Jr. and Theodora Kimball, eds., *Forty Years of Landscape Architecture*, vol. 2 (New York: G. P. Putnam's Sons, 1922), 268.

149 **To drain it:** David Karabell, Central Park tour guide, to JM, July 1, 2009.

151 **"Passages of scenery":** Sara Cedar Miller, *Central Park: An American Masterpiece* (New York: Abrams, 2003), 111.

151 **On December 11, 1858:** Date of first day of skating drawn from *New York Tribune*, December 16, 1858.

152 **Diocletian Lewis:** Notion that Lewis's ideas about outdoor fitness contributed to the park's popularity drawn from Clarence Cook, *A Description of the New York Central Park* (New York: Benjamin Blom, 1972), 64.

152 **rented for 10¢ an hour:** Rosenzweig and Blackmar, *The Park and the People*, 229.

152 armchairs for sliding: *New York Post,* January 28, 1862.

152 "Many a young fellow": Guidebook quoted in Rosenzweig and Blackmar, *The Park and the People,* 231.

152 Vaux went skating: Francis Kowsky, *Country, Park, and City: The Architecture and Life of Calvert Vaux* (New York: Oxford University Press, 1998), 138.

153 "members of the homo genus": *New York Herald,* December 20, 1858.

153 "all ages, sexes and conditions": *New York Times,* December 27, 1859.

153 "Masters Richard and William": *New York Herald,* December 17, 1858.

153 "a democratic development": FLO to Parke Godwin, August 1, 1858, reprinted in *Papers,* 3:201.

154 "blessed dandelions": Cook, *Description of Central Park,* 107.

154 boat right into the entrance: Detail checked on December 1, 2010, by JM with Sara Cedar Miller, Central Park Conservancy.

154 Strauss waltzes to Rossini marches: Examples of music taken from concert write-ups that appeared in *New York Herald,* August 28, 1859; *New York Tribune,* September 3, 1860; and *New York Times,* October 9, 1860.

155 orchestra play from the middle of the lake: FLO Jr. and Kimball, *Forty Years of Landscape Architecture,* 2:414.

155 clangs seemed to meld: *New York Herald,* July 31, 1859.

155 "Sabbath cracker": Rosenzweig and Blackmar, *The Park and the People,* 255.

156 thirty-four bridges and archways: Bridge count from the *Metropolitan Museum of Art Bulletin* (Winter 2008).

157 "Nature first, second, and third": Calvert Vaux to Clarence Cook, June 6, 1865, quoted in Louise Chipley Slavicek, *New York City's Central Park* (New York: Infobase Publishing, 2009), 79.

157 "Vast and beautiful": *New York Times,* September 3, 1859.

157 "A royal work": *Atlantic,* April 1861.

157 "Well, they have left it": Cook, *Description of Central Park,* 110.

157 240,000 trees: *Metropolitan Museum of Art Bulletin* (Winter 2008).

158 "red-brown line; indigo-blue moulding": Fred B. Perkins, *The Central Park: Photographed by W. H Guild Jr. with Descriptions and a Historical Sketch by Fred B. Perkins* (New York: Carleton, 1864), 36–37.

158 naturalistic, allegorical, or merely whimsical: Drawn in part from discussion of meaning of Mould carvings in Miller, *Central Park,* 49–53.

158 Secretly, Olmsted thought Green: FLO, manuscript fragment, reprinted in *Papers,* 3:57.

159 "for a rainy day": FLO to Kingsbury, July 16, 1848.

160 On June 13, 1859: *Papers,* 3:11.

Chapter 13: Growling Green

161 "There is not one": FLO to JO, September 23, 1859.

161 "thoroughly worn-out": Ibid.

161 lingo of the day for medicinal spirits: Interview, JM with Terry Reimer, director of research, National Museum of Civil War Medicine, May 7, 2009.

162 After seeing him off: Details of Mary watching boat depart contained in MPO to FLO, October 2, 1859.

163 "Dear little woman": FLO to MPO, October 6, 1859.

163 **On October 11:** Chronology and many details of trip drawn from FLO to Central Park board of commissioners, December 28, 1859, reprinted in *Papers*, 3:234–242, with annotations.

164 **"I must confess":** MPO to FLO, October 10, 1859.

164 **"Green here. . . . He growled":** MPO to FLO, October 24, 1859.

164 **"Upon my word Olmsted":** Vaux to FLO, October 1859 [no day specified in letter].

165 **a silver spoon:** Francis Kowsky, *Country, Park, and City: The Architecture and Life of Calvert Vaux* (New York: Oxford University Press, 1998), 140.

166 **"I return with greatly improved":** FLO to Central Park board of commissioners, December 28, 1859, reprinted in *Papers*, 3:236.

166 **"ignorant of a park, properly so-called":** Olmsted monthly report to Central Park board of commissioners, read on October 13, 1857, reprinted in FLO Jr. and Theodora Kimball, eds., *Forty Years of Landscape Architecture*, vol. 2 (New York: G. P. Putnam's Sons, 1922), 58.

166 **$1.50-a-day salaries:** FLO to Central Park board of commissioners, November 13, 1860, reprinted in *Papers*, 3:282.

166 **derisively called "sparrow cops":** Roy Rosenzweig and Elizabeth Blackmar, *The Park and the People* (Ithaca: Cornell University Press, 1992), 242.

166 **The park keepers made 228 arrests:** FLO to Andrew Green, April 29, 1860.

166 **No murders happened:** Rosenzweig and Blackmar, *The Park and the People*, 2.

167 **"direct strangers to different":** Notice posted in Keepers' Room, November 10, 1860, reprinted in *Papers*, 3:279.

167 **"Central Park Visitors are Warned":** *Regulations for the Use of the Central Park*, drawn up by FLO, November 3, 1860, reprinted in ibid., 279.

167 **"carriage rests":** FLO Jr. and Kimball, *Forty Years of Landscape Architecture*, 2;413.

168 **"It is quite expensive":** Andrew Green to FLO, November 12, 1860.

168 **"None were cut":** FLO to Green, November 15, 1860.

168 **"I recollect the willows":** Green to FLO, November 15, 1860.

169 **"Although an error":** Green to FLO, July 26, 1860.

169 **"Just in the earliest":** FLO to JO, June 14, 1860.

169 **"young pugilist":** MPO to JO, June 29, 1860.

170 **Olmsted and Vaux as "landscape architects":** *Papers*, 2:267.

170 **"unconscious influence":** Carla Yanni, *The Architecture of Madness: Insane Asylums in the United States* (Minneapolis: University of Minnesota Press, 2007), 9.

171 **Kill out the Lunatic Hospital:** John Butler to FLO, December 3, 1872.

Chapter 14: Swans

172 **would surely kill him:** FLO to JO, October 21, 1860.

173 **little John Theodore died:** Genealogy, FLO Papers, Library of Congress.

173 **She took to her bed:** FLO to JO, October 21, 1860.

173 **"Whilst expressing my deep regret":** Mr. Asboth to FLO, 1860 [date unspecified in letter].

174 **outlay of twelve and a half cents:** FLO to Central Park board of commissioners, January 22, 1861, reprinted in *Papers*, 3:307.

174 **"a systematic small tyranny":** FLO to Vaux, March 25, 1864.

174 **"Not a cent":** FLO to John Bigelow, February 9, 1861.

174 **"I have fixed":** FLO to JO, September 23, 1859.

175   "It is humiliating to me, Sir": FLO to Central Park board of commissioners, January 22, 1861, reprinted in *Papers*, 3:297–319.

175   a reporter for the *New York World*: *New York World*, March 11, 1861.

175   "The pitching appeared": *New York Times*, October 9, 1860.

176   The reporter counted about forty: *New York World*, March 11, 1861.

Chapter 15: In Search of a Mission

178   He considered joining the navy: FLO to JO, April 16, 1861.

179   "the most powerful organization": William Maxwell, *Lincoln's Fifth Wheel: The Political History of the U.S. Sanitary Commission* (New York: Longmans, Green, 1956), preface by Allan Nevins, viii.

180   One of these outfits: Charles Stillé, *History of the United States Sanitary Commission* (Philadelphia: J. B. Lippincott, 1866), 41–42.

180   "Without concert of effort": Maxwell, *Lincoln's Fifth Wheel*, 1.

181   Bellows assembled a board: Ibid., 8–9.

182   "I approve the above": Ibid., 8.

182   "good big work": FLO to Bertha Olmsted, January 28, 1862.

183   "Bloody 11th Camp C": FLO to MPO, June 28, 1861.

184   On his first night: Ibid.

184   Olmsted visited another nineteen camps: Stillé, *History of the United States Sanitary Commission*, 85.

185   "It is now hardly possible": Ibid., 86.

185   constantly battling the flies: FLO to MPO, July 2, 1861.

186   "cheap & nasty French": Ibid.

186   "Lincoln has no element": FLO to JO, August 3, 1861.

186   "The official machinery": FLO to MPO, July 2, 1861.

186   "Give me some good news": Ibid.

187   "A large portion": FLO to William Cullen Bryant, July 31, 1861, reprinted in *The Papers of Frederick Law Olmsted*, vol. 4, *Defending the Union* (Baltimore: John Hopkins University Press, 1986), 133.

187   "They, too, were dirty": FLO, "Report on the Demoralization of the Volunteers," September 5, 1861, reprinted in ibid., 165.

189   The first draft . . . hasn't survived: Ibid., 15.

189   "imbecility of the government": FLO to MPO, September 7, 1861.

189   "Did the government really": FLO, "Report on the Demoralization of the Volunteers," September 5, 1861, reprinted in *Papers*, 4:172.

190   "So it will become": FLO to JO, September 12, 1861.

190   twenty-six surgeons and eighty assistants: Stillé, *History of the United States Sanitary Commission*, 116.

190   5,000 vaccines: Maxwell, *Lincoln's Fifth Wheel*, 110.

190   "a self-satisfied, supercilious": FLO to John Murray Forbes, December 15, 1861, reprinted in *Papers*, 4:240.

191   McClellan's private quarters in Washington: Details of meeting with General McClellan drawn largely from FLO to JO, September 12, 1861.

191   "His mind is patient": Henry Bellows to James McKim, August 8, 1864.

191   "a severe judge": Bellows to Eliza Nevins Bellows, February 25, 1863.

191   "run the machine": George Templeton Strong, *Diary of the Civil War, 1860–1865* (New York: Macmillan, 1962), 188.

192   "Dear Charley": FLO to JCO, October 17, 1861.

192   It wasn't until six months: FLO to Bellows, December 20, 1861, reprinted in *Papers*, 4:242.

192   "I have discovered": Ibid.

192   It was October 28, 1861: Genealogy, FLO Papers, Library of Congress.

192   "We have a girl": FLO to Brace, November 8, 1861.

194   "I have, I suppose": FLO to Bellows, June 1, 1861, reprinted in *Papers*, 4:118.

194   "I shall go to Port Royal": FLO to JO, February 24, 1862.

195   "thoughts about the management": FLO to Abraham Lincoln, March 8, 1862.

195   "A hostile force": FLO letter, *New York Times*, November 29, 1861, signed "Yeoman."

195   didn't change a single word: FLO to JO, February 19, 1862.

195   circulated similar petitions: Laura Wood Roper, "Frederick Law Olmsted and the Port Royal Experiment," *Journal of Southern History* (August 1965).

195   "keep up a steady": FLO to Bellows, February 15, 1862, reprinted in *Papers*, 4:273.

Chapter 16: In the Republic of Suffering

196   "As for the Sanitary Commission": FLO to JO, April 19, 1862.

198   Union soldiers desperately ill: Charles Stillé, *History of the United States Sanitary Commission* (Philadelphia: J. B. Lippincott, 1866), 154.

199   "a death-place for scores": *Hospital Transports: A Memoir of the Embarkation of the Sick and Wounded from the Peninsula of Virginia in the Summer of 1862* (Boston: Ticknor and Fields, 1863), 24.

199   viewed as a stimulant: Interview, JM with Terry Reimer, director of research, National Museum of Civil War Medicine, May 7, 2009.

199   oldfangled name for hydrochloric acid: E-mail on June 16, 2009, from Michael Flannery, medical historian, University of Alabama at Birmingham.

200   "Poor, pale, emaciated, shivering": *Hospital Transports*, 33.

200   "sea fashion": Ibid., 18.

201   rubbing a little powdered opium: George Adams, "Fighting for Time," in *The Image of War, 1861–1865*, vol. 4 (Washington, DC: National Historical Society, 1957).

201   "catching for mother": FLO to Henry Bellows, June 3, 1862, reprinted in *Papers*, 4:357.

201   "Give him back": Katharine Prescott Wormeley, *The Other Side of War: On the Hospital Transports with the Army of the Potomac* (Gansevoort, NY: Corner House Historical Publications, 1998), 121.

201   Some of the women: See also "The Letters of Harriet Douglas Wetten," published in *Wisconsin Magazine of History* (Winter 1964–1965): 131–151.

202   "He is small": Wormeley, *Other Side of War*, 62–63.

202   One Sunday in late May: *Hospital Transports*, 85–88.

203   "Will you please engage": FLO to Bellows, June 13, 1862, reprinted in *Papers*, 4:371.

203   "I need not say": FLO to MPO, June 11, 1862.

204   "without beds, without straw": FLO to Bellows, June 3, 1862, reprinted in *Papers*, 4:357.

204   "not only more whimpering": *Hospital Transports*, 120.

204   **"In this republic of suffering"**: Ibid., 115.

205   **"the best army the world"**: FLO to Abraham Lincoln, July 6, 1862, reprinted in *Papers*, 4:393.

206   **"The summer's work has"**: FLO to Bellows, July 13, 1862, reprinted in *Papers*, 4:404.

206   **"the most important contribution"**: *Letters of Charles Eliot Norton*, vol. 1 (Boston: Houghton Mifflin, 1913), 211.

206   **Charles Dickens**: FLO, *The Cotton Kingdom* (New York: Da Capo Press, 1996), xxvi.

207   **Karl Marx**: Karl Marx, *Capital*, vol. 1, pt. 3, chap. 8, n. 17.

207   **Charles Darwin**: Speech by William Erasmus Darwin, Charles's son, delivered at Cambridge in 1909.

207   **606,000 words**: FLO, *The Cotton Kingdom*, xxxi.

207   **$1,400, adjusted for inflation**: Ibid., 13.

207   **his "impression" had hardened**: Ibid., 8.

207   **"It is said that"**: Ibid., 3.

208   **Great Britain was surprisingly ambivalent**: Characterization based on e-mail to JM dated June 17, 2009, from Sir Brian Harrison, history professor emeritus at Oxford University, and interview on July 2, 2009, JM with Charles Hubbard, professor of history at Lincoln Memorial University.

208   **"What would happen"**: *Congressional Globe*, 35th Cong., 1st sess., 961.

208   **"About America I think"**: Emma Darwin to J. D. Hooker, December 26, 1863, Darwin Correspondence Project, accessed online.

209   **"calm and dispassionate Mr. Olmsted"**: *Fraser's*, February 1862.

209   **Mercury was used**: Discussion of mercury drawn largely from interview, JM with Terry Reimer, director of research, National Museum of Civil War Medicine, May 7, 2009.

209   **"I itched furiously"**: FLO to MPO, August 30, 1862.

210   **"He has said, of course"**: FLO to MPO, September 15, 1862.

Chapter 17: Antietam to Gettysburg

211   **this odor would be remembered**: *Battle of Antietam: Carnage in a Cornfield*, HistoryNet.com.

212   **red-and-white USSC flag**: William Maxwell, *Lincoln's Fifth Wheel: The Political History of the U.S. Sanitary Commission* (New York: Longmans, Green, 1956), 273.

212   **"Most of our ladies"**: Henry Bellows to Mrs. R. Swain, November 13, 1862.

212   **"I have addressed large"**: Horace Howard Furnace to FLO, June 8, 1863.

213   **at Antietam a full day**: FLO to MPO, September 21, 1862.

213   **According to its records**: Charles Stillé, *History of the United States Sanitary Commission* (Philadelphia: J. B. Lippincott, 1866), 267.

213   **"It was very squalid"**: FLO to MPO, September 29, 1862.

214   **"The Proclamation of Emancipation"**: *New York Times*, September 28, 1862.

214   **"I shall stand by it"**: FLO to Charles Stillé, February 23, 1863.

214   **"Each would then become"**: FLO to John Nicolay, October 10, 1862.

214   **"You are too near the machinery"**: George Curtis to FLO, September 29, 1862, letter reprinted in Laura Wood Roper, *FLO: A Biography of Frederick Law Olmsted* (Baltimore: Johns Hopkins University Press, 1973), 212.

214   "Kiss all the young ones": FLO to MPO, September 29, 1862.

215   "Thank you for encouraging": FLO to MPO, October 11, 1862.

215   "We will be as frugal": Ibid.

215   "It is a day for heroes": Ibid.

216   "You understand . . . the glorious": Bellows to John Heywood, March 10, 1863.

217   "a friendly feeling amongst": FLO to Bellows, February 4, 1863, reprinted in *Papers*, 4:512.

218   "peculiar zest": FLO to JO, April 1, 1863.

218   "I am not always": Ibid.

219   *Carl* is a play on *carl*: *Papers*, 4:529.

219   "What else is necessary": FLO's diary, "A Journey in the West," reprinted in *Papers*, 4:527.

219   "It seems useless to describe Chicago": Ibid., 591.

220   briefly occupied Frederick: Stillé, *History of the United States Sanitary Commission*, 376–377.

220   steady stream of wagons: *New York Times*, July 16, 1863.

220   a pair of supply wagons: *New York Times*, July 31, 1863.

220   "Thank God!": Ibid.

221   "Private advices tend": George Templeton Strong, *Diary of the Civil War, 1860–1865* (New York: Macmillan, 1962), 329.

221   "Olmsted is wary, shrewd": Ibid.

221   During the week: Tally of relief items provided at Gettysburg drawn from *New York Times*, July 31, 1863.

222   "evidence of terrible fighting": FLO to Edwin Godkin, July 19, 1863, reprinted in *Papers*, 4:658.

222   Particularly touching, to Olmsted: Ibid.

Chapter 18: "The Country Cannot Spare You"

223   "beastly drunkenness": Cornelius Agnew to FLO, April 24, 1863.

224   "I chafe and fume": FLO to Henry Bellows, July 28, 1863, reprinted in *Papers*, 4:681.

224   "He is an extraordinary fellow": George Templeton Strong, *Diary of the Civil War, 1860–1865* (New York: Macmillan, 1962), 304–305.

224   "Olmsted is in an unhappy": Ibid., 183.

225   *principles of management*: FLO to JO, April 25, 1863.

225   "However wanting in sagacity": FLO to JO, May 2, 1863.

225   *Comment, Reviser, Scrutiny*: List of potential names drawn from FLO to Edwin Godkin, July 19, 1863, reprinted in *Papers*, 4:658, and FLO to MPO, July 2, 1863.

226   "I don't believe it will succeed": Charles Dana quoted in FLO to Edwin Godkin, August 7, 1863.

226   "You are less rooted": Dana to FLO, August 7, 1863.

227   "absolute poverty": FLO to Bellows, August 15, 1863, reprinted in *Papers*, 4:692.

227   "*The country can not spare you*": Bellows to FLO, August 13, 1863, reprinted in *Papers*, 4:702.

227   estimated $15 million: Charles Stillé, *History of the United States Sanitary Commission* (Philadelphia: J. B. Lippincott, 1866), 173.

228   **1,482 camp inspections:** William Maxwell, *Lincoln's Fifth Wheel: The Political History of the U.S. Sanitary Commission* (New York: Longmans, Green, 1956), 310.

228   **137,000 beds:** George Adams, "Fighting for Time," in *The Image of War, 1861–1865*, vol. 4 (Washington, DC: National Historical Society, 1957).

228   **"inestimable blessings and benefits":** Stillé, *History of the United States Sanitary Commission*, 180–181.

229   **"mid-wife to the Red Cross":** Maxwell, *Lincoln's Fifth Wheel*, 276.

Chapter 19: Gold Dust

232   **"perhaps the finest mining":** Horace Greeley, *An Overland Journey, from New York to San Francisco* (New York: C. A. Avord, 1860), 319.

232   **The 44,387 acres:** *The Mariposa Company*, prospectus, 3.

233   **"Why, when I came to California":** Samuel Bowles, *Across the Continent: A Summer's Journey to the Rocky Mountains, the Mormons, and the Pacific States* (Springfield, MA: Samuel Bowles, 1865), 312.

233   **"There seems to be no limit":** *The Mariposa Company*, prospectus, 67.

233   **$10,000 salary in gold:** Details of Olmsted's compensation drawn from FLO to JO, August 10, 1863, and *The Papers of Frederick Law Olmsted*, vol. 5, *The California Frontier* (Baltimore: Johns Hopkins University Press, 1990), 6.

234   **"The steamer on the Atlantic":** FLO's travel journal, New York to San Francisco, reprinted in *Papers*, 5:72.

235   **"makes all our model scenery":** FLO to MPO, September 25, 1863.

235   **"Remember to point out":** Ibid.

235   **"It's Fifth Avenue":** Ibid.

236   **"would under favorable natural":** FLO to Ignaz Pilat, September 26, 1863, reprinted in FLO Jr. and Theodora Kimball, eds., *Forty Years of Landscape Architecture*, vol. 2 (New York: G. P. Putnam's Sons, 1922), 347.

236   **"a dead flat, dead brown":** FLO to MPO, October 14, 1863.

237   **Olmsted checked into Oso House:** Description of Oso House and many Bear Valley details drawn from FLO to MPO, October 14, 1863, and FLO to JO, February 14, 1864.

238   **Mariposa was a high-tech operation:** Description of mines drawn partly from FLO to JO, February 11, 1864, and interview on October 22, 2009, JM with Randy Bolt, historical guide for California state parks.

238   **profit of $50,000 per month:** *Official Report of J. Ross Browne, U.S. Commissioner, &c., upon the Mineral Resources of the Mariposa Estate*, 7.

238   **"These facts, all new":** FLO to James Hoy, October 19, 1863.

239   **"Things are worse here":** FLO to MPO, October 31, 1863.

239   **"I can make nothing":** FLO to Frederick Knapp, November 21, 1863.

240   *California,* **he was certain:** FLO to MPO, October 15, 1863.

240   **"Evening services":** Ibid.

240   **a recurring dream:** *Harriet Errington Diary*, March 17, 1864, entry, Loeb Library.

241   **"I think something":** FLO to Frederick Knapp, November 21, 1863.

241   **"My special object":** Vaux to FLO, October 19, 1863, reprinted in *Papers*, 5:114.

242   **"superior education in certain directions":** FLO to Vaux, November 26, 1863.

243   **"helps to strengthen":** FLO to JO, January 1, 1864.

243   **"Think of it as 13 times":** FLO to MPO, October 15, 1863.

Chapter 20: Yosemite

244 "He (Fremont) seems": FLO to JO, October 30, 1863.

244 **Grass Valley section:** Contrast with Grass Valley provided during interview, on October 22, 2009, JM with Randy Bolt, historical guide for California state parks.

245 **Olmsted cut the miners' wages:** FLO to George Farlee, March 1, 1864.

245 "They hate regularity": FLO to James Hoy, March 2, 1864.

245 **Israel Raymond sent a letter:** Israel Raymond to John Conness, February 20, 1864, reprinted in Hans Huth, "Yosemite: The Story of an Idea."

247 "I know what stage say": FLO Jr. interview by Laura Wood Roper, Library of Congress.

247 "I was very busy sewing": JCO's Mariposa Journal, June 30, 1864, Loeb Library.

247 "Marion House": Francis Kowsky, *Country, Park, and City: The Architecture and Life of Calvert Vaux* (New York: Oxford University Press, 1998), 163.

248 **On March 25, 1851:** Details of Yosemite in the 1850s partly drawn from Ralph Kuykendall, *Early History of Yosemite Valley, California* (Washington, DC: U.S. Government Printing Office, 1919).

249 **Carleton Watkins:** Details about photographer drawn partly from "Carleton E. Watkins, Pioneer Photographer of the Pacific Coast," *Yosemite Nature Notes* (April 1953).

249 "Seven Weeks in the Great Yo-Semite": *Atlantic*, June 1864.

249 **Indians began to gather:** Details of Miwok gathering from FLO, "Notes on the Pioneer Condition," reprinted in *Papers*, 5:649–650.

250 "probably the noblest tree": FLO, "Yosemite and the Mariposa Grove: A Preliminary Report, 1865," accessed online at http://yosemite.ca.us.

250 "Previous expectations—photographs, sketches": FLO, "Plan of Narrative for Clarks & Yo Semite, & c," July 30, 1864.

251 "The union of the deepest sublimity": FLO, "Yosemite and the Mariposa Grove."

252 **As for choosing the committee:** "The Yosemite Valley and the Mariposa Big Trees," introductory note by Laura Wood Roper, *Landscape Architecture*, October 1952.

252 "There should be no": FLO to Clarence King, October 23, 1864.

252 **Recently, he had sold a block:** *Papers*, 5:307.

252 **He was alarmed by how quickly:** FLO to JO, October 30, 1863.

Chapter 21: Unsettled in the West

255 "The highlight of the trial": *New York Times*, December 22, 1864.

255 "Was any unfair advantage": Ibid.

255 "I-I-I think not": Account of stammering and its impact from Allan Nevins, *Frémont: The West's Greatest Adventurer*, vol. 2 (New York: Harper and Bros., 1928), 670.

255 **traded as high as $45:** *New York Times*, January 25, 1865.

256 **the first Olmsted heard of the Opdyke-Weed libel trial:** FLO to Edwin Godkin, January 9, 1865, reprinted in *Papers*, 5:292.

256 **Olmsted gathered up $4,000:** Ibid.

256 **Olmsted had sold much of his stock:** *Papers*, 5:307.

256 "I have made no progress": FLO to MPO, January 18, 1865.

257 "Should a few guarantee": Text of telegram appears in *Papers*, 5:305n7.

257 "**Bunsbyish impertinence**": FLO to Edwin Godkin, January 26, 1865, reprinted in ibid., 310.

258 "**But, today, singing *Glory! Hallelujah!*"**: FLO to Frederick Knapp, April 9, 1865, reprinted in ibid., 349.

259 "**I have never seen**": FLO to JO, April 29, 1865.

259 "**I can't help feeling**": FLO to Frederick Knapp, April 16, 1865, reprinted in *Papers*, 5:353.

259 "**At any rate**": Ibid.

259 "**I would do so simply**": FLO to MPO, April 16, 1865.

260 **elected in abstentia**: FLO to JO, February 11, 1865.

260 "**The business is one promising extraordinary profits**": FLO, *The Production of Wine in California: Particularly Referring to the Establishment of the Buena Vista Vinicultural Society*, April–May 1865, reprinted in *Papers*, 5:337.

262 "**Being an evergreen**": FLO, *Preface to the Plan for Mountain View Cemetery*, May 1865, reprinted in ibid., 480.

263 "**I trust you are getting**": Vaux to FLO, May 10, 1865, reprinted in *Papers*, 5:359.

264 "**I love beautiful landscapes**": FLO to Vaux, June 8, 1865, reprinted in ibid., 390.

264 "**Nobody cares two straws**": Vaux to FLO, May 20, 1865.

264 "**A scheme that can be upset**": Vaux to FLO, July 6, 1865.

264 "**Your objection to the plan**": Vaux to FLO, July 8, 1865.

264 "**stubborn cemetery maker in California**": Vaux to FLO, May 30, 1865.

264 "**Frederick the Great, Prince**": Vaux to FLO, July 31, 1865.

265 "**If I go on and do Brooklyn alone**": Vaux to FLO, May 20, 1865.

265 **Scott's tenure as president**: *Papers*, 5:418.

265 **eve of World War II**: Interview on October 22, 2009, JM with Randy Bolt, historical guide for California state parks.

265 "**Its business history**": Nevins, *Frémont*, 2:445.

265 **Hot on the heels**: Olmsted didn't receive Vaux's letters saying he'd won the Prospect Park design commission (June 22, 1865) and saying the Central Park board was ready to reappoint them landscape architects (July 21, 1865) until after he'd received Scott's letter that cut his ties to the Mariposa Company, according to *Papers*, 5:419.

266 **Olmsted replied at once**: FLO to Vaux, August 1, 1865, NYPL.

266 **as well as Samuel Bowles**: Details drawn partly from George Merriam, *The Life and Times of Samuel Bowles* (New York: Century, 1885).

266 **sang . . . Civil War anthems**: Samuel Bowles, *Across the Continent: A Summer's Journey to the Rocky Mountains, the Mormons, and the Pacific States* (Springfield, MA: Samuel Bowles, 1865), 232.

267 "**Yosemite should be held**": "Yosemite and the Mariposa Grove: A Preliminary Report, 1865," accessed online at http://yosemite.ca.us.

267 "**Before many years**": Ibid.

267 "**The establishment by the government**": Ibid.

268 **Several of them wound up writing books**: See also Albert Deane Richardson, *Beyond the Mississippi: From the Great River to the Great Ocean: Life and Adventure on the Prairies, Mountains, and Pacific Coast* (Hartford, CT: American Publishing, 1869).

Chapter 22: New Prospects

271 "**Whether bursting the fast**": Clay Lancaster, *Prospect Park Handbook* (New York: Greensward Foundation, 1988), 24.

271   **In January 1865:** Richard Berenson and Neil Demause, *The Complete Illustrated Guidebook to Prospect Park and the Brooklyn Botanic Gardens* (New York: Silver Lining Books, 2001), 25.

272   **view was breathtaking:** Account of view in 1860s drawn from multiple sources including *Brooklyn Eagle*, April 27, 1867.

273   **"Here is a suggestion":** FLO and Vaux, *Preliminary Report for Laying Out a Park in Brooklyn*, 1866, reprinted in *Landscape into Cityscape: Frederick Law Olmsted's Plans for a Greater New York* (Ithaca: Cornell University Press, 1968), 108.

273   **claret and orange-juice punch:** Francis Kowsky, *Country, Park, and City: The Architecture and Life of Calvert Vaux* (New York: Oxford University Press, 1998), 175.

274   **dreamed up a radical solution:** Description of Olmsted's design for a San Francisco park drawn from *Preliminary Report in Regard to a Plan of Public Pleasure Grounds for the City of San Francisco*, 1866, reprinted in *Papers*, 5:518–543.

274   **For the College of California:** Details of Olmsted's design for this college drawn from *Report upon a Projected Improvement of the Estate of the College of California, at Berkeley, Near Oakland*, 1866, reprinted in ibid., 546–570.

274   **"I like the plan myself":** Henry Coon to FLO, June 29, 1866.

275   **Launching a new publication:** Details of the *Nation*'s founding drawn from multiple sources, including William Armstrong, "The Freedmen's Movement and the Founding of the *Nation*," *Journal of American History* (March 1967).

275   **"substantially the same":** Ibid.

276   **"Olmsted's coming in relieves":** Edwin Godkin to Charles Eliot Norton, January 15, 1866, reprinted in Rollo Ogden, *The Life and Letters of Edwin Lawrence Godkin*, vol. 1 (New York: Macmillan, 1907), 243.

277   **articles on various agricultural topics:** See "The Progress of Horticulture," *Nation*, March 1, 1866.

277   **article on the migration from farm to city:** See "The Future of Great Cities," *Nation*, February 22, 1866.

277   **piece about proper nutrition for soldiers:** *Nation*, January 18, 1866.

277   **There was a review of *Short Sermons*:** *Nation*, May 8, 1866.

277   **a review of Samuel Bowles:** *Nation*, January 11, 1866.

277   **review of a memoir, *Life of Benjamin*:** *Nation*, May 18, 1866.

277   **Another piece titled "Hint for Tourists":** *Nation*, March 15, 1866.

278   **"I wanted Olmsted's name":** Edwin Godkin to Charles Eliot Norton, July 1866.

279   **"It grows upon me":** FLO to Norton, July 15, 1866, reprinted in *The Papers of Frederick Law Olmsted*, vol. 6, *The Years of Olmsted, Vaux & Co.* (Baltimore: Johns Hopkins University Press, 1992), 99.

280   **Worthington duplex pump:** *Brooklyn Eagle*, November 11, 1870.

280   **marked by a series of red flags:** *Brooklyn Eagle*, October 18, 1867.

281   **pedestrian paths . . . depressed below ground level:** Interview on May 5, 2010, JM with Christian Zimmerman, Prospect Park landscape architect.

282   **"He must be an exceptional":** *Brooklyn Eagle*, November 14, 1879.

283   **a constant reminder:** See FLO to JCO, January 29, 1873, Loeb Library.

283   **Olmsted suggested that the children's section:** Kowsky, *Country, Park, and City*, 189.

285   **"the wealth in which she":** FLO to Edward Bright, February 1, 1867, reprinted in *Papers*, 6:189.

285   **"It remains to be seen":** FLO, *Last Report of the Southern Famine Relief Commission*, reprinted in ibid., 228.

Chapter 23: City Planning: Buffalo and Chicago

287 "commercial Constantinople": Henry Perry Smith, *History of the City of Buffalo and Erie County*, vol. 2 (Syracuse: D. Mason, 1884), 180.

288 "What was my horror": FLO to MPO, August 25, 1868.

288 "Mr. Olmsted has a mastery": *Brooklyn Eagle*, August 5, 1870.

289 "I think it will go": FLO to MPO, August 26, 1868.

289 a "big speculation": FLO to Vaux, August 29, 1868, NYPL.

289 "They want to go": FLO to MPO, August 23, 1868.

290 "be the first consideration": FLO and Vaux, *Preliminary Report upon the Proposed Suburban Village at Riverside, Near Chicago*, reprinted in *Civilizing American Cities: Writings on City Landscapes*, 292.

290 "absence of sharp corners": Ibid.

291 "There will probably": FLO to Vaux, August 29, 1868, NYPL.

292 "a character of magnificence": *Century Illustrated Magazine*, October 1886.

294 Olmsted and Vaux had even coined a term: Interview on August 4, 2009, JM with Francis Kowsky, author of *Country, Park, and City: The Architecture and Life of Calvert Vaux* (New York: Oxford University Press, 1998).

295 advertisement . . . in the *Nation*: *Nation*, May 1, 1866.

295 "the best planned city": FLO to George Waring, April 13, 1876.

297 "You certainly cannot set": FLO and Vaux, *Report Accompanying Plan for Laying Out South Park*, reprinted in *Civilizing American Cities: Writings on City Landscapes*, 164.

297 dubbed it the Midway Plaisance: Interview on June 9, 2010, JM with Julia Bachrach, Chicago Park District.

298 "in stone beyond recovery": Mariana Griswold van Rensselaer, *Henry Hobson Richardson and His Works* (New York: Dover Publications, 1969), 118.

299 "I feel myself so nearly": FLO to Samuel Bowles, June 2, 1871.

300 "I am looking": FLO to Kingsbury, October 8, 1871.

300 Unbenownst to Olmsted: Detail that Kingsbury letter and Chicago fire on same day noted by Witold Rybczynski, *A Clearing in the Distance: Frederick Law Olmsted and America in the Nineteenth Century* (New York: Scribner, 1999), 310.

300 Vaux designed but a single house: Interview on June 12, 2010, JM with Lonnie Sacchi, Riverside local historian.

301 firm of William Le Baron Jenney: Promotional brochure, *Riverside in 1871 with a Description of Its Improvements*, 7.

Chapter 24: Battling Boss Tweed, Splitting with Vaux

303 "like little dollars": Alexander Callow Jr., *The Tweed Ring* (New York: Oxford University Press, 1966), 40.

304 to several thousand: Jump in Central Park employment under Tweed drawn from ibid., 127.

304 "circulation of air": FLO Jr. and Theodora Kimball, eds., *Forty Years of Landscape Architecture*, vol. 2 (New York: G. P. Putnam's Sons, 1922), 90.

304 pumice those archways: *New York Times*, September 2, 1871.

304 fittingly lavish monument: *New York Times*, December 30, 1870.

305 "It is disheartening": FLO to Kingsbury, October 8, 1871.

305 **"Church's name was first suggested"**: FLO to Charley Brace, November 24, 1871.

306 **"The Park has suffered"**: FLO to Columbus Ryan, February 27, 1872, letter reprinted in FLO Jr. and Kimball, *Forty Years of Landscape Architecture*, 2:350.

307 **He obtained Olmsted and Vaux's reports**: Terence Young, *Building San Francisco's Parks, 1850–1930* (Baltimore: Johns Hopkins University Press, 2004), 71.

307 **"Please excuse the liberty"**: William Hammond Hall to FLO, August 22, 1871, letter reprinted ibid., 74.

307 **"I have given the matter"**: FLO to William Hammond Hall, October 5, 1871.

308 **plant succession**: Discussion of plant succession drawn partly from Young, *Building San Francisco's Parks*, 85.

309 **"seems to have nearly"**: *New York Tribune*, June 22, 1872.

309 **"My name was used"**: *New York Post*, June 22, 1872.

309 **"I am surprised & gratified"**: FLO to James McKim, June 28, 1872, reprinted in *Papers*, 6:566.

310 **"relief to me"**: FLO to Alfred Bloor, October 4, 1882.

310 **a pair of huge and prestigious commissions**: Francis Kowsky, *Country, Park, and City: The Architecture and Life of Calvert Vaux* (New York: Oxford University Press, 1998), 205–206.

310 **The air hung thick**: Description of grounds of McLean in 1872 drawn in part from Alex Beam, *Gracefully Insane: Life and Death Inside America's Premier Mental Hospital* (New York: Public Affairs, 2001), 30.

311 **"decided advantage in the great"**: FLO to Henry Rogers, August 17, 1873.

311 **Olmsted also suggested a building scheme**: FLO to Henry Rogers, December 13, 1872, reprinted in *Papers*, 6:584.

311 **Two months after**: Details of John Olmsted's death drawn largely from FLO to Kingsbury, January 28, 1873, and FLO to JCO, January 29, 1873, Loeb Library.

312 **"He was a very good man"**: FLO to Kingsbury, January 28, 1873.

Chapter 25: Blindness and Vision

313 **The brownstone was located**: Details about brownstone's layout drawn mostly from FLO Jr., "Random Notes About F.L.O.'s office at 209 West 46th Street," June 1952, Library of Congress.

314 **Everywhere, all over the house**: Titles drawn from inventory, "List of Books Belonging to F. L. Olmsted, December 1882," Library of Congress.

315 **"a great deal of disappointed love"**: FLO to Calvert Vaux, November 26, 1863.

316 **"on the least provocation"**: FLO to Frederick Knapp, July 11, 1870.

316 **"To saddle & bridle"**: FLO to Knapp, October 8, 1866.

317 **"Just the nicest"**: FLO to Kingsbury, September 6, 1893.

317 **he'd be rechristened**: Henry Olmsted's rechristening as FLO Jr. discussed in *The Papers of Frederick Law Olmsted*, vol. 7, *Parks, Politics, and Patronage* (Baltimore: Johns Hopkins University Press, 2007), 139.

318 **"the enemy/mother"**: Albert Olmsted to FLO, August 4, 1873.

318 **"I write that you"**: Albert Olmsted to FLO, October 15, 1873.

318 **"I remain your affectionate, Mother"**: See MAO to FLO, August 18, 1873.

318 **"relieved of responsibilities"**: FLO to S. H. Wales, September 17, 1873, reprinted in *Papers*, 6:651.

319 **Olmsted was confined to a darkened bedroom:** Melvin Kalfus, *Frederick Law Olmsted: The Passion of a Public Artist* (New York: New York University Press, 1990), 62.

319 **P. T. Barnum wrote inquiring:** P. T. Barnum to FLO, September 15, 1873.

319 **"I hope you have":** Board of Ed., Elmira, New York, to FLO, September 22, 1873.

319 **"Suppose a man":** FLO to Brace, December 21, 1873.

320 **"In short, the capital":** FLO to Justin Morrill, January 22, 1874, reprinted in *Papers*, 7:36.

320 **"to form and train":** Charles Beveridge and Paul Rocheleau, *Frederick Law Olmsted: Designing the American Landscape* (New York: Universe Publishing, 1998), 155.

321 **twenty-one different streets . . . forty-six different places":** Interview on July 12, 2010, JM with Steve Livengood, chief guide, U.S. Capitol Historical Society.

321 **"The building will appear":** FLO to Edward Clark, October 1, 1881, reprinted in *Papers*, 7:557.

322 **"The larger part":** Ibid.

322 **"I heard that it":** *Papers*, 7:509.

323 **"the genius of the place":** *Report of Fred. Law Olmsted on the Mount Royal Park*, 1874, reprinted in *Papers*, 7:89.

324 **"mountain more mountain-like":** FLO, *Mount Royal, Montreal* (New York: G. P. Putnam's Sons, 1881), 44.

324 **"power of their scenery":** *Report of Fred. Law Olmsted on the Mount Royal Park*, 1874, reprinted in *Papers*, 7:89.

324 **"prophylactic and therapeutic":** FLO, *Mount Royal, Montreal*, 22.

324 **"feebler sorts of folks":** Beveridge and Rocheleau, *Frederick Law Olmsted*, 77.

325 **Now, Dalton invited Olmsted:** Cynthia Zaitzevsky, *Frederick Law Olmsted and the Boston Park System* (Cambridge: Harvard University Press, 1982), 43.

325 **"any boy who had":** FLO to Horatio Admiral Nelson, June 6, 1876.

326 **"farcical failure":** FLO to JCO, October 7, 1877, reprinted in *Papers*, 7:333.

Chapter 26: A Troubled Wander Year

328 **"I could not keep":** FLO to MPO, August 15, 1877.

328 **"read over and committed":** FLO to JCO, autumn of 1877, undated, Loeb Library.

329 **"Everywhere examine closely":** Ibid.

329 **"Steep your mind":** Ibid.

329 **"They show that you":** FLO to JCO, October 7, 1877, reprinted in *Papers*, 7:333.

330 **"The Greensward Ring":** FLO Jr. and Theodora Kimball, eds., *Forty Years of Landscape Architecture*, vol. 2 (New York: G. P. Putnam's Sons, 1922), 109.

330 **"too much in haste":** FLO to JCO, October 23, 1877, Loeb Library.

330 **"When I have reminded you":** FLO to JCO, December 1, 1877, Loeb Library.

331 **"I have been to":** JCO to FLO, December 3, 1877, Loeb Library.

331 **"It is evident that":** FLO to JCO, December 18, 1877, Loeb Library.

332 **"His mention of a long":** JCO to MPO, January 13, 1878, Loeb Library.

332 **"It is not unnatural":** *New York World*, January 22, 1878.

332 **"greedy misrepresentations":** *New York Tribune*, February 19, 1878.

332 **Owen to pen a brief statement:** *New York Tribune*, February 21, 1878.

332 **"chivying English disposition":** MPO to JCO, February 24, 1878.

333 **"He is continually fearing":** JCO to Owen Olmsted, March 8, 1878, Loeb Library.

333 "one of the worst nights": JCO to MPO, March 13, 1878, Loeb Library.

334 "It all makes me sick": FLO to Horace Cleveland, February 9, 1881.

334 "being without a single": E. W. Howe, a Boston city engineer, date unknown, quotation provided by the Emerald Necklace Conservancy.

334 "childish": *American Architect and Building News*, quoted in Cynthia Zaitzevsky, *Frederick Law Olmsted and the Boston Park System* (Cambridge: Harvard University Press, 1982), 47.

Chapter 27: Stringing Emeralds

335 "They must have you": H. H. Richardson to FLO, May 21, 1878.

335 "Offensive exudations arise": FLO to the Board of Commissioners of the Department of Parks of the City of Boston, January 26, 1880, reprinted in *Papers*, 7:451.

336 He requested a meeting: FLO, "Paper on the Back Bay Problem and Its Solution Read Before the Boston Society of Architects," in *The Papers of Frederick Law Olmsted*, supplement 1, *Writings on Public Parks, Pathways, and Park Systems* (Baltimore: Johns Hopkins University Press, 1997), 442.

337 Oregon holly grape: Cynthia Zaitzevsky, *Frederick Law Olmsted and the Boston Park System* (Cambridge: Harvard University Press, 1982), 189.

337 "The collection of water-birds": FLO to the Board of Commissioners of the Department of Parks of the City of Boston, January 26, 1880, reprinted in *Papers*, 7:451.

337 Olmsted owned a dictionary: FLO to W. Bowen Murphy, August 3, 1895.

337 "Sedgeglade": FLO to Charles Dalton, December 9, 1879.

338 rhododendron show: Theodora Kimball timeline, Library of Congress.

338 didn't think this was a very good idea: See FLO to Charles Sargent, July 8, 1874.

339 Bentham and Hooker: Interview on June 23, 2010, JM with Lisa Pearson, librarian, Arnold Arboretum.

340 "This is a civilized community": Cynthia Zaitzevsky, *Fairsted: A Cultural Landscape Report* (Brookline, MA: National Park Service, Olmsted Center for Landscape Preservation, 1997), 9.

340 "very low": FLO to Charles Eliot Norton, October 19, 1881, reprinted in *Papers*, 7:561.

340 "We are again under": Ibid.

341 "The whole thing seems": John Platt to FLO, November 23, 1881.

341 "John certainly felt": Calvert Vaux to FLO, December 9, 1881.

341 "tranquilizing": FLO to Brace, March 7, 1882.

342 February 1883: Terms of Olmsted's salary, Zaitzevsky, *Fairsted*, 9–10.

342 "Your house—a beautiful thing": Richardson to FLO, February 6, 1883.

342 stepson John would build them a cottage: Interview on June 22, 2010, JM with Alan Banks, supervisory ranger, Fairsted, Frederick Law Olmsted National Historic Site.

342 Olmsted converted the large: Details on Fairsted interior drawn from Alan Banks tour of Fairsted for JM, June 22, 2010, and FLO Jr.'s "Random Notes About FLO's Brookline Office," June 1952, Library of Congress.

343 Richardson's flamboyant home office: Details from Mariana Griswold van Rensselaer, *Henry Hobson Richardson and His Works* (New York: Dover Publications, 1969), 124–125.

343 gave Olmsted a cucumber magnolia: Alan Banks tour of Fairsted for JM, June 22, 2010.

344   **"I'll plan anything"**: Richardson, quoted in Cynthia Zaitzevsky, *Frederick Law Olmsted and the Boston Park System* (Cambridge: Harvard University Press, 1982), 176.

344   **"I enjoy this suburban"**: FLO to Brace, March 7, 1882.

345   **"throw more upon Eliot"**: FLO to JCO, December 15, 1884, Loeb Library.

345   **"Nothing else compares"**: FLO quoted in Zaitzevsky, *Frederick Law Olmsted*, vii.

346   **"Jeweled Girdle"**: Interview on June 23, 2010, JM with Jeanie Knox, director of external affairs, Emerald Necklace Conservancy.

346   **An unknown someone:** Detail checked on December 10, 2010, by JM with Alan Banks, supervisory ranger, Fairsted.

Chapter 28: Saving Niagara, Designing Stanford

347   **"From this hour"**: Pierre Berton, *Niagara: A History of the Falls* (Albany: State University of New York Press, 1992), 193.

348   **"To drive around"**: *Boston Daily Advertiser*, September 14, 1881.

348   **"Carlyle signs"**: Charles Eliot Norton to FLO, December 23, 1878.

348   **"I don't see that"**: *Washington Post*, September 14, 1882.

349   **"Governor Cleveland *strongly*"**: H. H. Richardson to FLO, February 6, 1883.

349   **"I congratulate you"**: Norton quoted in Berton, *Niagara: A History of the Falls*, 191.

349   **"particularly offensive"**: Laura Wood Roper, *FLO: A Biography of Frederick Law Olmsted* (Baltimore: Johns Hopkins University Press, 1973), 397.

350   **"life seems a struggle"**: Jervis McEntee, quoted in Francis Kowsky, *Country, Park, and City: The Architecture and Life of Calvert Vaux* (New York: Oxford University Press, 1998), 306.

351   **"I have followed the Appalachian"**: "Notes by Mr. Olmsted," *Special Report of New York State Survey on the Preservation of the Scenery of Niagara Falls*, reprinted in *Papers*, 7:477–478.

351   **"He helped me"**: FLO to Mariana Griswold van Rensselaer, May 17, 1887.

351   **"well windward of expenses"**: FLO to Calvert Vaux, April 16, 1887, quoted in Kowsky, *Country, Park, and City*, 306.

352   **"He went on discussing"**: FLO to van Rensselaer, May 2, 1887.

352   **in excruciating pain:** Mariana Griswold van Rensselaer, *Henry Hobson Richardson and His Works* (New York: Dover Publications, 1969), 36.

352   **after having her third child, Charlotte:** Mac Griswold's afterword in *Fairsted: A Cultural Landscape Report* (Brookline, MA: National Park Service, Olmsted Center for Landscape Preservation, 1997), 134.

352   **"changes in our time"**: FLO to Brace, November 1, 1884.

353   **"It's a pity"**: Kingsbury to Brace, January 10, 1885.

354   **"There is not any word"**: FLO to Charles Eliot, June 8, 1886, Stanford Library, Special Collections.

355   **"The site is settled"**: FLO to JCO, September 18, 1886.

356   **The quads and arcades:** Interview on March 29, 2010, JM with Dave Lenox, Stanford University architect.

356   **"I find Governor Stanford"**: FLO to Eliot, July 20, 1886, Stanford Library, Special Collections.

356   **"not a tree, nor a bush"**: FLO to Leland Stanford, November 27, 1886, Stanford Library, Special Collections.

357   **"Gov. replied a Landscape Arch't"**: Charles Coolidge to FLO, May 3, 1887, Stanford Library, Special Collections.

357   **simply cribbed one:** Reference to Shepley, Rutan & Coolidge borrowing H. H. Richardson designs drawn from Paul Turner et al., *The Founders and the Architects: The Design of Stanford University* (Palo Alto: Department of Art, Stanford University, 1976), 40.

358   **"We are now compelled":** FLO to Stanford, May 14, 1890, Stanford Library, Special Collections.

358   **"We are gradually improving":** Stanford to FLO, November 9, 1891, Stanford Library, Special Collections.

Chapter 29: Big House in the Big Woods

360   **"delicate, refined, and bookish":** FLO to Kingsbury, January 20, 1891.

361   **"What do you imagine":** Ibid.

361   **During recent travels:** Interview on August 30, 2010, JM with Bill Alexander, landscape and forest historian, the Biltmore Estate.

362   ***The Cultivation and Management:*** Bill Alexander, *The Biltmore Nursery: A Botanical Legacy* (Charleston, SC: Natural History Press, 2007), 23.

362   **"There is no experience":** FLO to George Vanderbilt, July 12, 1889.

362   **"Such land in Europe":** FLO to Kingsbury, January 20, 1891.

363   **"private work of very rare public interest":** FLO to W. A. Thompson, November 6, 1889.

363   **"earnest, tempestuous and used":** FLO, quoted in John Bryan, *The Biltmore Estate: The Most Distinguished Private Place* (New York: Rizzoli International Publications, 1994), 23.

365   **"fall tripingly [*sic*] off":** FLO to Vanderbilt, July 12, 1889.

366   **"My office is much better":** FLO to Brace, January 18, 1890.

366   **"His death was a shock":** FLO to Kingsbury, January 20, 1891.

366   **"dosed me excessively":** Ibid.

366   **Woozy, half out of his mind:** Details of Olmsted's composing his first letter to Elizabeth Baldwin Whitney from *Papers*, 1:66.

366   **"in vino veritas":** Ibid.

367   **"queer note":** FLO to Elizabeth Baldwin Whitney, December 16, 1890.

367   **"I know that in the minds":** Ibid.

367   **"stating on honor":** FLO to FLO Jr., [about] December 1, 1890.

368   **"I have, with an amount":** FLO to FLO Jr., September 5, 1890.

368   **"It would be no use":** FLO Jr. to FLO, November 25, 1890.

Chapter 30: A White City Dreamscape

370   **"toothless, witless old dotard":** R. Reid Badger, *The Great American Fair: The World's Columbian Exposition and American Culture* (Chicago: Nelson Hall, 1979), 45.

370   **"cattle show":** Donald Miller, *City of the Century: The Epic of Chicago and the Making of America* (New York: Simon and Schuster, 1996), 379–380.

371   **"Chicago Shall Rise Again!":** Badger, *Great American Fair*, 33.

371   **"In all the world":** Ibid., 31.

371   **"When can you be here?":** Erik Larson, *The Devil in the White City: Murder, Magic, and Madness at the Fair That Changed America* (New York: Vintage Books, 2004), 52.

372 "We have carried our": FLO to JCO, November 24, 1890.
373 "some big strong tree": Miller, *City of the Century*, 317.
374 "looked as if he were drawing": Ibid., 328.
374 "Do you mean to say": Ibid., 382.
375 "Gentlemen, 1893 will be": Larson, *The Devil in the White City*, 97.
375 "a place of relief": FLO to Henry Codman, November 4, 1891.
376 "You're dreaming, gentlemen": Larson, *The Devil in the White City*, 115.
376 Staff is a kind: Description of staff drawn in part from interview, June 9, 2010, JM with Julia Bachrach, Chicago Park District.
377 "I suspect that even": FLO to Daniel Burnham, December 23, 1891.
377 In a follow-up memo: FLO to Burnham, December 28, 1891.
377 "You know that if boats": FLO to Burnham, December 23, 1891.
378 "Turkey red" wallpaper: FLO to FLO Jr., June 28, 1891.
378 "grandiloquent pomp": "Report of Frederick Law Olmsted," April 1892, fragment, Library of Congress.
379 "peculiarity of my case": FLO to Henry Codman, June 16, 1892.
380 "You know that I am": Ibid.
380 "A most capital school": FLO to partners, July 19, 1892.
381 "I am tired": FLO to JCO, October 11, 1892.
381 "I have worked, I have schemed": Miller, *City of the Century*, 382.
381 "I am as one standing on a wreck": FLO to Gifford Pinchot, January 19, 1893.
381 The temperature on February 4, 1893: FLO to JCO, February 4, 1893.
382 "It looks as if": FLO to JCO, February 17, 1893.
382 "The dirt of the provisional": FLO to JCO, April 27, 1893.
382 "I am living": FLO to JCO, April 20, 1893.
383 "paints with lakes and wooded slopes": Daniel Burnham speech of March 25, 1893, Ryerson and Burnham Libraries, the Art Institute of Chicago.
383 "I doubt if a man": Kingsbury to FLO, July 8, 1893.
384 "Everywhere there is growing interest": FLO to Burnham, June 20, 1893.
385 "Mr. Olmstead Talks": *Atlanta Constitution*, March 18, 1894.
385 "Words fail": Badger, *Great American Fair*, 97.

Chapter 31: "Before I Am the Least Prepared for It"

388 a forty-nine-page pamphlet: Bill Alexander, *The Biltmore Nursery: A Botanical Legacy* (Charleston, SC: Natural History Press, 2007), 27.
388 "Am I needed at Kansas City?": FLO to JCO, October 27, 1893.
388 "My health is extremely frail": FLO to JCO, October 28, 1893.
388 "*This* is a place and G. W. V.": FLO to partners, November 1, 1893.
389 "breaks suddenly and fully": FLO to George Vanderbilt, July 12, 1889.
389 "Hasn't Olmsted done wonders": Alexander, *Biltmore Nursery*, 48.
390 "Write in a personal way": FLO to FLO Jr., December 23, 1894.
391 "I am compelled to answer": FLO Jr. to FLO, January 1, 1895.
392 The letters were nearly identical: J. G. Langston "reminiscence" from January 31, 1921, Library of Congress.
393 "I can't think that you": FLO to partners, August 31, 1895, Loeb Library.
393 "It would help us very much": JCO to FLO, September 2, 1895.
393 "In my flurry": FLO to Charles Eliot, September 26, 1895, Loeb Library.
394 "in a dreadful state": MPO to JCO, September 27, 1895.

394 **"I am lying awake nights"**: FLO to FLO Jr., July 11 or August 11 [unclear], 1895.
394 **"Observe, inquire, read"**: FLO to FLO Jr., [date unclear but appears to be autumn 1895].
394 **"I write only in yielding"**: FLO to FLO Jr., October 15, 1895.
394 **"I am thinking more"**: FLO to FLO Jr., October 14, 1895.
395 **"You cannot think how much"**: FLO to FLO Jr., October 1895 [no day specified in letter].
396 **"I am going down hill rapidly"**: FLO to JCO, December 12, 1895, Loeb Library.
396 **His wife had died**: Francis Kowsky, *Country, Park, and City: The Architecture and Life of Calvert Vaux* (New York: Oxford University Press, 1998), 312.
396 **a man told the *Brooklyn Eagle***: *Brooklyn Eagle*, November 21, 1895.
397 **"I am quite equal"**: MPO to "my dear boys," April 22, 1896.
397 **In a separate letter**: Marion Olmsted to JCO and FLO Jr., March 31, 1896.
397 **Then Mary traveled to the Continent**: MPO to JCO, April 10, 1896.
398 **"They didn't carry"**: Laura Wood Roper, *FLO: A Biography of Frederick Law Olmsted* (Baltimore: Johns Hopkins University Press, 1973), 474.
398 **"I said you could"**: JCO to FLO Jr., December 15, 1897, Loeb Library.

Chapter 32: Fade

399 **At two o'clock in the morning on August 28, 1903:** Theodora Kimball timeline, Library of Congress.
399 **Three days later:** A small funeral service was held at Fairsted; it appears that Mary Olmsted attended this service but not the interment of Olmsted's ashes at the Old North Cemetery in Hartford. See JCO to Sophia White Olmsted, September 8, 1903, Loeb Library.

Epilogue: Olmsted's Wild Garden

401 **Much of its business involved circling back around:** Detail based on interviews with a number of current caretakers of Olmsted green spaces, including April 2, 2010, JM with Barbara Smith and Dennis Evanosky, docents, Mountain View Cemetery.
402 **Rick also served alongside Daniel Burnham:** Interview on July 12, 2010, JM with Steve Livengood, chief guide, U.S. Capitol Historical Society.
402 **"one of the finest planned communities ever":** Susan Klaus, *A Modern Arcadia: Frederick Law Olmsted Jr. and the Plan for Forest Hills Gardens* (Amherst: University of Massachusetts Press, 2002), back cover.
402 **contributions of an Olmsted sister:** Details about Marion Olmsted's role in the firm drawn from interview on June 22, 2010, JM with Alan Banks, supervisory ranger, Fairsted, Frederick Law Olmsted National Historic Site.
403 **all the way to 2000:** Details about Olmsted firm after no Olmsteds involved from ibid.
403 **"With my work":** Interview on December 2, 2010, JM with Peter Walker, founder of PWP Landscape Architecture.
404 **"the nearest thing posterity":** FLO, *The Cotton Kingdom* (New York: Da Capo Press, 1996), ix.

INDEX

Note: In subheadings, references to Frederick Law Olmsted are shown with the initials FLO; subheadings referring to Frederick Law Olmsted Jr. "Rick" are shown with the name Rick.

Abbott, James, 106–107
Abolitionist, FLO as
  FLO's initial gradualist stance on slavery, 75–76
  FLO's opposition to slavery on economic grounds, 82–86, 192–195
  FLO's view that slavery causes cultural stagnation, 86–87, 93, 139–140
  Contrast provided by Texas German free-soilers, 97–101, 103–105
  FLO's aid to Kansas free-soilers, 106–107
  FLO's abolitionist stance stiffens, 106–107, 115, 207–208, 214, 259
  FLO's reaction to Emancipation Proclamation, 214
Across the Continent (Bowles), 268, 277
Ahwahneechee Indians, 248, 249
Akerly, Samuel, 53, 54, 55
Allison, Samuel, 92–93
Alphand, Jean-Charles Adolphe, 164
Alzheimer's or some other form of senile dementia afflicts FLO, 392–399
American Association for the Relief of the Misery of Battlefields (AARMB), 228
American Freedmen's Aid Union, 275
American Institute of Architects, 137
American Red Cross (Olmsted's USSC as forerunner), 228–229
The American Spelling Book (Webster), 11
Anderson, Robert, 179–180

Arboretums
  Biltmore Estate (proposed), 364, 389, 393
  Boston's Arnold Arboretum, 338–339
  Stanford University (proposed), 357
Architecture (structures vs. landscape)
  of Biltmore mansion, 360–364, 387, 389
  for buildings at Chicago World's Fair, 374–376, 380, 383
  Downing and Vaux collaborations, 136
  Richardson and FLO collaborations, 337–345
  See also under names of specific architects
Arendt, Hannah, 404
Aristotle, 285
Arnold Arboretum, Boston, 338–339
Arthur, Chester, 229
Ashburner, William, 248, 252, 266
Asheville, North Carolina, 4, 360–363, 390–391
Atlanta, Georgia. *See* Druid Hills
Atlantic magazine, 157, 182, 183, 249

Bache, Alexander, 181
Back Bay Fens (park), Boston, 335–338, 404
Baldwin, Elizabeth, 40–43, 70, 366–367
Barnum, P. T., 286, 319, 320
"Bartleby the Scrivener" novella (Melville), 111
Barton, Clara, 228–229

437

Barton, F. A., 18
Baseball games in Central Park, 175
Beadle, Chauncey, 364, 390
Bear Valley, California, 237–238
Beck, James, 322
Beecher, Henry Ward, 106–107
Beecher Bibles (Sharps rifles), 106–107
Belle Isle park, Detroit, 345
Bellows, Henry
  as USSC creator, administrator,
    180–182, 206, 212
  relationship with FLO, 191, 216–217,
    221, 224–227
  founds AARMB, 228
  supports Geneva treaty, 228–229
  death, 352
Belmont, August, 145–147, 156
"Benito Cereno" story (Melville), 113
Benkard and Hutton importer, 19–20, 31
Bennett, James Gordon, 77, 127
Bentham and Hooker classification
  system, 339
Bierce, Ambrose, 353
Bierstadt, Albert, 249, 332
Biltmore Estate, Asheville, North Carolina
  design of mansion by Hunt, 363–364,
    387
  landscape design by FLO, 4, 361–365,
    372, 387–389
  Rick serves as apprentice on project,
    389–391, 394–395
  naming of estate, 365
  See also Forest management
Birge, George, 294
Birkenhead Park, Liverpool, England, 62
Blackwood's Magazine, 113–114
Bleeding Kansas, 106, 107, 118
Bois de Boulogne, Paris, 164
Boone and Crockett Club, 377
Boston, Massachusetts
  Arnold Arboretum, 338–339
  Back Bay Fens, 335–338
  Franklin Park, 345–346
  park commissions, 325, 334
  park system (Emerald Necklace),
    341–346, 392
Boulder, Colorado, 402
Bow Bridge in Central Park, 157, 405
Bowles, Samuel, 266–268, 277, 299

Brace, Charles Loring "Charley"
  background and youth, 36–37, 55, 56,
    61–65
  as abolitionist, 76–77, 104, 107
  as author, 77, 80, 277, 314
  Children's Aid Society founder, 80, 93,
    277, 353
  hires Vaux for children's housing, 350
  imprisoned in Hungary, 65, 69
  marriage and family, 69, 317
  as USSC inspector during Civil War,
    188
  death, 366
Brace, Joab, 16–17
Brady, Mathew, 141, 165
Bridge designs (FLO parks), 156–157,
  294, 337–338
Bright, Edward, 285
Bright's disease, 351–352, 366
British Sanitary Commission, 181
Brookline, Massachusetts (FLO's home).
  See Fairsted
Brooklyn park. *See* Prospect Park,
  Brooklyn
Brooks, David, 38
Brooks–Sumner incident in U.S.
  Congress, 117–118
Bryant, William Cullen, 55, 127, 317
Bryn Mawr College, Pennsylvania, 401
Buena Vista Vinicultural Society, 260
Buffalo park system, New York, 287–289,
  292–296
Buffalo State Asylum for the Insane, New
  York, 297–299
Bull, Mary Ann. *See* Olmsted, Mary Ann
Burnham, Daniel
  as Chicago World's Fair director,
    373–378, 381–385
  gives tribute honoring FLO, 1, 3, 383
  on McMillan Commission, 402
Burritt, Elihu, 46–47
Bushnell, Horace, 170
Butler, Benjamin, 343
Butler, John, 171

Capital (Das Kapital, Marx), 207
Capitol project, Washington, D.C. *See*
  U.S. Capitol building and
  landscaping

Carl (pseudonym for F. L. Olmsted), 219

Carl of Solms-Braunfels (prince of Germany), 98

Carlyle, Thomas, 45–46, 291, 348

Carson, Kit, 232

Cat, FLO's named Minna, 51

Central Park, New York
background and early history of park, 124–131
FLO as park superintendent, 131–133, 135
park design competition, 138–147. *See also* Greensward Plan
administration and policing, 166–167, 173–175
features, 142–159, 283–284, 305, 404
FLO's battles with Andrew Green over money, 167–169, 173–175
FLO and Vaux ongoing role with park, 210, 265, 283–284, 295, 303–306, 318, 329, 338, 370, 379
FLO's special passion for the park, 210, 235, 305, 315, 333, 343, 370
damaged by Tammany Hall, 303–306
Vaux's complaint that he's denied credit for park, 241–242, 309, 332
FLO ousted 329–332
tribute to FLO's design, 404–405
See also park features: Bow Bridge, the Dairy, the Lake, Pavilion, the Ramble, Sheep's Meadow

Chase, Salmon, 194, 196

Chicago Great Fire (1871), 300–302, 370–371, 372

Chicago park system
original 1871 design, 296–297, 301–302
Jackson Park, 372, 374, 386
Midway Plaisance, 296–297, 302, 372, 385, 404
Washington Park, 301–302, 362, 372
See also World's Fair of 1893

Children's Aid Society, 80, 93, 277, 353

Childs, Emery, 289–292, 300–301

China voyage (FLO's), 4, 24–34, 178, 375

Chirk Castle in Wales, 64

Cholera, 129, 173, 181

Church, Frederic, 137, 305, 349

Civil War (1861–1865)
as viewed in England, 3, 208–209
camp conditions reported by USSC, 184–185
end of slavery demanded in Emancipation Proclamation, 213–214
medical relief by USSC, hospital ships, 178–181, 197–206
final stages, 223, 258–259
See also United States Sanitary Commission

Civil War Battles (and USSC's relief efforts)
Antietam, 211–213
Bull Run, 186–190
Fair Oaks, 203–205
Gettysburg, 219–222
Vicksburg campaign, 216–218
Williamsburg, 200–201

Clark, Abby, 39

Clark, Galen, 248, 252, 266, 268, 354

Cleveland, Grover, 349, 384

Cleveland, Horace W. S., 301–302, 362, 403

Codman, Henry
as FLO's apprentice, 344–345
and Stanford University project, 354–355
as partner of F. L. Olmsted and Company, 366
role in World's Fair project, 371–373, 378
death, 381

Codman, Philip, 378

Colfax, Schuyler, 266–268

College of California, 262, 274

Columbian Exposition. *See* World's Fair of 1893

Commissioner of contrabands, 194–196

Common spaces as design concept, 291, 295, 301, 356, 401

Commonwealth Avenue, Boston, 346

"Communitiveness," 356

Compromise of 1850, 75

Concerts in Central Park, 154–155, 158

Condit, Frances, 39

Confederacy
  effects of Emancipation Proclamation,
    213–214
  scrip and war bonds, 220, 223
Congregationalist church, 41, 319
Conness, John, 245–246, 251–252, 268
Conservation of natural places. *See*
  Environmentalism
Constitution steamship, 235
Contoit's New York Garden, New York,
  126
Cook, Clarence, 144, 317
Cook, Sarah, 39
Coolidge, Charles, 357
Coon, Henry, 262, 274
Cornell, Alonzo, 348–349
Cottingham, Lewis, 135
The Cotton Kingdom (F. L. Olmsted), 3,
  207–209, 403–404
  helps shift Britain's support to Union, 3,
    208–209
Croquet mania (Prospect Park, New York
  City), 282
*The Cultivation and Management of Our
  Native Forests . . .* (H. W. S.
  Cleveland), 362
Culture
  Downing as critic, 68
  of Gullahs of Port Royal plantations, 193
  insecurities of Americans, 111, 369
  poverty of South/primacy of North, 86,
    93, 190
  of Texan Germans, 99
Culyer, John, 280
Curtis, George, 112, 120–122

Dairy, Central Park, 284, 304
Dalton, Charles, 325, 334, 339
Dame schools, 9–12
Dana, Charles, 112, 146, 226
Dana, Richard Henry, Jr., 21–22
Daniel Webster hospital ship, 198–199, 205
Darwin, Charles, 207, 314
Darwin, Emma, 208
David Parker and Company, 241
Davis, Alexander Jackson, 52, 67
Davis, Henry, 49
Davis, Jefferson, 208
Davis, Mrs. (Henry's wife), 49, 51

Day, Ellen, 51
Day, Mary, 51
Deer Isle, Maine, 392–395, 397, 398
Defoe, Daniel, 314
Degener, Edouard, 100–101
Delano, Sara, 136
Delaware Park. *See* Buffalo park system,
  New York
Democratic equality of people. *See*
  Egalitarianism *and* Social reform and
  social vision
Dennett, J. R., 276
Denver, Colorado, 366
Detroit, Michigan, 402
Dickens, Charles, 116, 206–207, 257
Dillon, Robert, 145–147
Dix, Edwards & Company, 109–116, 120
Dix, Joshua, 109, 112, 119–120
Dodworth, Harvey, 154–155, 158
Dogs (FLO's companions)
  Neptune, 49, 51, 54
  Judy, 95, 102
Dombey and Son (Dickens), 257
Domes of Yosemite painting (Bierstadt),
  249
Donkeys (Fanny, Kitty, and Beppo, ridden
  by FLO's children), 247
Dorsheimer, William, 287, 292, 294, 298,
  347–349
Douai, Adolph, 100, 103–105
Douglas, Stephen, 105
Downing, Andrew Jackson
  as 19th century taste-maker, 50–51,
    67–68, 127
  calls for a New York City park, 127
  employs architect Vaux, 67–68,
    135–136
  landscape commission for U.S. Capitol,
    130, 136, 183, 288
  edits *Horticulturist*, 50–51
  death, 130, 136
Druid Hills planned suburb in Atlanta,
  365, 373, 388

Eastman, George Clinton Van Vechten,
  17–18
École des Beaux-Arts, Paris, 263, 297, 344
École Nationale Forestière, Nancy, France,
  387

Economic crisis (panic of 1857), 132–133
Edwards, Arthur, 109, 112
Egalitarianism
    FLO taken by democratic spirit of
        Birkenhead Park, 63
    FLO's view that Central Park is for
        everyone, 140, 152–155
    FLO's view that Yosemite is for
        everyone, 267
    See also Social reform and social vision
Eidlitz, Leopold, 330
Eliot, Charles
    apprentice, 344–345
    as partner with FLO, 382, 388, 393
Ellicott, Joseph, 292–293
Ellington grammar school, Connecticut,
    15–16
Elliott, Charles (Central Park board
    member), 124
Elliott, Ezekiel, 188
Ellsworth, James, 371, 375
Elm City hospital ship, 202–203
Emancipation Proclamation (September
    1862), 213–214
Emerald Necklace park system, Boston,
    341–346
Emerson, Ralph Waldo, 40, 45, 112, 136,
    145–146, 348
Emerson, William, 122
Endale Arch, Prospect Park, New York
    City, 281
England and Europe travels
    walking tour (1850), 61–65
    for *Putnam's Magazine*, 116–120
    with stepson John Charles, 328–333
    for health, nervous disorders, 162,
        378–380, 396–398
The Englishman in Kansas . . .
    (Gladstone), 121
Environmentalism
    youthful appreciation of nature by
        FLO, 11–12, 13, 15, 18, 48, 56, 63,
        69, 81, 96
    Yosemite, 2, 245–246, 251–252,
        266–268
    Niagara Falls, 2, 298, 339–340,
        347–351
    wetlands restoration (Back Bay Fens), 2,
        337

Rick's role in creating national parks, 402
    See also Forest management
Epistle IV to Richard Boyle (Pope), 323
Errington, Harriet (Olmsted family
    governess), 246–247, 248, 251
Essay on the Picturesque . . . (Price), 15

F. L. & J. C. Olmsted Company, 345
F. L. Olmsted and Company, 366
Fairmount Farm of George Geddes, 44
Fairsted (FLO's home in Brookline,
    Massachusetts), 340–344, 392–393
Famine at Home circular, 285
Farming (scientific)
    apprenticeships, 37–38, 44–47
    in England, 63–64
    under Geddes, 44–47
    Sachem's Head (FLO's Connecticut
        farm), 48–53, 66
    of Texas Germans, 97, 99
    Tosomock (FLO's Staten Island, New
        York, farm), 59–60
Fenton, Roger, 165
Fenway Park, Boston, 404
Fillmore, Millard, 130, 136, 288
Finley, Clement Alexander, 190–191, 197
Forest Hills Gardens, New York, 402
Forest management (FLO's efforts),
    361–363, 387–388, 395–396
'48ers (German-Americans), 100
Foster, Lafayette, 195, 196
Fox, Warren, 23–34, 276
Franklin Park, Boston, 345–346
Frémont, John Charles
    background, 232–233
    owns Mariposa Estate, 226
    as debtor, 239–240, 244
    testifies in Opdyke–Weed trial, 255
    dies nearly penniless, 265
French, Daniel Chester, 383
Froebel, Julius, 100
Fugitive Slave Act of 1850, 75, 105
Furness, Horace Howard, 212

Gage, Lyman, 374–375, 376
Garden and Forest magazine, 362
Gardening for Ladies (Loudon), 314
Garrison, William Lloyd, 76
Geddes, George, 44–47, 69, 352

Geneva treaty, 228–229

A Geography and Atlas (Olney), 11

German Americans
anti-slavery attitudes, 98–101, 103–104
erect Central Park statue of Schiller,
155–156
'48ers, 100–101
free-soilers in Texas, 98–99

Gerster, Anton, 157, 308

Gibbs, Oliver Wolcott, 181, 228

Gilpin, William, 15, 63, 139, 342

Gladstone, Thomas, 118, 121

Godkin, Edwin
abortive publishing project with FLO,
225–226
as FLO's friend, supporter, 241, 332,
344, 383
as journalist, 89
runs *Nation* magazine with FLO, 260,
274–275

Gold mining. *See* Mariposa Estate
gold-mining property

Gold Rush in California
causes inflation, 132
and Frémont's floating land grant,
232–233
impact on Yosemite, 246, 248

"Gold Under Gilt" story (F. L. Olmsted),
90

Golden Gate Park, 306–308, 354. *See also*
San Francisco park

Goldsmith, Oliver, 15

Goodloe, Daniel, 207

Goodrich, Samuel (Peter Parley), 11

Goodwin, Jim, 22–23, 25–26, 32

Gradualist position on slavery, 75–76,
115, 214

Gramercy Park, Manhattan, 127

Grammar schools and boarding schools
(FLO's), 12–17

Grant, Ulysses, 215, 217, 223, 226, 234,
308

Grass Valley gold-mining operations,
244–245

Gray, John, 137, 141

Greeley, Horace, 107, 157, 232, 308–309

Green, Andrew
battles over Central Park with FLO,
158–159, 164–169, 174–175
conflict with an ill and delirious Vaux,
210
on Tweed Ring park board, 304, 306
on Niagara Falls improvement board,
349–350

Greensward Plan, 139–147, 151, 156,
158, 280

Greensward Ring, 329, 330

Green-Wood Cemetery, Brooklyn, 127

Griffin, Christine Kean, 198

Grinnell, Moses, 180

Groesbeck, William, 309

Grundel, Hermann, 334, 335

Gullah community of Sea Islands, 193–194

Hale, Edward Everett, 106

Hall, William Hammond, 306–308, 354,
403

Halleck, Fitz-Greene, 156

Hamilton, James Alexander, 124–125

Hammond, James, 208

Hammond, William, 197, 314

Haraszthy, Agoston, 260–261

Harper's New Monthly Magazine, 111,
112, 116, 241

Harris, Elisha, 181

Harrison, Jonathan, 349

Hartford, Connecticut, 6–12, 312,
317–318, 399

Hartford Female Seminary, 39

Hartford Grammar School, 14, 15

Hartford Retreat for the Insane, 8,
170–171, 394

Hartford Young Men's Institute library,
15, 63, 307

Harvard University
Arnold Arboretum's unique public/
university partnership, 338–339
attended by Rick, 367
confers honorary degree on FLO,
383–384
Rick sets up first landscape architecture
course in America, 402

Hawthorne, Nathaniel, 314

Henry Clay steamship, 62, 68–69, 130

Hillside Cemetery in Middletown, New
York, 169

History of England (Macaulay), 314

Hitchcock, Sophia, 116–117

Hoe, Richard, 111
Horses (FLO and John Hull Olmsted's)
    Fanny, 94, 98, 102
    Nack, 94, 98, 102
    Belshazzar, 102
Horticulturist journal, 50–51, 67–68, 127
Hudson River School art and painters,
    136–137, 156–157, 305
Hughes, Langston, 404
Hungary in 1851 (Brace), 77
Hunt, Richard Morris
    battles with Vaux, 263, 297
    as architect of Biltmore mansion,
        360–364, 387, 389
    painted by Sargent, 391–392
    as architect of building at 1893 World's
        Fair, 374–375, 383
    death, 392

Ice-skating in Central Park, 151–153
Incidents of a Whaling Voyage (Francis
    Olmsted), 21
Indian Hunter statue (Ward), 156
Infantile Chemistry Association, 38, 43, 277
Irving, Washington, 125

Jackson Park, Chicago, 372, 374, 386
Jefferson, Thomas, 40, 85, 146
Jenney, William Le Baron
    as engineer during Civil War, 217–218
    involvement in Riverside suburb
        project, 301
    as architect involved in 1893 World's
        Fair, 374, 375
Jesup, Morris, 125, 332
Jewett, Helen, 77
Jewett, Sherman, 288
Jones Wood, Manhattan, 128
Journalism (FLO's involvement in),
    68–69, 77–89, 91–102, 108,
    115–120, 124, 135, 207–208
The Journal of Gideon Olmsted (G.
    Olmsted), 21
A Journey in the Back Country (F. L.
    Olmsted), 124, 135, 163, 208
A Journey in the Seaboard Slave States (F. L.
    Olmsted), 115–116, 119, 207
A Journey Through Texas (F. L. Olmsted),
    120

Kansas Territory, 105–107, 121
Kansas-Nebraska Act of 1854, 105–107
Kapp, Ernst, 100
Kapp, Friedrich, 352
Kern, G. M., 314
Kessler, George, 403
King, Thomas Starr, 216
Kingsbury, Frederick
    background, friendship with FLO, 37,
        69
    on FLO's honorary degrees, 383–384
    on FLO's idealism, perseverance, 50, 52
    letters to/from FLO, 38–39, 305, 312,
        353, 361, 366
Kingsley, Charles, 118
Kirkbride, Thomas, 311
Kirkbride Plan (mental institution
    design), 311
Klein, Naomi, 404

The Lake at Central Park, 149–153, 155
Lake Champlain, Vermont, 360
Landscape architecture
    FLO's prescient interest in park-
        making, 62–63, 69, 93,
    FLO's earliest efforts while living on
        Staten Island, 56–57, 360
    FLO–Vaux partnership, 150–151,
        271–272, 283–284, 295–296,
        305–306
    FLO as pioneer in field 1, 150–151,
        170, 225, 285–286, 328, 344–345,
        354–355
    "landscape architect" as term for new
        profession, 170
    FLO's aesthetics as a landscape
        architect, 144–145, 150, 151, 155,
        323, 345, 363, 377
    FLO as expert at foliage composition,
        153–154, 157, 235–236, 261–262,
        297, 336–337, 343, 376, 380, 390
    FLO as undistinguished gardener and
        botanist, 157, 337, 364, 380, 390
    FLO as big-idea person, deficient
        draftsman, 261, 313, 336
    reliance by FLO on technology and
        engineering in park-making,
        148–150, 163, 279–280, 290,
        336–337, 373, 375

Landscape architecture (*continued*)
reliance by FLO on artificial means to
create natural-looking parks, 149,
151, 153, 279–280, 292, 324,
335–336, 375
similarity to FLO between landscape
architecture and music, 154–155
apprenticeships offered by FLO, 344–345
Horace Cleveland's practice, 362
Harvard course, 402
See also individual projects: Arnold
Arboretum, Back Bay Fens, Biltmore
Estate, Buffalo park system, Buffalo
State Asylum for the Insane, Central
Park, Franklin Park, McLean Asylum,
Mountain View Cemetery, Mount
Royal, Prospect Park, Niagara Falls,
Riverside, IL, Stanford University,
U.S. Capitol, World's Fair
Larkin, John, 294
Lathrop, Ariel, 357–358
Law, Jonathan, 6
Lawrenceville School, 345, 355
Lee, Robert E., 211, 219–221, 258
Leland Stanford Jr. University. *See*
Stanford University
L'Enfant, Pierre-Charles, 292–293, 322
Lenox, Massachusetts, 360
Lewes, George Henry, 118
Lewis, Diocletian, 152
Liberator abolitionist newspaper, 76, 275
Life of Benjamin Silliman, M.D.
(Silliman), 277
Lincoln, Abraham
earliest photograph of, 35
as president during Civil War, 186–187,
208, 211, 213–214, 220, 226, 251
lukewarm toward USSC, 181–182, 191
FLO's impressions and dealings with,
185–186, 191–192, 195, 205, 214
issues Emancipation Proclamation,
213–214
signs Yosemite Valley bill, 251
death, 258–259
statue in Prospect Park, 280–281
Lincoln, Mary Todd, 186
Little Dorrit (Dickens), 116
Liverpool, England, 62–63, 72, 162–163,
378, 396

Llewellyn Park in West Orange, New
Jersey, 52
Longfellow, Henry Wadsworth, 112, 113,
348
Long Meadow, Prospect Park, New York
City, 272, 281–282
Longstreet, James, 220
Loudon, Jane, 314
Loudon, John Claudius, 307
Louisville, Kentucky, 378, 388, 401
Low, Frederick, 252
Lowell, James Russell, 40, 112, 276
Ludlow, Fitz Hugh, 249
Lynch, Anne Charlotte, 10, 90

Macaulay, Thomas Babington, 314
MacMonnies, Frederick, 384
Maine College of Agriculture and the
Mechanic Arts, 286, 299, 355
Malaria, 131–132, 193, 210, 234, 360
Malcolm X, 404
Manhattan brownstone, FLO's home-
office, 313–314
Marble Faun (Hawthorne), 314
Mariposa Estate gold-mining property
history including Frémont's ownership,
226, 232–233
FLO wrestles with whether to accept
job in California, 226–227
FLO's tenure as superintendent, 237–241,
244–245, 253, 256–257, 259
financial collapse due to board
members' swindle, 254–259
reorganizes, fails repeatedly, 265
Mariposa Grove of Big Trees, 250–252,
266, 354
Mayne, Richard, 163
McAdam, John Loudon, 290
McClellan, George, 191, 197, 203, 205,
213, 220
McEntee, Jervis, 136–137, 141–142, 143,
350
McEntee, Mary Swan, 137. *See also* Mary
Vaux
McKim, Charles, 374
McKim, James, 275–276, 309, 374
McLean Asylum, Belmont, Massachusetts,
310–311, 398–399
McMillan, William, 296

McMillan Commission, 402

Meade, George, 220

Medical Bureau, U.S. Army, 180–181, 190–197

Melville, Herman, 111, 113

Mental illness
    FLO's breakdowns, depression, dementia, 161–162, 209–210, 224, 318–319, 392–398
    FLO's decline and admission to McLean Asylum, 397–398
    and mercury for medicinal use, 209
    FLO's mother and stepdaughter, 9, 316, 352, 397
    FLO's special sympathy for sufferers, 170–171, 189, 298–299, 310–311

Mental institutions (featuring Olmsted landscape designs)
    Bloomingdale Asylum New York, 170, 203
    Buffalo State Asylum for the Insane, 298–299
    Hartford Retreat, 8, 170–171, 394
    McLean Asylum, Belmont, 310–311, 398

Metropolitan Museum of Art, New York, 310, 350, 361

Michaux, François André, 290–291

Midway, as term coined by Olmsted and Vaux, 385, 404

Midway Plaisance, Chicago, 296–297, 302, 372, 385, 404

Mill, John Stuart, 118, 208–209, 314

Millbrae, California, 262, 404

Miller, J. W., 120–121

Miller & Company, 121–122

Mills, Darius, 262, 404

Mills, Robert, 136

Milwaukee, Wisconsin, 366

Minturn, Robert, 309

Miss Rockwell's school, 10–12, 90

Miwok Indians, 249

Modern Painters (Ruskin), 58–59, 70

Mongredien, Augustus, 314

Montreal (Mount Royal park), 323–326

Morgan, J. P., 284

Morrill, Justin, 320

Mould, Jacob Wrey, 141–143, 158

Mounds, Maria, 39

Mount Royal, Montreal, 323–326

Mount St. Vincent, Manhattan, 160, 164, 169, 204

Mountain View Cemetery, Oakland, California, 170, 261–262, 401

Muir, John, 268

Mule (Mr. Brown, used by FLO and John Hull Olmsted), 94, 96, 102

Museum of Natural History, New York, 310, 350, 361

My Diary North and South (Russell), 219

Nader, Ralph, 404

Nation
    early efforts to start a national weekly publication, 225–226
    founding by abolitionists, 260, 275
    FLO's involvement, 276–278, 404
    ad for Olmsted, Vaux & Company, 295

National American Democratic Republican Party, 309

Nature
    youthful appreciation by FLO, 11–12, 13, 15, 18, 48, 56, 63, 69, 81, 96
    FLO relies on artificial means to create natural-looking parks, 149, 151, 153, 279–280, 292, 324, 335–336, 375
    as architect Vaux's credo, 156–157
    eases melancholy, 170
    appreciation by Hudson River School painters, 136–137

Neu Braunfels, Texas, 97–99, 100

Nevins, Allan, 179, 265

New England Emigrant Aid Company, 106

New York Daily Times/New York Times newspaper
    background on paper and FLO being hired, 78
    FLO's "The South" column, 3, 77–89
    FLO's Texas dispatches, 91, 94, 99, 102
    on Central Park, 153, 157
    exposes Tweed Ring, 305

Niagara Falls
    degradation of this landmark, 347–348
    FLO's early preservation efforts, 298, 339–340, 348–349
    FLO–Vaux partnership on preservation project, 349–351

Niblo's Garden, New York, 126

Nicolay, John, 214
Norman, Henry, 349
North America (Trollope), 219
North American Sylva (Nuttall), 291
Norton, Charles Eliot
  friendship with FLO, 279, 344, 383
  Niagara Falls preservation efforts,
    348–349
  on Southern trilogy, 206
Nuttall, Thomas, 290–291

Ocean Queen hospital steamship, 199–200
Olmsted, Aaron (great-uncle), 8, 21, 22
Olmsted, Albert (half-brother), 311–312,
  317–318
Olmsted, Benjamin (grandfather), 14–15,
  22
Olmsted, Bertha (half-sister), 32,
  116–117, 182, 312
Olmsted, Charlotte (mother), 6, 8–9, 42
Olmsted, Charlotte (stepdaughter)
  birth, 110
  adopted by FLO, 160
  marries, has children, 344
  mental illness, 316, 352, 397
Olmsted, Content Pitkin (grandmother),
  14–15, 192
Olmsted, Denison, 113
Olmsted, Francis (cousin), 21
Olmsted, Frederick Law
  childhood, early education, vocational
    apprenticeships, 6–20
  as sailor, 21–34
  at Yale, 38–39
  as farmer, 37–38, 43–61, 63–66
  romantic life as a young man, 39–41,
    43, 51, 57–59, 69–72
  as reporter, writer, publisher, 68–69,
    77–89, 91–102, 108, 115–120, 124,
    135, 207–208
  as head of USSC, Civil War medical
    relief outfit, 182–192, 196–206
  in California, 232–263
  as landscape architect. *See* Landscape
    architecture for detailed subject
    breakdown and list of some of FLO's
    major projects
  as early environmentalist. *See*
    Environmentalist

  as futurist, 142–143, 267, 293
  as social reformer. *See* Social reform and
    social vision
  marriage and family life, 159–162, 169,
    192, 203–204, 214–215, 235,
    246–247, 282–283, 299–300,
    313–319, 330–-331, 333, 340–344,
    391–399
  religion, experience and views, 10,
    13–14, 16–18, 28–29, 41–43,
    45–46, 319
  social life, 35–37, 182, 317, 344
  travel, 2, 61–65, 79–88, 92–102,
    116–120, 162–165, 215–219,
    234–237, 332–334, 361–362,
    378–380, 396–397
  health problems, physical and mental, 4,
    17–18, 25–26, 32, 34, 120, 161–162,
    172–174, 209–210, 318–319, 330,
    333, 378–382, 392–398
  death, 399
  legacy of, 401–405
Olmsted, Frederick Law, Jr. "Rick" (son)
  rechristened from Henry Perkins
    Olmsted, 317
  youth, 300, 344, 354
  as FLO's chosen successor, 366–368,
    390–393, 398, 402
  apprenticeship on World's Fair project,
    376, 378
  apprenticeship at the Biltmore Estate,
    390–392
  and FLO's failing memory, death,
    391–392, 393–395, 399
  as partner in Olmsted Brothers, 398,
    401–402
  death, 402
Olmsted, Gideon (great-uncle), 21
Olmsted, Henry Perkins (son). *See*
  Olmsted, Frederick Law, Jr. "Rick"
Olmsted, James (ancestor), 8
Olmsted, John Charles (stepson)
  youth 160–161, 247, 283
  character and personality traits
    315–316, 328–333, 344, 398
  as FLO's employee, 325, 336, 342, 345,
    373, 388,
  tension with FLO, his stepfather and
    boss, 330–333, 393

attends to dying brother Owen,
    340–341
and FLO's failing memory, 393–397
partnership with Rick, 398, 401–402
death, 402
Olmsted, John (father)
    background, character, 6–12, 18, 38,
        52–53, 91, 225, 312, 391
    charitable donations, 8, 15, 171
    letters from FLO, 30, 44, 45, 61–62,
        72, 80, 90, 112, 113, 114, 115, 161,
        169, 174, 178, 190, 194, 196–197,
        225, 242–243, 244, 259
    money, property, given to FLO, 48–49,
        52–53, 61–62, 108–109, 114–115,
        210
    death, 311–312
Olmsted, John Hull (brother)
    childhood, 8–9, 17, 19
    at Yale, 19, 35–37
    medical training, 55, 91, 172
    observations about his brother, FLO,
        50, 58
    walking tour of England with FLO,
        61–65
    courtship and marriage to Mary
        Perkins, 58–59, 69, 72
    Texas trip with FLO, 91–102
    A Journey Through Texas, 119–120
    special relationship with FLO, 134,
        258, 283
    tuberculosis and death, 55, 71–72, 91,
        120, 133–134, 277–278
Olmsted, John Theodore (son), 169,
    172–173, 367
Olmsted, Maria (aunt), 24, 54
Olmsted, Marion (daughter)
    birth, 192
    character and personality traits, 247,
        317, 397
    unacknowledged artistic talent, 398, 402
    and FLO's failing health and memory,
        392–393, 396–398
    death, 402
Olmsted, Mary Ann née Mary Ann Bull
    (stepmother)
    marriage to FLO's father and family life,
        10–12, 17, 314
    on FLO living at home, 38

puritanical streak, participation in
    religious revivals, 10, 13, 42
contests husband John's will, 317–318
Olmsted, Mary (half-sister), 116
Olmsted, Mary Perkins (sister-in-law and
    wife)
    background, 57–58
    courtship and marriage to John Hull
        Olmsted, 58–59, 69, 72
    children with John Hull Olmsted, 110,
        160, 315–316
    death of John Hull Olmsted, 133–134
    as widow, marries FLO, 159–160
    married life with FLO, 161–162, 169,
        192, 203–204, 214–215, 235,
        246–251, 282–283, 314–319,
        391–399
    children with FLO, 169, 192, 282–283,
        300
    deaths of children, 173, 282–283,
        340–341
    daughter Charlotte's mental illness, 316,
        397
    and FLO's failing health, memory,
        393–398
    death, 402
Olmsted, Olmsted & Eliot Company, 382
Olmsted, Owen (stepson)
    adopted by FLO, 160
    resemblance to father John Hull
        Olmsted, 283, 316–317
    ranches in Montana, 340, 355
    death from tuberculosis, 340–341
Olmsted Brothers, 398, 401–403
Olney, Jesse, 11
Opdyke, George
    as Mariposa mines financial backer,
        226, 233, 240
    loses libel suit against Thurlow Weed,
        252–255
Opium wars, 30
Origin of Species (Darwin), 314
Orwell, George, 404

Panama route for Atlantic–Pacific travel,
    234–236
Panic of 1857, 132–133
Paris Exposition Universelle of 1889,
    369–370

Parish, Daniel, 136
Park making. *See* Landscape architecture
    for detailed subject breakdown and a
    list of some of FLO's major projects
Park systems
    Boston park system (Emerald
        Necklace), 341–342
    Buffalo park system, New York,
        287–289, 292–296
    Chicago park system, 296–297,
        301–302, 372–373
Parker, John, 118
Parker, Theodore, 76
Parker, Willard, 172–173, 332
Parkways
    early proposal for metro New York City,
        272–273
    in Buffalo, 293–294
    in Boston, 342, 346
    as concept and term, 293–294, 404
Parley, Peter (Samuel Goodrich), 11
Parsons, Samuel, 165
Pavilion, Central Park, 283
Paxton, Joseph, 62
Peabody, Robert, 374
Pemberton, John, 223
Perkins, Cyrus, 57
Perkins, Emily, 70–72, 106, 117
Perkins, Mary. *See* Olmsted, Mary Perkins
Philadelphia World's Fair of 1876,
    369–370
Phoenix Park, Dublin, 165
Pickett, George, 220–221
Pilat, Ignaz, 157, 235–236
Pinchot, Gifford, 387–388, 390,
    395–396
Pisgah National Forest, North Carolina, 396
Pittsburgh, Pennsylvania, 402
Planned communities, designed by FLO
    Riverside, 289–292, 301
    Atlanta, 365, 373, 388
    Denver, 366
    designed by Rick, 402
    See also Suburban communities
Poe, Edgar Allan, 90
Policing parks, 163, 166–167
Pope, Alexander, 323
Poppey, Frederick, 308
Post, George, 380

Practical Landscape Gardening (Kern), 314
Preservation. *See* Environmentalism,
    Forest management
Price, Uvedale, 15, 63, 139, 307
Principals of Political Economy (Mill), 314
Prospect Park, Brooklyn
    Vaux pursues and wins preliminary
        design project, 263–266
    Olmsted and Vaux design park, 270–273
    construction, 278–282
    Endale Arch, 281
    The Long Meadow, 272, 281–282
    sunken pathways, 281–282
    and parkway concept, 272–273, 294
    Croquet mania, 282
    special unity of design, 270–272, 281
    personnel, 279–280, 296, 301, 308,
        322, 362
Proto-environmentalism. *See*
    Environmentalism
Publishing (FLO's work as an editor as
    opposed to as a writer). *See Nation*
    and Putnam's Monthly Magazine
Punch magazine, 118–119
Putnam, George, 55, 66–69, 90, 109,
    125, 317
Putnam's Monthly Magazine
    FLO publishes short story "Gold Under
        Guilt," 90–91
    magazine's history, 110–111
    FLO's tenure as owner and editor,
        108–122
    nativist approach, publishing American
        authors, 111–114
    magazine's financial troubles and
        collapse, 114–115, 119–122

Radford, George, 296
The Ramble in Central Park, 153–154,
    235–236, 304, 380, 404–405
Raymond, Henry, 77–78, 80, 91, 146
Raymond, Israel, 245–246, 252, 268
Rayner, Henry, 379–380, 396
Red Cross (Olmsted's USSC as
    forerunner) 228–229
Reformer, FLO as. *See* Social reform and
    social vision
Regent's Park, London, 165, 332
Reid, Whitelaw, 332

Religious beliefs/religious education
  FLO's schooling, 10, 13–14, 16–18
  FLO, views and experiences, 28–29,
    41–43, 45–46
  FLO as agnostic, 319
  of Olmsted family, stepmother Mary
    Ann, 10, 13, 42
  revivals, 9, 41–43
Remarks on Forest Scenery (Gilpin), 15
*Report on the Demoralization of the
  Volunteers* (USSC), 189–190
Repton, Humphrey, 307
Republican Party, 233, 308–309
Retreat for the Insane, Hartford,
  Connecticut, 170–171. *See also*
  mental institutions
Richardson, Henry Hobson
  architectural style, 298
  Buffalo asylum architecture, 297–299
  in collaboration with FLO, 337–340, 345
  as FLO's friend, 298, 317, 335, 342,
    344
  on Niagara Falls preservation, 298, 349
  death, 351–352
Richmond, Virginia, 183, 258
Richmond County Agricultural Society,
  59–60
Riverside Improvement Company (RIC),
  289–292, 300–301
Riverside, Illinois (model suburb), 287,
  289–292, 300–301
Roads in parks and other landscape
  architecture projects
  in Back Bay Fens, 337
  for Biltmore Estate, 389
  proposed to connect New York City
    green spaces, 272–273
  macadamization in Riverside, 290
  at Niagara Falls, 351
  parkways in Buffalo design, 294
  plank roads, 47, 60
  proposed for Montreal park design,
    324–326
  separation of ways for park traffic,
    156–157, 272
  sunken transverse roads in Central Park,
    142, 145, 149, 156
Robinson Crusoe (Defoe), 314
Rochester, New York, 366

Rockwell, Naomi, 10–12
Ronaldson ship, 23–34, 276
Roosevelt, Theodore, 284, 377, 396
Root, John, 373–375, 381
Ruskin, John, 58–59, 70, 165, 342, 348
Russell, Howard, 219

Sachem's Head Farm, Connecticut,
  48–53, 66
Sailor
  FLO's time as, 21–34
Sampson Low, Son & Company,
  206–207
San Antonio Zeitung newspaper, 96,
  99–100, 103–104
San Francisco park, FLO's rejected design,
  262–263, 273–274. *See also* Golden
  Gate Park
Sargent, Charles Sprague, 338–339, 343,
  362, 389
Sargent, John Singer, 391–392
Sartor Resartus (Carlyle), 45–46, 291
Schiller, Johann Christoph Friedrich von,
  155–156
Schlesinger, Arthur, 404
Scott, William B., 265
Sea Islands, Port Royal Sound, South
  Carolina, 192–195
Second Great Awakening religious revival,
  41
Seneca Village black community,
  Manhattan, 129–130
Senile dementia or perhaps Alzheimer's
  FLO suffers from, 392–399
*Sentimental Journey Through France and
  Italy* (Sterne), 15
Separation of ways as design concept,
  156–157, 272
SFRC. *See* Southern Famine Relief
  Commission
Sheep Meadow (Central Park), 235
Shepley, Rutan & Coolidge, 356–357
Sherman, Roger, 40
Sherman, Thomas, 192–193
Sherman, William, 217
Short Sermons to News Boys (Brace), 277,
  314
Shurcliff, Arthur, 402
Silliman, Benjamin, 38, 277

Slavery
abolitionist position vs. gradualism,
75–78
FLO affected by *Uncle Tom's Cabin*,
74–75
Emancipation Proclamation issued,
213–214
as flawed economic/cultural system in
FLO's view, 83–86, 93, 192–195
plantation life as witnessed by FLO,
81–82, 92–94
punishment of slave witnessed by FLO,
87–88
anti-slavery attitudes of German settlers
in Texas, 98–101, 103–104
See also Abolitionist; *The Cotton
Kingdom*
Sleep and Its Derangements (Hammond),
314
Social reform and social vision
FLO's youthful development as a
reformer and early calls for reform,
45–47, 51, 59–60, 62–64, 93
in landscape designs, 139–140, 146,
153, 273, 274, 283–284, 291, 320,
324–325, 350–351, 356, 377–378
for the mentally ill, 170–171, 288–289,
310–311
USSC battlefield-relief in Civil War,
178–195, 228–229
attempted in Bear Valley, California, 241
SFRC aid to stricken post-war South,
284–285
progressive view of alcoholism, 218
FLO's legacy, 403
Solitude (Zimmermann), 15, 170,
342–343
"The South" column (F. L. Olmsted), 3,
80–89
Southern Famine Relief Commission
(SFRC), 284–285
Southern travels, antebellum by FLO,
79–88, 92–102
Southern trilogy (F. L. Olmsted), 124,
135, 206, 219, 403
Spaulding hospital/military transport ship,
202–203
The Spoils of the Park pamphlet (F. L.
Olmsted), 333

St. Botolph Club, Boston, 344
St. John's Park, Manhattan, 127
Stanford, Leland, 353–358
Stanford, Leland, Jr., 353
Stanford University, Palo Alto, California,
353–358
Stanton, Edwin, 196
Staten Island farm. *See* Tosomock Farm,
Staten Island
Statue of the Republic (French), 383, 384
Statues and stone carvings
in Central Park, 155–156, 158
at Chicago World's Fair, 383, 384
of Lincoln in Prospect Park, 280–281
Stearns, George, 276, 278
Stebbins, Henry, 306
Stern, Robert A. M., 402
Sterne, Laurence, 15
Stevens, Sophia, 70
Stowe, Harriet Beecher, 42, 74–76, 79
Stranahan, James, 170, 271, 279, 282
Strong, George Templeton, 181, 224, 228
Suburban communities
Brookline, 342–344
Llewellyn Park, West Orange, New
Jersey, 52
designed by Rick, 402
See also Planned Communities
(designed by FLO)
Sullivan, Louis, 301, 374, 375, 386
Sunken transverses (Central Park) 142,
145, 149, 156
Surveyor apprenticeship, 18
Sweeny, Peter "Sly," "Spider," 303–305, 329

Tammany-controlled Central Park board
damages park, 303–305
ousts FLO, 329–332
Taylor, Bayard, 125
Tebbel, John, 111
Texas travels of Olmsted brothers, 92–102
encounters with German farmers and
'48ers, 96–99, 100–101
book collaboration between brothers,
119–120
Thackeray, William Makepeace, 113–114,
118–119
Thompson, Hunter S., 404
Thoreau, Henry David, 113

Tosomock Farm, Staten Island, 53–60,
65, 91, 110
Trask, Charley, 37, 69, 172–173, 353
Trees and other foliage
for Capitol grounds design, 320–321
in Central Park, 149, 151, 157, 280
for Chicago World's Fair, 376–378,
380–382
cypress in Mountain View cemetery,
261–262
for Hartford Retreat design, 170–171
for Montreal design, 324
for Biltmore Estate approach road, 389
need for ones suited to Mediterranean
climate for Stanford University, 356
nurseries, 59, 65, 364
in Panama, 234–236
plant succession technique, 308
for salt marsh of Back Bay Fens,
336–337
sequoias in California, 250
tree-moving machine invented, 280
See also Arboretums; Forest
management
Trees and Shrubs for English Plantations
(Mongredien), 314
The Trent Affair, 208
Trinity Church, Boston, 335, 352
Trinity Church, New York, 243
Trollope, Anthony, 219
Trotter, Laura, 198
Tull, Jethro, 64
Tweed, William Marcy "Boss," 303–305,
329
Tweed Ring, 304–306
The Two Paths (Ruskin), 165
Two Years Before the Mast (Dana), 21–22
Typhoid fever, 198–199, 353

Uncle Tom's Cabin (Stowe), 74–75, 207
"Unconscious influence" of the
environment, 170
United States Sanitary Commission
(USSC)
founding and background, 178–182
and Bull Run, 186–190
aid provided at Antietam, 211–213
aid provided at Gettysburg, 220–222
hospital ships, 197–206, 218

localism problems, 215–216
medical reform efforts, 182–192,
211–214
wartime medical treatments described,
199, 201, 203
FLO's resignation, 223–227
record of battlefield relief, post-war
activity, 227–229
See also Civil War battles
Urban planning, 142, 292–295, 354, 402.
See also Planned communities
U.S. Capitol building and landscaping
FLO's design, 320–323
L'Enfant's 18th century plan, 292–293,
322
U.S. Congress, 105, 117–118, 196, 251,
320–323, 370–371
U.S. Forest Service, 396
USSC. *See* United States Sanitary
Commission

Valley of the Shadow of Death photo
(Fenton), 165
Valley of Yosemite painting (Bierstadt), 249
Vanderbilt, Cornelius, 199, 234
Vanderbilt, George Washington,
360–389, 391–392
Vanderbilt, William, 55, 57, 360
Vanderbilt family mausoleum, 361
Vaux, Bowyer, 160
Vaux, Calvert
as architect working with Downing, 68,
135–136
first meeting with FLO, 68
Central Park collaboration with FLO,
137–143, 150–153, 156–157,
283–284
feels slighted over credit given to FLO,
241–242, 332
marriage and family life, 137, 160, 396
Metropolitan Museum, Museum of
Natural History, 310, 350
Prospect Park collaboration with FLO,
263–266
Niagara collaboration with FLO,
350–351
partnership with FLO dissolved, 309–310
professional setbacks, 361, 379–380
death, 396–397

Vaux, Downing, 137–138
Vaux, Julia, 160, 165–166
Vaux, Mary née Mary Swan McEntee, 137, 396
Vauxhall Gardens, 126
The Vicar of Wakefield (Goldsmith), 15
Viele, Egbert Ludovicus
  background, 130–131
  Central Park plan submitted, rejected, 137–138, 144–145, 147
  Brooklyn park design submitted, rejected, 271–273
  as FLO's nemesis, 323, 333

Waite, Morrison, 348
Walker, Francis, 354–356
Walker, Peter, 403
"Walks Among the New-York Poor" articles (Brace), 80
Walks and Talks of an American Farmer . . . (F. L. Olmsted), 68–69, 90, 108, 139
Ward, John Quincy Adams, 156
Washington, D.C.
  during Civil War, 183–185, 187–188
  public spaces reorganized by Rick, 402
  slavery, 79
  See also U.S. Capitol grounds
Washington Monument, 136, 183
Washington Park, Chicago, 301–302, 362, 372
Watkins, Carleton, 246, 249, 314
Webster, Noah, 11
Weed, Thurlow, 254–256
Welton, Joseph, 38
Wetlands restoration (Back Bay Fens), 337
White City. *See* World's Fair
White, Richard Grant, 146–147
Whitmore, Zolva, 12–14
Whitney, Elizabeth Baldwin. *See* Baldwin, Elizabeth
Whittier, John Greenleaf, 111, 348
Whittredge, Worthington, 137
Wikoff, Henry, 186
Williams, Andrew, 129–130
Wilson, Edmund, 86
Wilson, Henry, 192
Wine making and FLO as consultant to upstart industry, 260–261

Wisedell, Thomas, 322
Wm. C. Bryant & Company, 143
Women volunteers
  on Civil War hospital ships, 198–202
  provide food, clothing to USSC, 211–213
Women's Central Association of Relief, 180
World's Fair of 1893 (Chicago)
  background, 369–372
  boats for fairgoers, 375, 376, 377–378
  building architecture, construction, 374–376, 380
  Ferris wheel, 385, 404
  grounds designed, constructed, by FLO, 1, 4, 373, 376–378, 380–384
  Wooded Island with Japanese pavilion, 375–377, 383, 386
Wormeley, Katharine Prescott, 198, 202, 205
Wright, Frank Lloyd, 301, 386
Wright, Frank Lloyd, Jr., 402

Yale University
  brother John Hull Olmsted attends, 17, 23, 35
  confers honorary degree on FLO, 383–384
  encounter with John's classmate, Allison, 92–93
  FLO's brief enrollment, 38, 50, 277
  stepson John Charles attends, 315, 325
  and uncommon set of friends, 35–36, 48–49
Yeoman (pseudonym for F. L. Olmsted), 80, 90, 195
Yosemite
  FLO's first glimpse, 243
  history and early representations in art, 248–249
  local Indians, 237, 248, 249, 365
  Olmsted family trip, 248–251
  FLO serves on Yosemite preservation commission, 245–246, 251–252, 266–268
  becomes national park, 268

Zimmermann, Johann Georg, 15, 170
Zouave regiments in Civil War, 184, 189
Zuckerman, Mary Ellen, 111

APPENDIX
The Olmsted Views

I enjoyed visiting all these incredible sites while researching this book. For each, I've selected choice spots, some of which are remarkably unsullied and have changed little in appearance since Olmsted's day. Of course, you'll have to use your imagination to shut out cars and people using cell phones.

OAKLAND, CALIFORNIA
Mountain View Cemetery

Go to the highest point on the hill. Legend has it that Olmsted stood here, lifted his finger, and pointed down toward the bay, declaring, "This is the spot." In his day, one would have had an incredible view of two bustling boomtowns, Oakland and San Francisco. Your view today is of the same two cities, now all grown up. Notable people buried here include chocolate baron Domingo Ghirardelli and Julia Morgan, architect of the Hearst Castle at San Simeon.

PALO ALTO, CALIFORNIA
Stanford University

The layout of the university's grounds was the result of a compromise—more like a showdown really—between Olmsted and iron-willed Leland Stanford. Visit the Main Quad, the area of the campus most true to Olmsted's vision. Stanford wanted this space covered in grass, but Olmsted fought to pave it and include the round oases filled with flowers and palms. The idea for the quad itself was Olmsted and Stanford's jointly. Olmsted pushed for the arcades that unify the buildings. As someone who came to landscape architecture circuitously—as a sailor then farmer then journalist—Olmsted believed in mixing disciplines. The Main Quad was intended as a common space where students pursuing diverse studies could meet and mingle their ideas.

YOSEMITE, CALIFORNIA

Olmsted was an environmentalist before the term even existed. He led the early efforts to preserve this natural wonder. One of his favorite spots here is Yosemite Falls, where water cascades over three separate tiers, plummeting a total of 2,425 feet. Olmsted put great effort into positioning the tents of his large camping parties so that everyone would have a view of the falls.

GUILFORD, CONNECTICUT

Sachem's Head Farm Site

From Guilford, drive three miles south to Sachem's Head, a little spit of land jutting into Long Island Sound. Park on Chimney Corner Circle. You are now at the approximate site of Olmsted's seaside Connecticut farm. The farmhouse is long gone, but the view out across the sound remains. Meanwhile, if you visit Staten Island, New York, Olmsted's farmhouse remains, but the view is long gone. Unfortunately, the house is situated on a busy modern thoroughfare, lined with shops. Address: 4515 Hylan Boulevard. The New York Parks Department purchased Olmsted's old farmhouse in 2006. During my visit it was under renovation, surrounded by scaffolding.

CHICAGO, ILLINOIS

Jackson Park

Stand on the Clarence Darrow Bridge. During the 1893 Columbian Exposition, the Brazilian Bridge occupied this same site. The big building you see: That was once the Palace of Fine Arts. It's the only large structure from the White City that remains. Today, it's the Museum of Science and Industry. The water flowing under the bridge: It is one of the languid waterways Olmsted designed for the fair. Continue over the bridge onto the Wooded Island, a natural-looking place that Olmsted built out with dredged lakeshore muck. It was intended to provide a respite from the bustle of the fair. Enjoy a stroll on the Wooded Island, which remains a calm spot in hectic modern Chicago.

RIVERSIDE, ILLINOIS

This model suburb was designed by Olmsted, Vaux & Company. Go to the intersection of Fairbank and Barrypoint roads. Looking in one direction, note the long stretch of green. Ample communal spaces such as this are the hallmark of Riverside's design. Now, find 100 Fairbank, a gray two-story house with Gothic accents. This is the work of Calvert Vaux. Sadly, it's one of the few houses designed by this exceptional architect that's still standing.

LOUISVILLE, KENTUCKY

Cherokee Park

This is one of Olmsted's most beautiful parks—and that's saying a lot. You might want to start out by car to get the lay of this 400-acre masterpiece. Use the Eastern Parkway entrance, then drive the scenic loop— Olmsted's original carriage road. You'll get a good flavor for what makes this a unique place: it's a valley park. Much of the landscape is on a gentle, downhill grade. Per his usual tricks, Olmsted made the valley more valley-like, reshaping the land so it undulates with a near symphonic harmony, more natural than nature. Park your car and take a walk along the Baringer Spring Trail. Now you have the opposite vantage: You're at the bottom of the valley looking up those gently undulating hillsides.

Iroquois Park

Olmsted's vision of parkways connecting the Louisville park system was never fully realized. But stretches were built, sufficient to provide dramatic entrances into the parks. Where Eastern Parkway is an ideal route into Cherokee Park, Southern Parkway is the best approach to Iroquois. And where Cherokee Park is a valley, Iroquois Park is a thickly forested hill. You can drive to the top via Uppill Road (quirky spelling courtesy of Olmsted). Or you can hike the Corbly Trail, which is roughly two miles to the hilltop and back. From the highest point on the hill, the view is breathtaking. Indians once used this spot to study the movement of buffalo herds along the Ohio River. Nowadays, you're treated to a great view of the Louisville skyline.

BOSTON, MASSACHUSETTS

Arnold Arboretum

This is a unique piece of the Emerald Necklace, an ambitious park system that Olmsted created for Boston. It's a tree museum jointly maintained by Harvard University and the city. Walk along the path; it follows nearly the same course that Olmsted laid out. The trees are still planted in the same order prescribed by Olmsted and his friend and founder of the arboretum Charles Sprague Sargent. Some of these trees are original plantings such as a cucumber magnolia (1880) and a silver maple (1881).

Back Bay Fens

Your ideal view is from the Boylston Street Bridge. This monumental structure, hewn of Cape Ann granite, was designed by Olmsted's friend architect H. H. Richardson. Take a look at all the rushes and other aquatic plants growing along the creek bank. Believe it or not, this was once a fetid swamp where Bostonians dumped their garbage. Olmsted turned it into a marsh, a type of landscape that he remembered fondly from growing up in Connecticut. In Olmsted's day, this was a saltwater marsh. Today, it's freshwater, thanks to the damming of the Charles River in 1910. But the landscape looks generally the same. It's fair to say that Olmsted's work here was America's first act of wetland restoration.

Franklin Park

Franklin Park and Back Bay Fens are also segments of the Emerald Necklace. Walk through the Ellicott Arch, designed by stepson John Olmsted. Follow the path, and very soon you'll come to the 99 Steps, a wonderful and whimsical Olmsted touch. The steps are made of Roxbury pudding-stone and lead up into a wilderness area grown thickly with trees. Listen carefully. You may not even be able to hear traffic noises. It's hard to fathom, but you are right in the middle of Boston right now.

B R O O K L I N E ,   M A S S A C H U S E T T S

Fairsted

Olmsted worked out of this home office at 99 Warren Street from 1883 to 1895, one of the most productive stretches in his career. As a landscape architect, Olmsted was sometimes required to design grounds to be secondary to structures. (His design for the grounds surrounding the Capitol building in D.C. is a good example.) Not at Fairsted. Here, foliage trumped structures. Note how the south face of the house is utterly blanketed in vines. The house is a National Historic Site, open to the public for tours. But make sure and walk around Olmsted's "yard," too. Look for the cucumber magnolia, a gift from Charles Sargent, his Brookline neighbor. (Olmsted and Sargent collaborated on the Arnold Arboretum, discussed above.)

D E T R O I T ,   M I C H I G A N

Belle Isle

Belle Isle is a large island park (982 acres) in the Detroit River. Visiting this much loved but hard-used place is bittersweet, as it retains few traces of Olmsted's design. An exception is the system of canals. Olmsted touted these as "highways of pleasure, in which boats would be used instead of carriages." Even the canals, as built, didn't hew to Olmsted's blueprint, but at least they are faithful to his intent and full of sinuous curves.

During the summer, paddleboats are available for rent. Whole sections of Belle Isle have fallen into terrible disrepair, but this boat's-eye view shows the park in its best light. You can paddle past a skating pavilion designed by Eero Saarinen, a botanical garden featuring a greenhouse by Albert Kahn, and the country's only marble lighthouse.

MARQUETTE, MICHIGAN
Presque Isle

With work on the Chicago world's fair underway, Olmsted and FLO Jr. visited Marquette in Michigan's Upper Peninsula. Olmsted was shown this island, three miles outside the town, and asked: How do we turn this into a proper park? His answer: Don't. In an 1891 letter, Olmsted implored the citizens of Marquette to leave this "beautiful and picturesque" place just as it was. For generations now, Olmsted's letter has been used to ward off developers. Presque Isle remains a pint-sized (323-acre) sliver of untrammeled wilderness. It's endlessly interesting; you can spend a whole day just hiking around the island. Check out the curious formations of *serpentinized peridotite*, black rocks formed by volcanic activity one billion years ago. A Presque Isle sunset—vast Lake Superior, sky that's bigger still, Huron Mountains in the distance, and everything awash in bands of color—is a natural drama not to be missed.

BUFFALO, NEW YORK
Delaware Park

Olmsted and Vaux dreamed up the park system, a set of connected parks. How do you connect parks? Why, with "parkways," a phrase the pair coined. In Buffalo, they got their first real opportunity to put the idea into practice. Delaware Park is the jewel of the Buffalo system. Enter it via Olmsted and Vaux's parkways. Here's an ideal route: Follow Chapin Parkway onto Lincoln Parkway under a canopy of trees the whole way and down a now-paved old bridal path and right into Delaware Park. Walk around the lake. Appreciate its lovely, meandering shoreline, and realize that it's entirely man-made, designed by Olmsted and Vaux.

NEW YORK, NEW YORK
Central Park

Enter at Fifth Avenue and 59th Street. The diagonal roadway gets you quickly out of the bustling city and into the peaceful heart of the park, per Olmsted and Vaux's design. Walk the quarter-mile length of the Mall to Bethesda Terrace. Note Jacob Wrey Mould's wildly imaginative stone carvings. Walk down the steps, past Bethesda Fountain, to the Lake. When the park opened in 1858, this was the most popular feature. Some winter days, thousands of people skated on it. A nineteenth-century engineering marvel, it was possible to raise the water level in the warmer months for boating. Follow the Lake's shore westward to the Bow Bridge. This is Vaux's masterpiece. Cross the Bow Bridge into the Ramble. This is Olmsted's wild garden, his favorite part of the park. He tinkered with its plantings endlessly, like a mad botanist.

Prospect Park

Start at Grand Army Plaza. This is Olmsted and Vaux's original park entrance, though the monument dates to 1892, after their involvement in the project. Head into the park and pass through Endale Arch, a subtle, rustic stonework designed by Vaux. Emerging from Endale Arch you'll be in the Long Meadow. It remains one of Olmsted and Vaux's finest creations, nearly a mile of stretching, rolling, invitingly green lawn. Note the sunken pathways. They're a canny original touch that keeps the view across the Long Meadow unbroken. When the park first opened, visitors were intrigued by the fact that, thanks to the sunken pathways, one couldn't see people's feet moving as they walked. A woman in one of those long nineteenth-century dresses would appear to glide across the meadow.

NIAGARA FALLS, NEW YORK

As an environmentalist, a role separate but related to his better-known work as a landscape architect, Olmsted was deeply involved in the preservation of this place. The plan he and Vaux drew up covered more than just Niagara Falls. Olmsted especially loved the islands in the headwater rapids before the water plunges over the falls. Visit Goat Island. You might also want to stop at the nearby Three Sisters Islands, which are especially unspoiled. In 1875, Olmsted took a trip here with H. H. Richardson. Together, they spent many hours enjoying the scenery on these headwater islands. This was Olmsted's idea: He knew the falls would be like an exclamation point, overwhelming anything else they might see. So he wanted to work his way to them by way of some quieter, gentler scenery.

Rochester, New York

Highland Park

One of Olmsted's favorite concepts was "passages of scenery." Highland Park features one of his greatest passages. Enter at the Lamberton Conservatory. Walk down the stairs and then proceed to wend your way through a series of "rooms" of trees. Each room is a small, open space surrounded by groupings of the same species, or visually complementary species of trees. The tree rooms have various gaps. Think of these gaps as doors. What's on the other side, you naturally wonder? That's just what Olmsted wanted. Walk through a door and you'll be in another, different, room of trees. Repeat. Repeat again. Pretty soon, you'll have experienced "passages of scenery."

Seneca Park

Olmsted was drawn to the idea of building a park along the bank of a river, and he thought this stretch of water—sometimes called the "cannon of the Genesee"—was perfect. Go past the zoo, and near the Trout Lake, pick up one of the wooded paths. Walking along, trees all around, great view of the Genesee River below, you might half expect to see someone paddle by on a wooden raft. This is a little slice of the nineteenth century right in downtown Rochester.

ASHEVILLE, NORTH CAROLINA

Biltmore Estate

Enjoy the meandering three-mile approach road, incredibly faithful to Olmsted's original route. The lush planting scheme—rhododendrons, white pines, even bamboo—is also faithful. Olmsted designed the approach to be full of visual variety, while shutting out all distant vistas. He wanted to save those for the house itself. Once inside, proceed to the loggia for an amazing view. Incredibly, much of the woodland you see stretching for miles didn't exist when George Vanderbilt bought the land. It was scruffy, abused for generations. Vanderbilt agreed to Olmsted's idea to plant trees as part of America's first experiment in managed forestry. Today, much of Vanderbilt's original acreage has become Pisgah National Forest. But the estate's 8,000 acres still contain plenty of woodland. Make your way down through the Olmsted-designed gardens on the hillside beneath the South Terrace. At the base of the hill, you can pick up the Woodland Trail for a short walk through forest planted by FLO.

MONTREAL, QUEBEC

Mount Royal

Enter the park at the intersection of Rue Peel and Avenue des Pins, at the edge of McGill University's campus. Make the brief walk to Chemin Olmsted. When the park opened, this was a carriage road. Olmsted was furious that it didn't follow his intricate scheme. But it still turned out plenty winding, plenty Olmstedian, and nowadays, it's for pedestrians only. Follow Chemin Olmsted to the chalet, requiring a winding gentle-grade climb of roughly a mile and a half. From here the view is amazing. You immediately grasp why Olmsted was so taken with this mountain-park site. Montreal is arrayed below, and in the distance, across the St. Lawrence River, Mont St. Bruno and Mont St.-Hilaire are visible. From the chalet, you can return via Chemin Olmsted or take a shortcut, marked *sentier de l'escarpment*—a steep stairway that will take you quickly and dramatically down the mountainside.

Washington, D.C.

Capitol Grounds

Coming off the Mall, enter the Capitol grounds via Pennsylvania Avenue. Walk up the hill until you find the Summerhouse. Olmsted devoted a great deal of thought and energy to this little gem, making sure it was just so. The Summerhouse is a great place to sit down and rest after a long day of seeing the sights. Make sure and explore the rest of the grounds, too, still nearly exactly as Olmsted designed them. Take a look at the photo insert in this book, where Olmsted's 1874 plan and a modern aerial shot are presented side by side for comparison.

Milwaukee, Wisconsin

Lake Park

Make sure to explore the ravines, laced with walking paths true to Olmsted's plan. You'll feel like you're deep in the woods. That's by design, as the original 1893 scheme called for planting trees to block distant views, a classic Olmsted trick. Keep walking, and soon enough you'll encounter an intentional break in the trees, opening to a vista. The effect is both startling and satisfying. Yes, you're in a wooded ravine. But the ravine, in turn, is cut into a steep bluff overlooking Lake Michigan, now spread endlessly before you.

Riverside Park

Riverside Park and Lake Park are just one mile apart. Newberry Boulevard was designed by Olmsted to connect the two, so it's the ideal route to take, either by car or on foot. You'll pass a series of grand houses, once homes to the tannery and glue barons of nineteenth-century Milwaukee. Once you enter Riverside Park, look for a very old-growth stand of Norway maples near Oakland Avenue. These centenarian trees, planted in a semi-circle, are what remains of a carriage drop-off in the original park plan. Otherwise, this first section of the park—given over to athletic fields and facilities—has strayed pretty far from Olmsted's vision. But head west, cross a footbridge, and you'll be in the untamed section of Riverside Park. Here, the footpaths meander as Olmsted intended. Wend your way to the Milwaukee River. People once used it to swim and ice skate. Today, it's used to fish and kayak.

ABOUT THE AUTHOR

Justin Martin is the author of two other biographies, *Greenspan: The Man Behind Money* and *Nader: Crusader, Spoiler, Icon*. As one of the few journalists to gain access to Greenspan, Martin produced a best-selling biography of the secretive Fed chairman that was also selected as a notable book for 2001 by the *New York Times Book Review*. Martin's Nader biography served as a primary source for *An Unreasonable Man*, an Academy Award–nominated documentary. Martin's articles have appeared in a variety of publications, including *Fortune, Newsweek*, and the *San Francisco Chronicle*. Martin is a 1987 graduate of Rice University in Houston, Texas. He was married in Central Park, Olmsted's masterpiece. He lives with his wife and twin sons in Forest Hills Gardens, New York, a neighborhood designed by Frederick Law Olmsted Jr.

READER'S GUIDE

For book clubs, classrooms, and others who are interested, a readers' guide to *Genius of Place* is available online at dacapopressreadersguides.com.

Additional information can be found at the author's website (www.justinmartin1.com) and this book's Facebook page (www.facebook.com/OlmstedBook).

Made in the USA
Middletown, DE
12 May 2023

30466334R00295